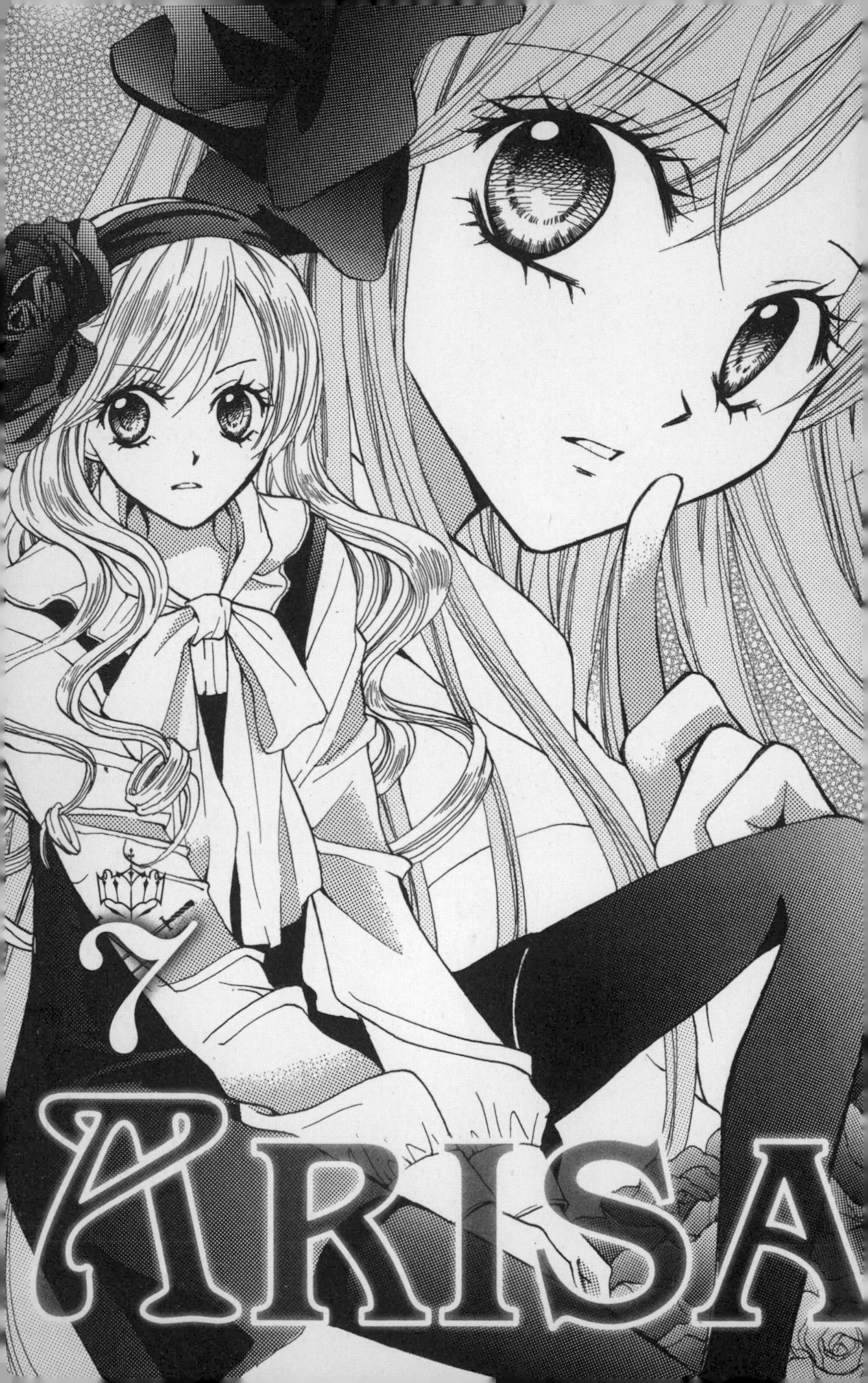
7
ARISA

Contents

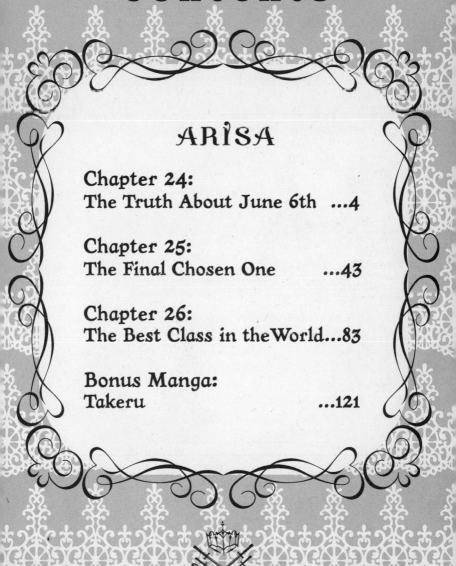

ARISA

Secret King's Room

The story so far

Tsubasa and Arisa are twin sisters separated by their parents' divorce. They finally reunited after three years of being apart, but their happy time together came to a sudden end when Arisa jumped out of her bedroom window right in front of Tsubasa, leaving behind a mysterious card...

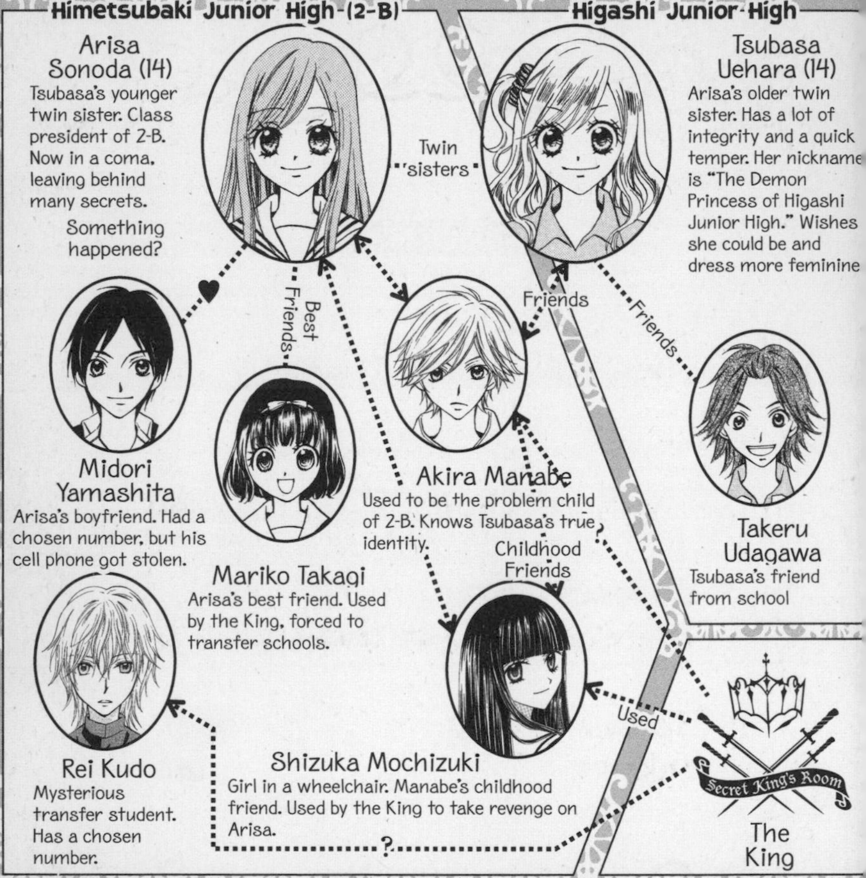

Himetsubaki Junior High (2-B)
Higashi Junior High
Arisa Sonoda (14)
Tsubasa's younger twin sister. Class president of 2-B. Now in a coma, leaving behind many secrets.
Twin sisters
Tsubasa Uehara (14)
Arisa's older twin sister. Has a lot of integrity and a quick temper. Her nickname is "The Demon Princess of Higashi Junior High." Wishes she could be and dress more feminine
Something happened?
Best Friends
Friends
Friends
Midori Yamashita
Arisa's boyfriend. Had a chosen number, but his cell phone got stolen.
Akira Manabe
Used to be the problem child of 2-B. Knows Tsubasa's true identity.
Takeru Udagawa
Tsubasa's friend from school
Childhood Friends
Mariko Takagi
Arisa's best friend. Used by the King, forced to transfer schools.
Used
Secret King's Room
The King
Rei Kudo
Mysterious transfer student. Has a chosen number.
Shizuka Mochizuki
Girl in a wheelchair. Manabe's childhood friend. Used by the King to take revenge on Arisa.
?
?

In order to discover the secrets Arisa was hiding, Tsubasa pretended to be her and attended Himetsubaki Junior High. In Class 2-B, a mysterious internet presence called "The King" led strange incidents and bullying.

Shizuka thought Tsubasa was really trying to be her friend until the King interfered with a text message, leading Shizuka to believe she had been deceived by Tsubasa. Shizuka tried to get revenge on "Arisa," but instead fell right into the King's trap. Shizuka has always trusted Manabe, and told him about Arisa's secret, which was a chat room. There Tsubasa and Manabe found a chat log between Arisa and the mysterious "K." Tsubasa sends a message to K, and he responds back...

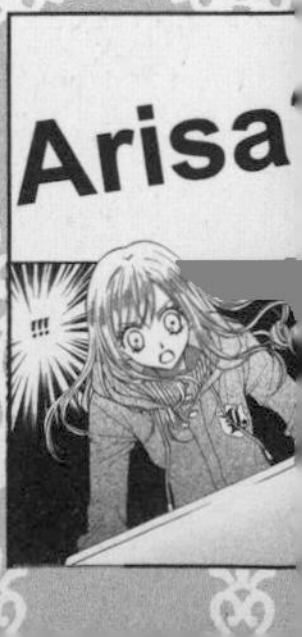

Arisa
!!!

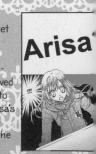

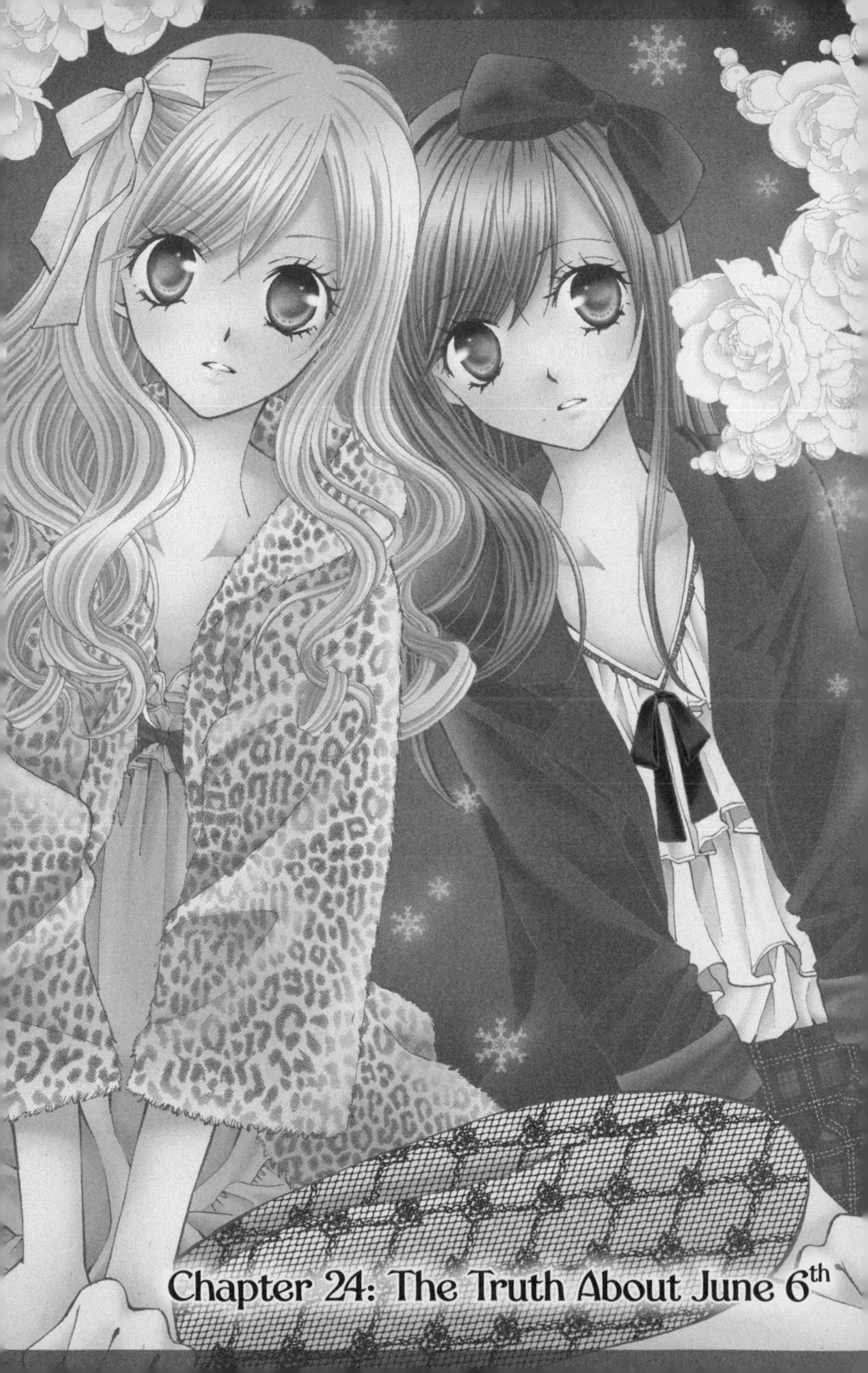
Chapter 24: The Truth About June 6th

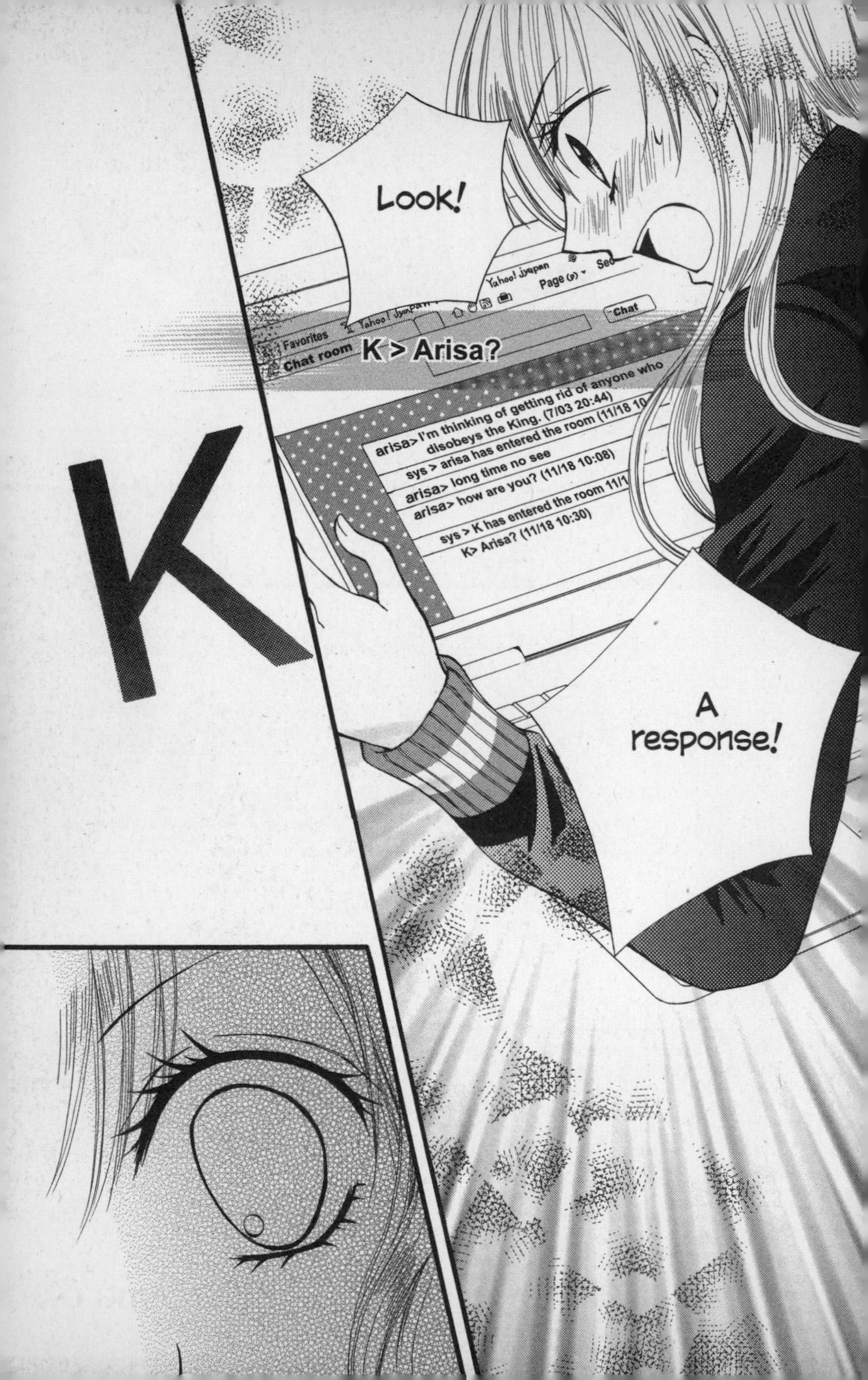
Look!
Yahoo! jyapan
Page (P)
Chat
Favorites
Chat room
K > Arisa?
arisa> I'm thinking of getting rid of anyone who disobeys the King. (7/03 20:44)
sys > arisa has entered the room
sys > long time no see
arisa> how are you? (11/18 10:08)
arisa> how are you?
sys > K has entered the room (11/18 10:30)
K> Arisa? (11/18 10:30)
A response!
K

K> is this really Arisa?

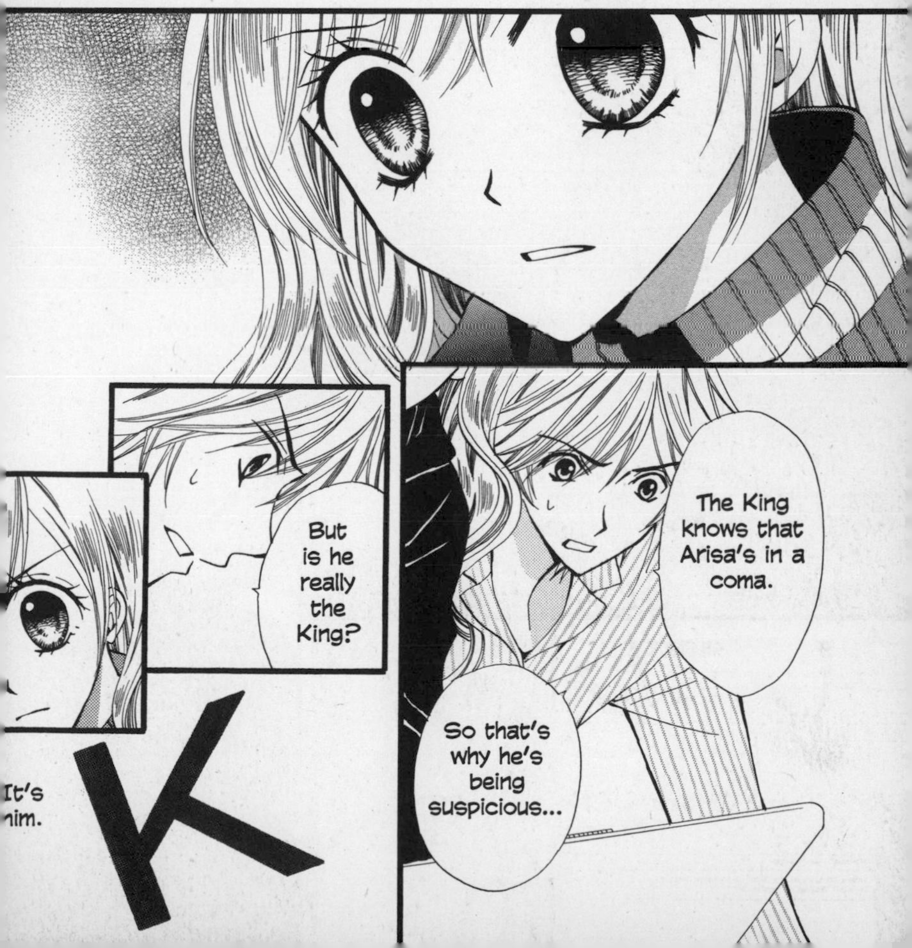
The King knows that Arisa's in a coma.
So that's why he's being suspicious...
But is he really the King?
K
It's

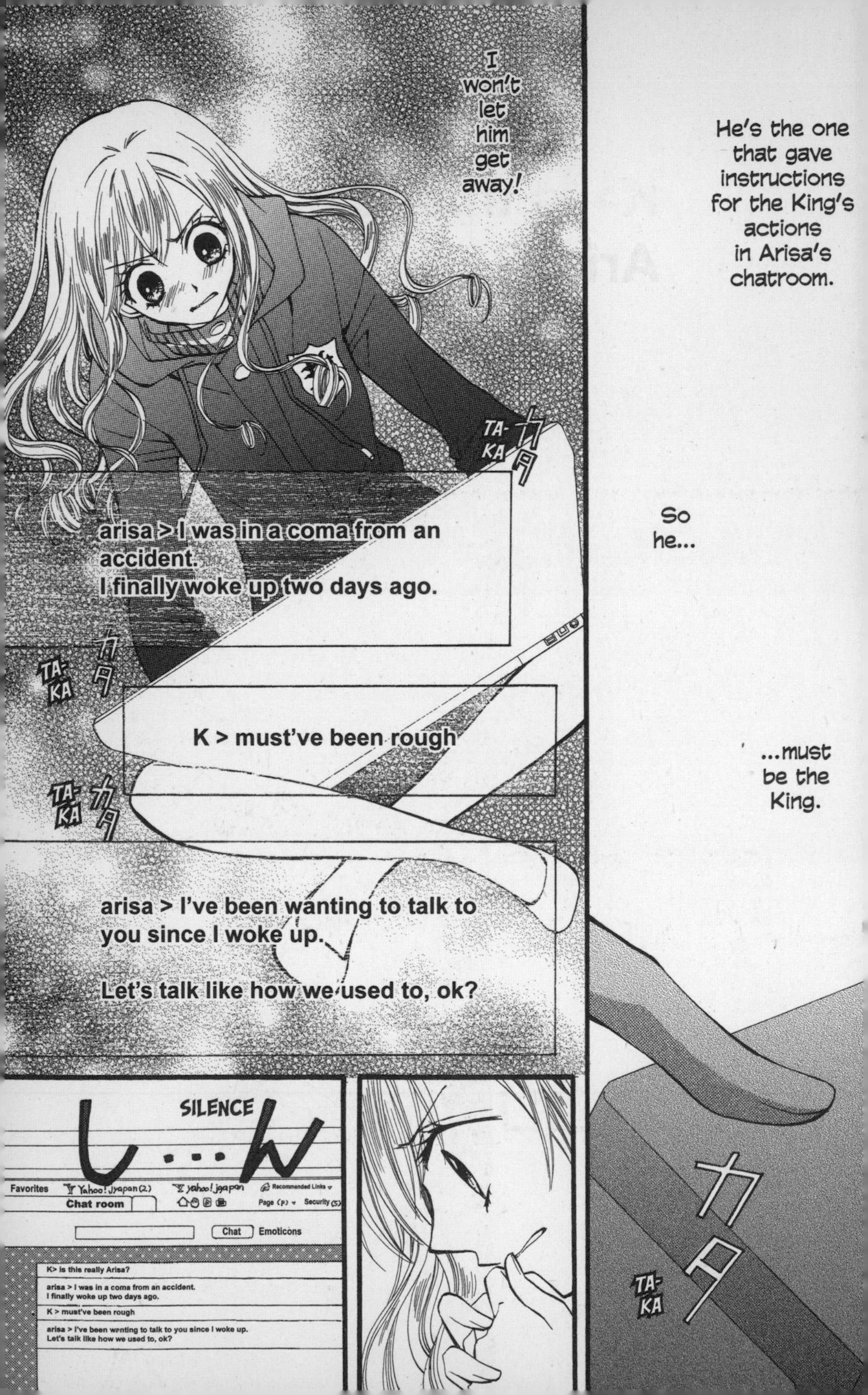
He's the one that gave instructions for the King's actions in Arisa's chatroom.
So he...
...must be the King.
TA-KA
I won't let him get away!
TA-KA
arisa > I was in a coma from an accident.
I finally woke up two days ago.
TA-KA
K > must've been rough
TA-KA
arisa > I've been wanting to talk to you since I woke up.
Let's talk like how we used to, ok?
SILENCE
Favorites
Chat room
Chat
Emoticons
K> is this really Arisa?
arisa > I was in a coma from an accident.
I finally woke up two days ago.
K > must've been rough
arisa > I've been wanting to talk to you since I woke up.
Let's talk like how we used to, ok?

K >

K > I wanted to talk to you too

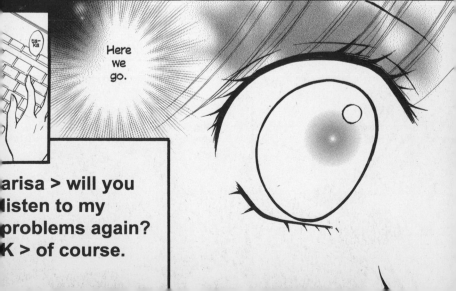

Here
we
go.

arisa > will you
listen to my
problems again?
K > of course.

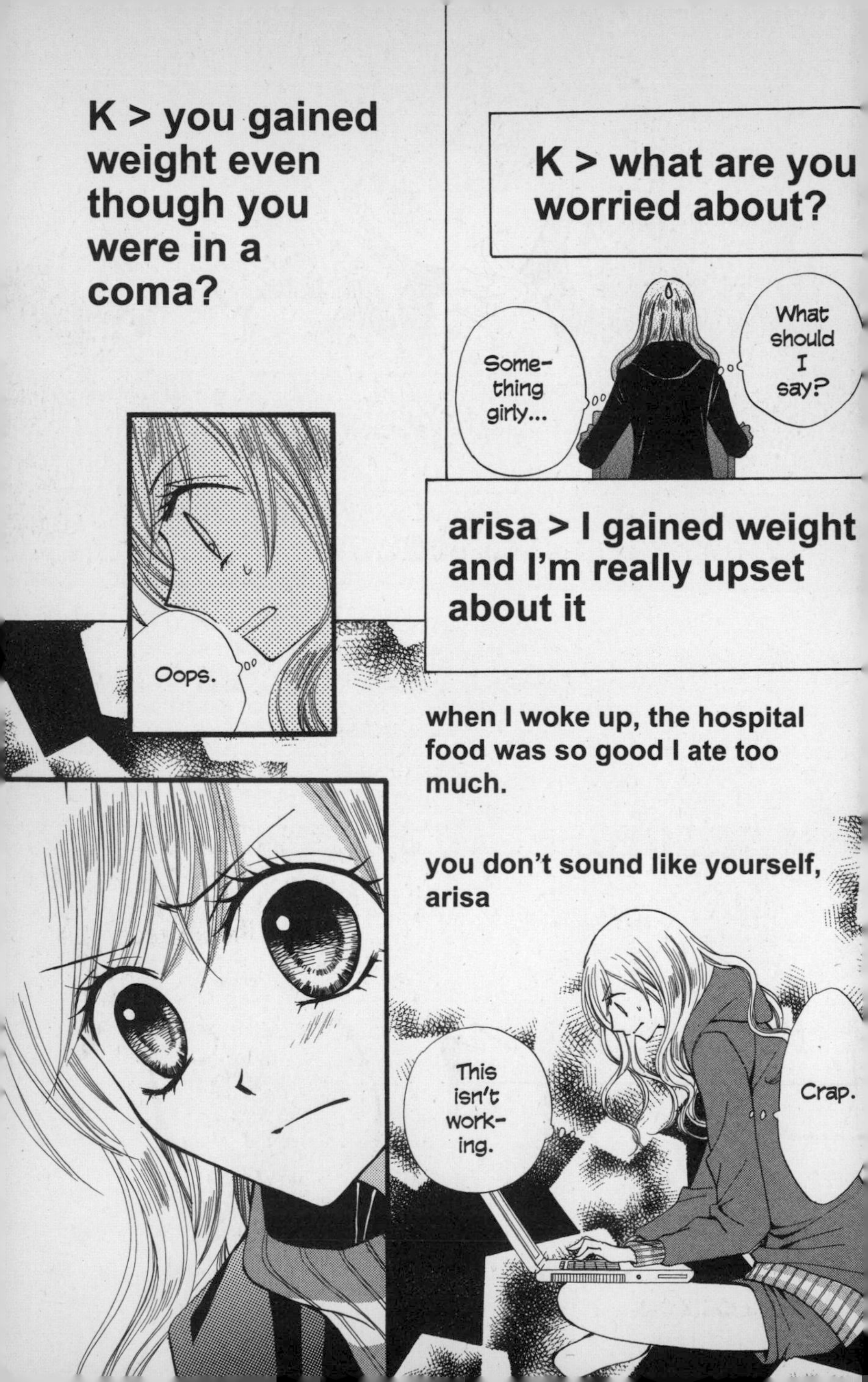
K > what are you worried about?
What should I say?
Something girly...
arisa > I gained weight and I'm really upset about it
when I woke up, the hospital food was so good I ate too much.
K > you gained weight even though you were in a coma?
Oops.
you don't sound like yourself, arisa
Crap.
This isn't working.

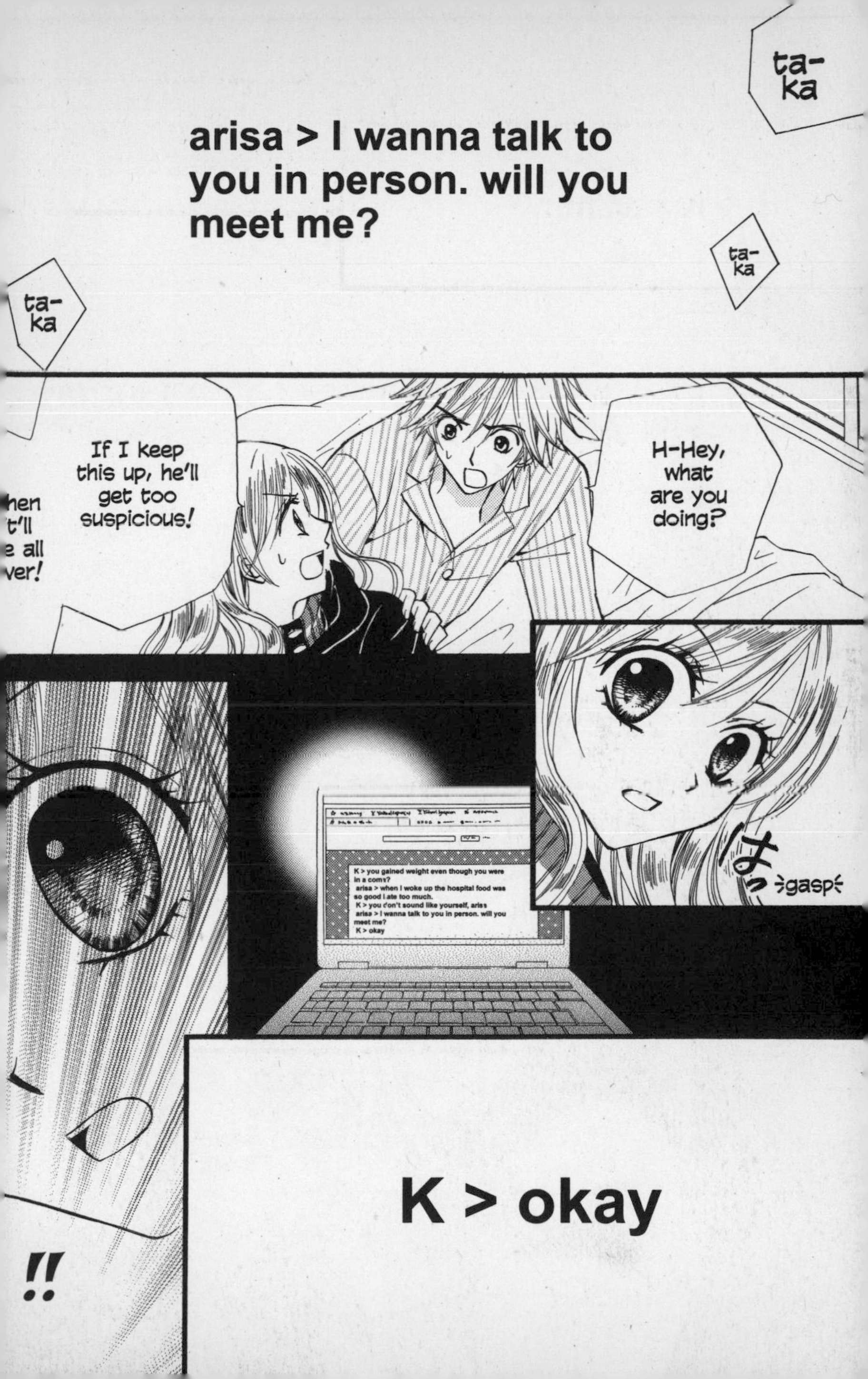
ta-ka
arisa > I wanna talk to you in person. will you meet me?
ta-ka
ta-ka
H-Hey, what are you doing?
If I keep this up, he'll get too suspicious!
はっ
gasp
K > you gained weight even though you were in a coma?
arisa > when I woke up the hospital food was so good I ate too much.
K > you don't sound like yourself, arisa
arisa > I wanna talk to you in person. will you meet me?
K > okay
K > okay
!!

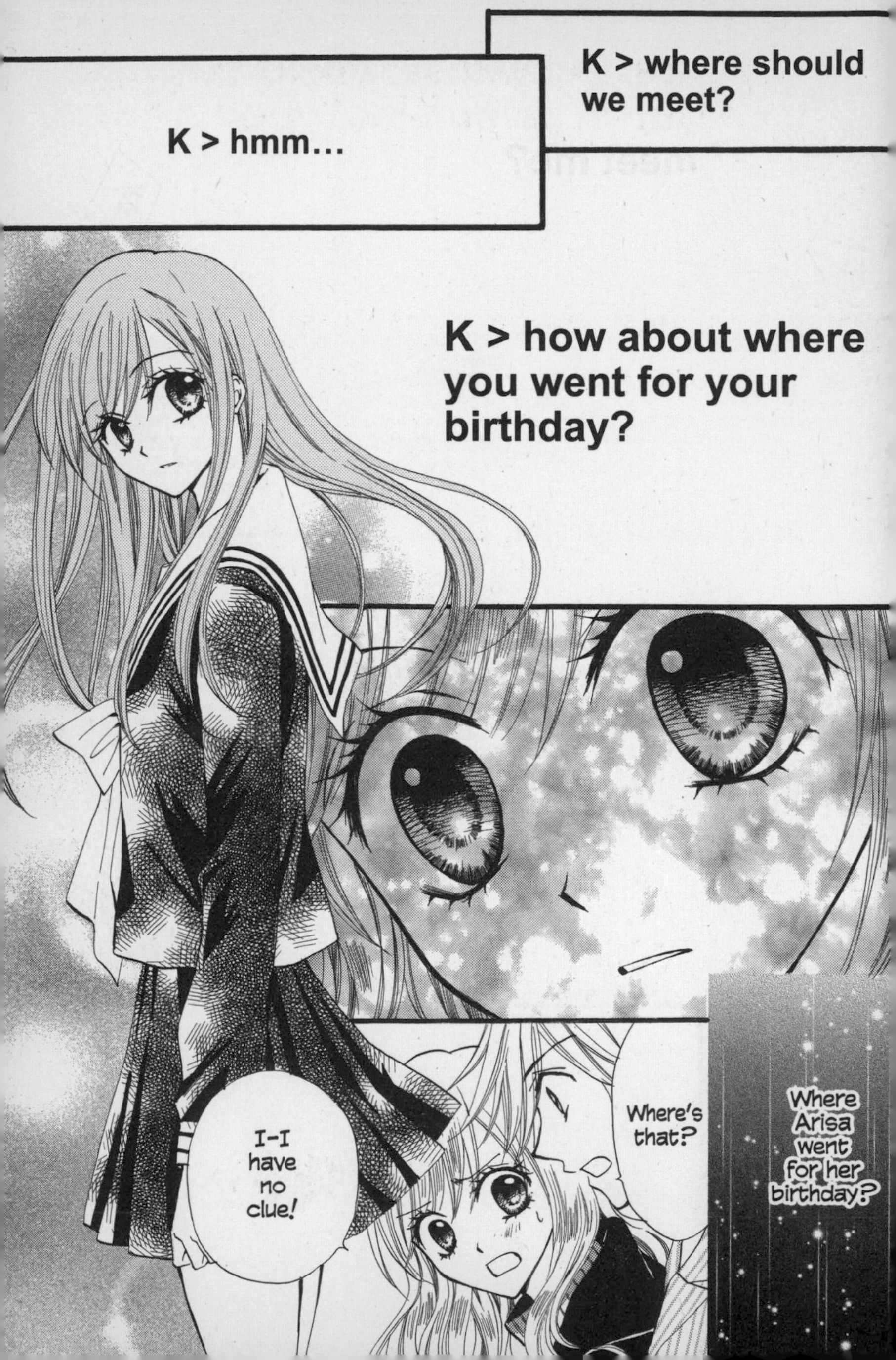
K > where should we meet?
K > hmm…
K > how about where you went for your birthday?
Where Arisa went for her birthday?
Where's that?
I-I have no clue!

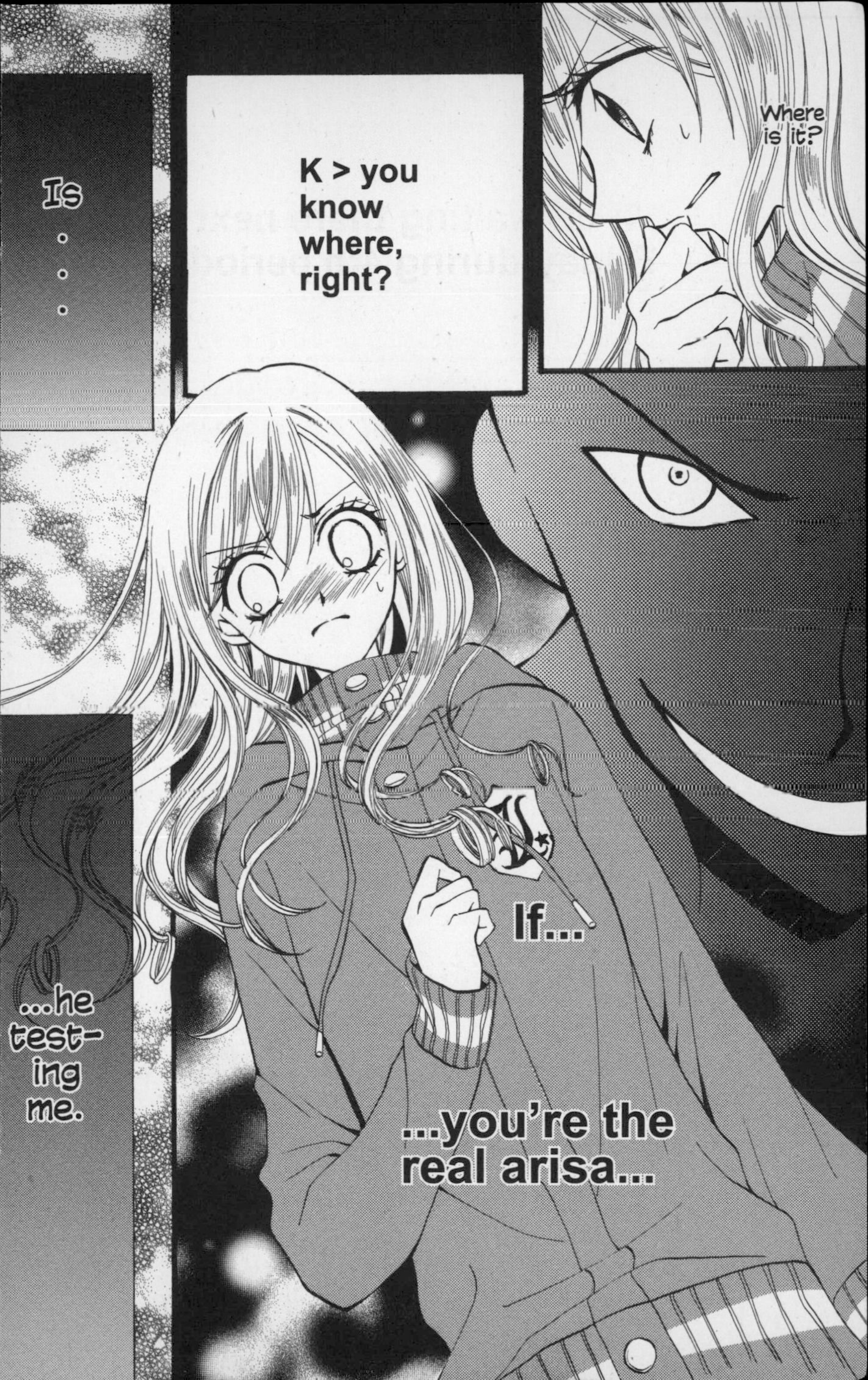
Where is it?
K > you know where, right?
Is . . . .
If...
...you're the real arisa...
...he testing me.

I'll be waiting there next Friday during 4th period.

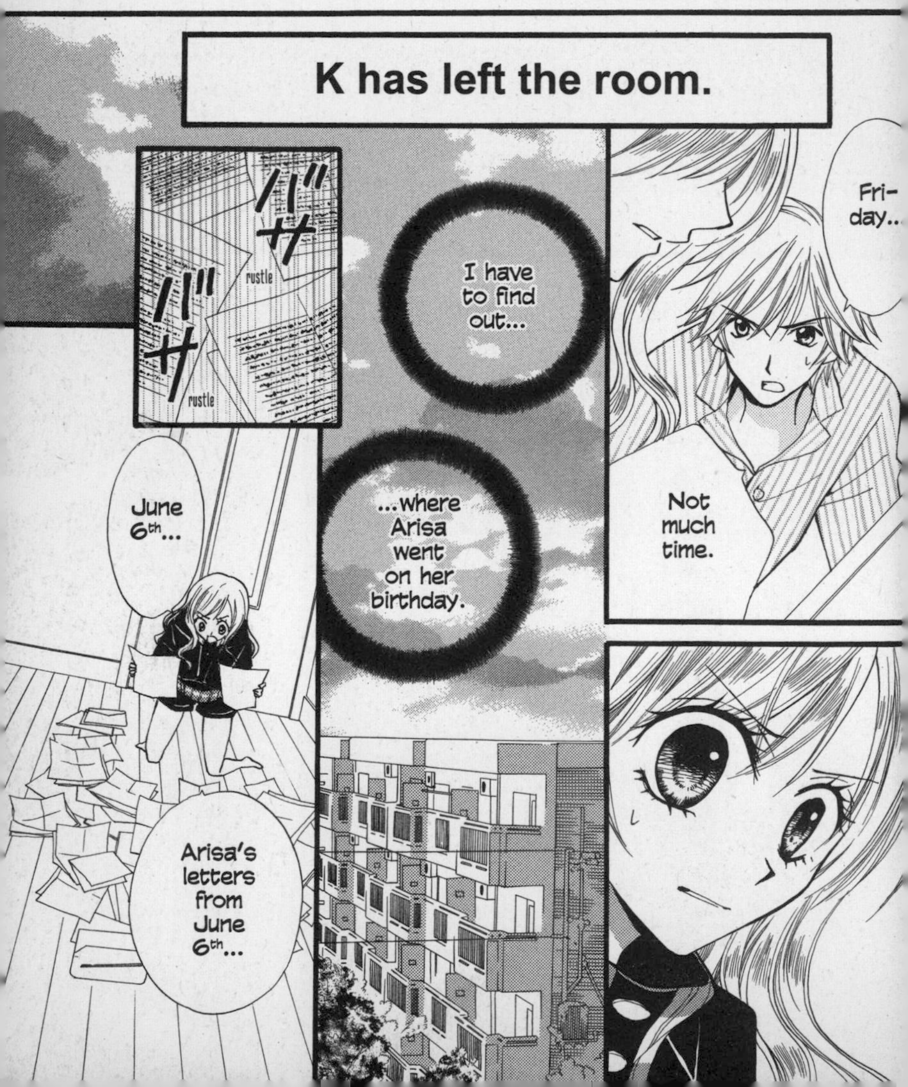
K has left the room.
Fri-day..
Not much time.
I have to find out...
...where Arisa went on her birthday.
rustle
rustle
June 6th...
Arisa's letters from June 6th...

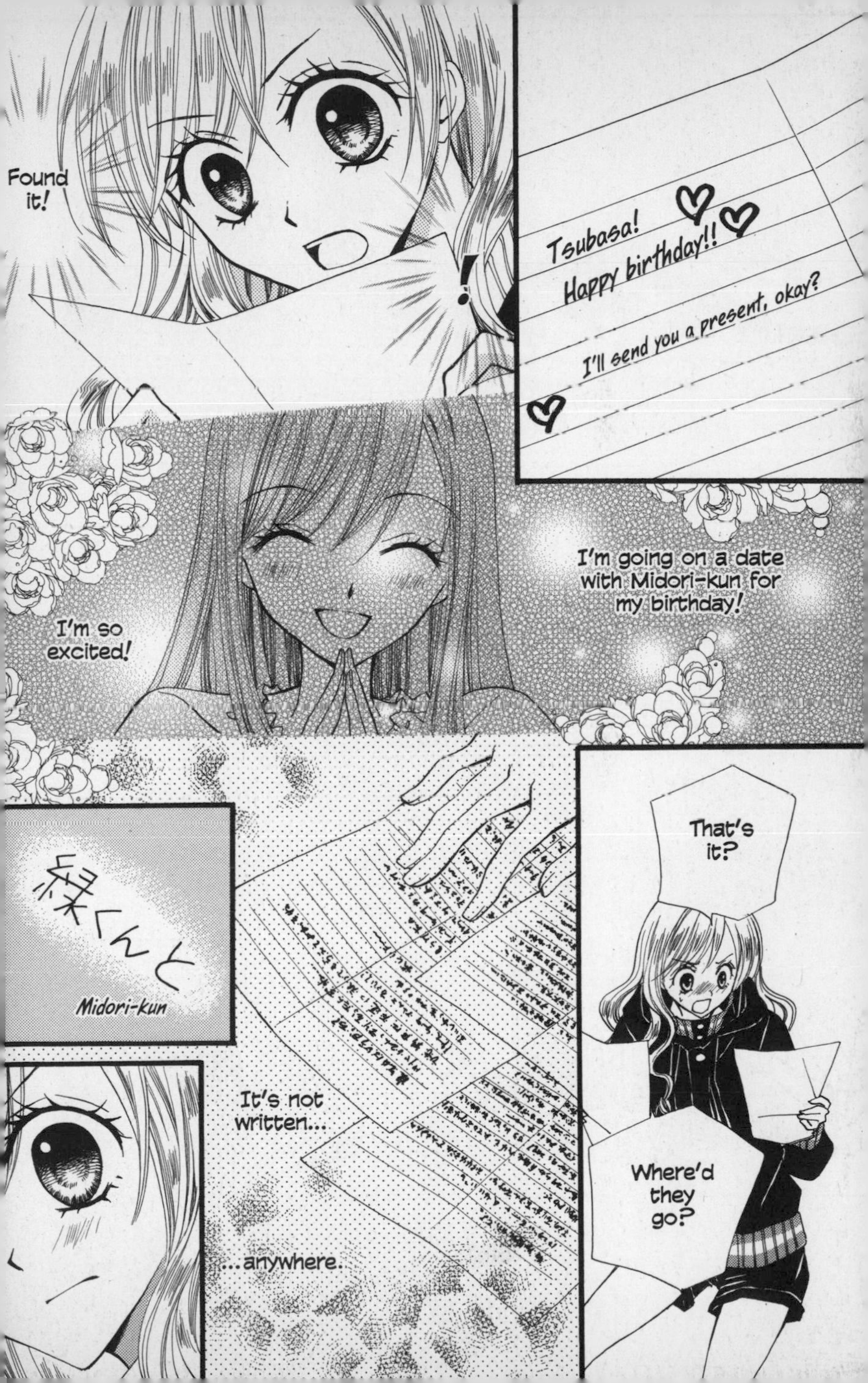
Tsubasa!
Happy birthday!!
I'll send you a present, okay?
Found it!
I'm going on a date with Midori-kun for my birthday!
I'm so excited!
That's it?
Where'd they go?
It's not written...
...anywhere.
緑くんと
Midori-kun

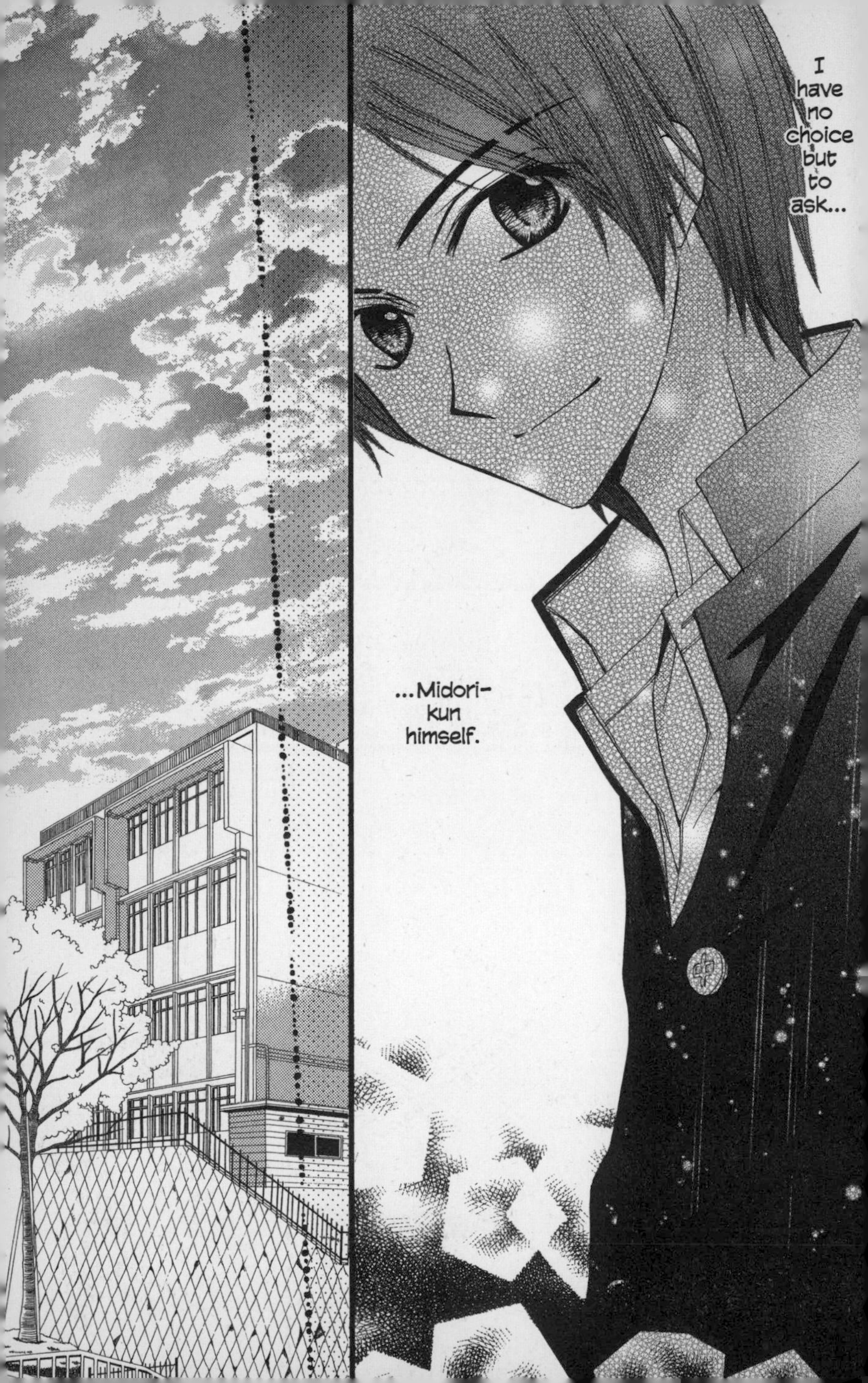
I have no choice but to ask...
...Midori-kun himself.

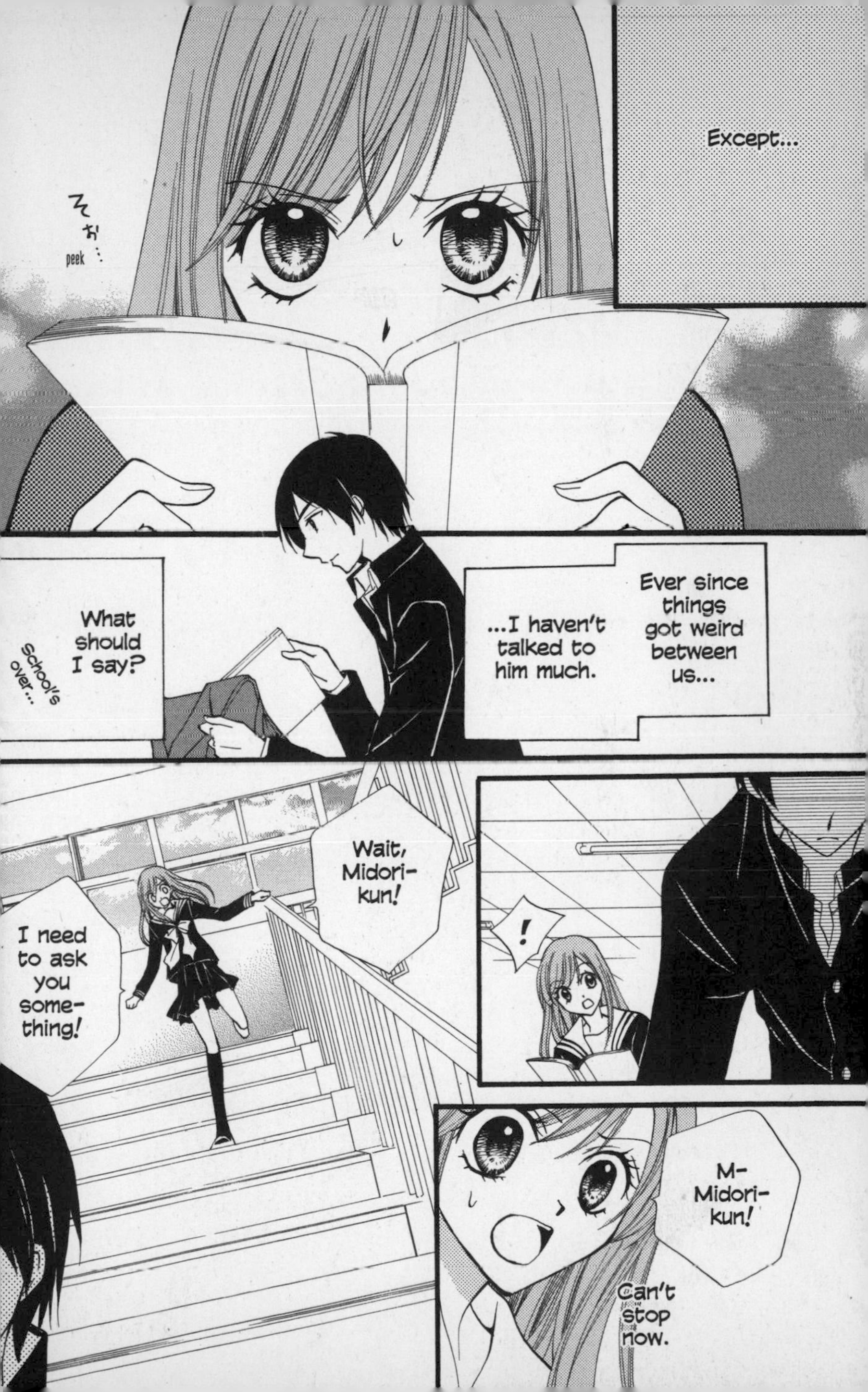

Except...
そお…
peek
Ever since things got weird between us...
...I haven't talked to him much.
What should I say?
School's over...
!
M-Midori-kun!
Can't stop now.
Wait, Midori-kun!
I need to ask you something!

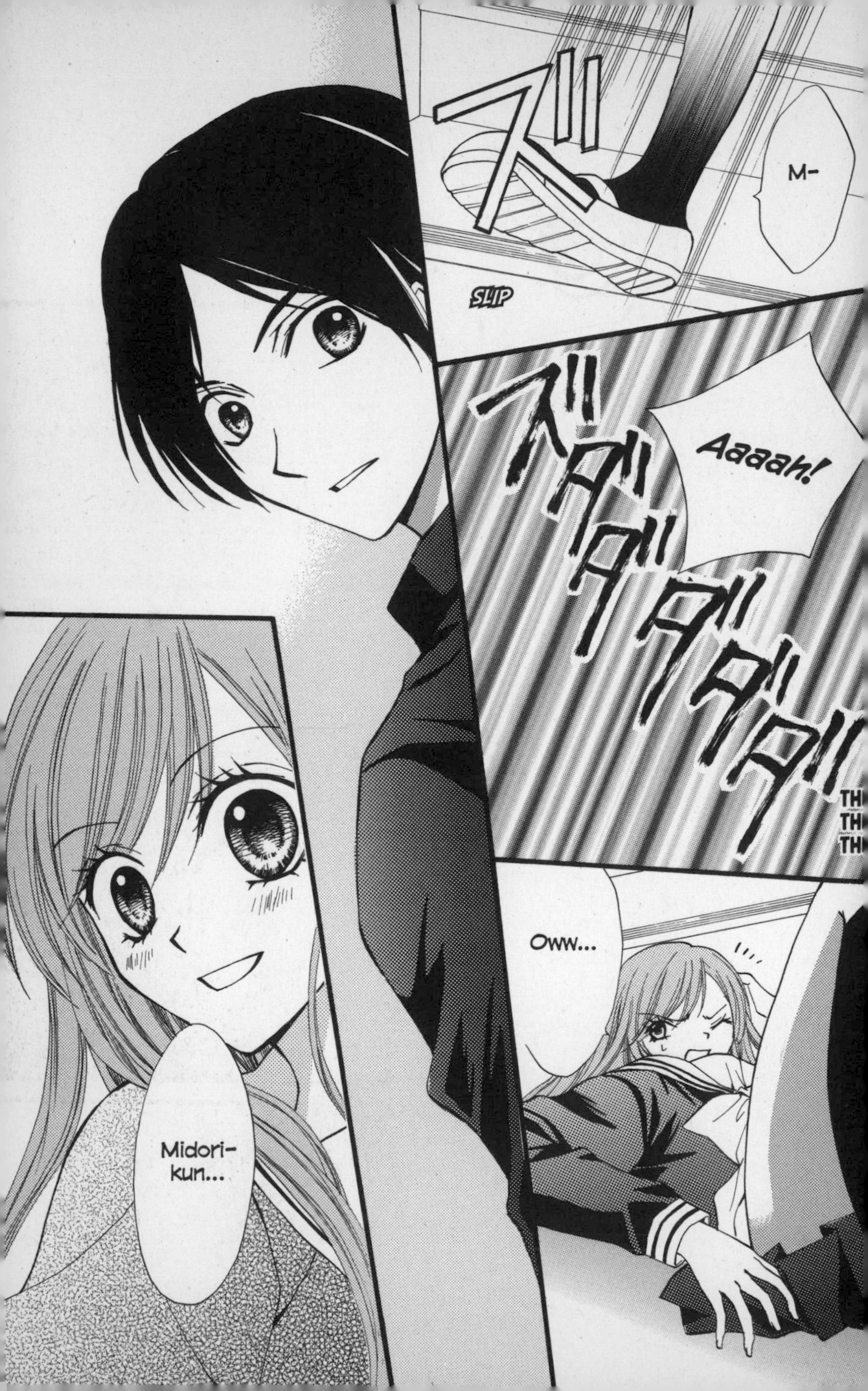
M-
SLIP
Aaaah!
TH
TH
TH
Oww...
Midori-kun...

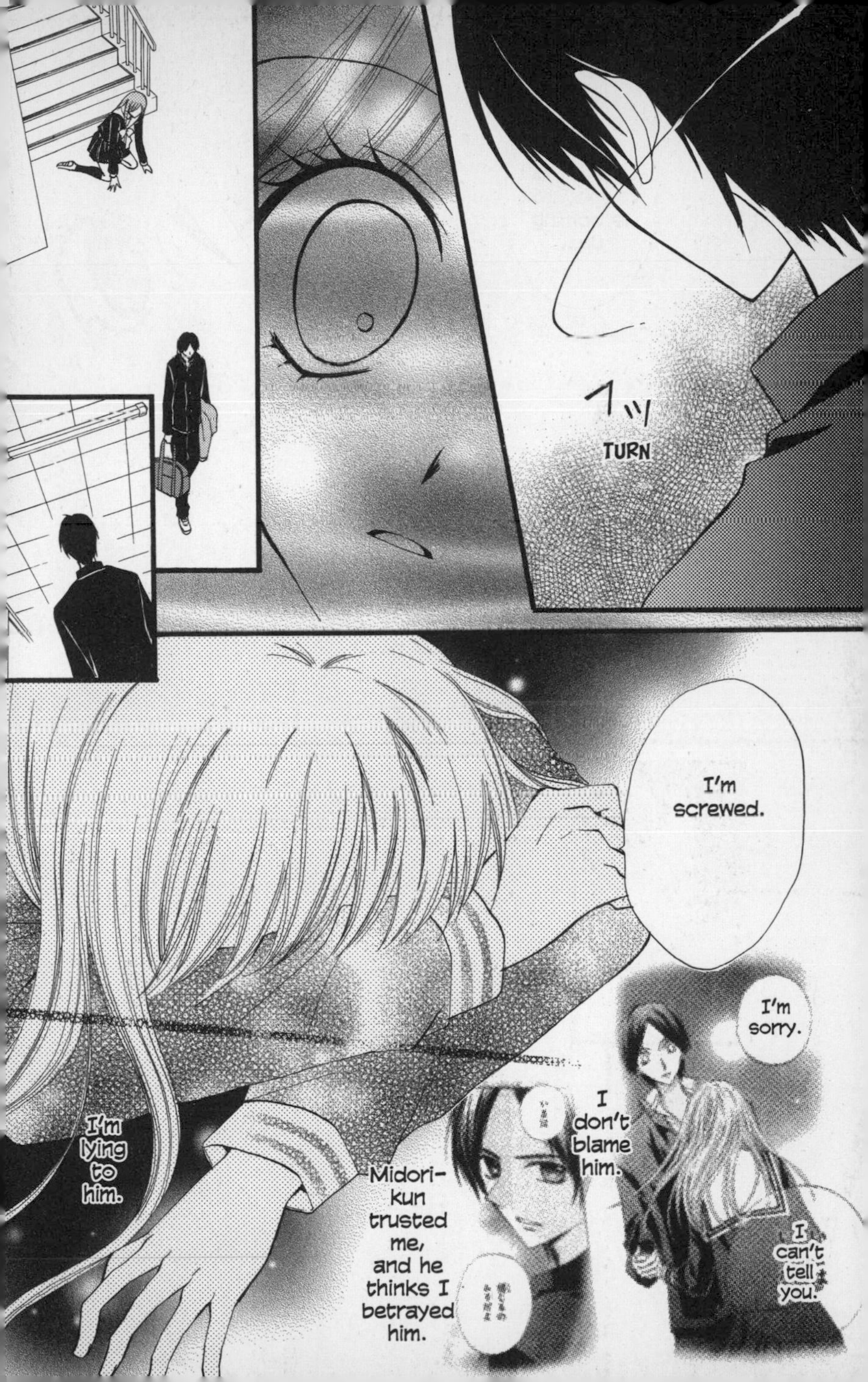
フッ
TURN
I'm screwed.
I'm sorry.
I can't tell you.
I don't blame him.
Midori-kun trusted me, and he thinks I betrayed him.
I'm lying to him.

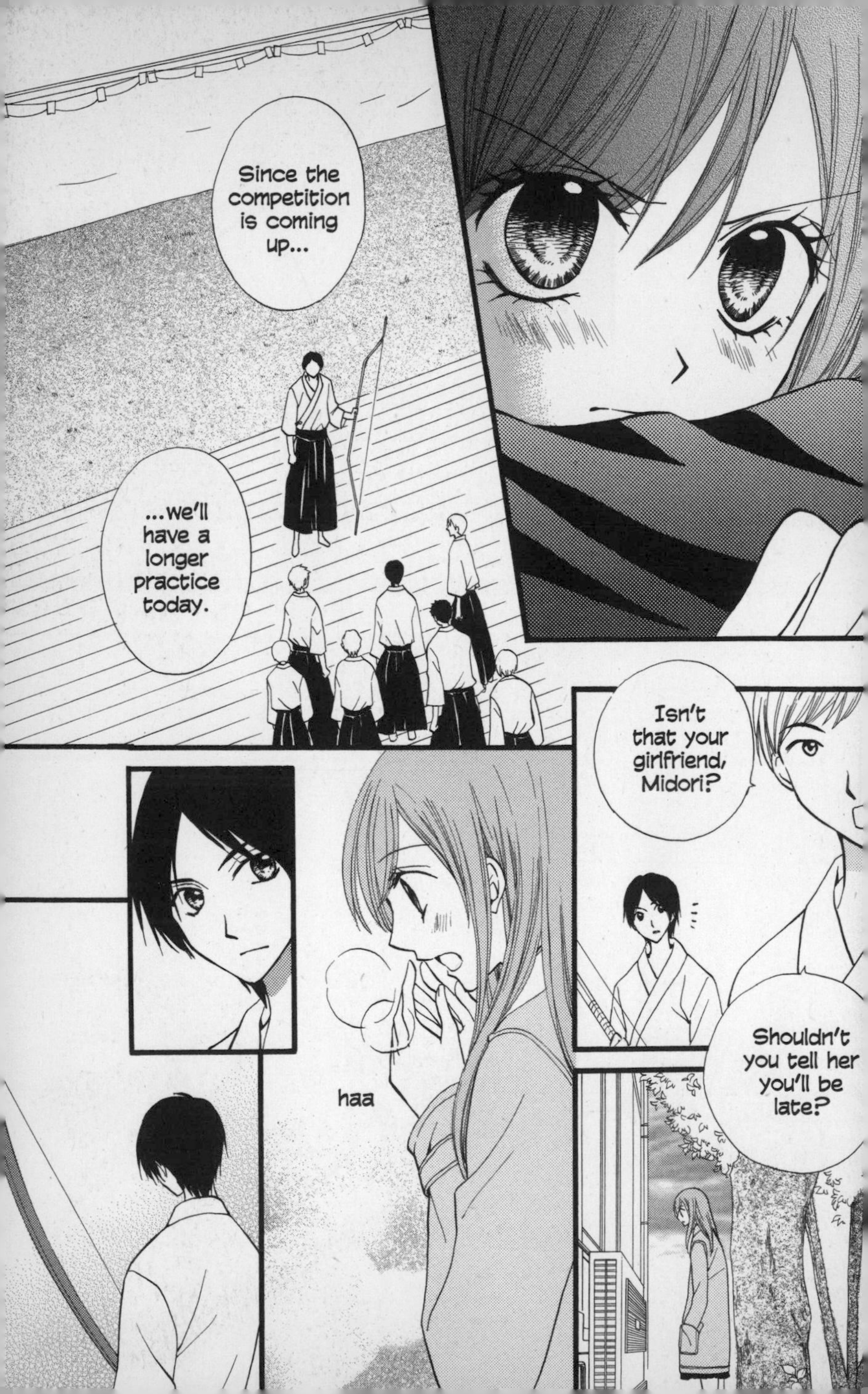
Since the competition is coming up...
...we'll have a longer practice today.
Isn't that your girlfriend, Midori?
Shouldn't you tell her you'll be late?
haa

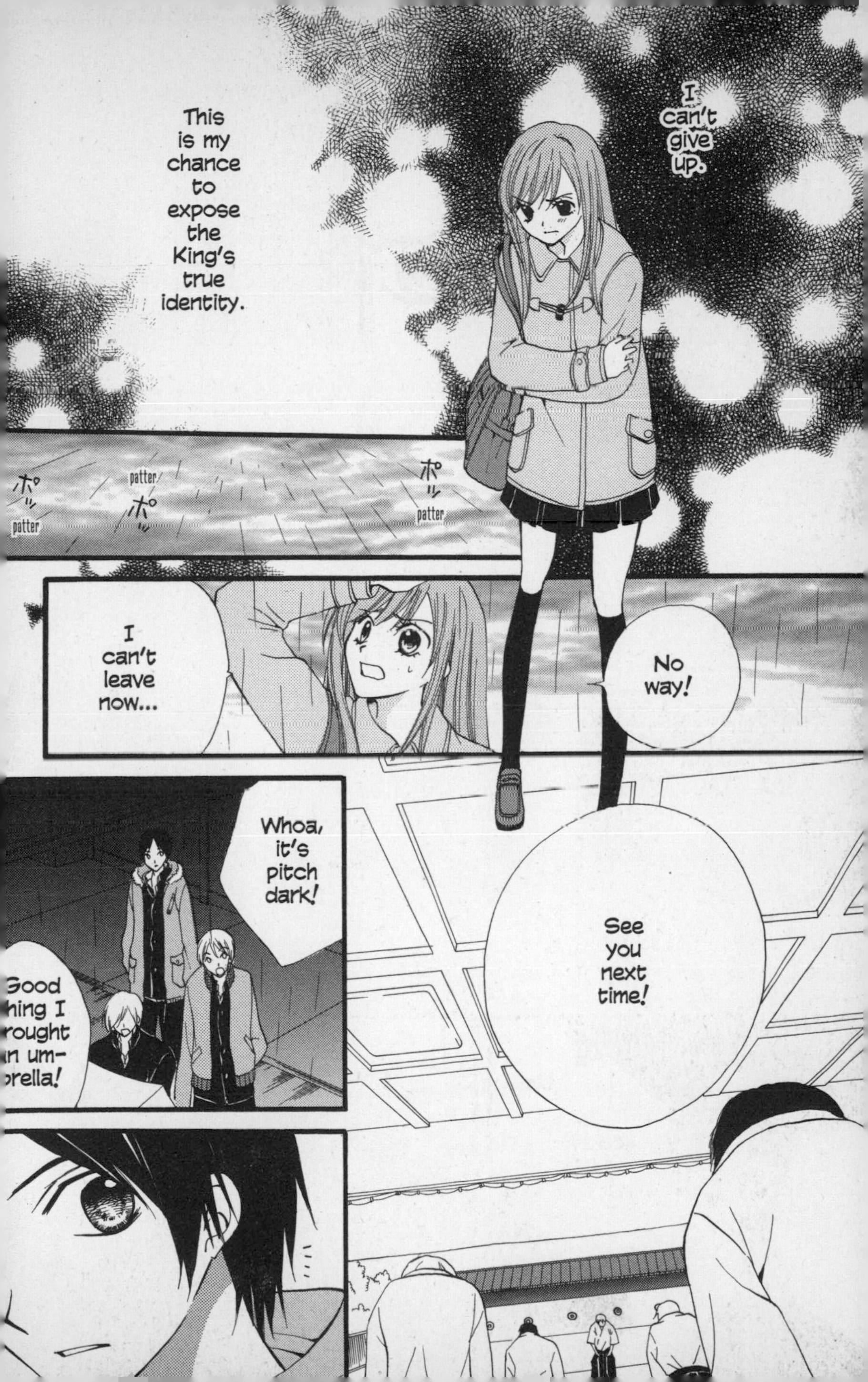
I can't give up.
This is my chance to expose the King's true identity.
ポツ patter
patter ポツ
ポツ patter
No way!
I can't leave now...
See you next time!
Whoa, it's pitch dark!
Good hing I rought an um- brella!
...

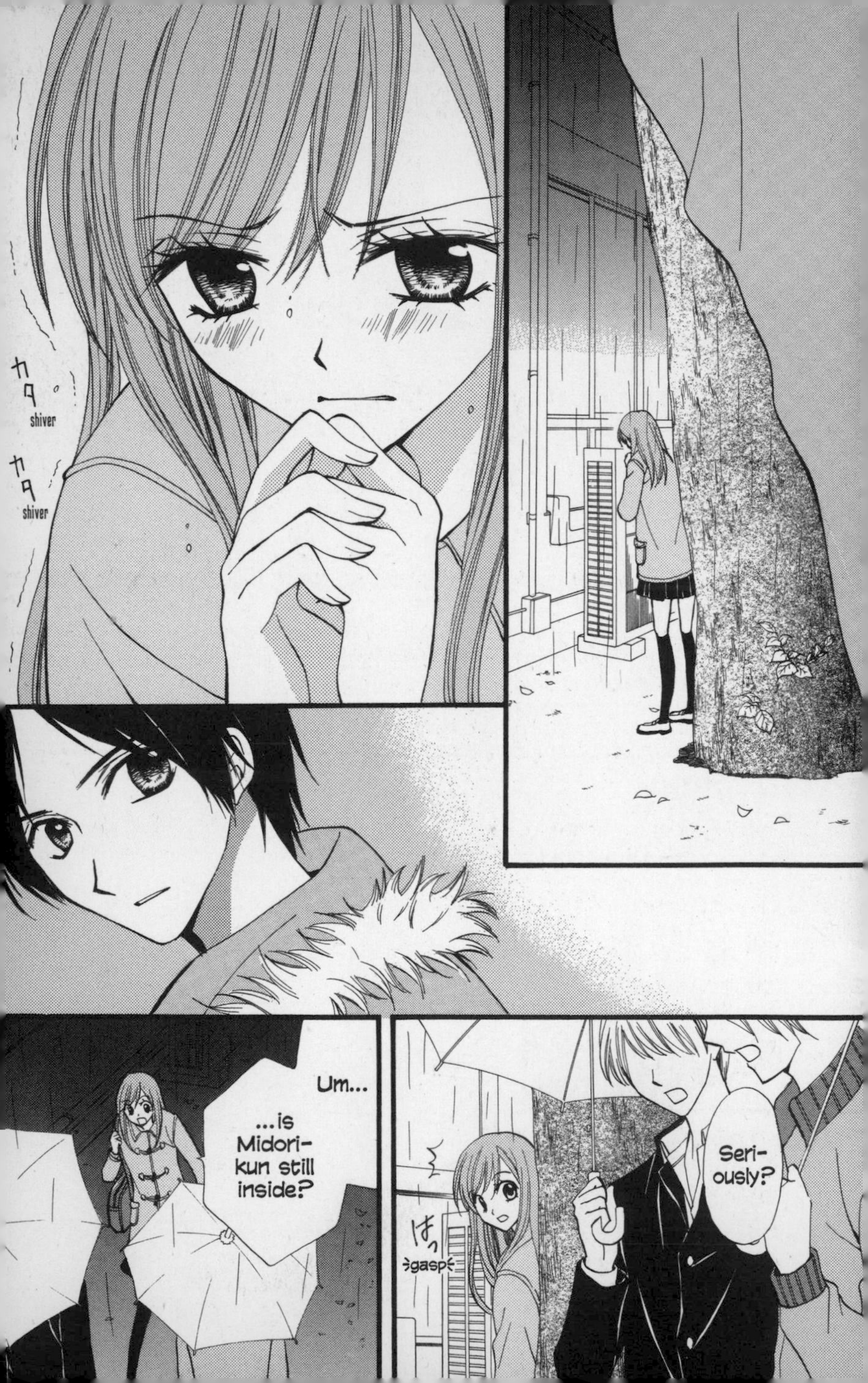
カタ
shiver
カタ
shiver
Seri-
ously?
はっ
gasp
Um...
...is
Midori-
kun still
inside?

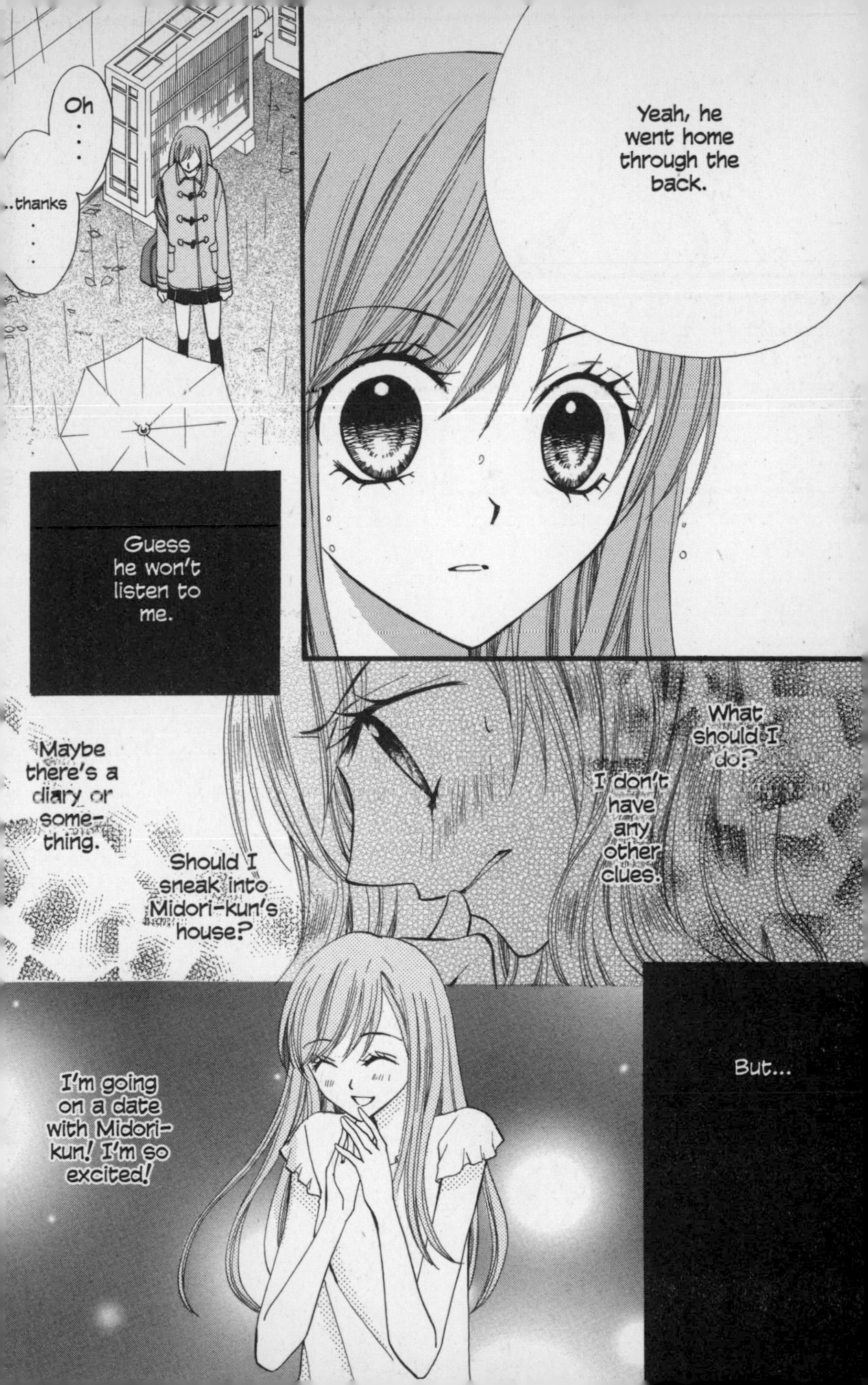
Yeah, he went home through the back.
Oh...
...thanks...
Guess he won't listen to me.
What should I do?
I don't have any other clues.
Maybe there's a diary or some-thing.
Should I sneak into Midori-kun's house?
But...
I'm going on a date with Midori-kun! I'm so excited!

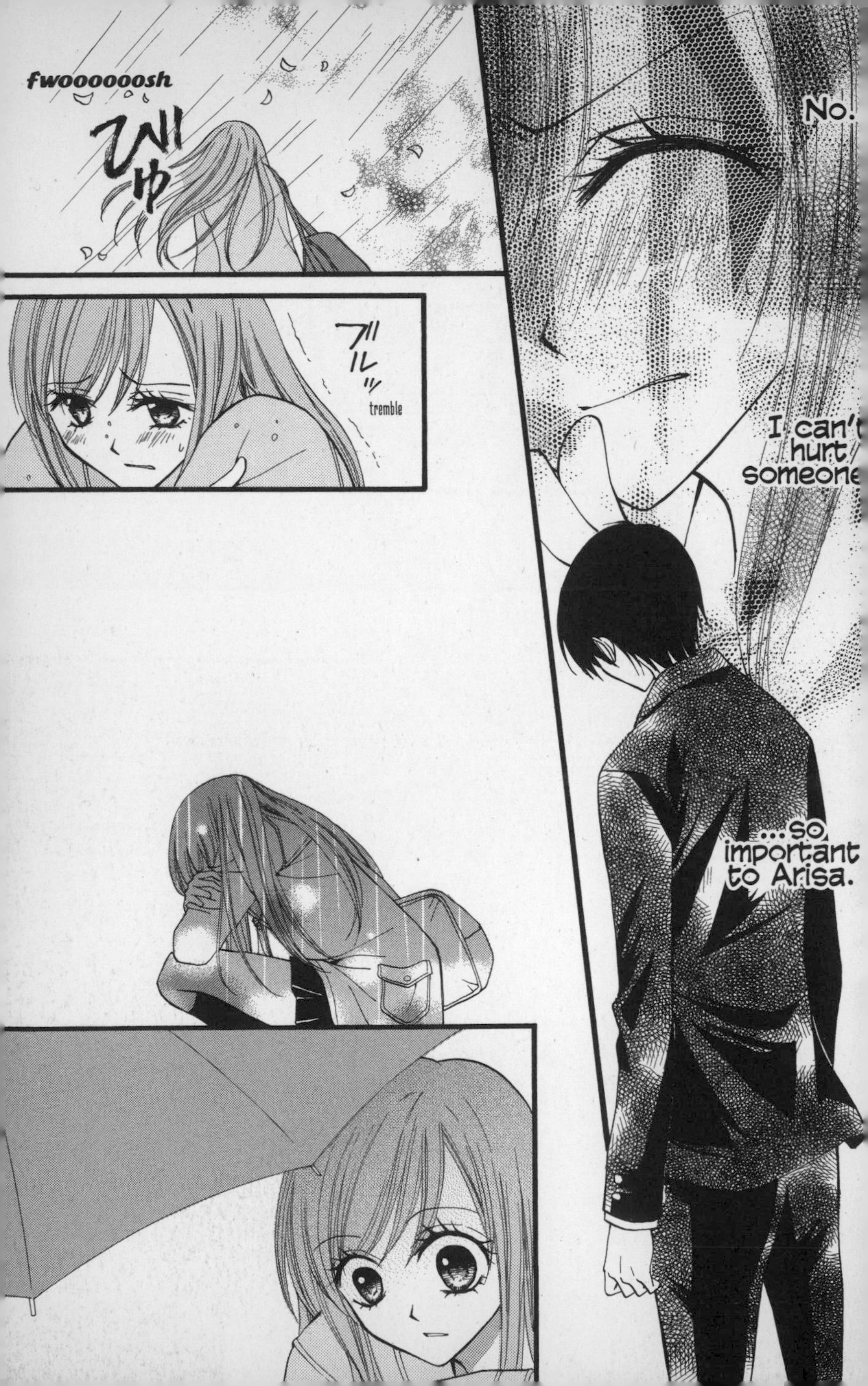
No.
I can't hurt someone
...so important to Arisa.
ひゅ
fwoooooosh
ブルッ
tremble

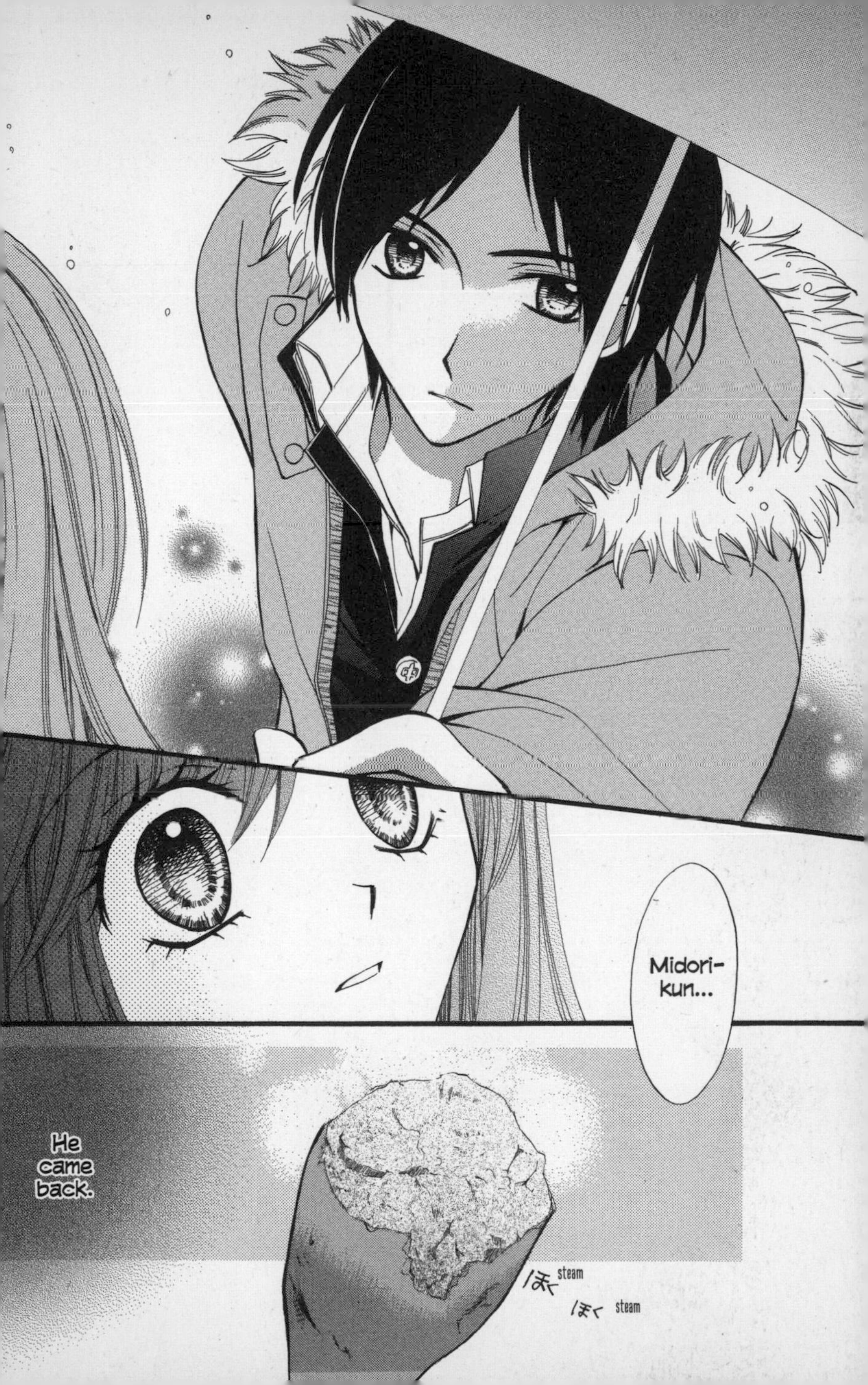
Midori-kun...
He came back.
ほく steam
ほく steam

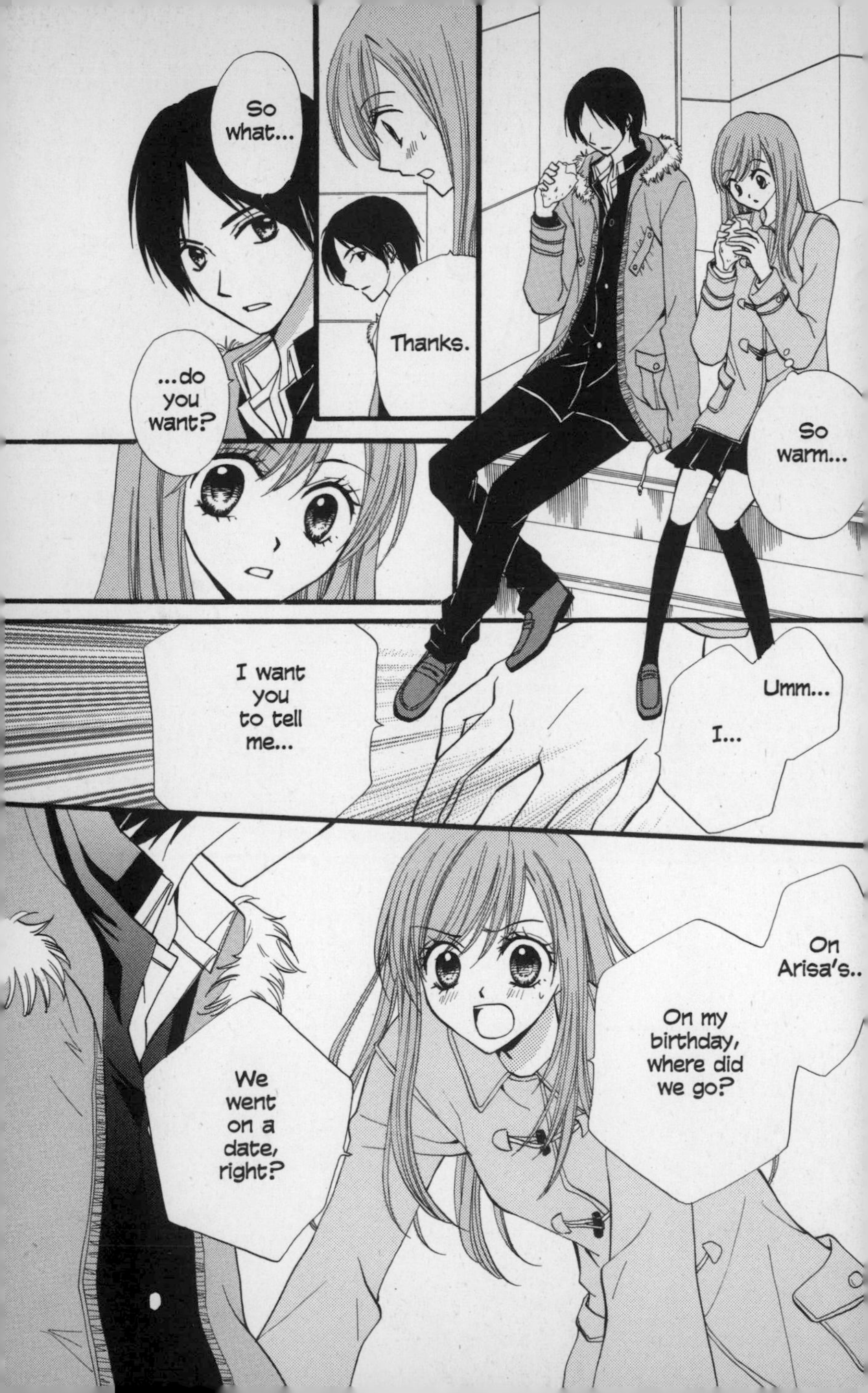
So warm...
Thanks.
So what...
...do you want?
Umm...
I...
I want you to tell me...
On Arisa's..
On my birthday, where did we go?
We went on a date, right?

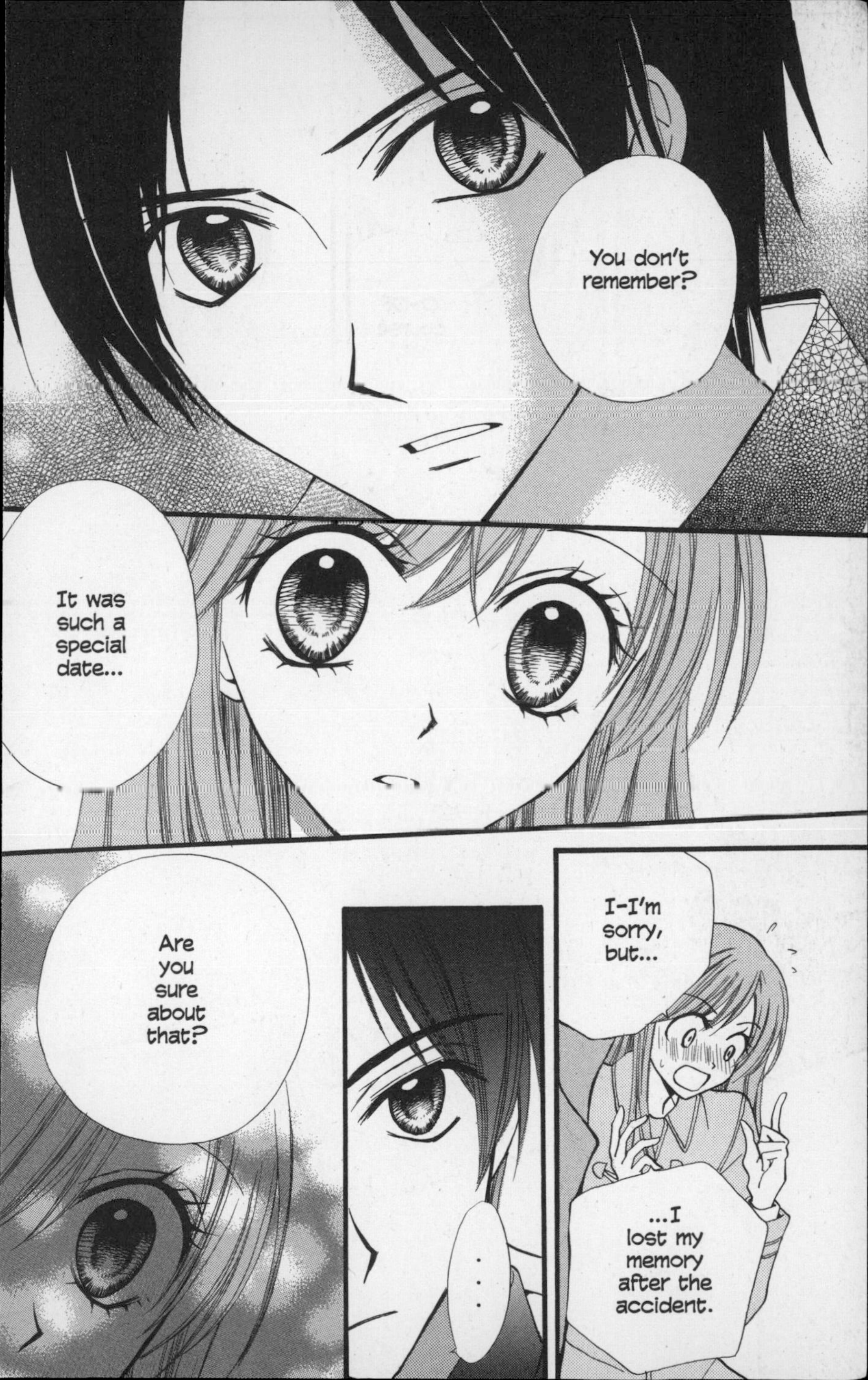
You don't remember?
It was such a special date...
I-I'm sorry, but...
...I lost my memory after the accident.
...
Are you sure about that?

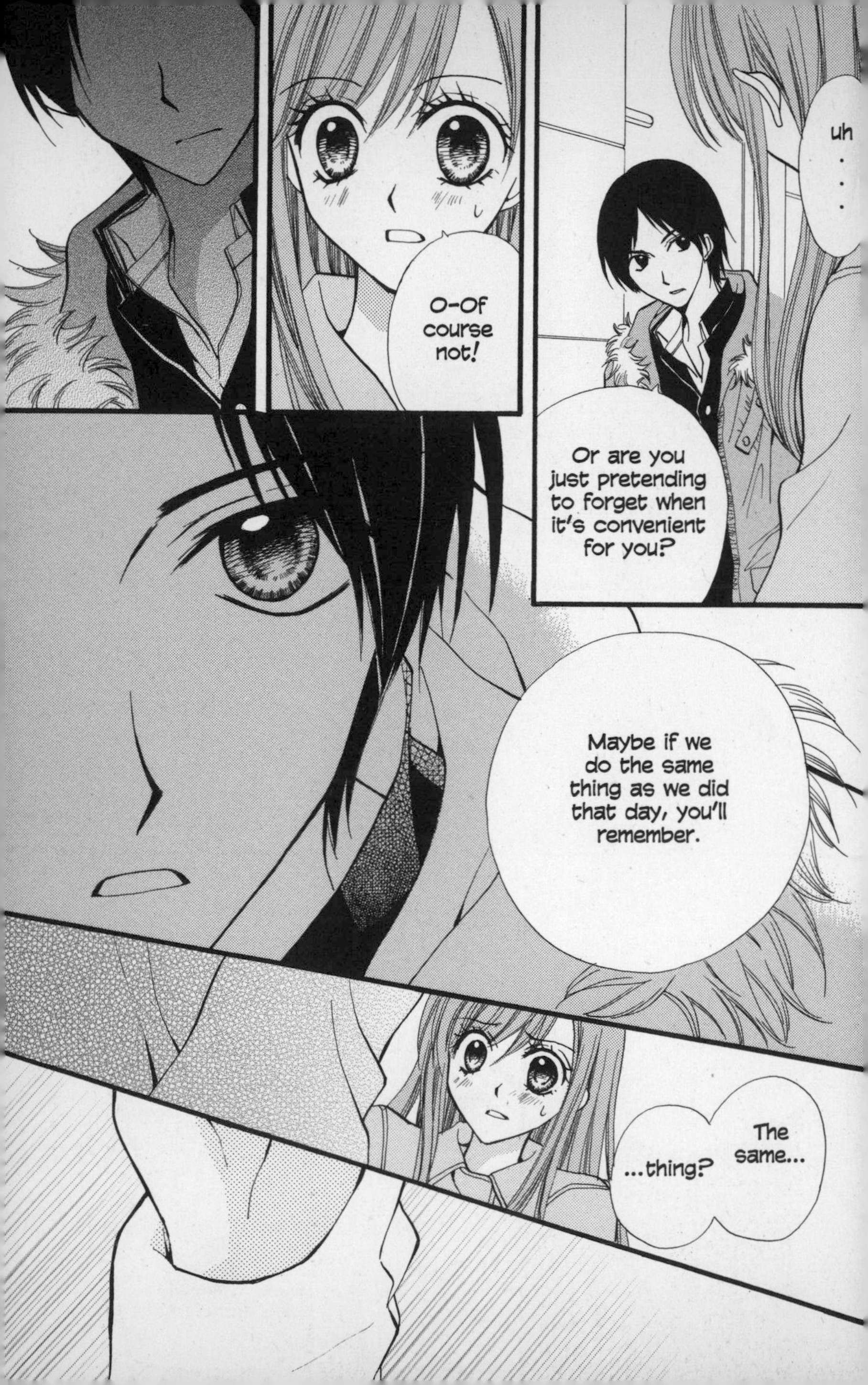
uh...
Or are you just pretending to forget when it's convenient for you?
O-Of course not!
Maybe if we do the same thing as we did that day, you'll remember.
The same...
...thing?

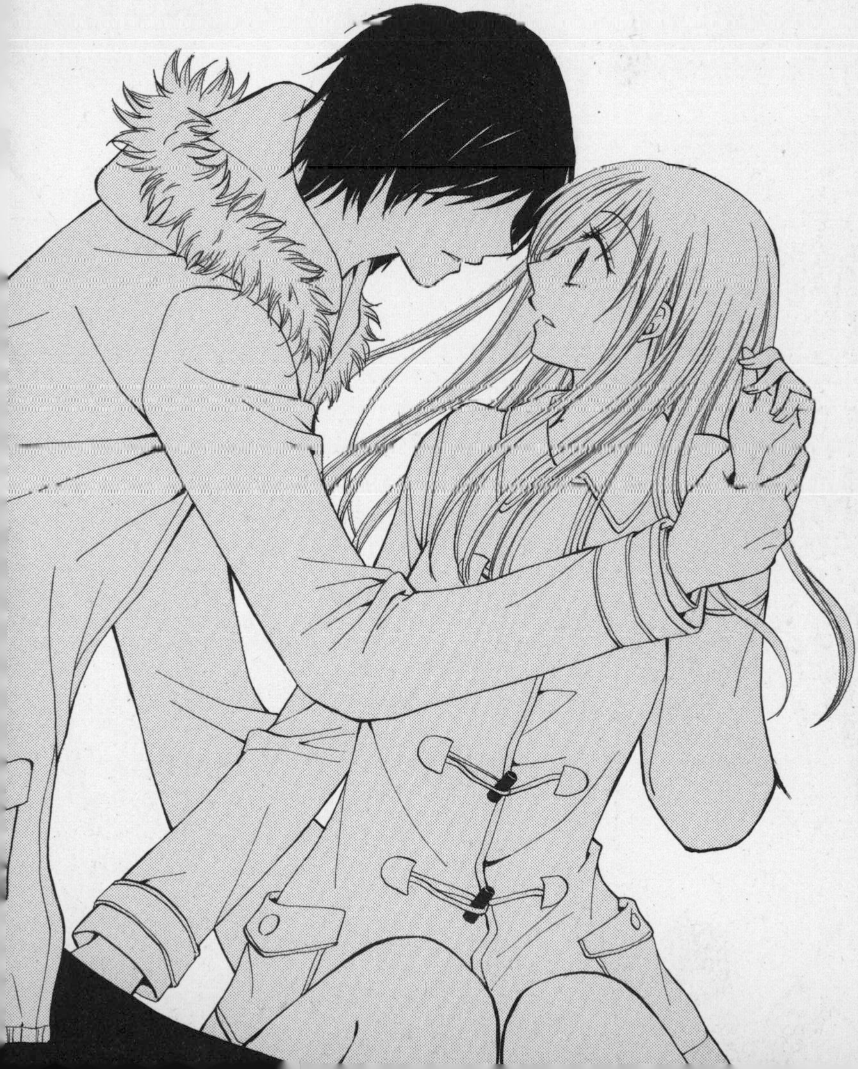

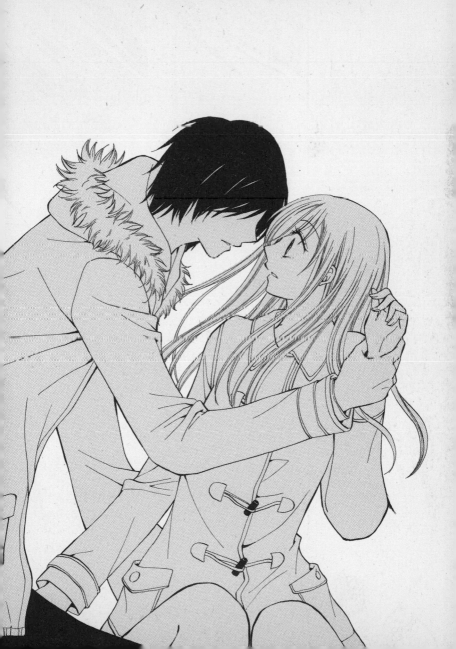

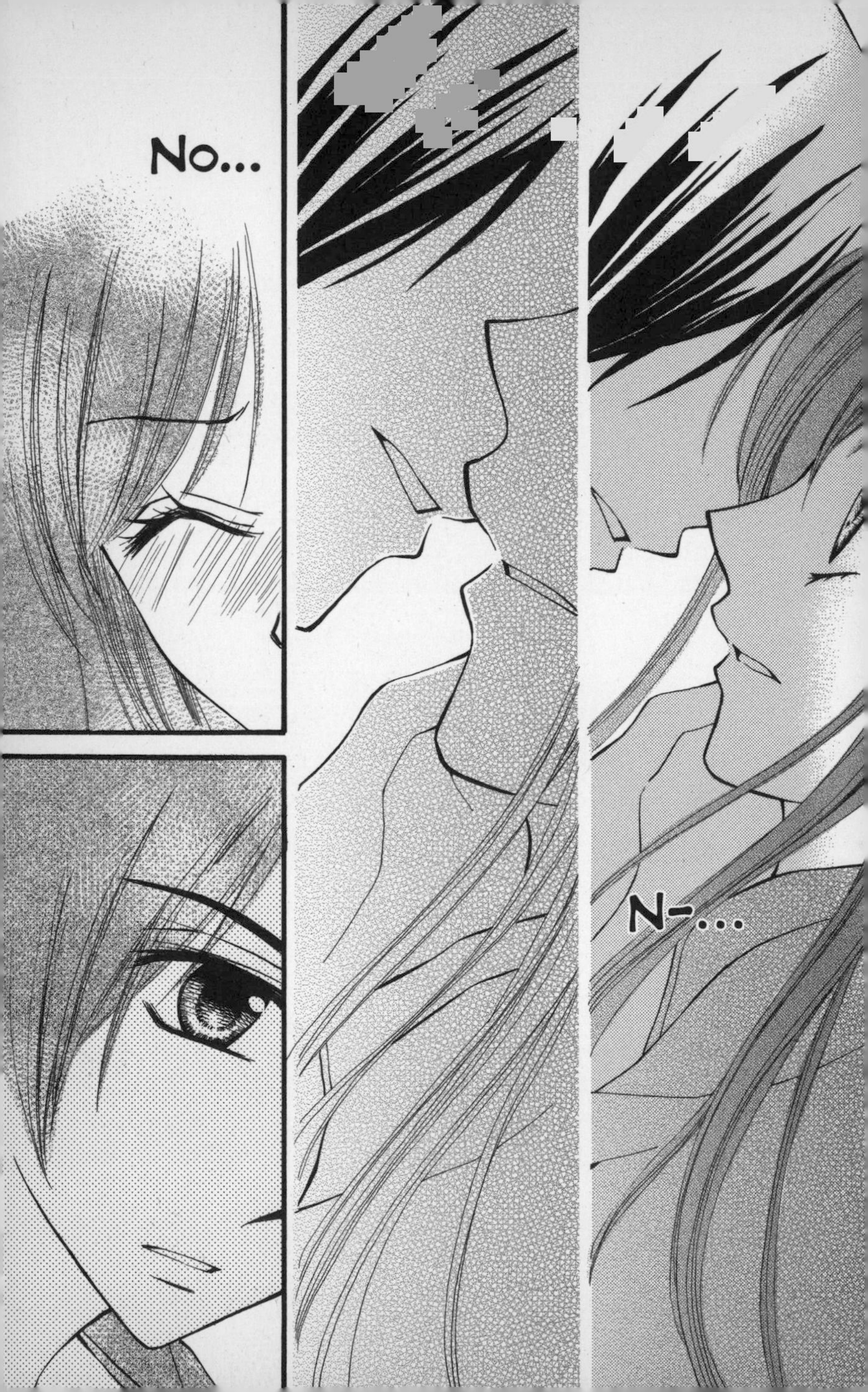
N-...
No...

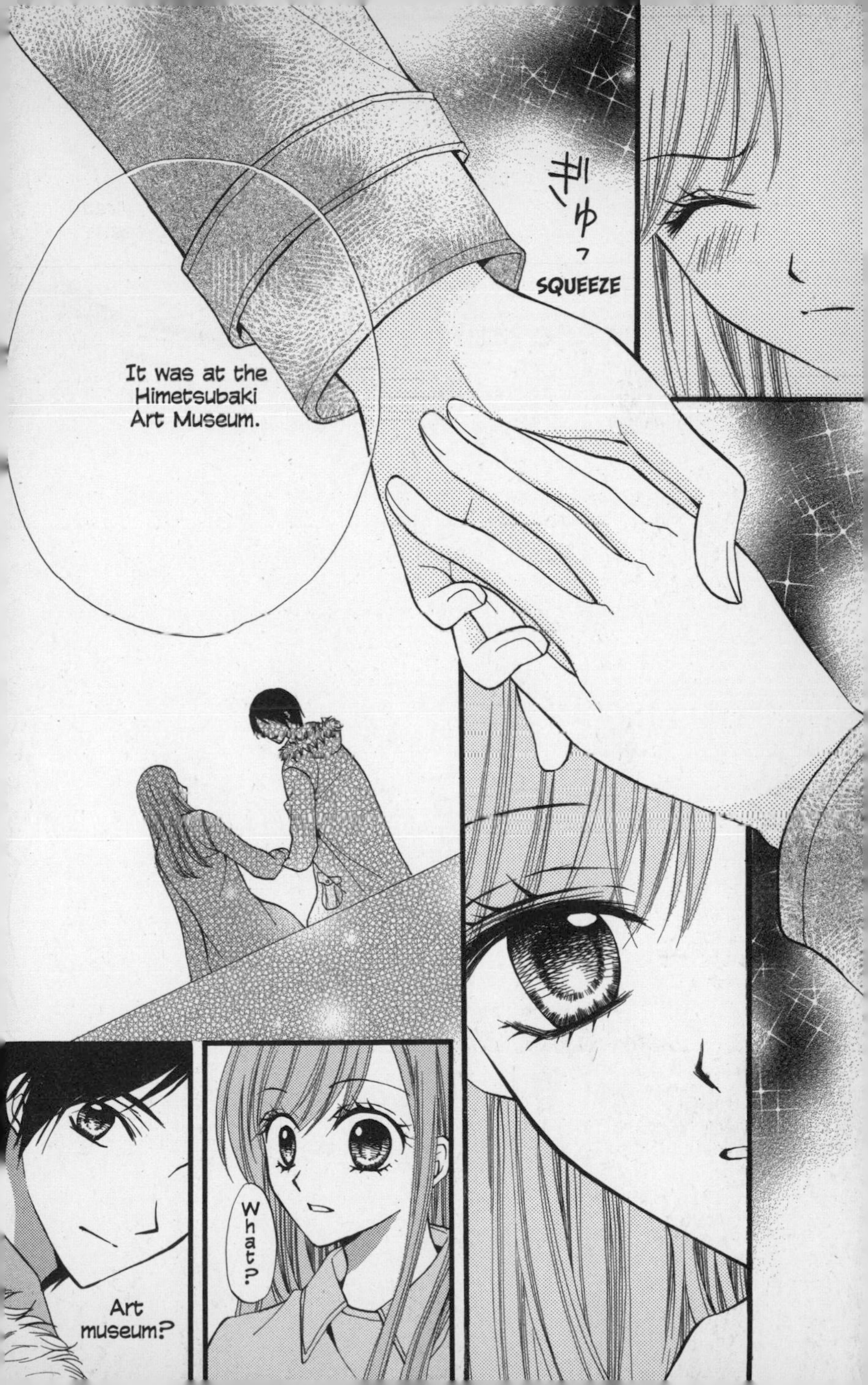
ぎゅっ
SQUEEZE
It was at the Himetsubaki Art Museum.
What?
Art museum?

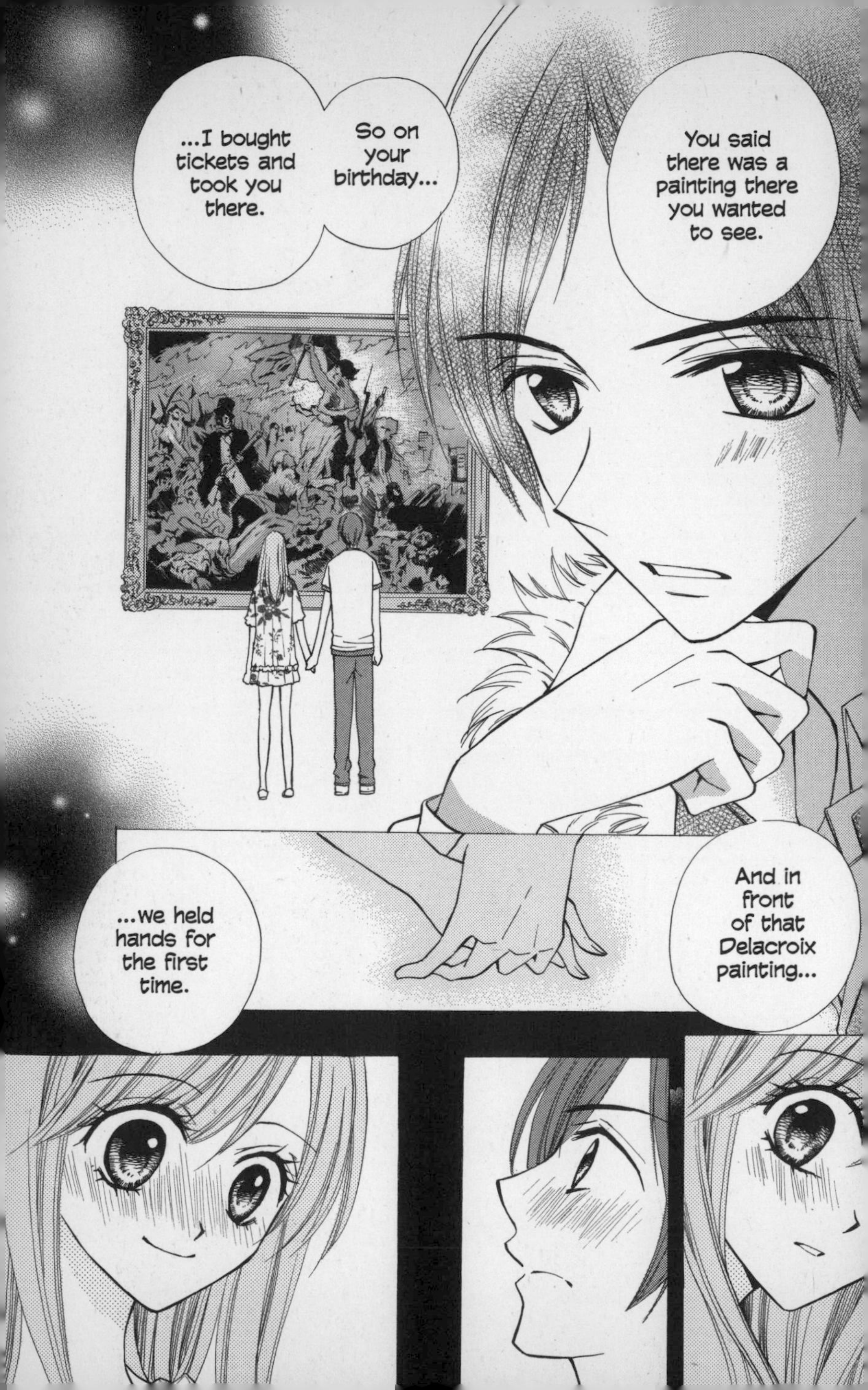
You said there was a painting there you wanted to see.
So on your birthday...
...I bought tickets and took you there.
And in front of that Delacroix painting...
...we held hands for the first time.

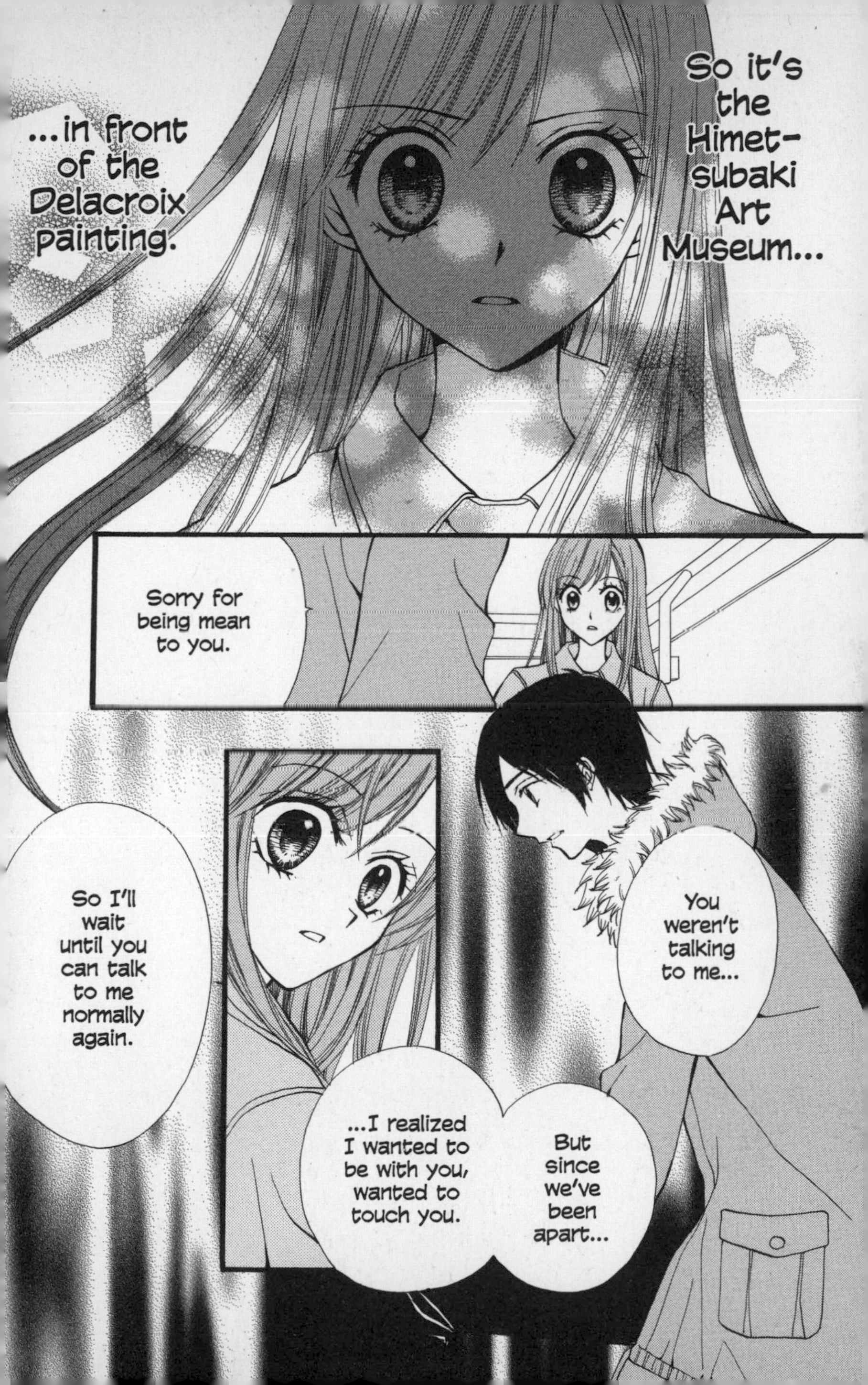
So it's the Himet-subaki Art Museum...
...in front of the Delacroix painting.
Sorry for being mean to you.
You weren't talking to me...
But since we've been apart...
...I realized I wanted to be with you, wanted to touch you.
So I'll wait until you can talk to me normally again.

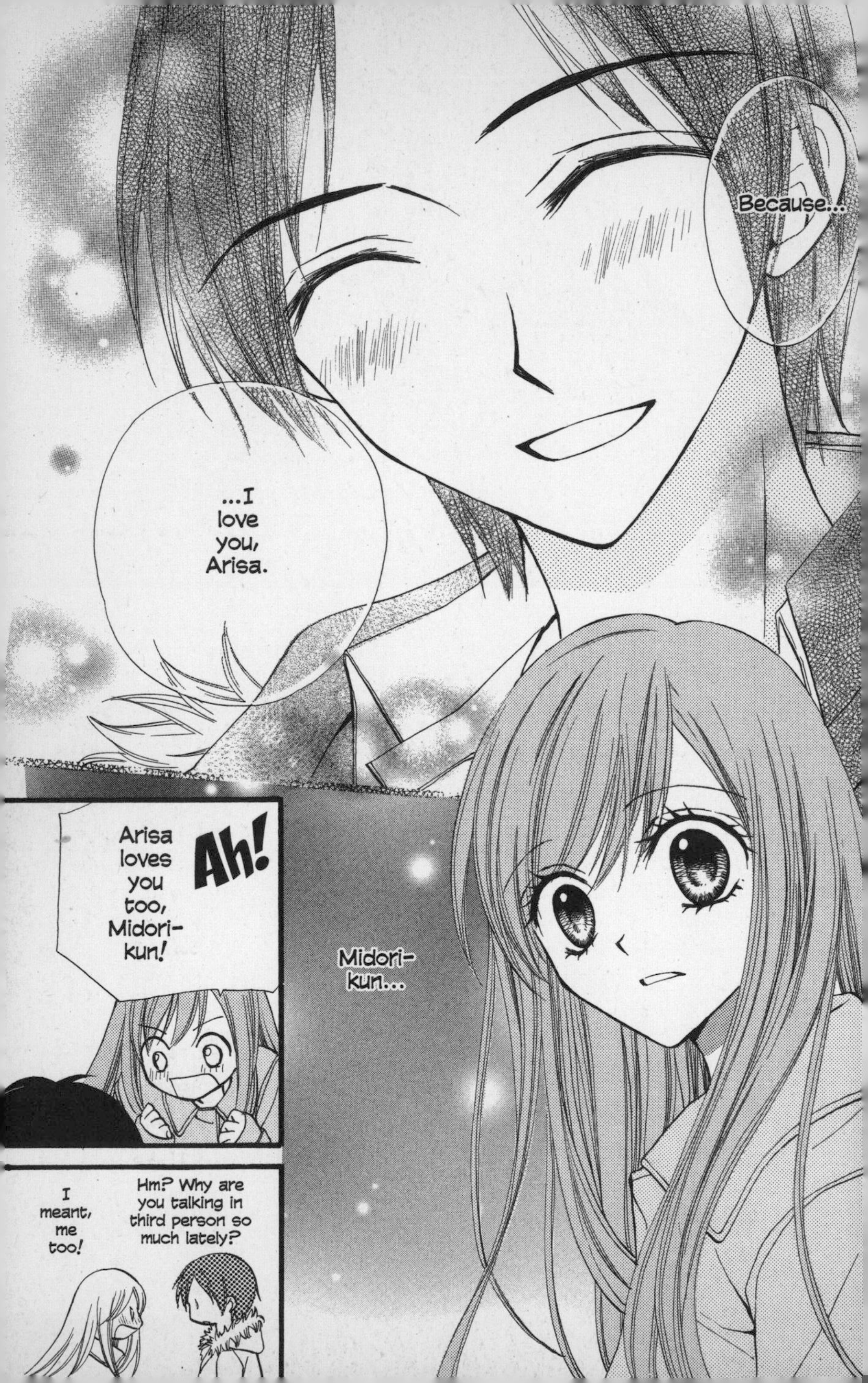
Because...
...I love you, Arisa.
Midori-kun...
Ah!
Arisa loves you too, Midori-kun!
Hm? Why are you talking in third person so much lately?
I meant, me too!

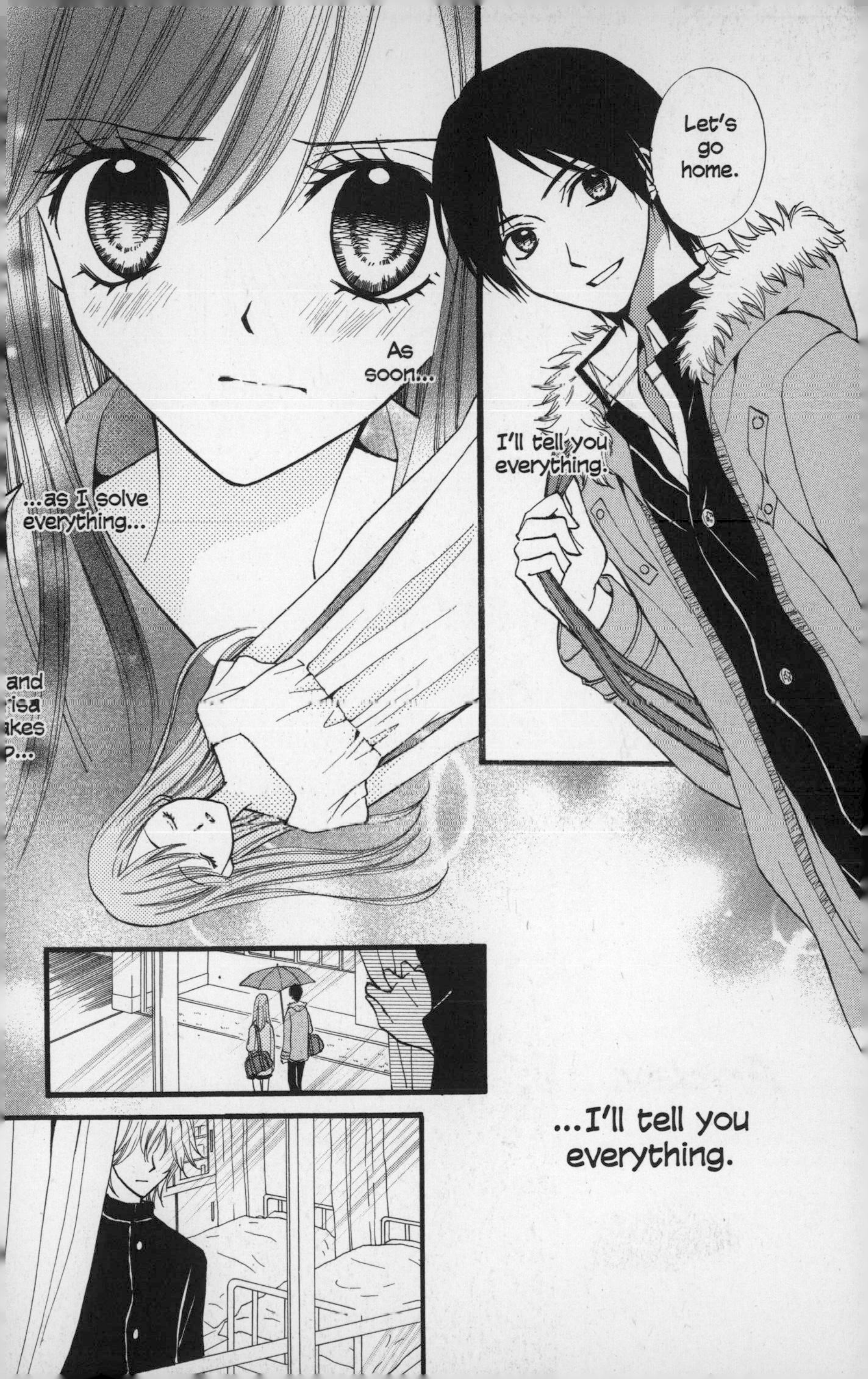
Let's go home.
I'll tell you everything.
As soon...
...as I solve everything...
and risa akes p...
...I'll tell you everything.

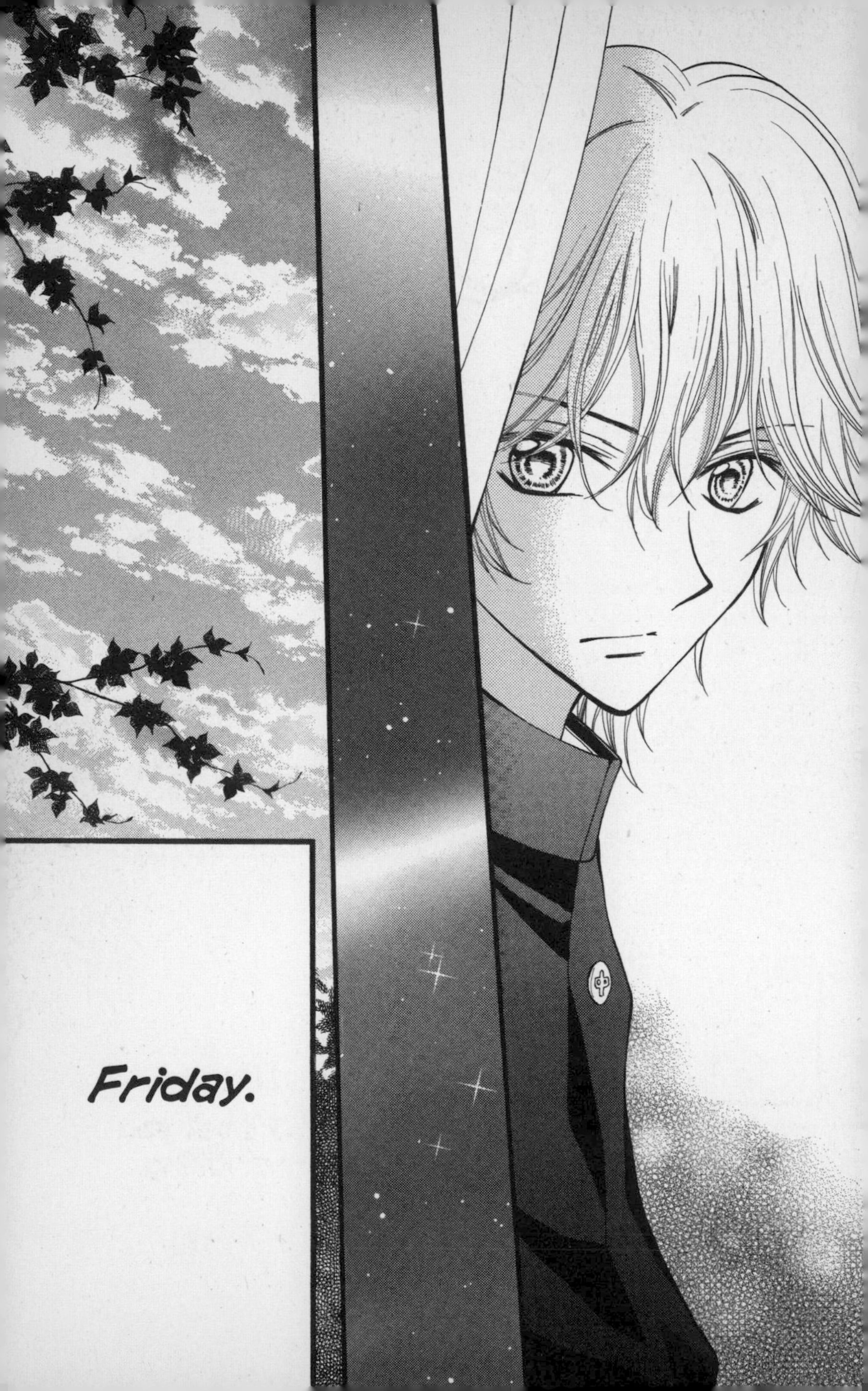
Friday.

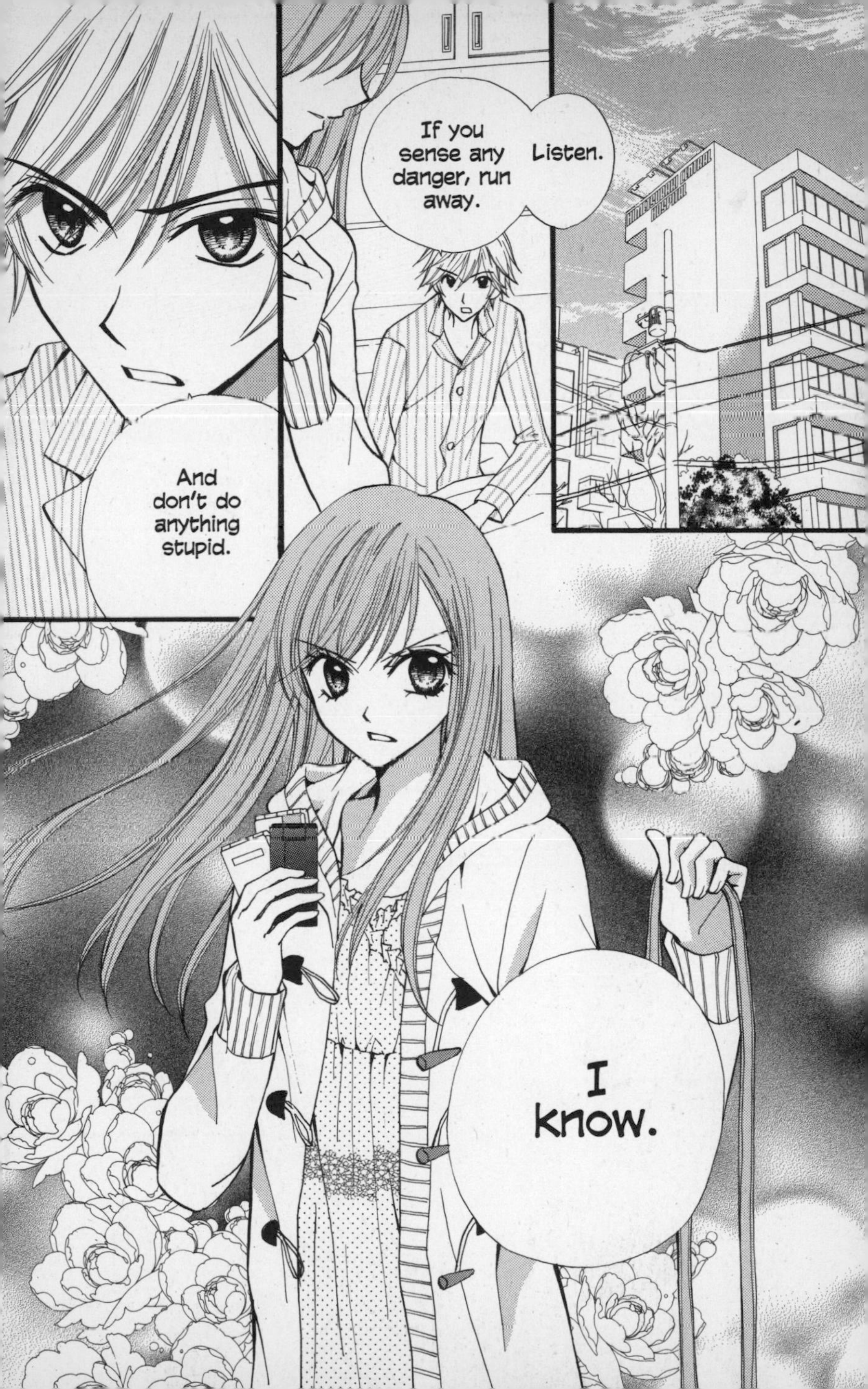
Listen.
If you sense any danger, run away.
And don't do anything stupid.
I know.

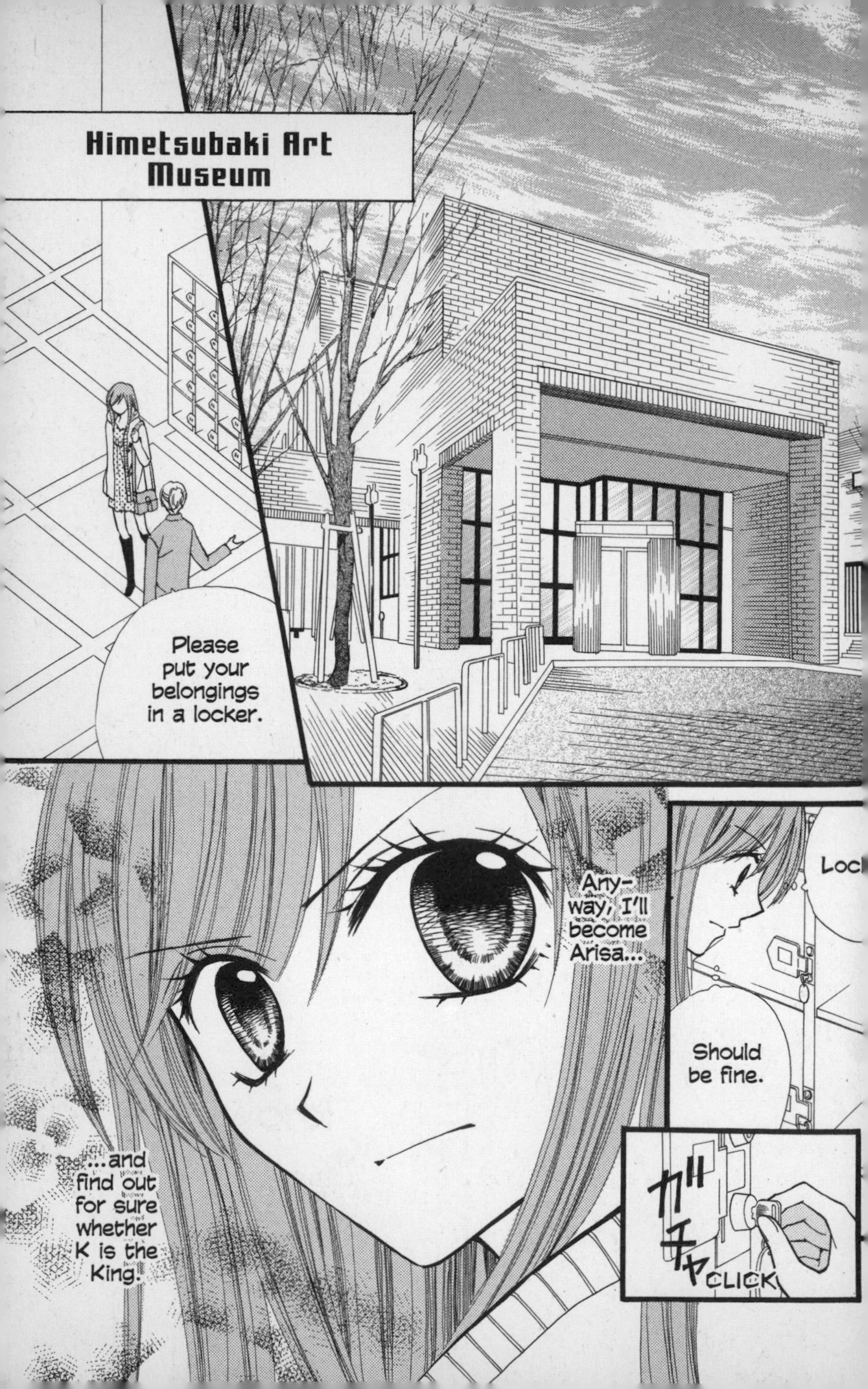
Himetsubaki Art Museum
Please put your belongings in a locker.
Loc
Should be fine.
ガチャ CLICK
Any-way, I'll become Arisa...
...and find out for sure whether K is the King.

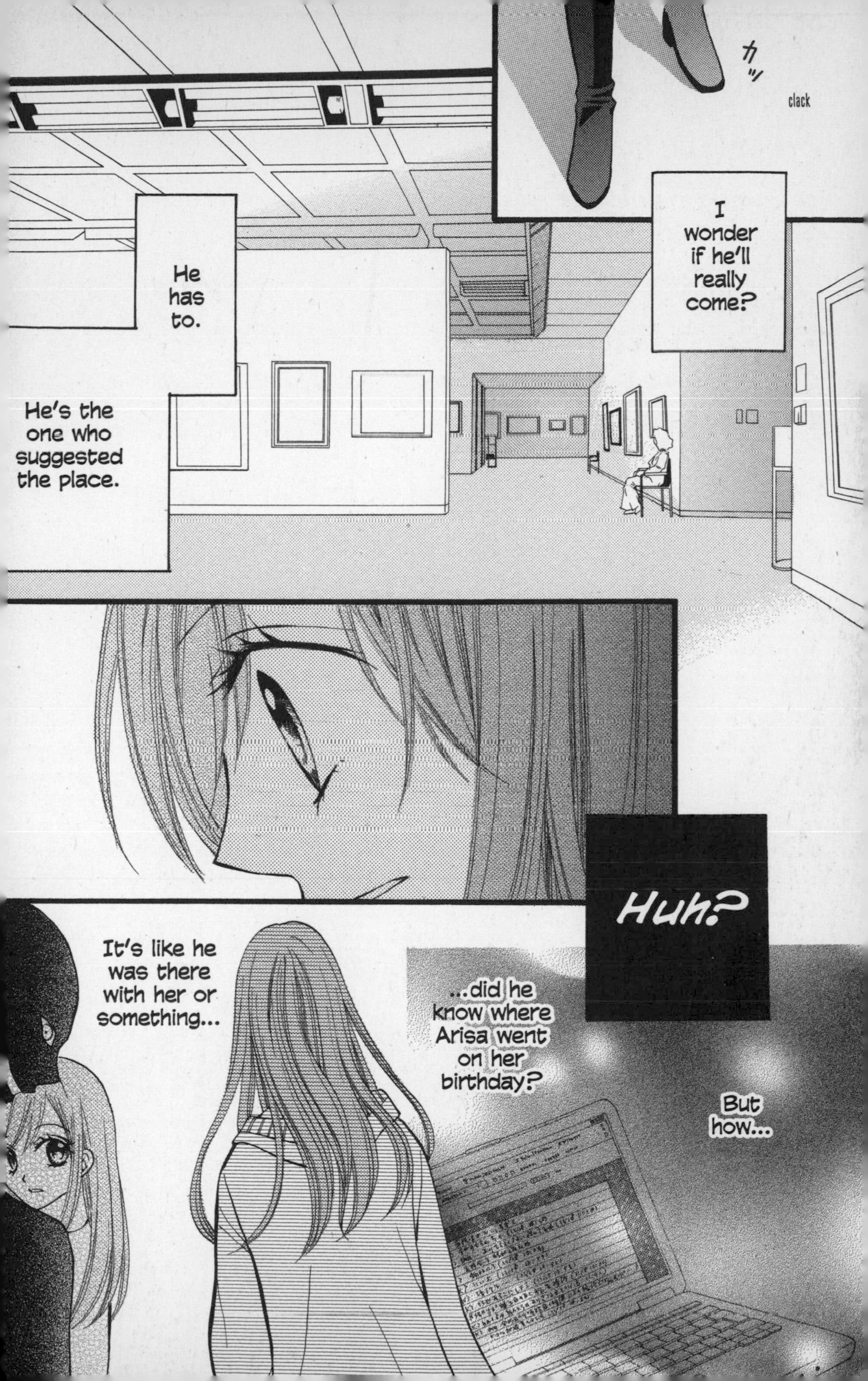
カッ
clack
I wonder if he'll really come?
He has to.
He's the one who suggested the place.
Huh?
But how...
...did he know where Arisa went on her birthday?
It's like he was there with her or something...

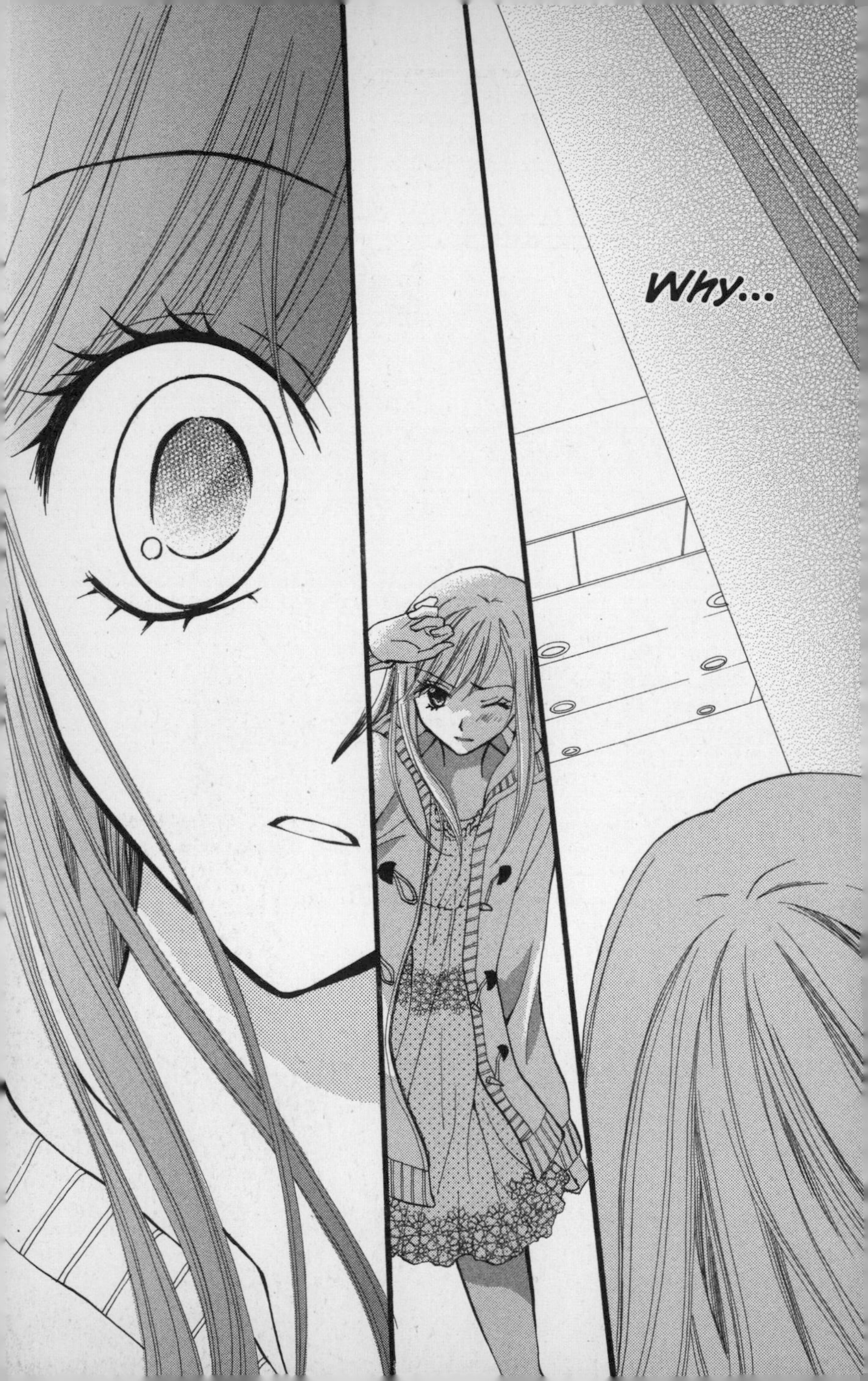
Why...

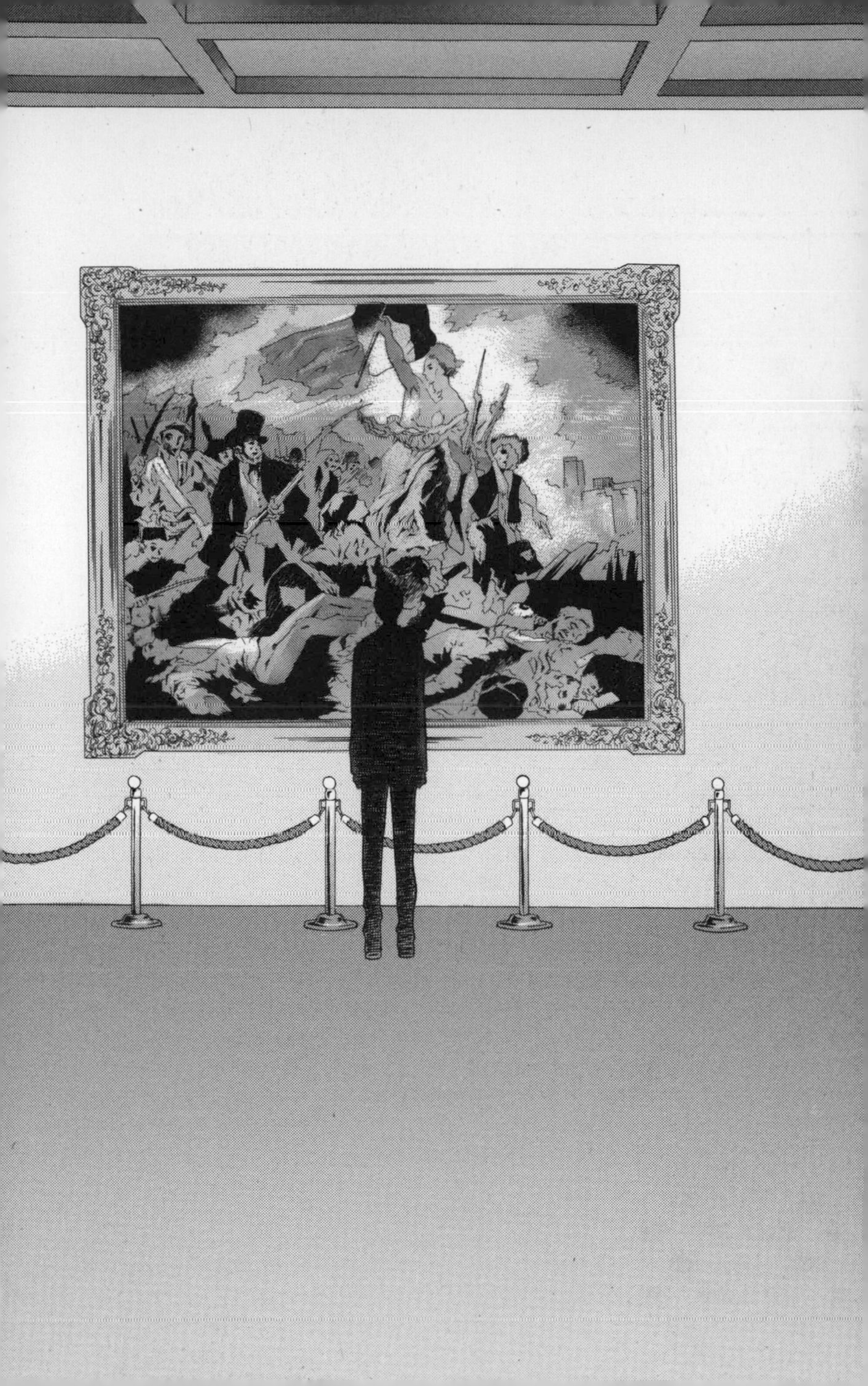

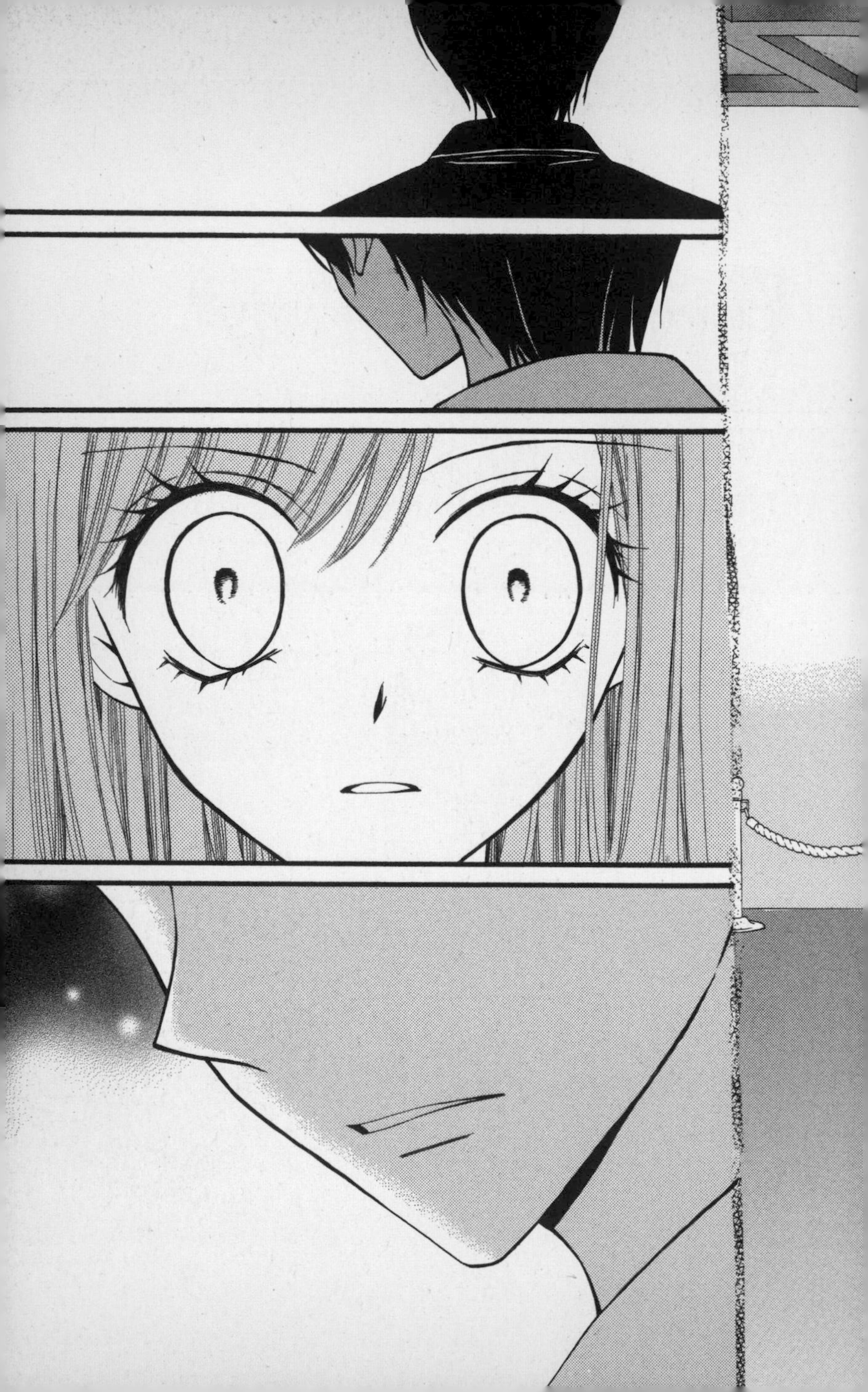

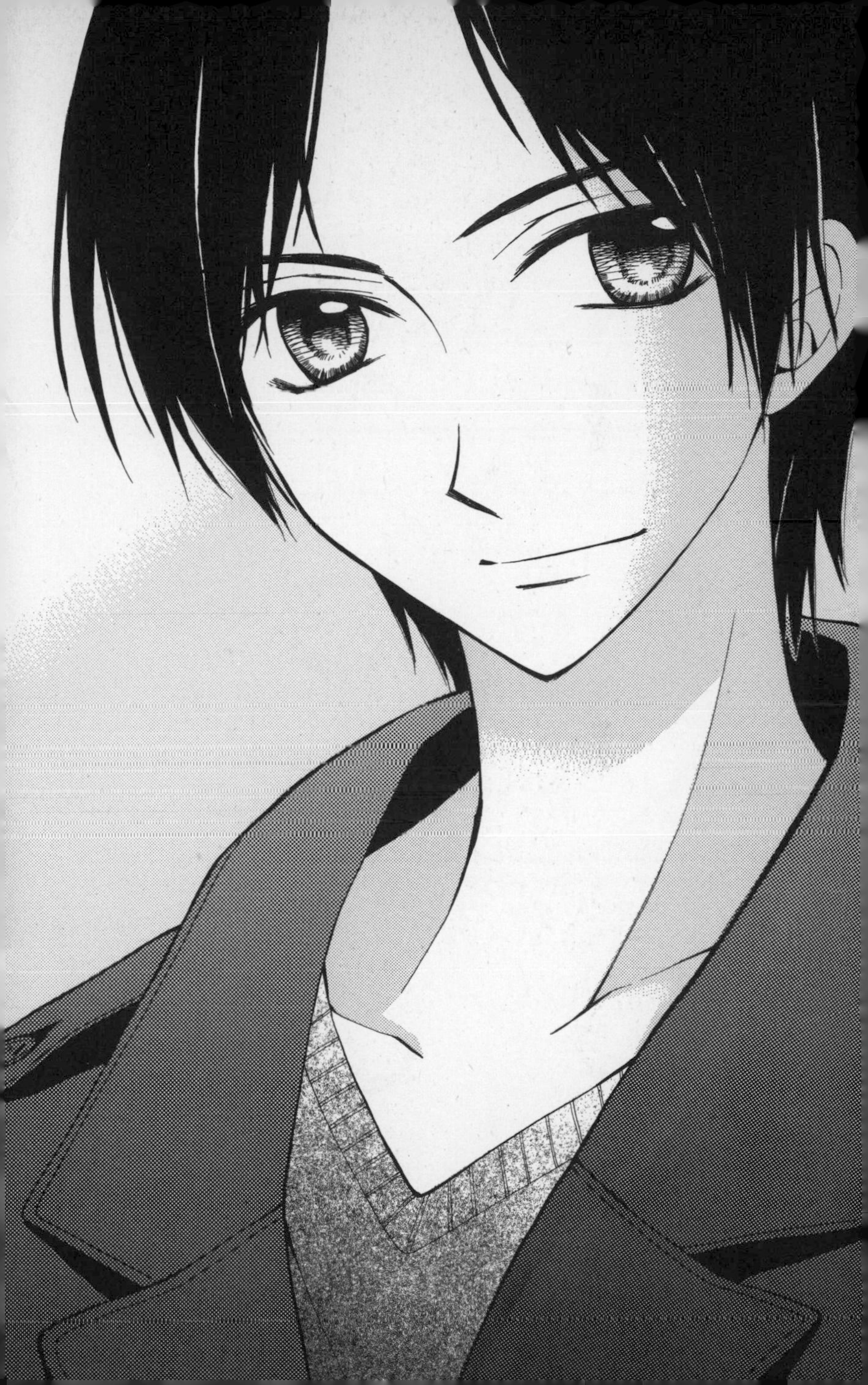

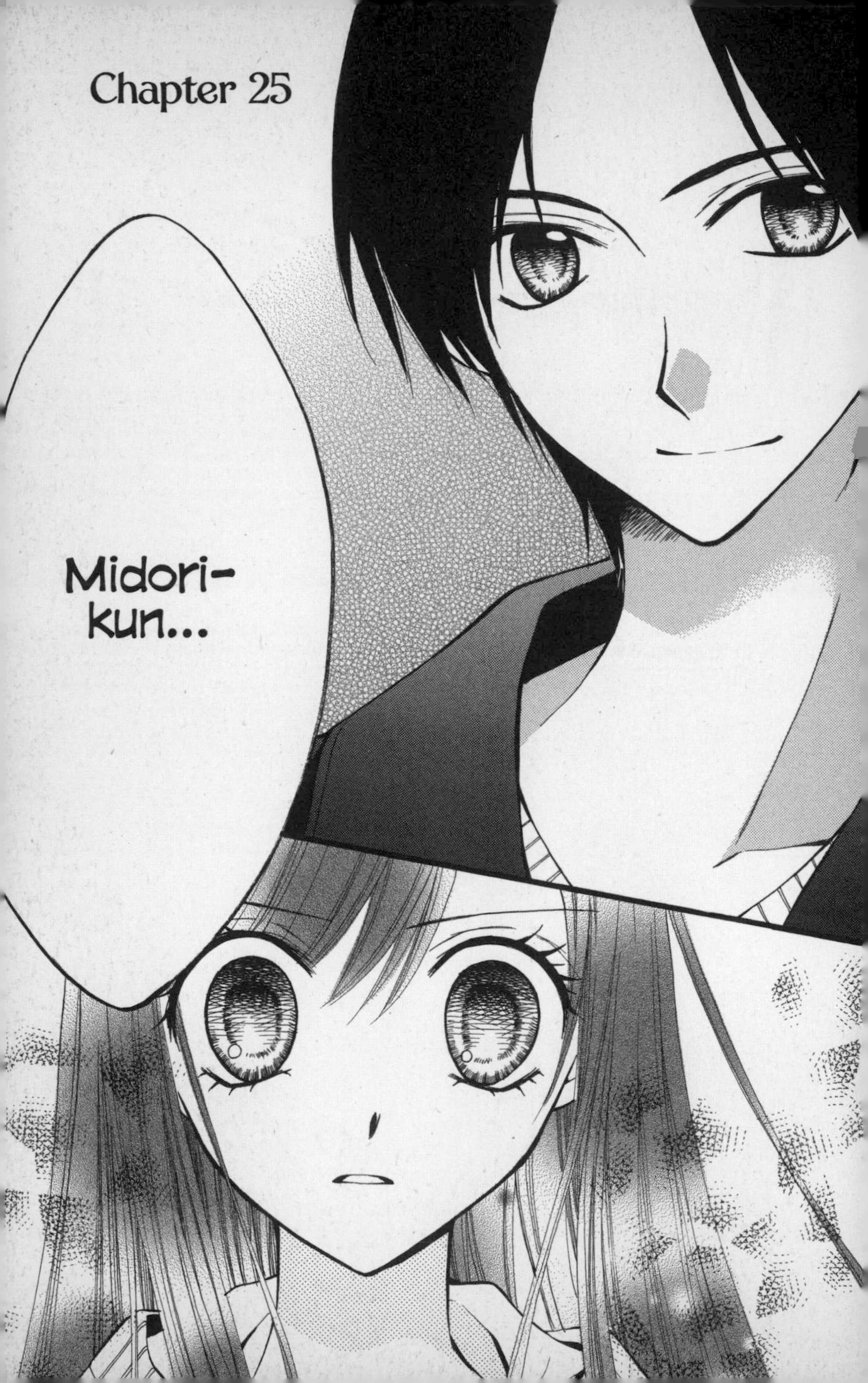
Chapter 25
Midori-kun...

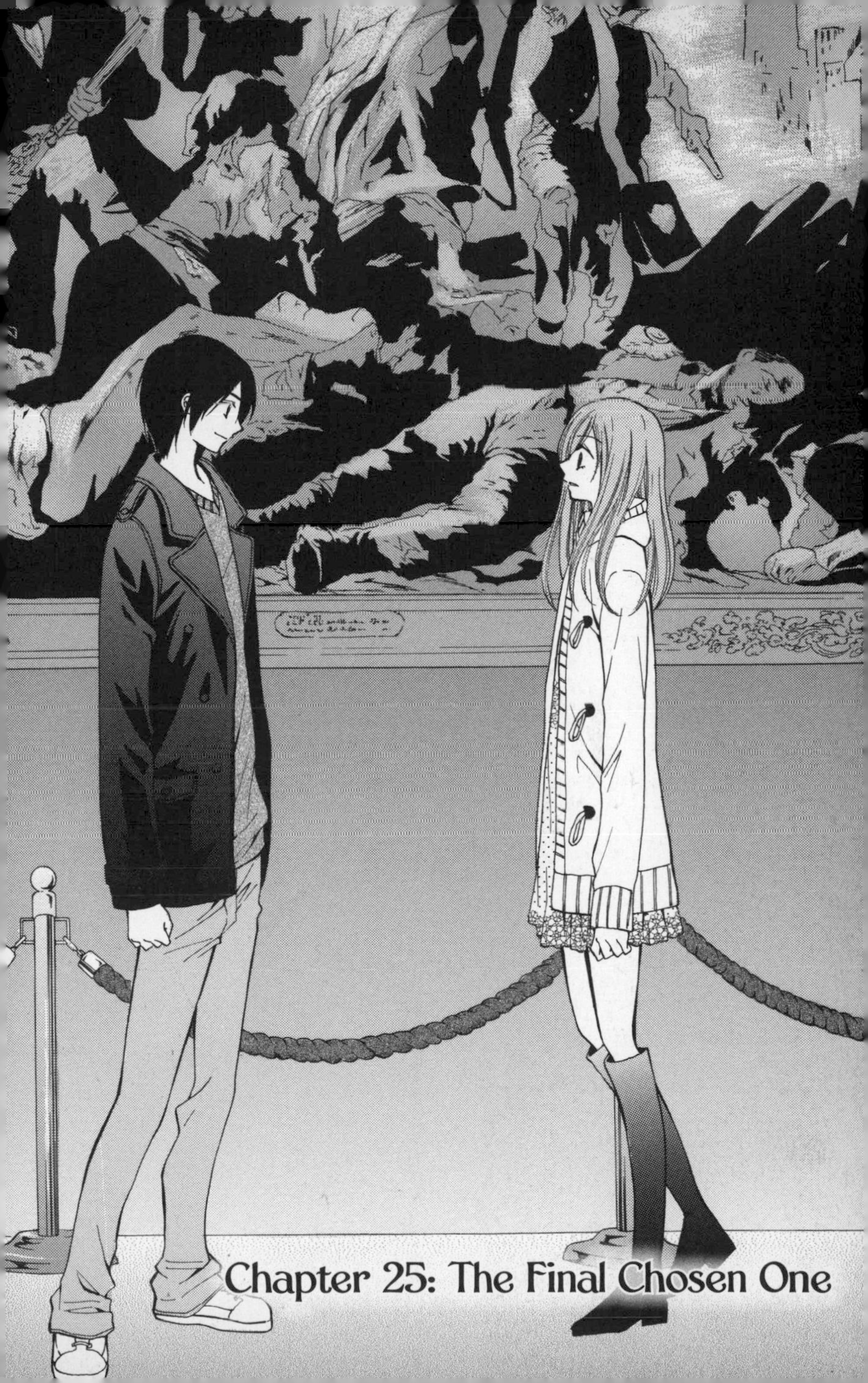
Chapter 25: The Final Chosen One

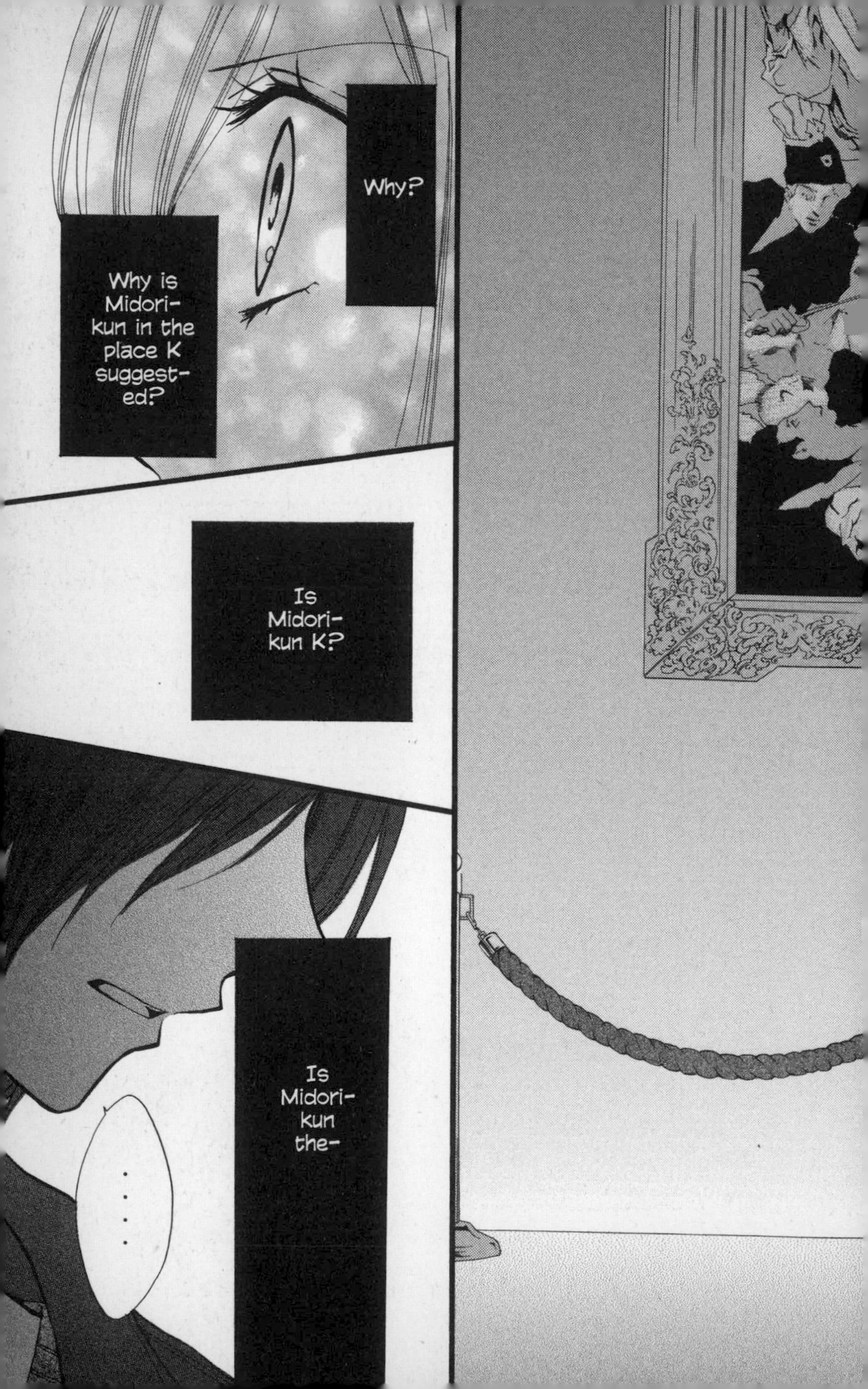
Why?
Why is Midori-kun in the place K suggest-ed?
Is Midori-kun K?
Is Midori-kun the-
. . . .

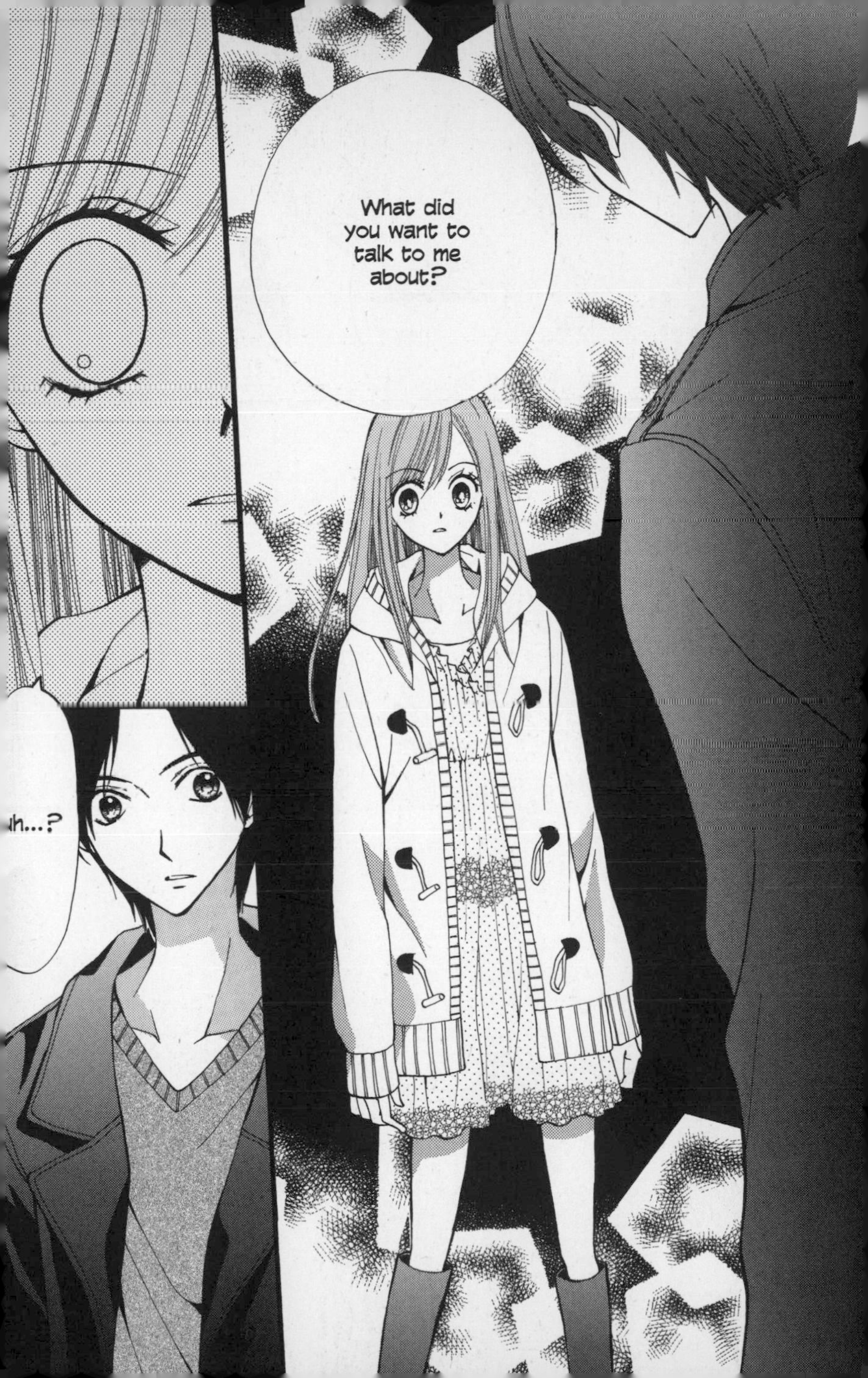
What did you want to talk to me about?
h...?

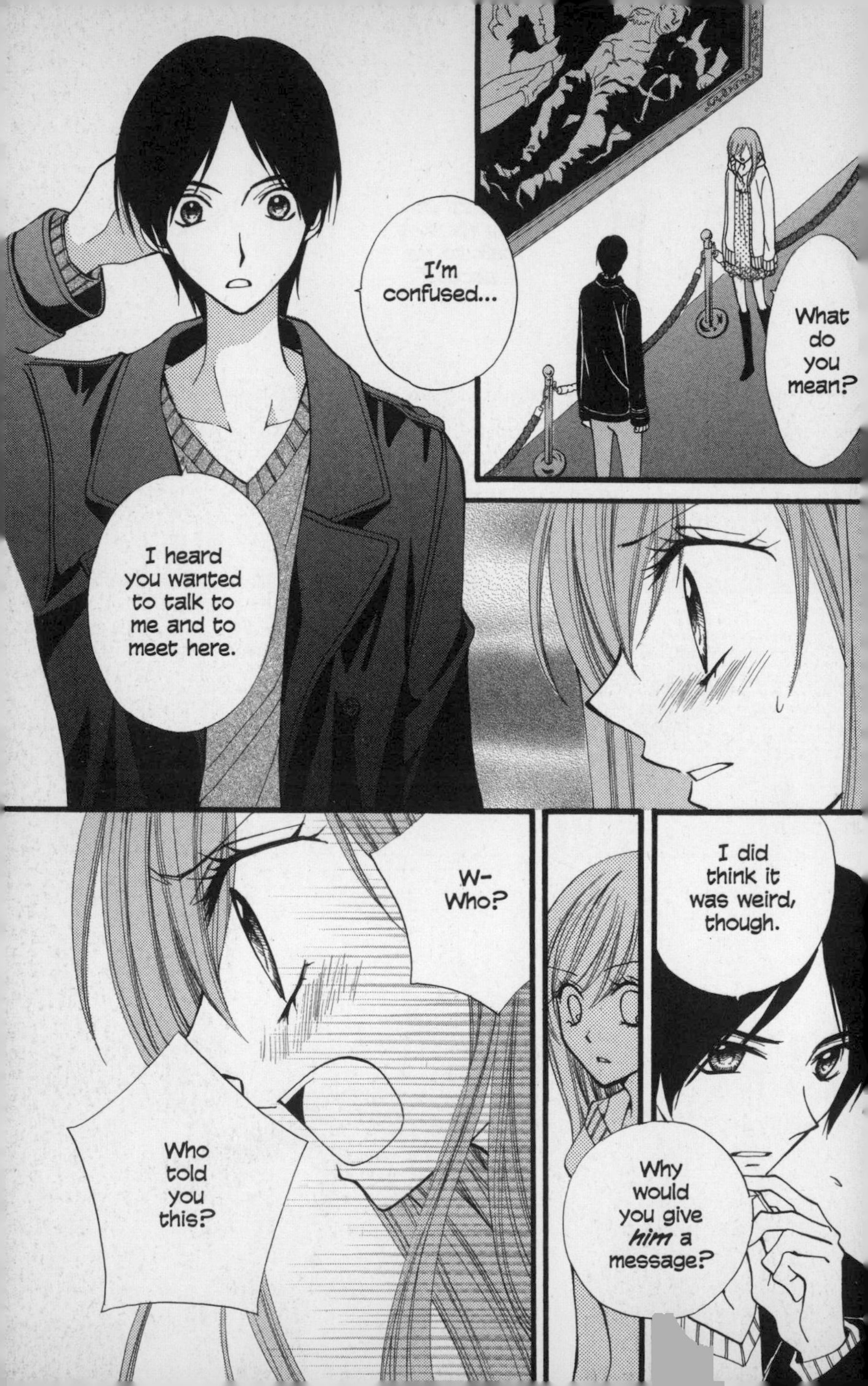
What do you mean?
I'm confused...
I heard you wanted to talk to me and to meet here.
I did think it was weird, though.
Why would you give *him* a message?
W-Who?
Who told you this?

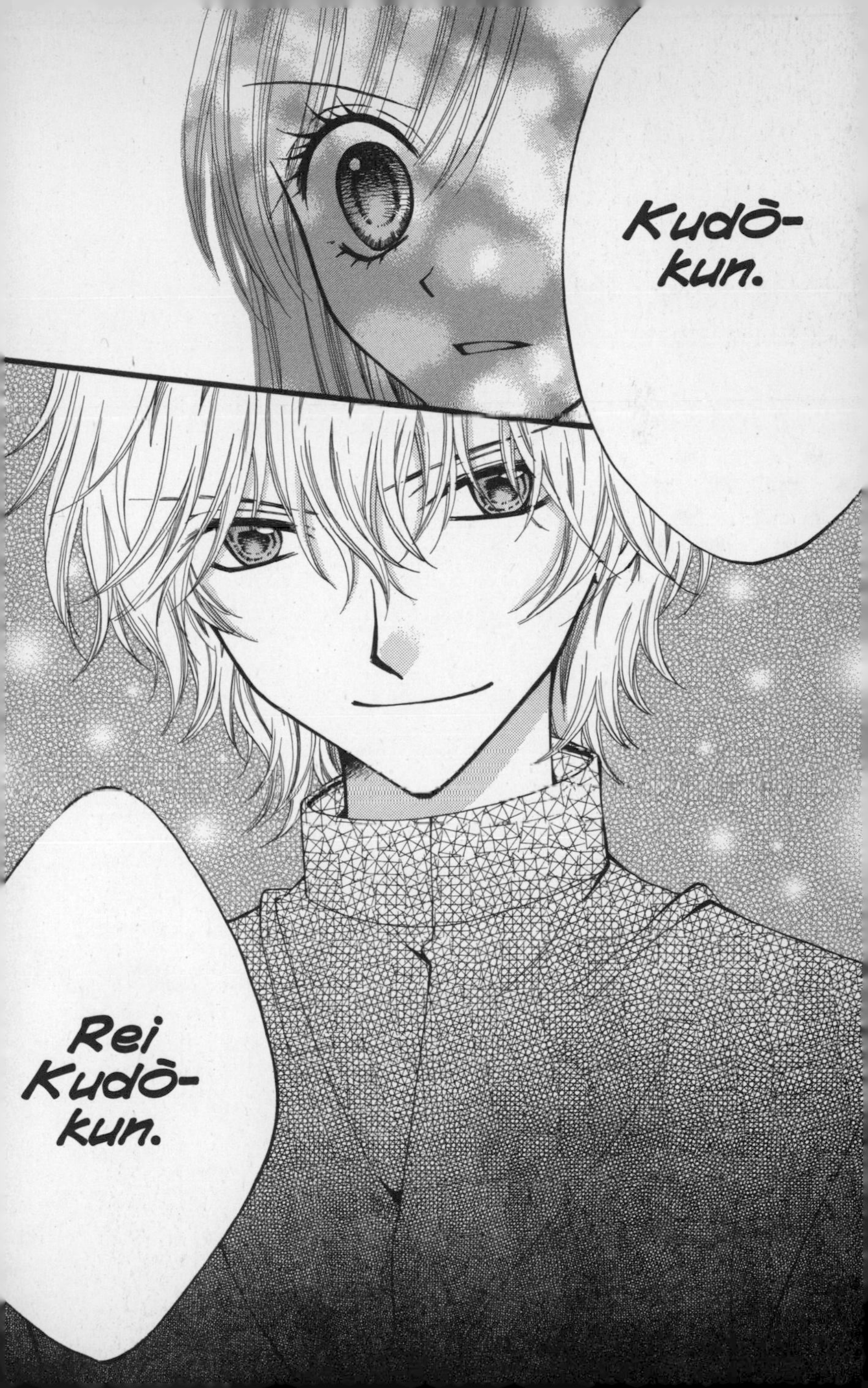
Kudō-kun.
Rei Kudō-kun.

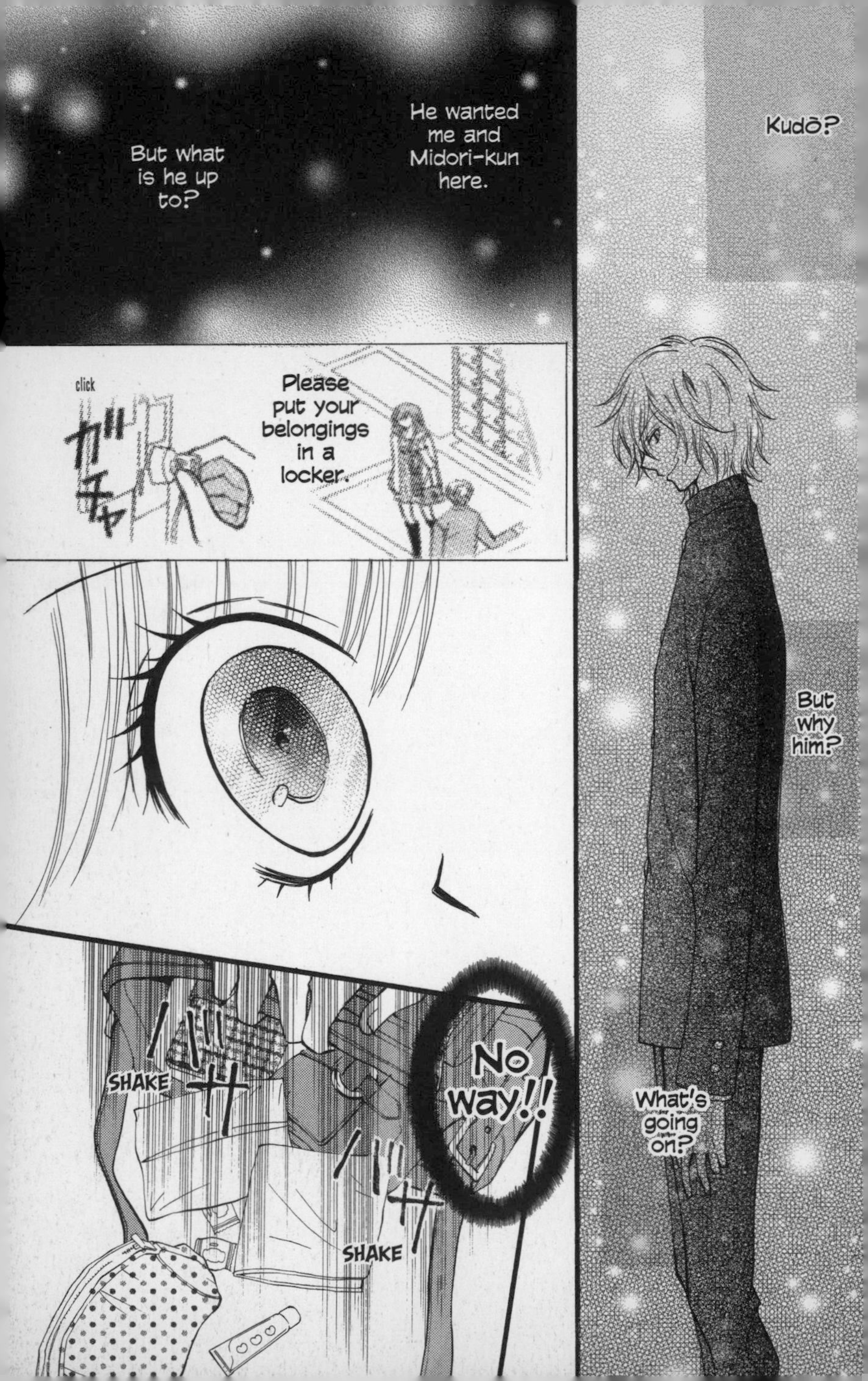
Kudō?
But why him?
What's going on?
He wanted me and Midori-kun here.
But what is he up to?
Please put your belongings in a locker.
ガチャ
click
No way!!
SHAKE
SHAKE

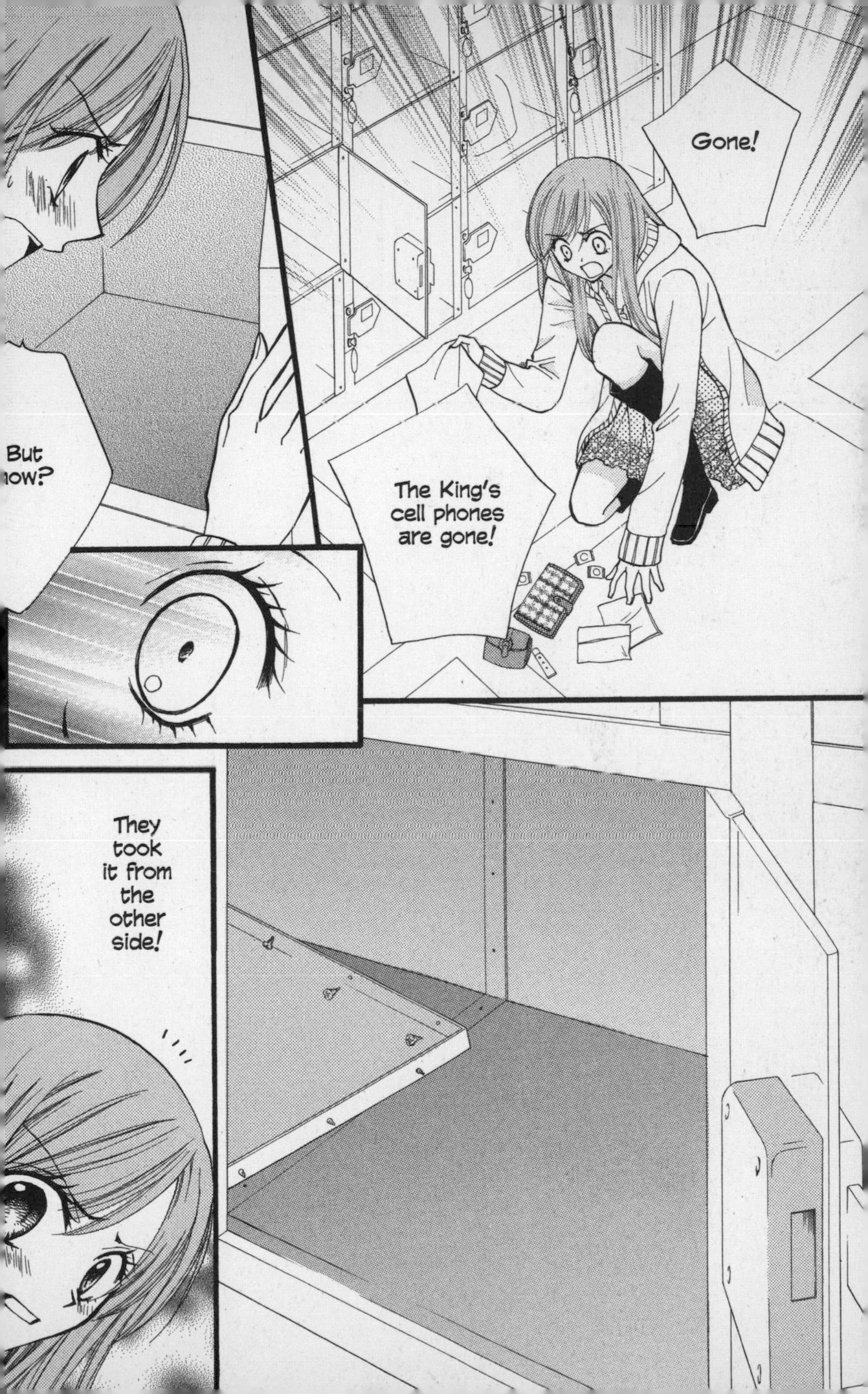
Gone!
The King's cell phones are gone!
But
They took it from the other side!

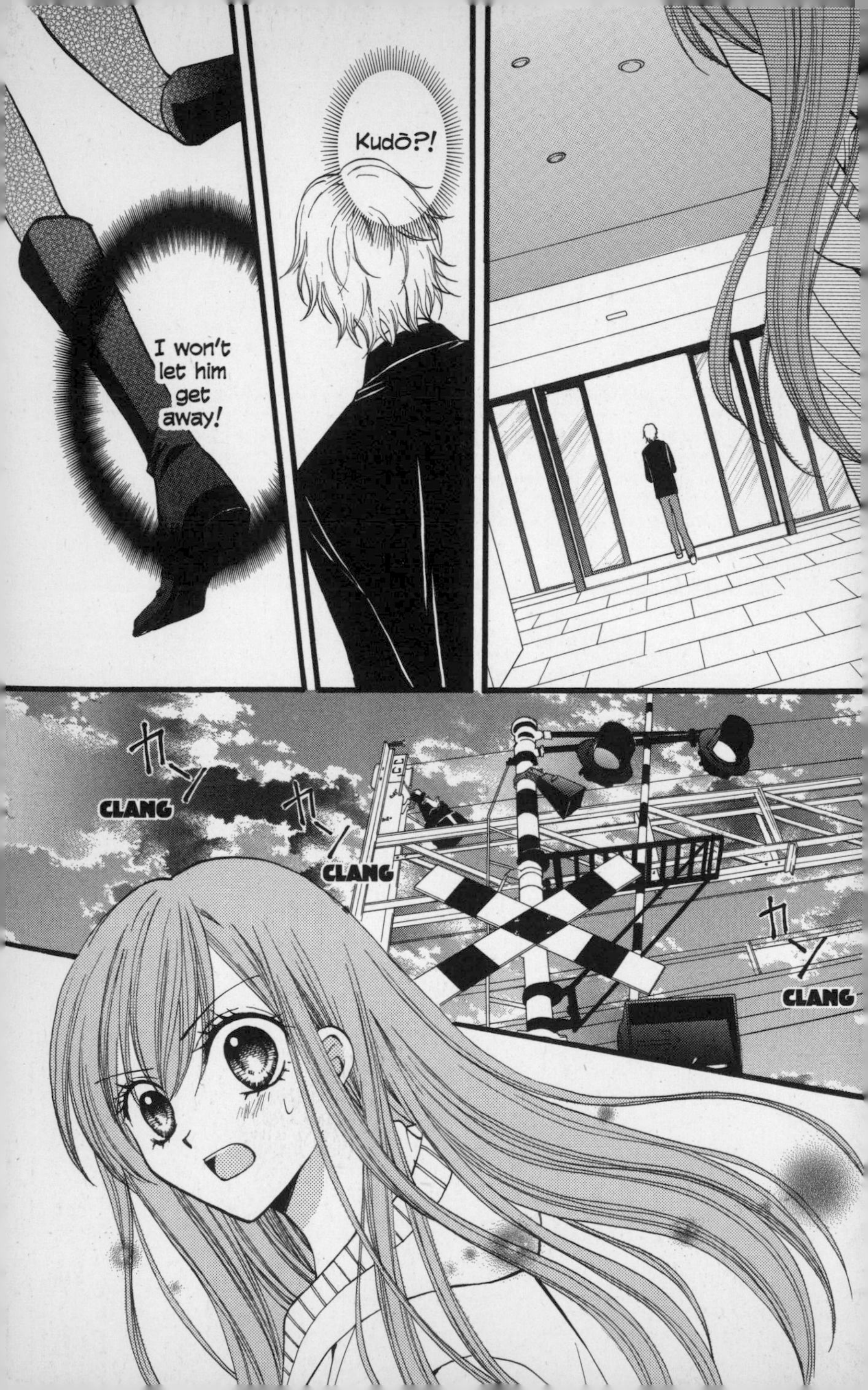

Kudō?!
I won't let him get away!
カーン
CLANG
カーン
CLANG
カーン
CLANG

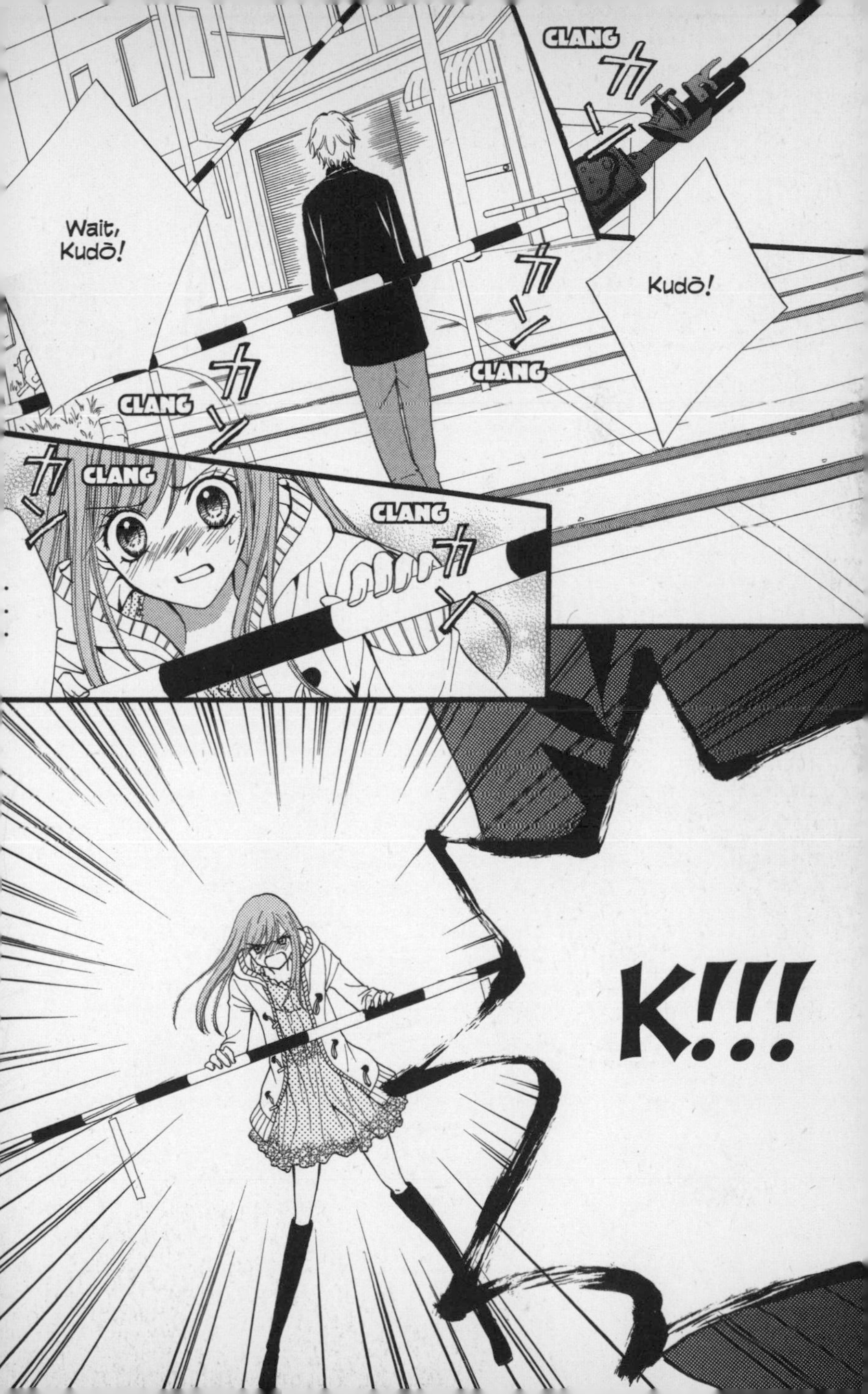
CLANG
Kudō!
CLANG
Wait, Kudō!
CLANG
CLANG
CLANG
K!!!

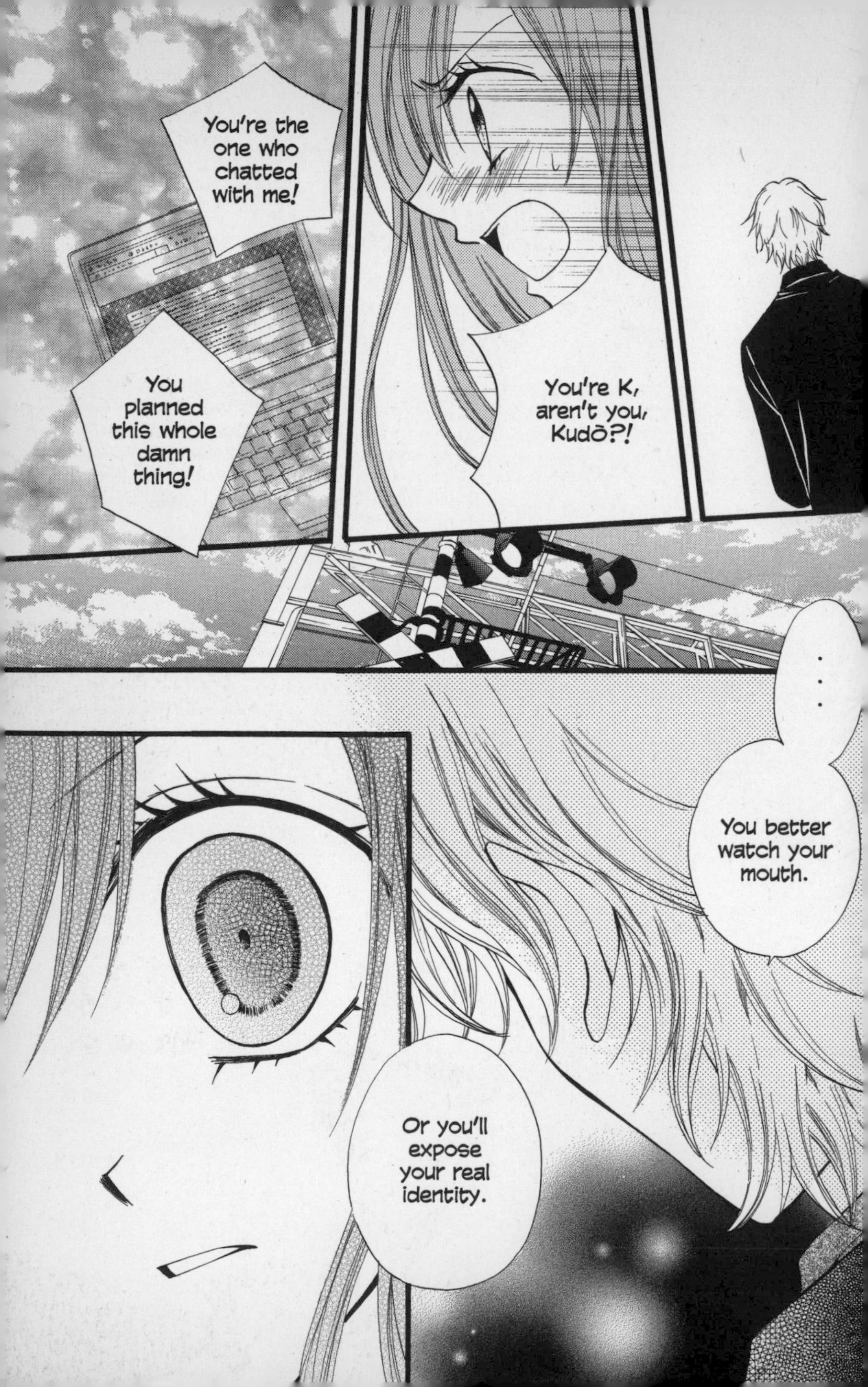
You're K, aren't you, Kudō?!
You're the one who chatted with me!
You planned this whole damn thing!
...
You better watch your mouth.
Or you'll expose your real identity.

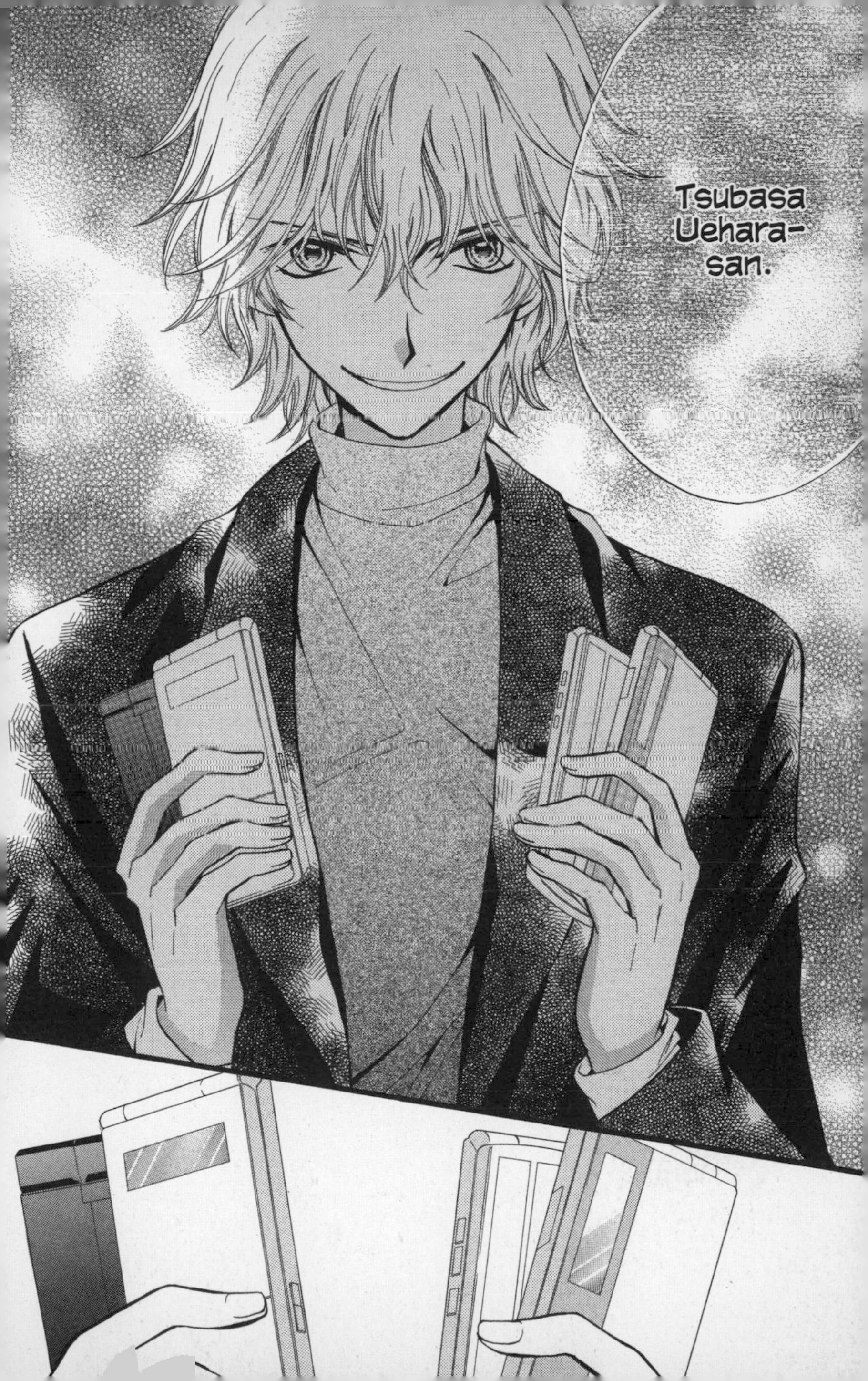
Tsubasa Uehara-san.

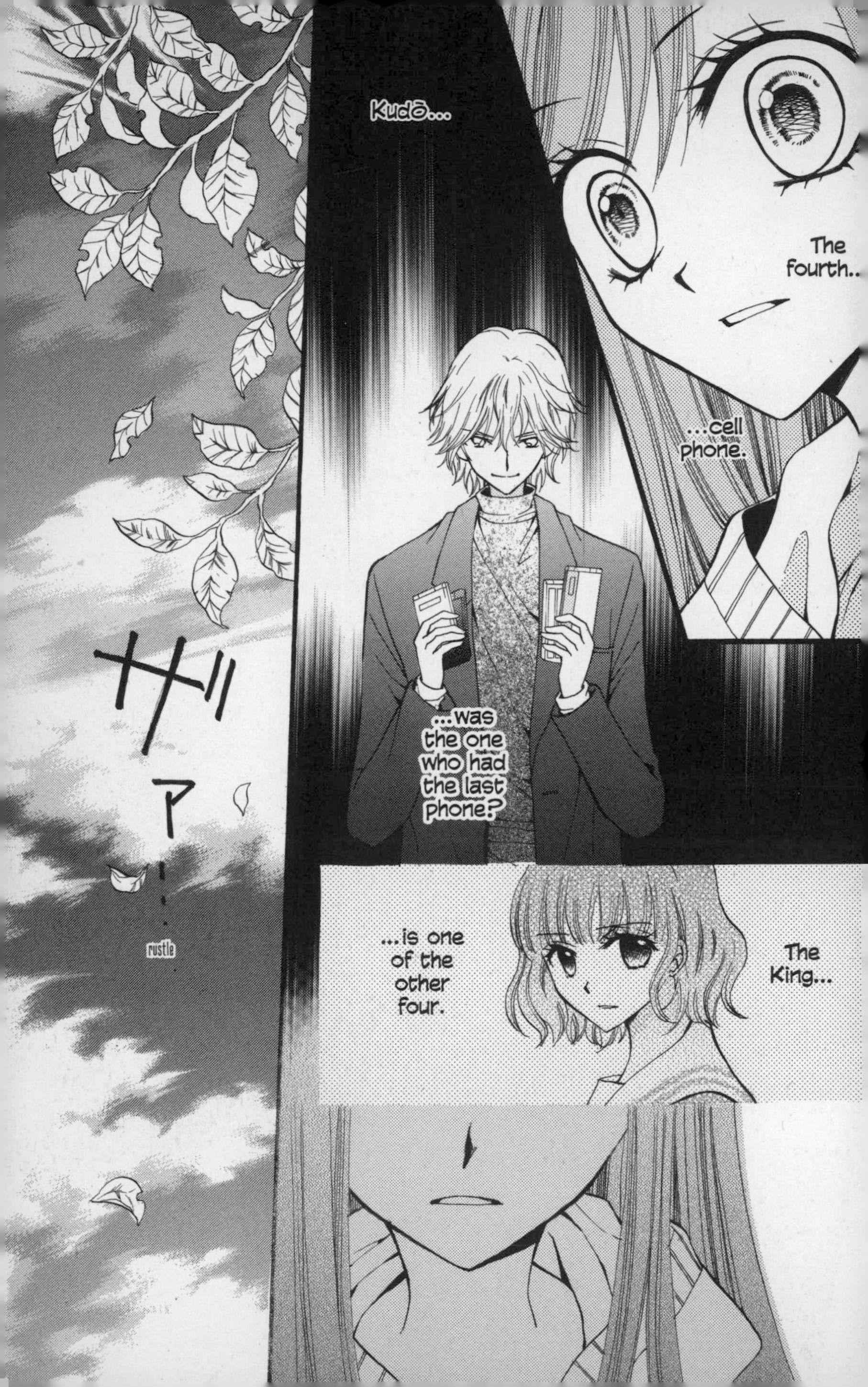
The fourth..
...cell phone.
Kudō...
...was the one who had the last phone?
The King...
...is one of the other four.
ザワ…
rustle

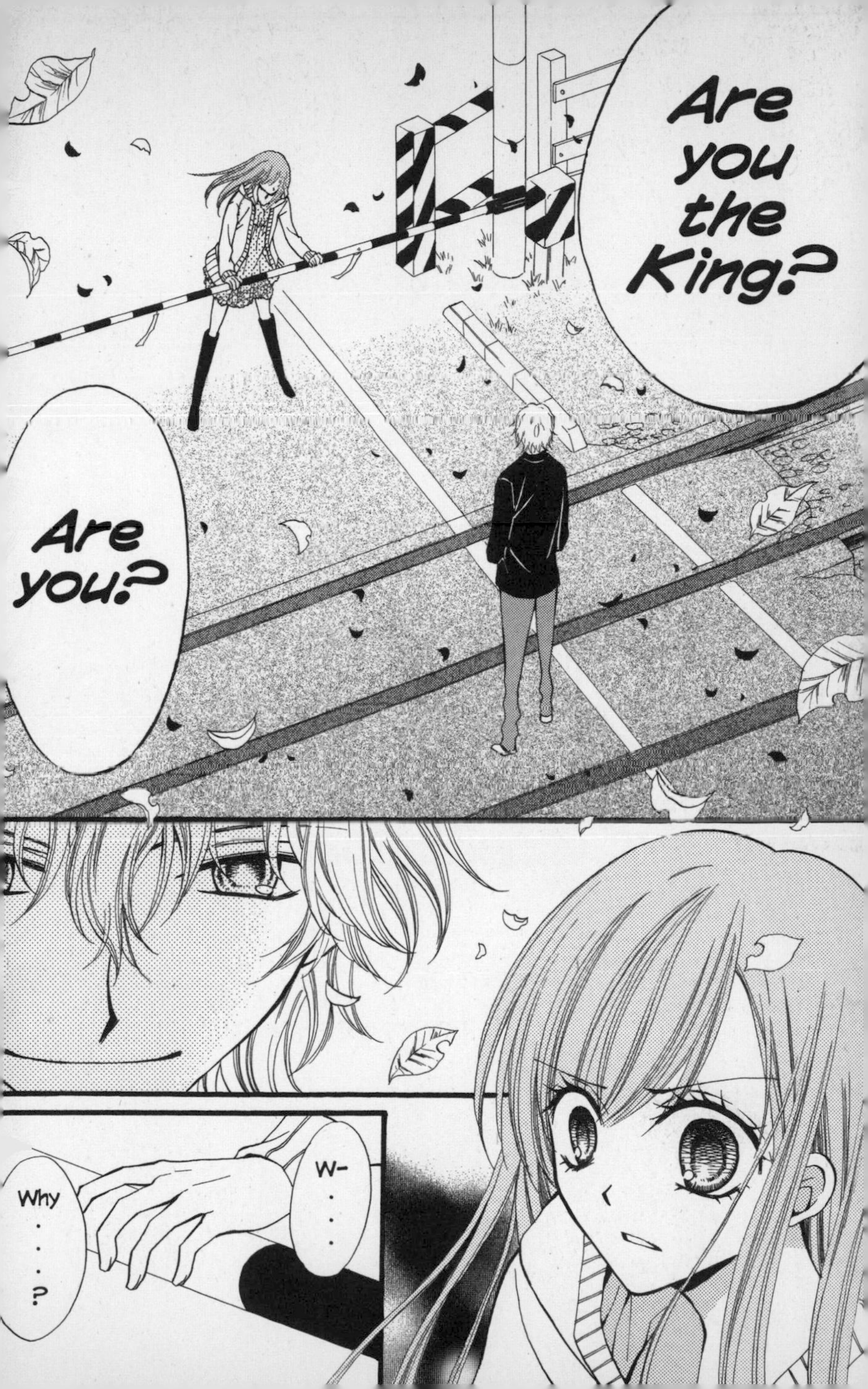
Are you the King?
Are you?
W-...
Why...?

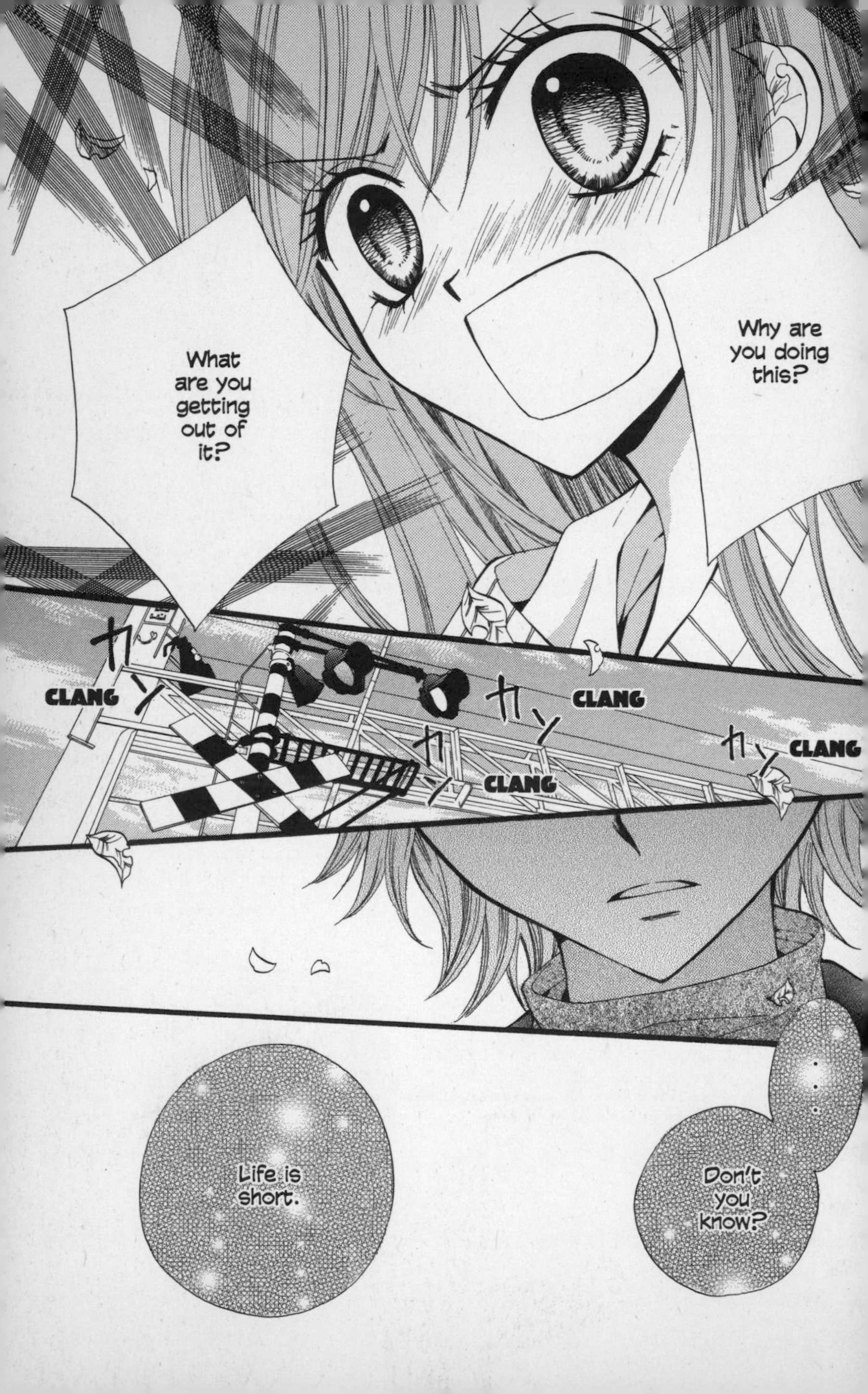
Why are you doing this?
What are you getting out of it?
カン
CLANG
カン
CLANG
カン
CLANG
カン
CLANG
Life is short.
Don't you know?

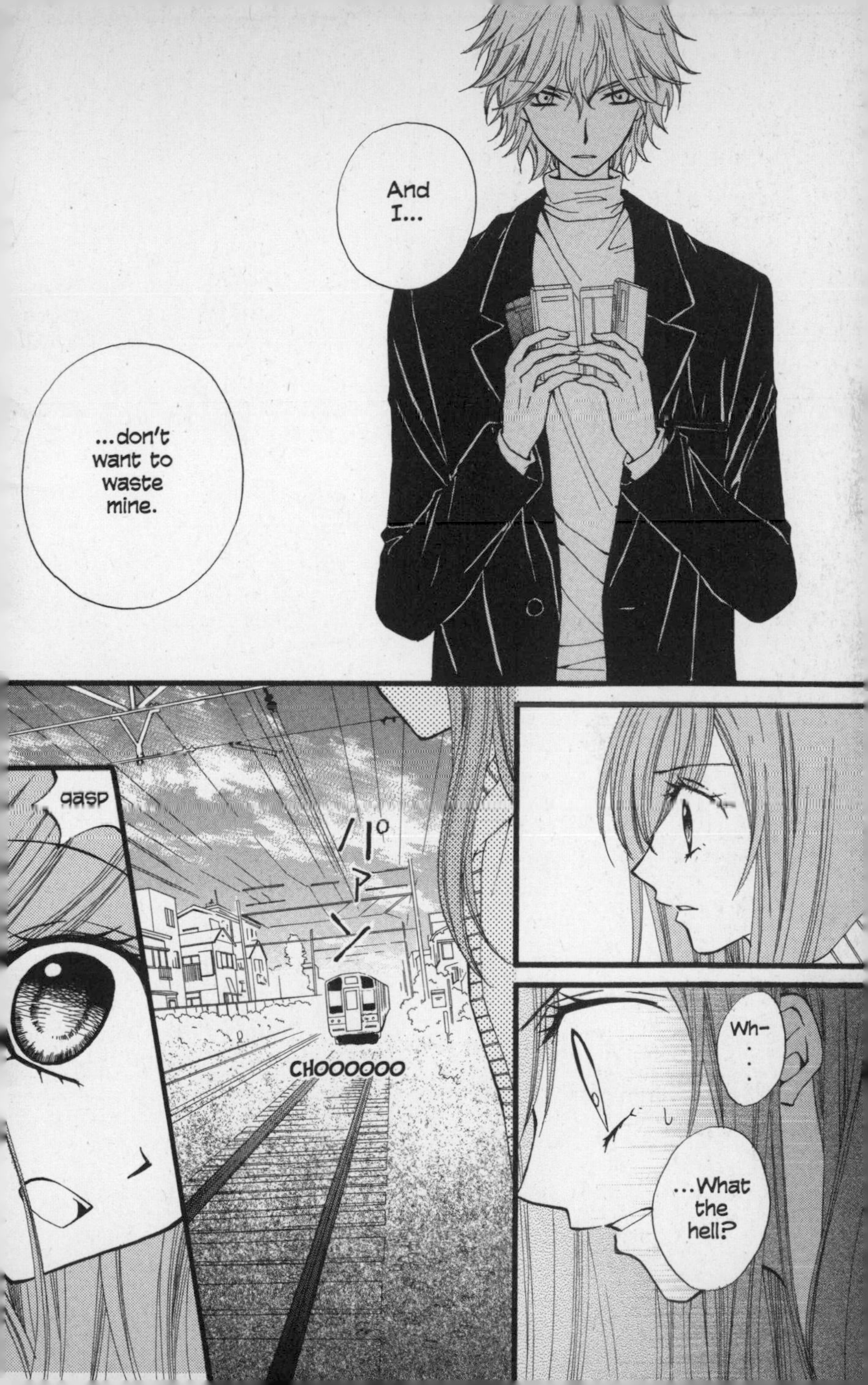
And I...
...don't want to waste mine.
Wh-...
...What the hell?
パアーン
CHOOOOOO
gasp

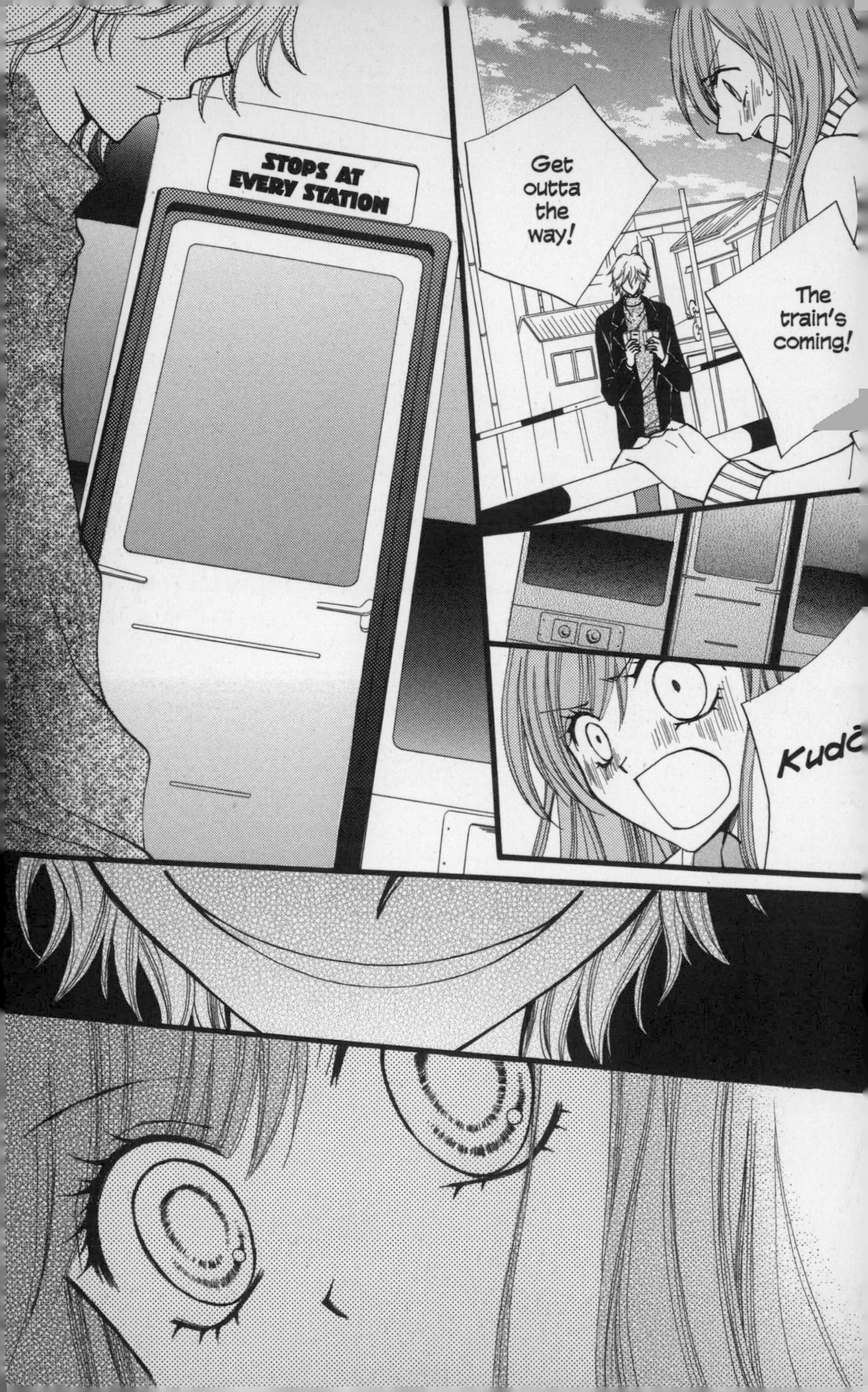
Get outta the way!
The train's coming!
STOPS AT EVERY STATION
Kudo

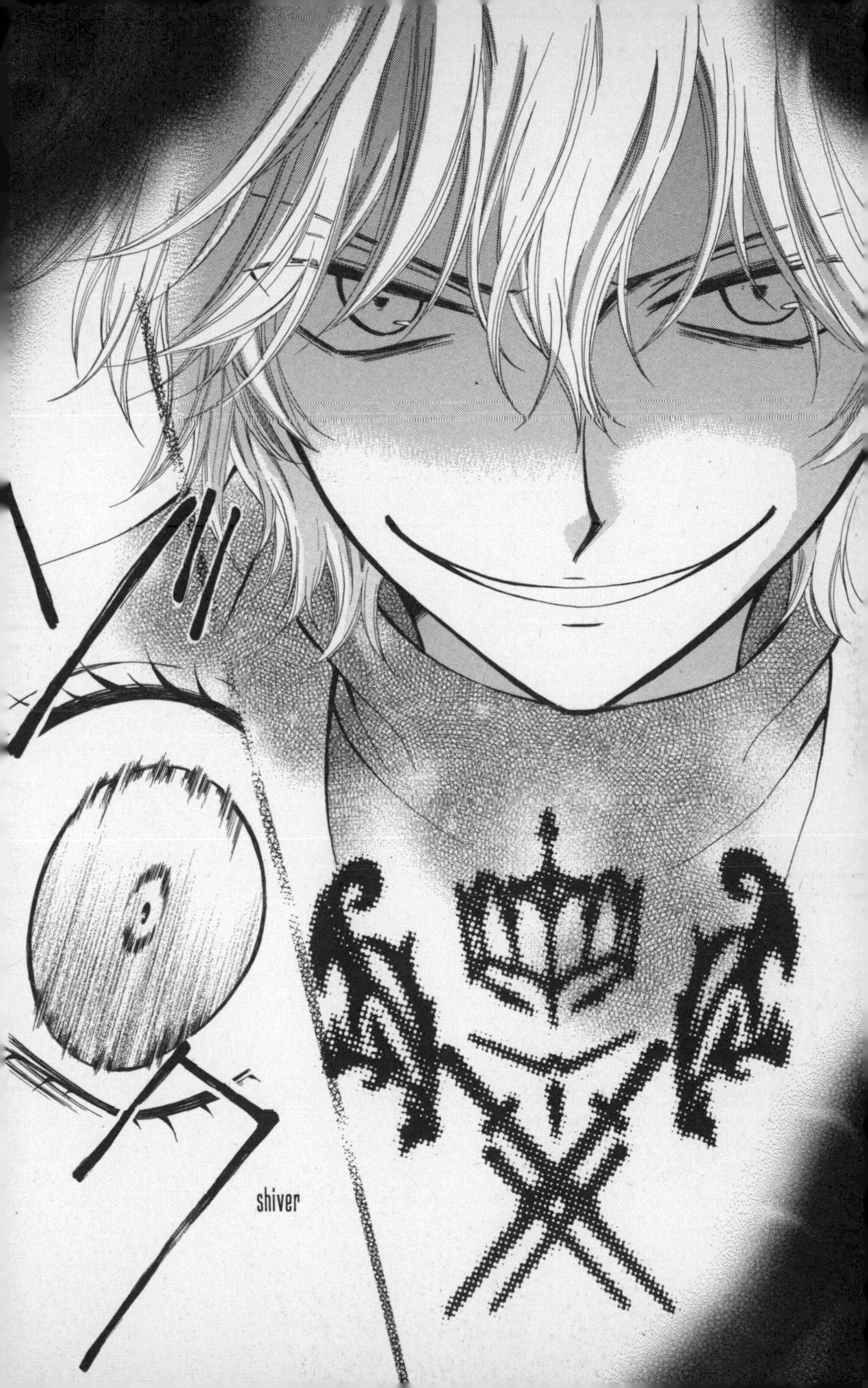
shiver

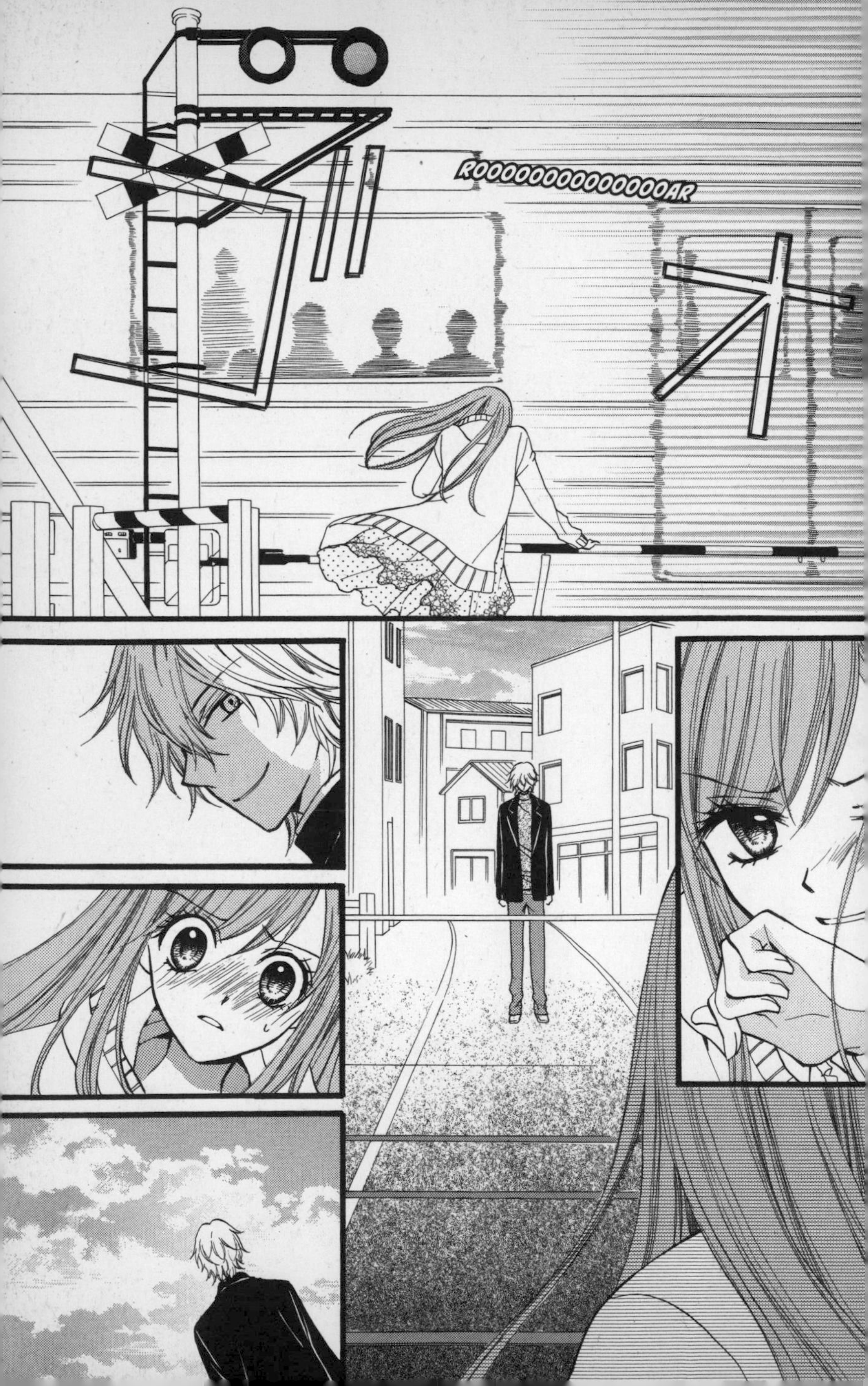
ROOOOOOOOOOOOOOOAR

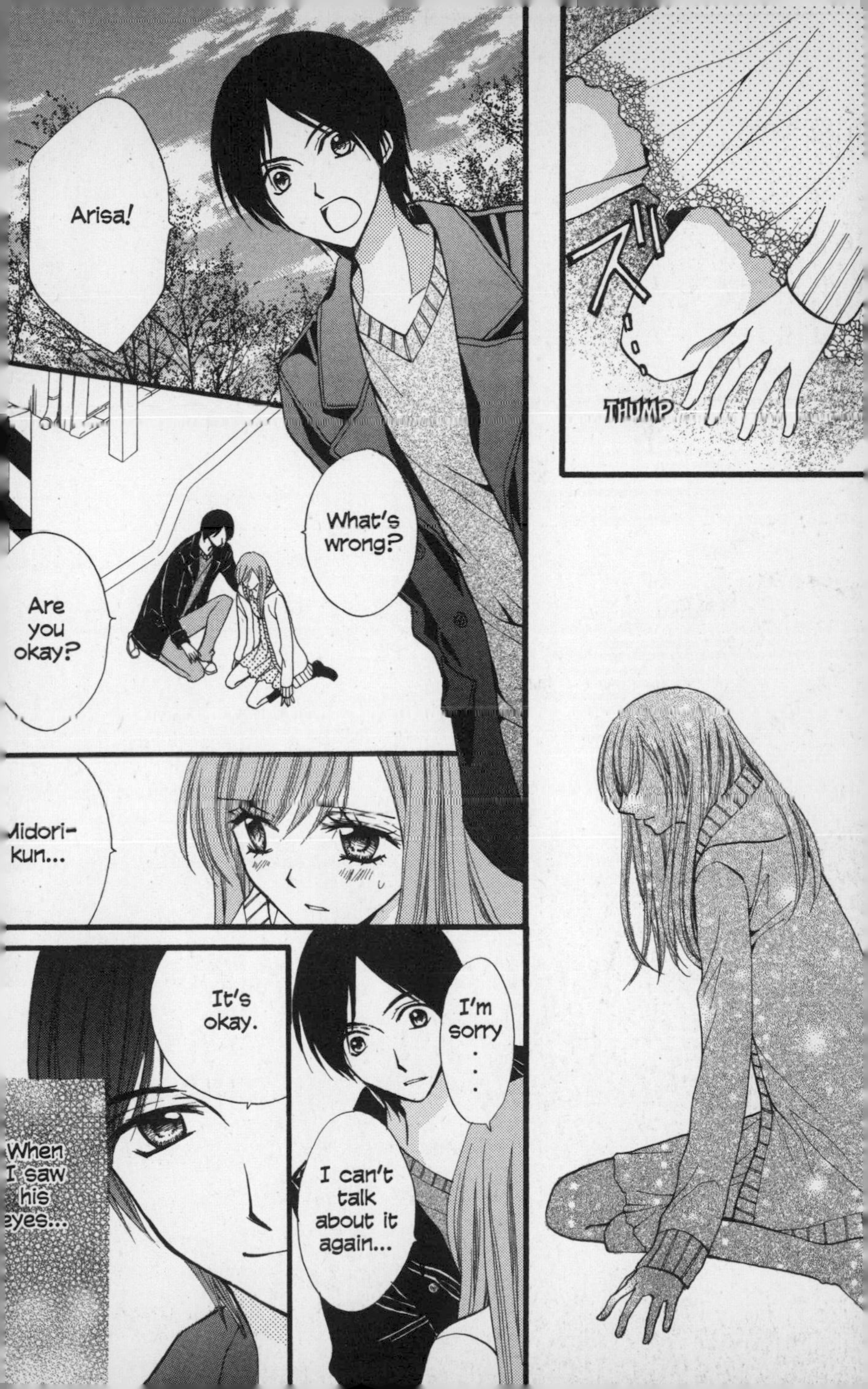
ズ
THUMP
Arisa!
What's wrong?
Are you okay?
Midori-kun...
I'm sorry . . .
It's okay.
I can't talk about it again...
When I saw his eyes...

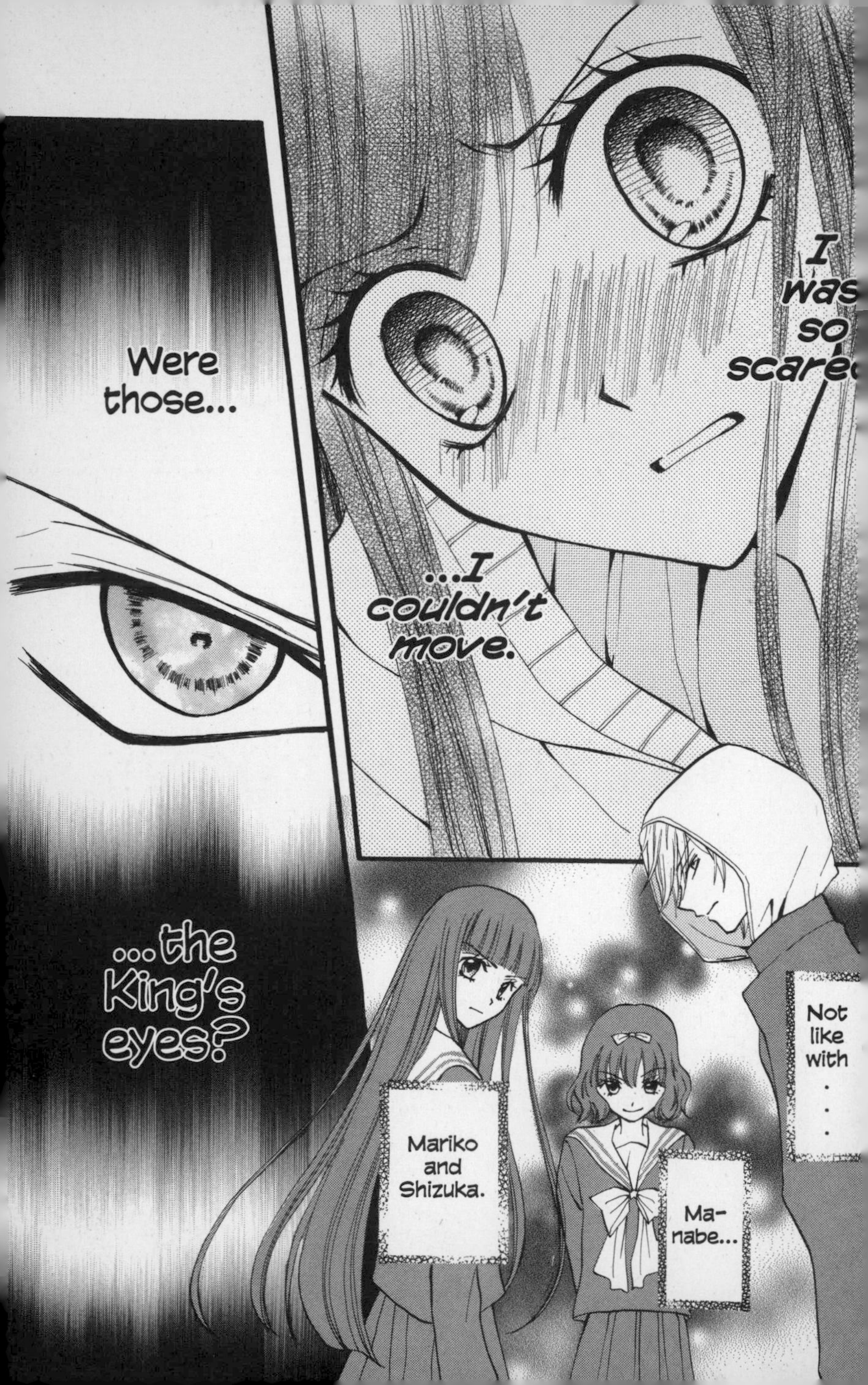
I was so scared
...I couldn't move.
Not like with . . .
Ma-nabe...
Mariko and Shizuka.
Were those...
...the King's eyes?

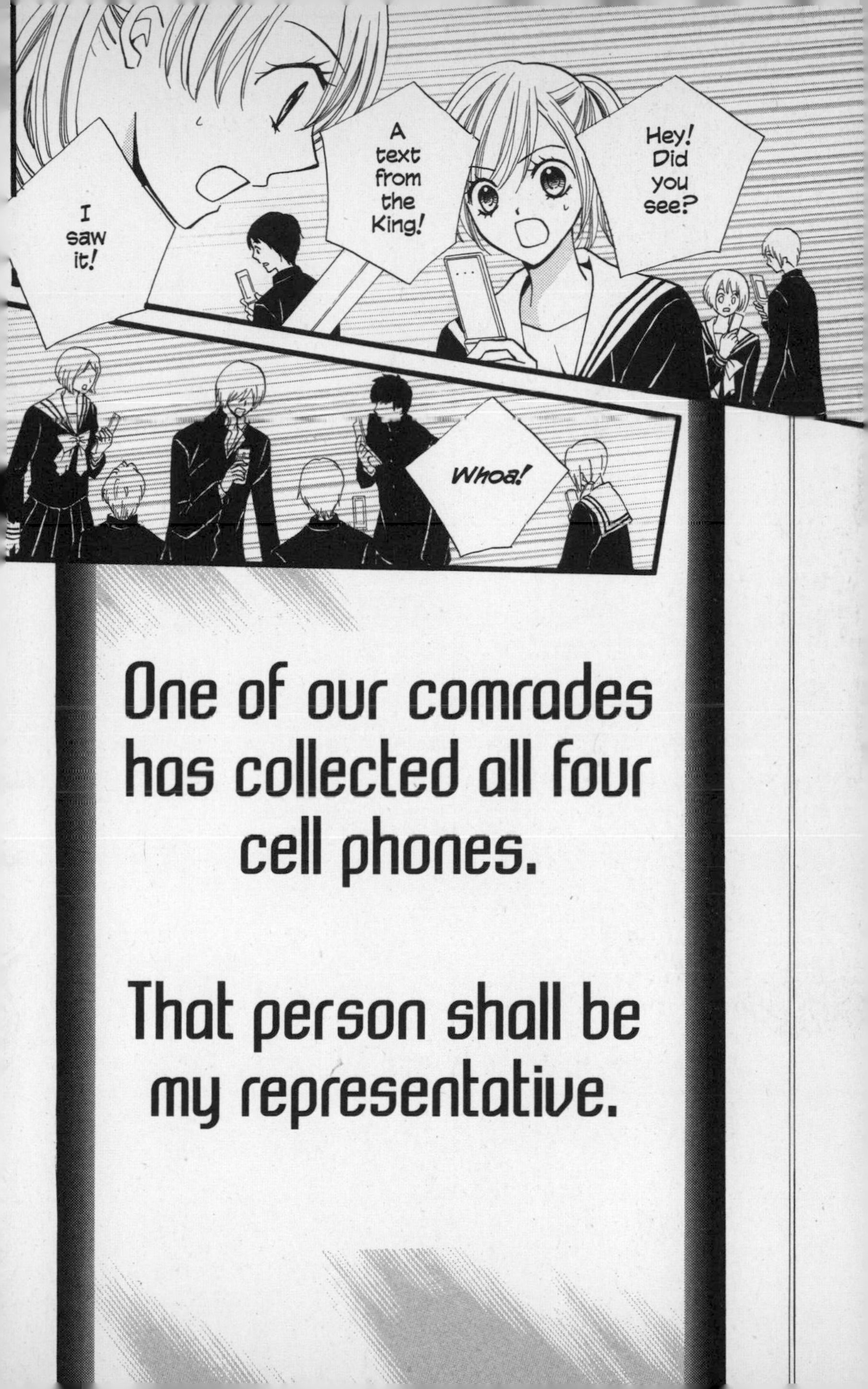
Hey! Did you see?
A text from the King!
I saw it!
Whoa!
One of our comrades has collected all four cell phones.
That person shall be my representative.

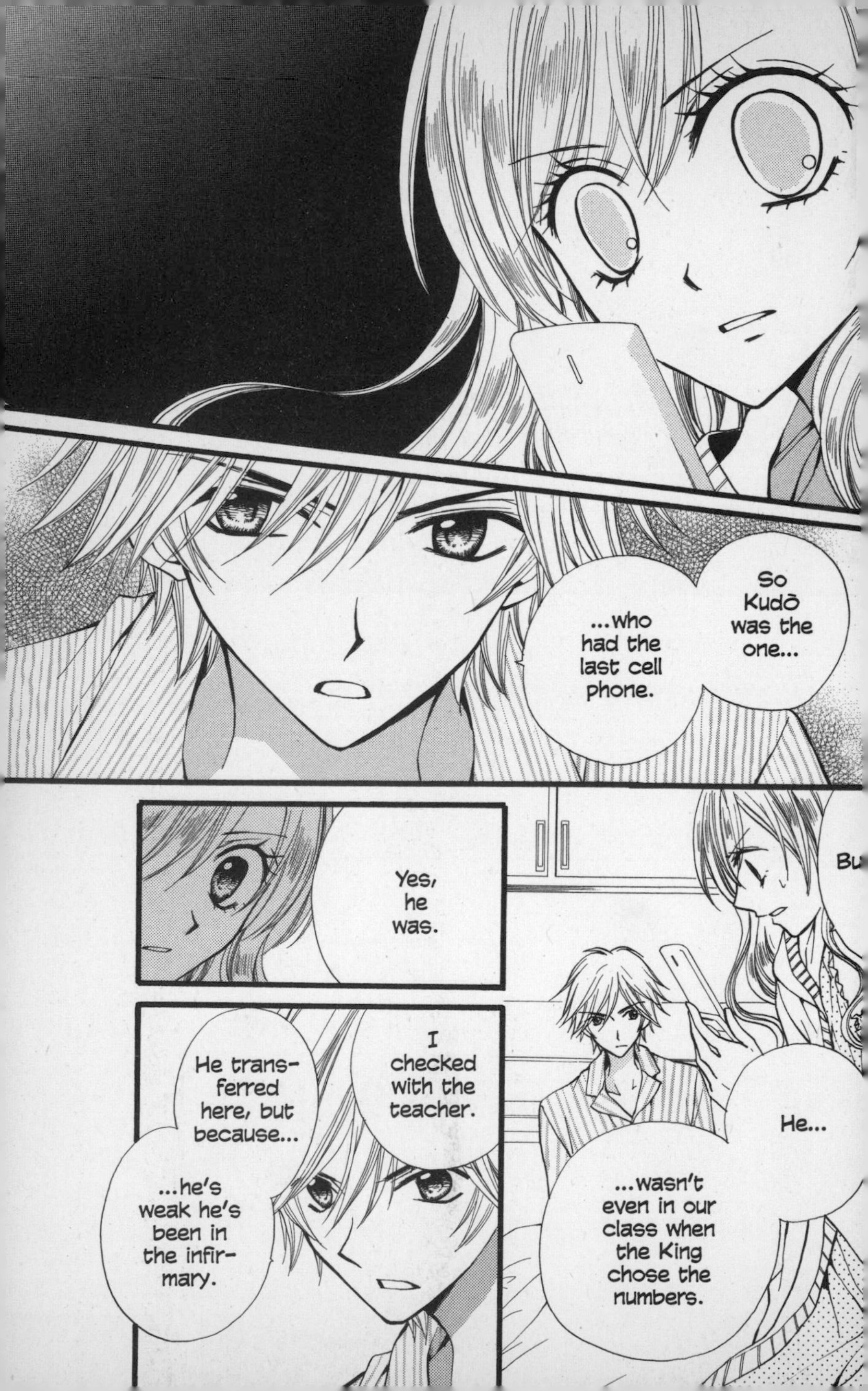
So Kudō was the one...
...who had the last cell phone.
Bu
He...
...wasn't even in our class when the King chose the numbers.
Yes, he was.
I checked with the teacher.
He trans-ferred here, but because...
...he's weak he's been in the infir-mary.

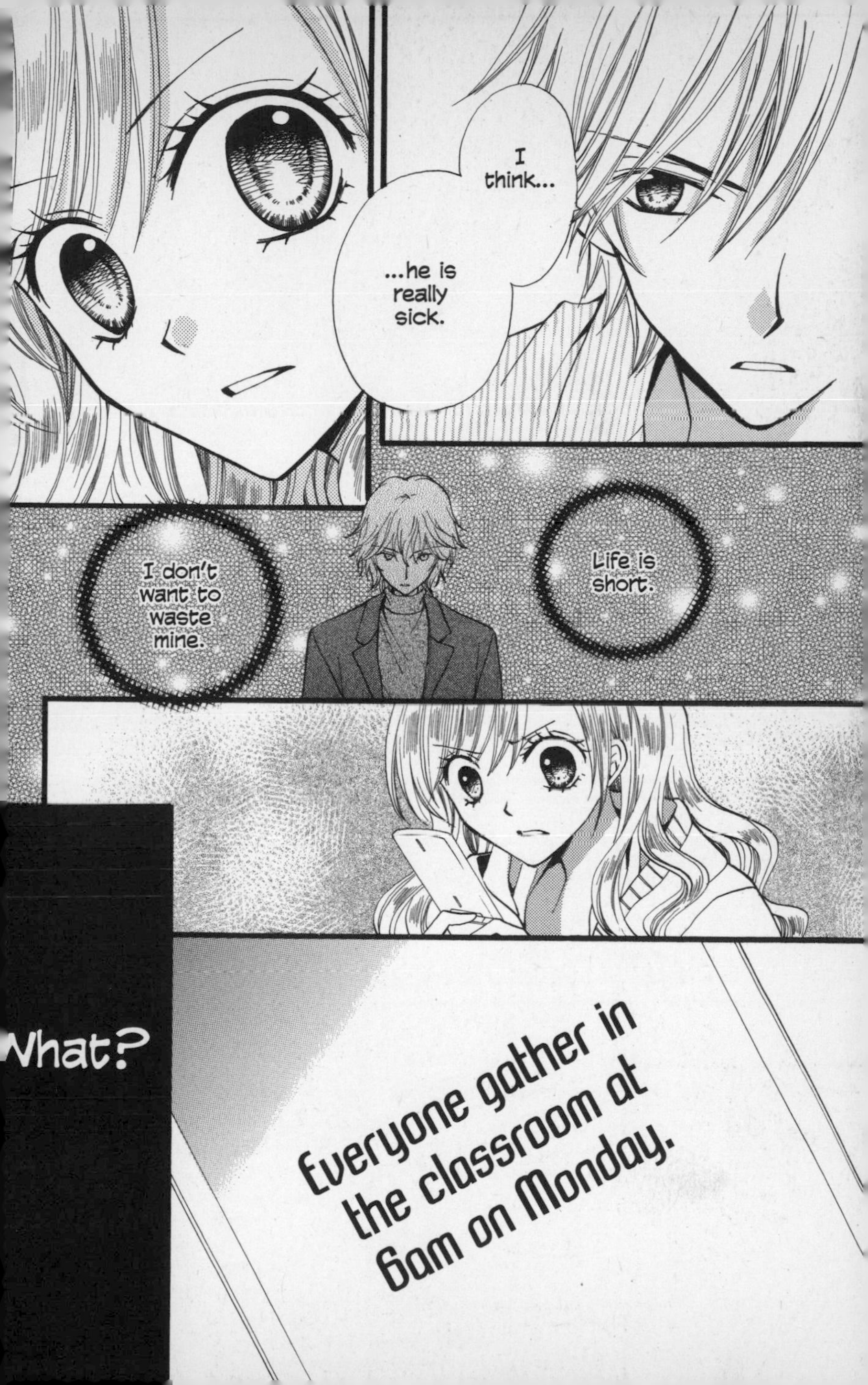
I think...
...he is really sick.
Life is short.
I don't want to waste mine.
Everyone gather in the classroom at 6am on Monday.
What?

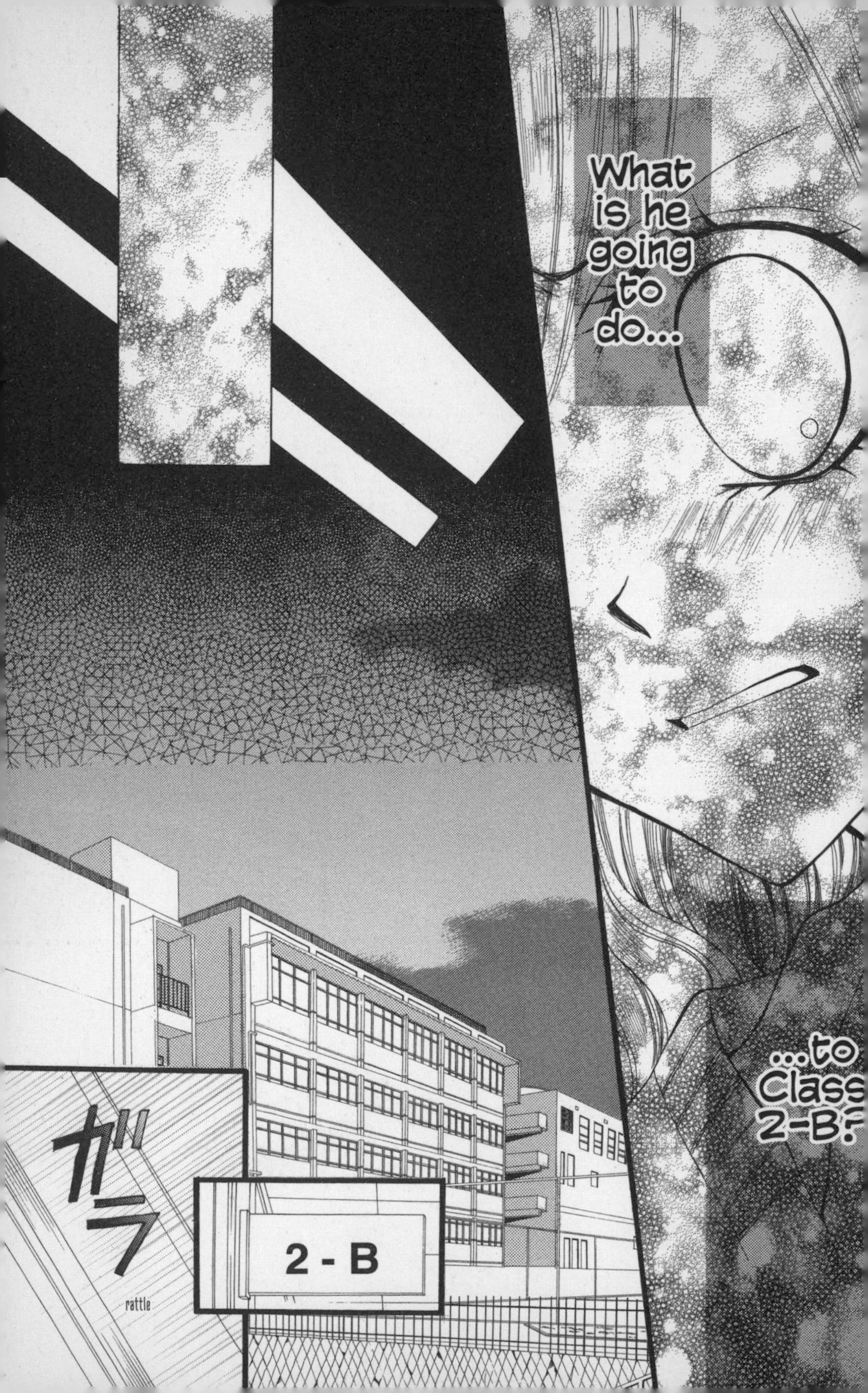
What is he going to do...
...to Class 2-B?
ガラ
rattle
2 - B

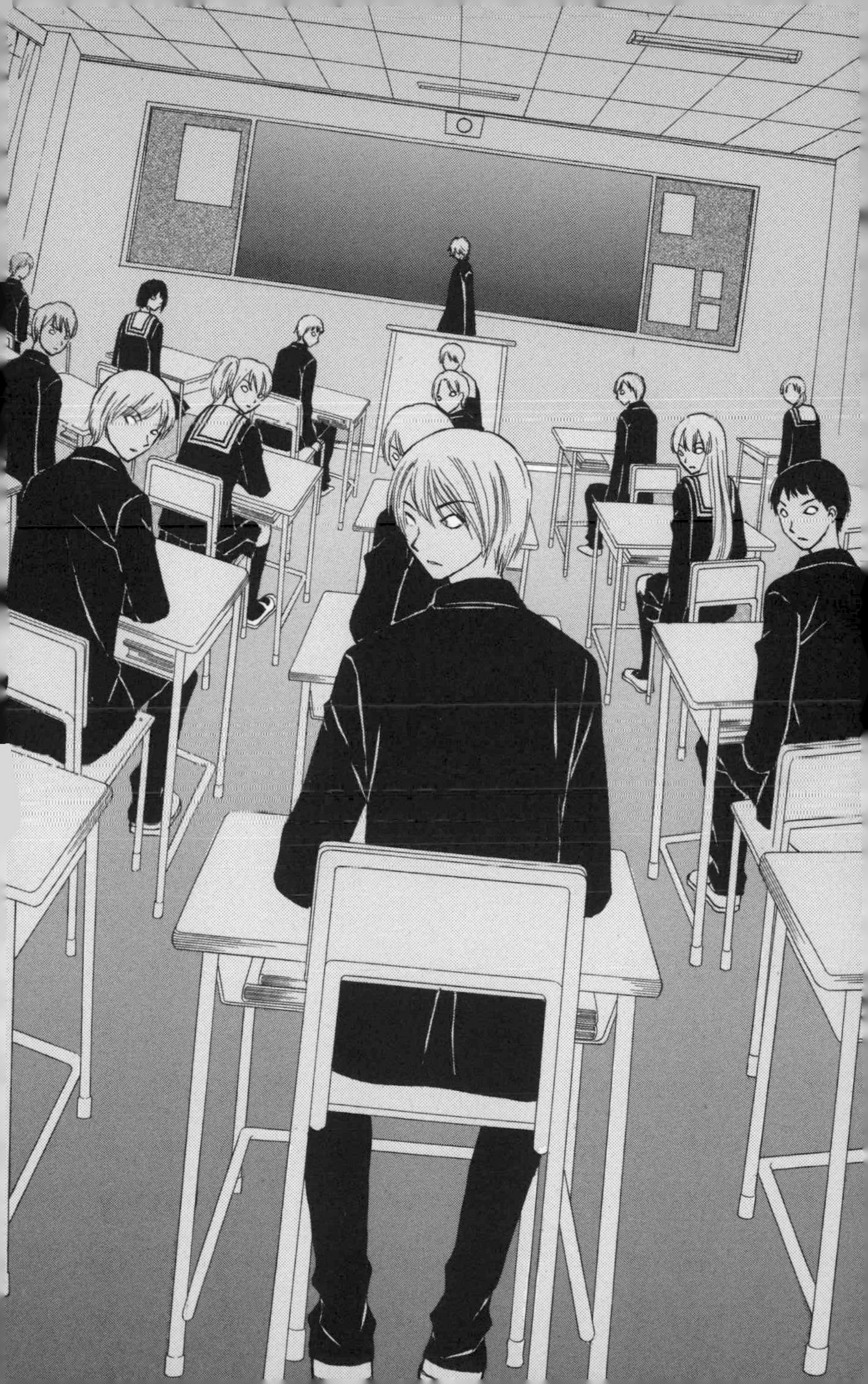

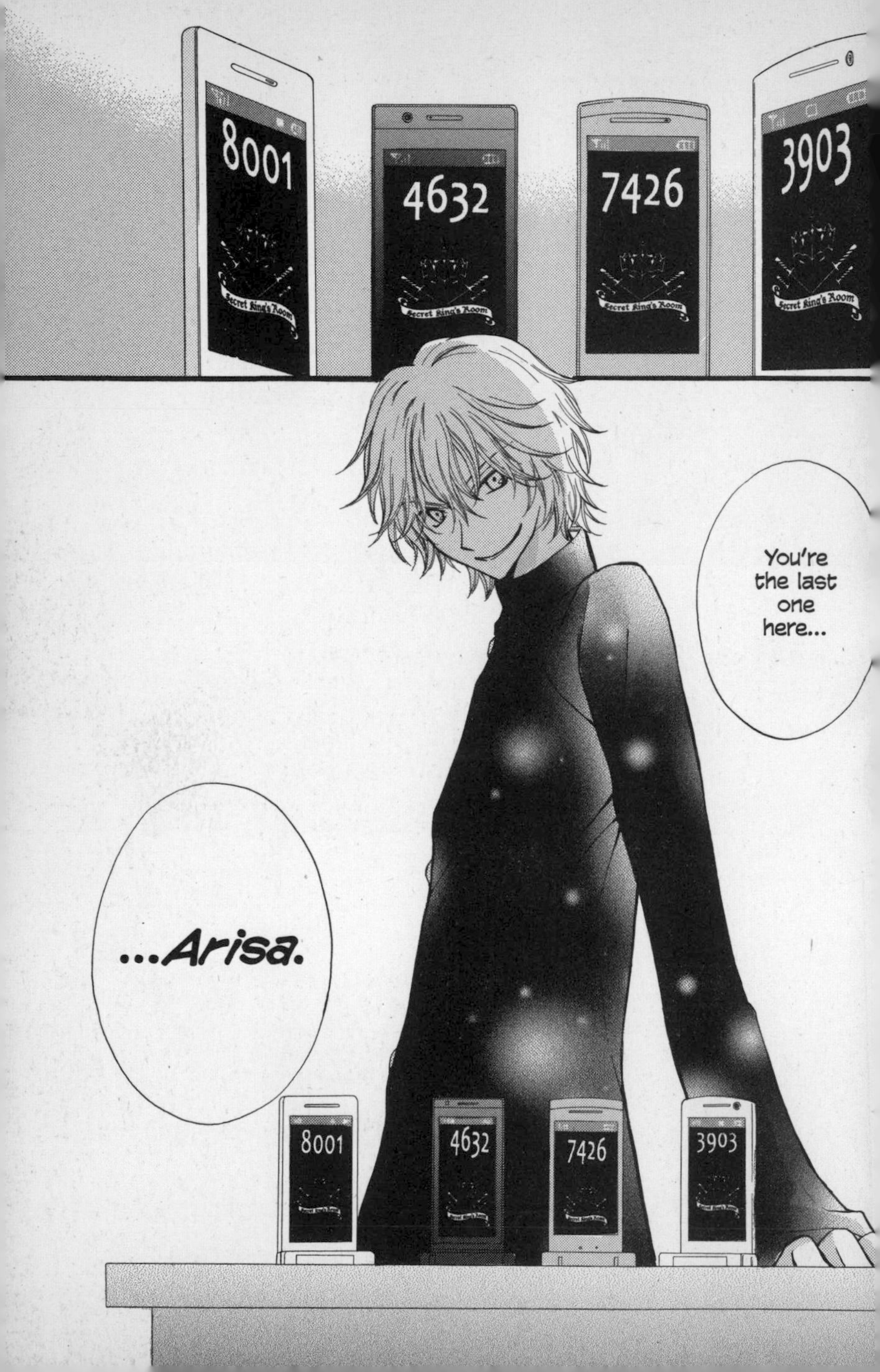
8001
4632
7426
3903
Secret King's Room
Secret King's Room
Secret King's Room
Secret King's Room
You're the last one here...
...Arisa.
8001
4632
7426
3903

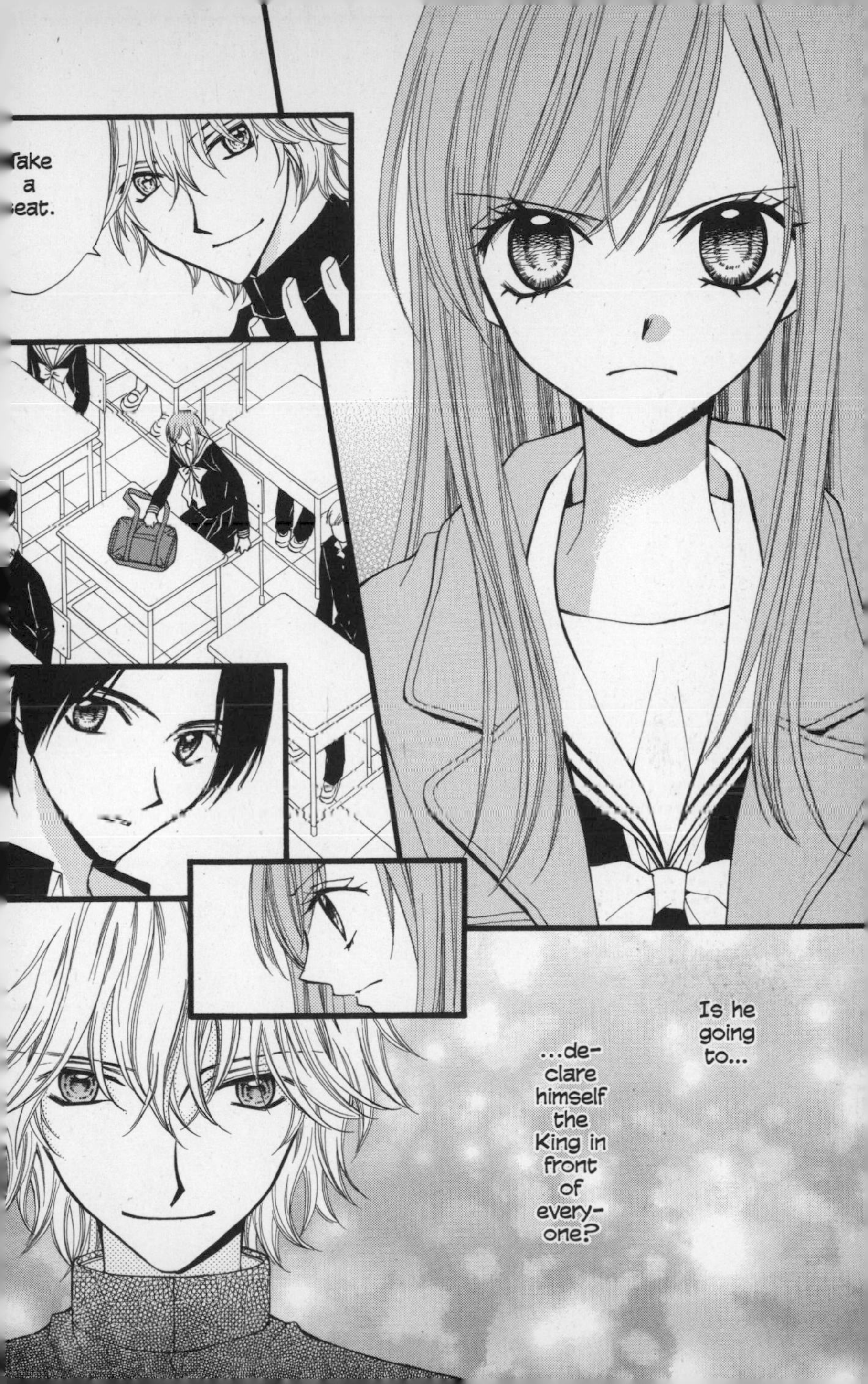
Take a seat.
Is he going to...
...de-clare himself the King in front of every-one?

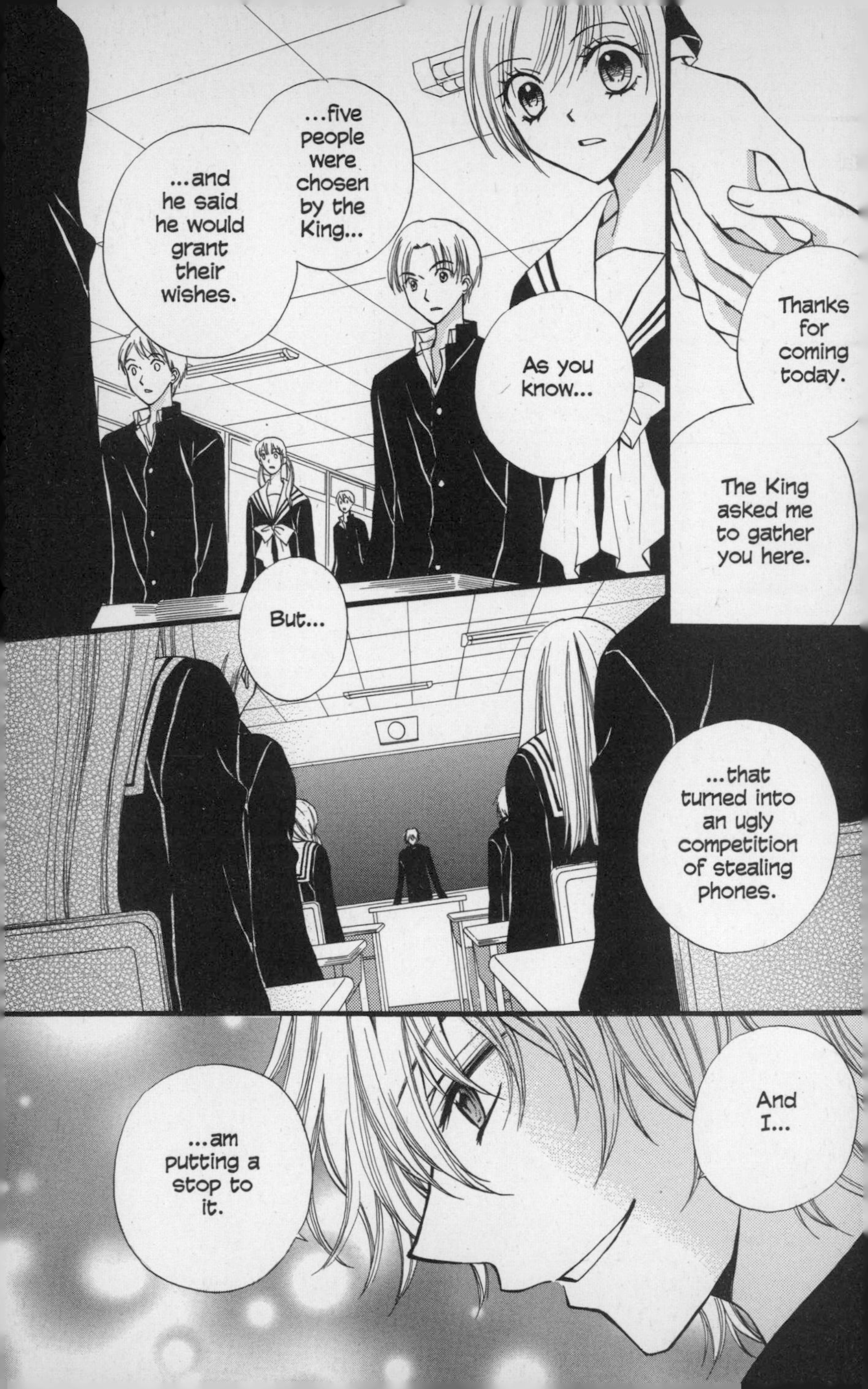
Thanks for coming today.
The King asked me to gather you here.
As you know...
...five people were chosen by the King...
...and he said he would grant their wishes.
But...
...that turned into an ugly competition of stealing phones.
And I...
...am putting a stop to it.

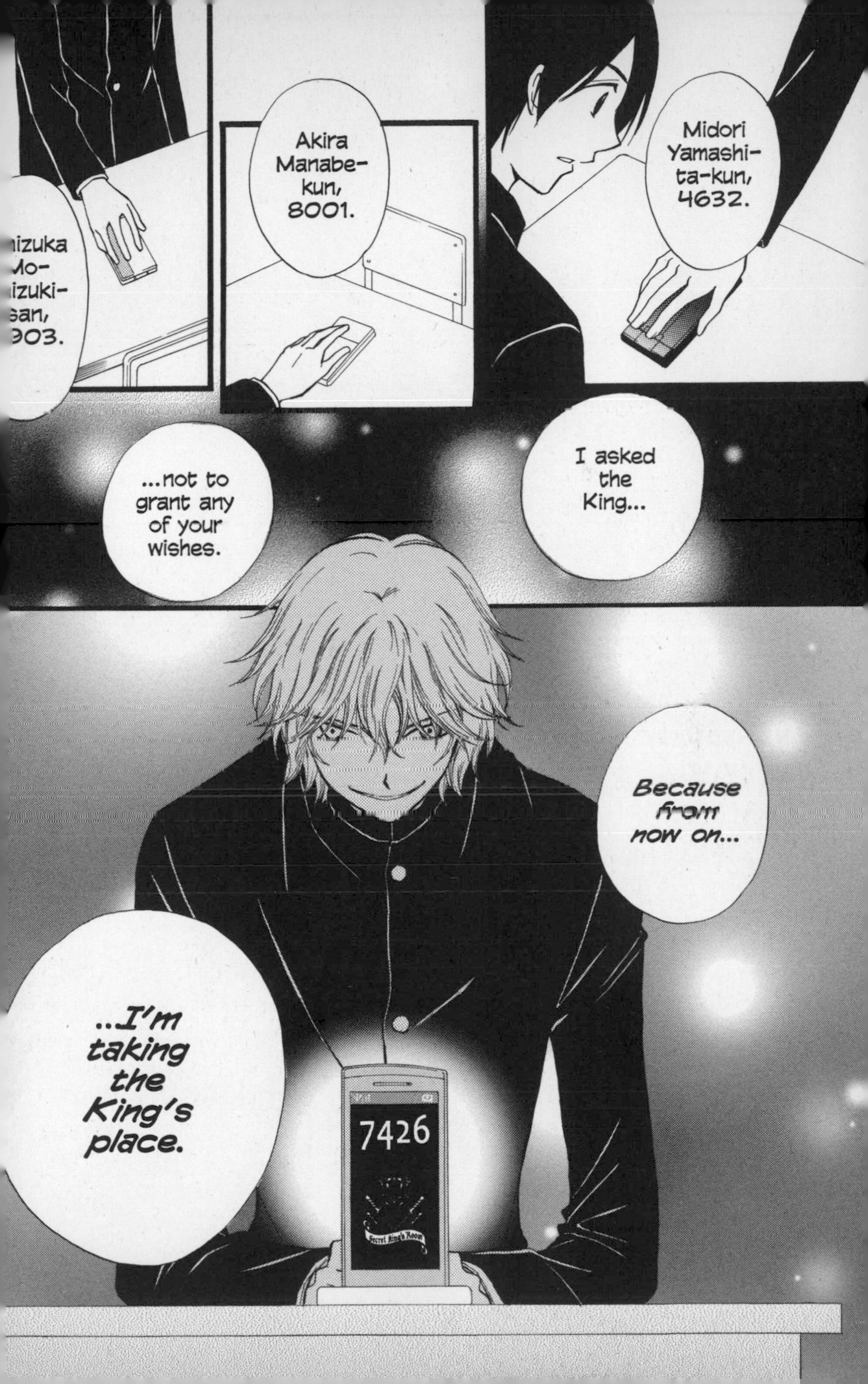

Midori Yamashita-kun, 4632.
Akira Manabe-kun, 8001.
izuka Mo-izuki-san, 903.
I asked the King...
...not to grant any of your wishes.
Because from now on...
...I'm taking the King's place.
7426
Secret King's Room

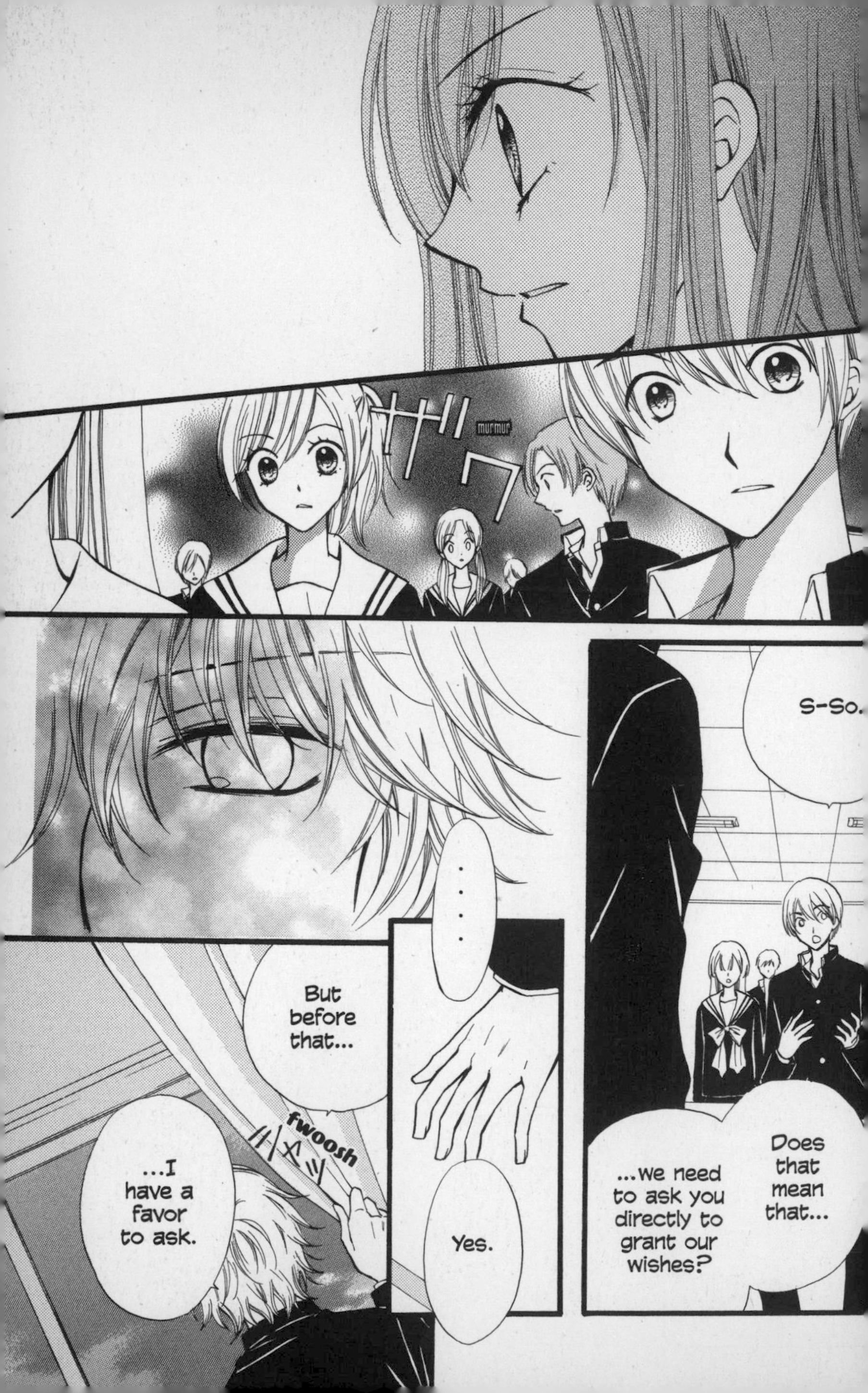
ザワ
murmur
S-So.
Does that mean that...
...we need to ask you directly to grant our wishes?
....
Yes.
But before that...
fwoosh
...I have a favor to ask.

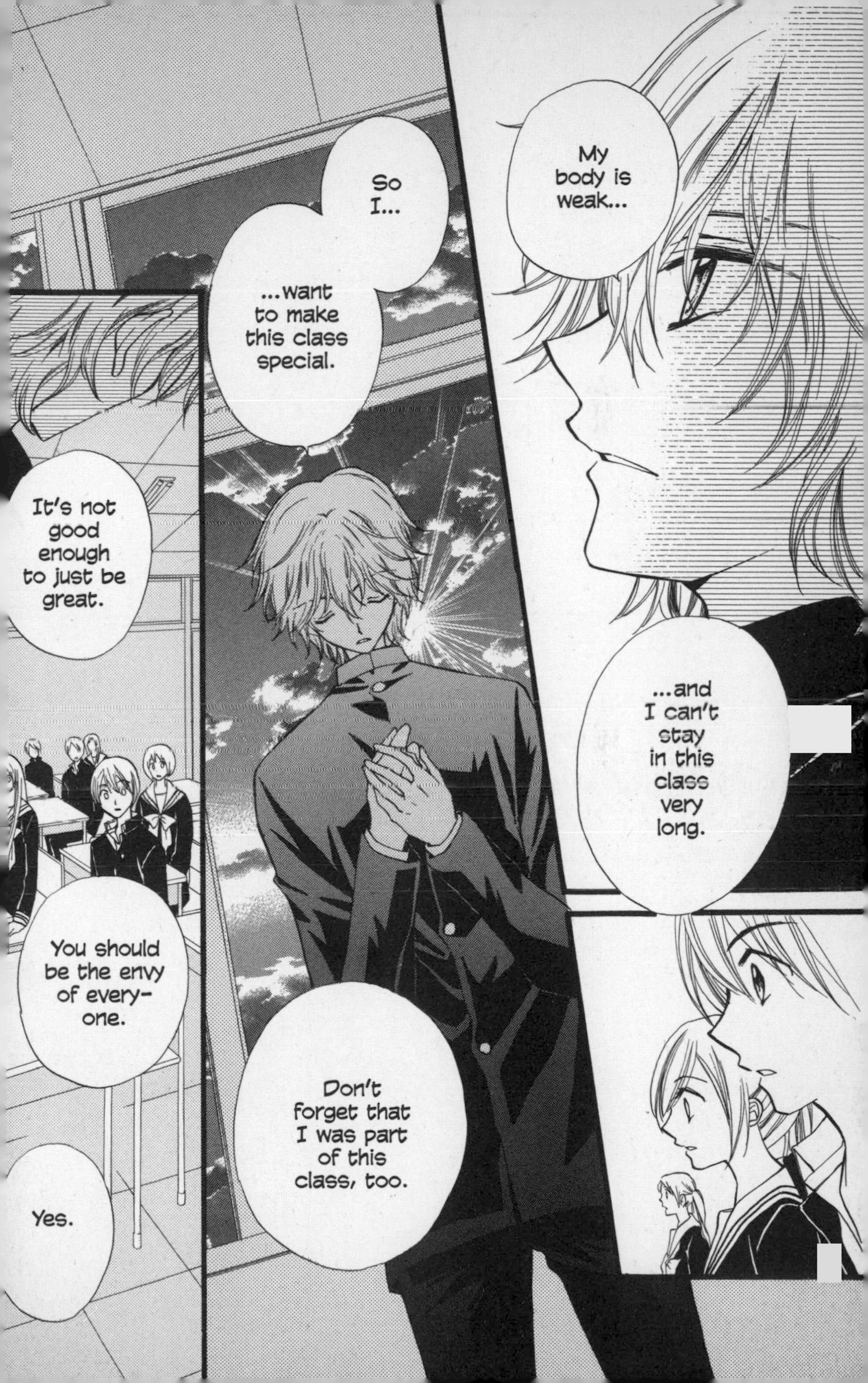
My body is weak...
...and I can't stay in this class very long.
So I...
...want to make this class special.
Don't forget that I was part of this class, too.
It's not good enough to just be great.
You should be the envy of every-one.
Yes.

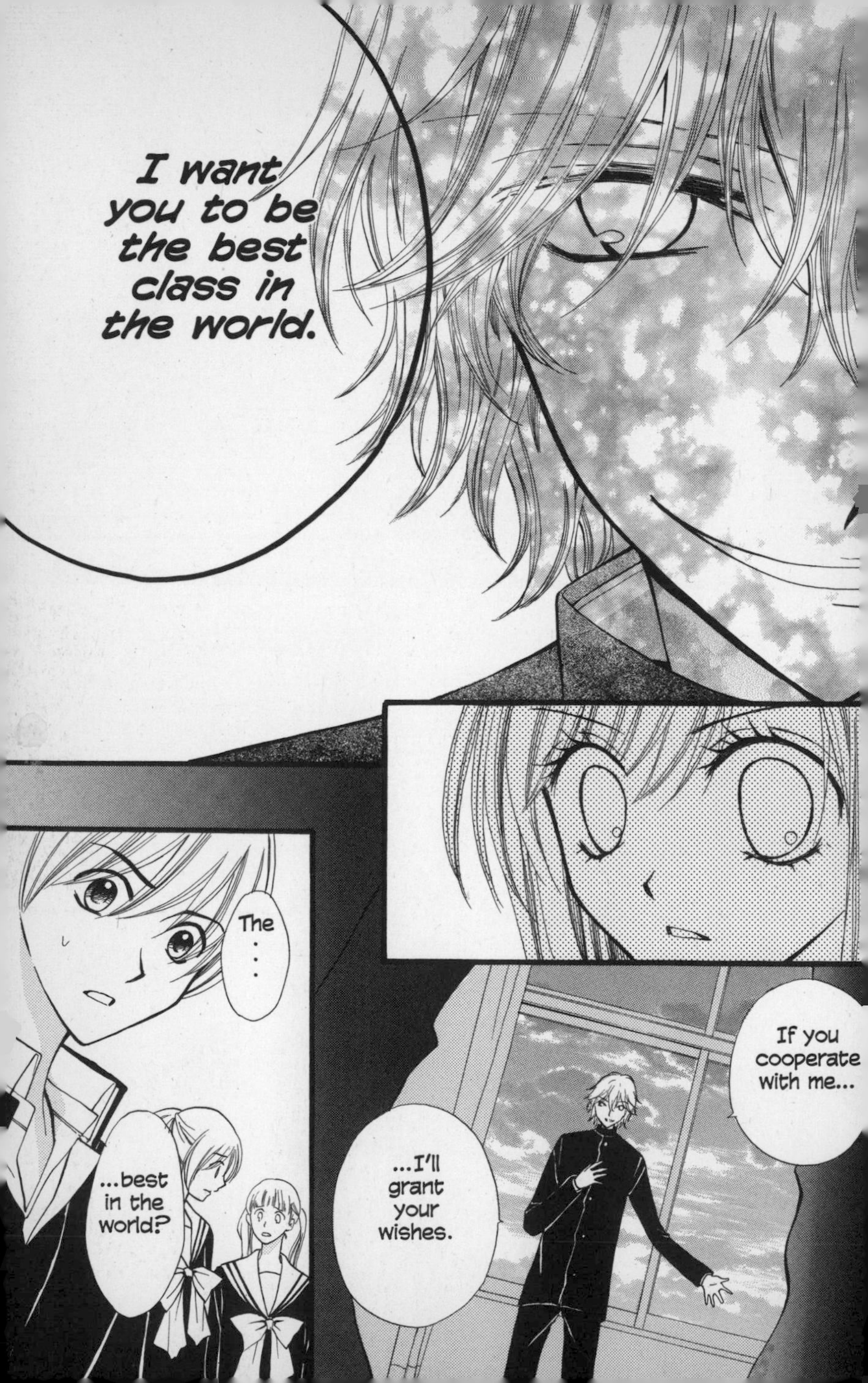
I want you to be the best class in the world.
If you cooperate with me...
...I'll grant your wishes.
The...
...best in the world?

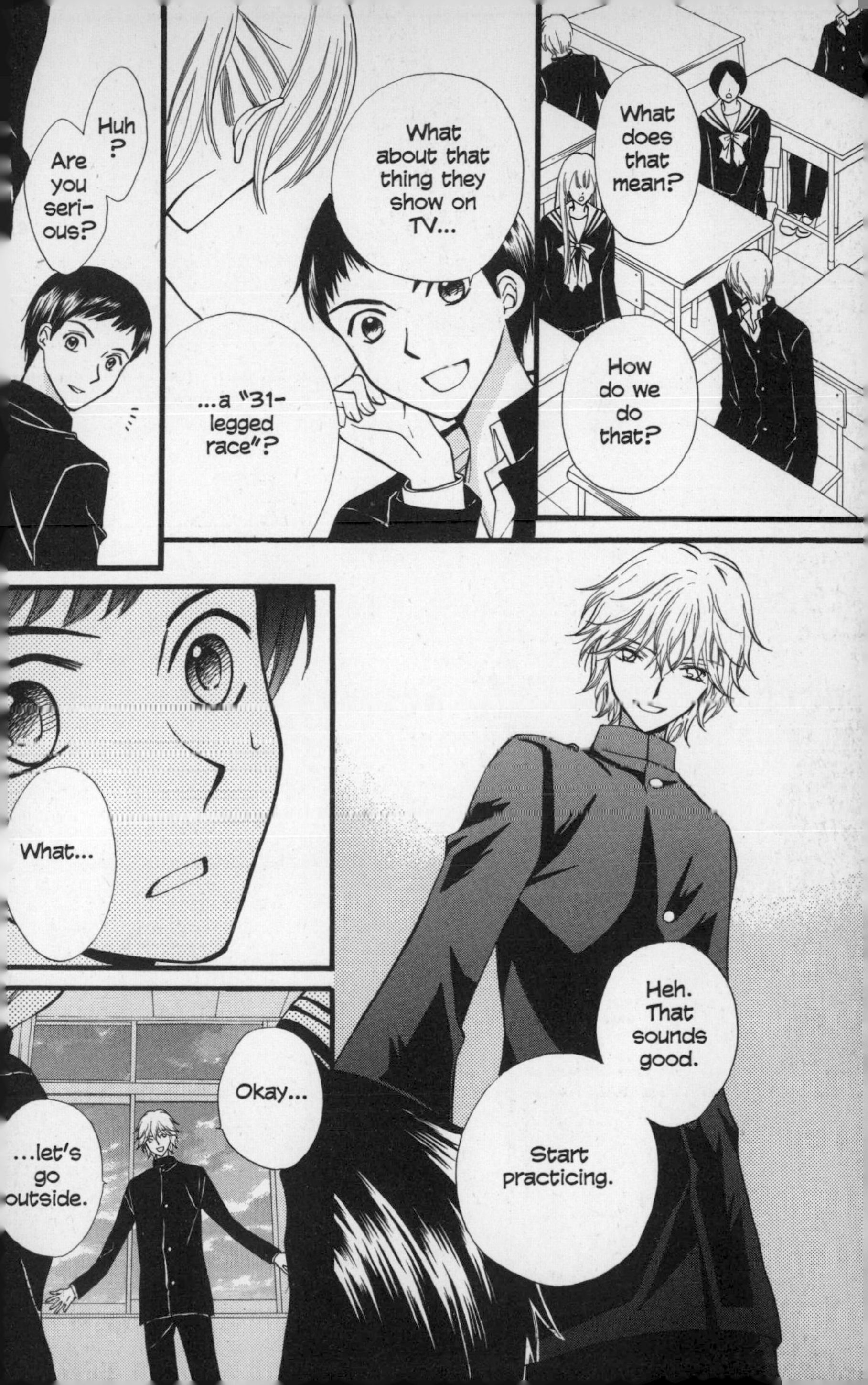
What does that mean?
How do we do that?
What about that thing they show on TV...
...a "31-legged race"?
Huh? Are you serious?
Heh. That sounds good.
Start practicing.
What...
Okay...
...let's go outside.

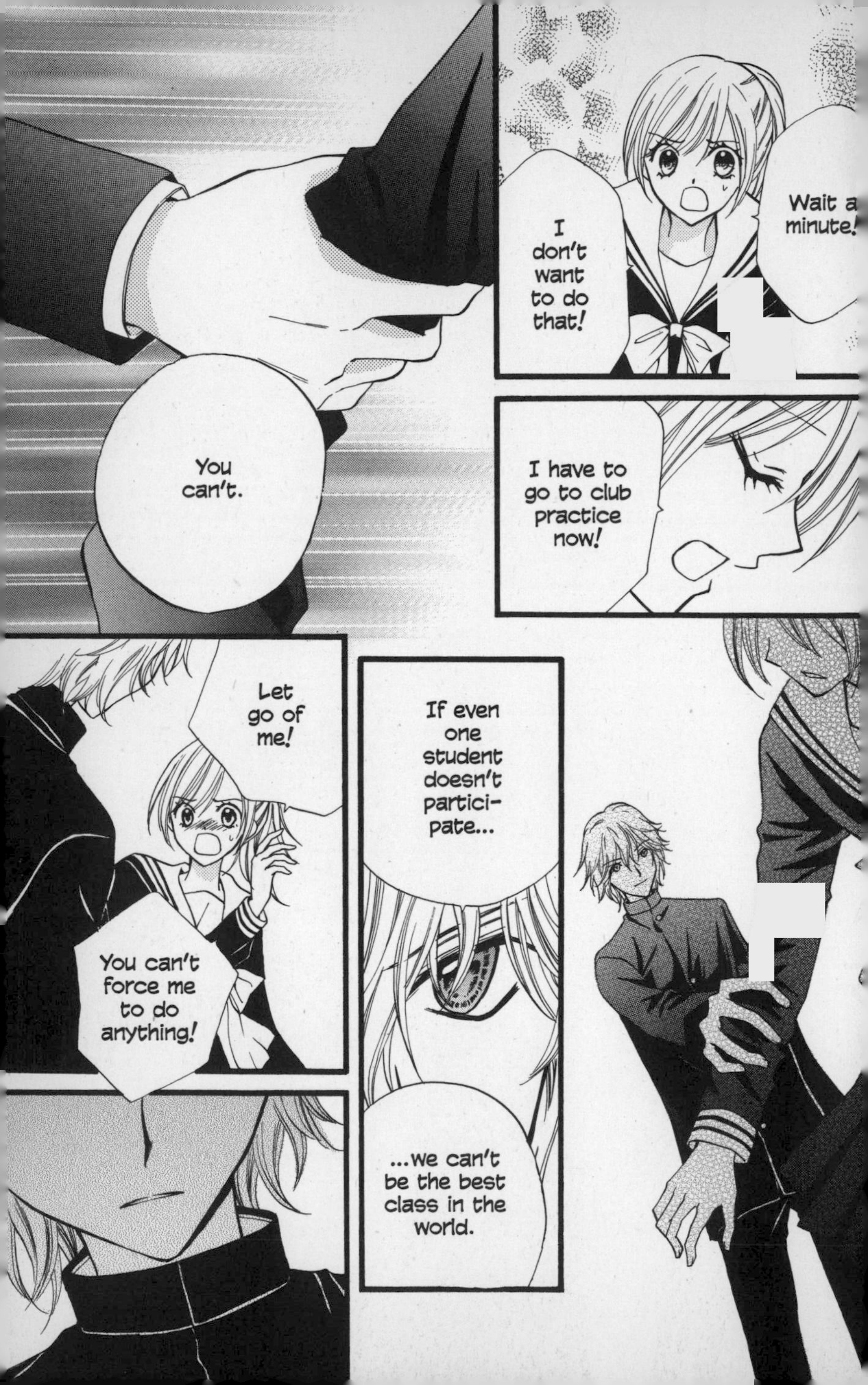
Wait a minute!
I don't want to do that!
I have to go to club practice now!
You can't.
If even one student doesn't partici-pate...
...we can't be the best class in the world.
Let go of me!
You can't force me to do anything!

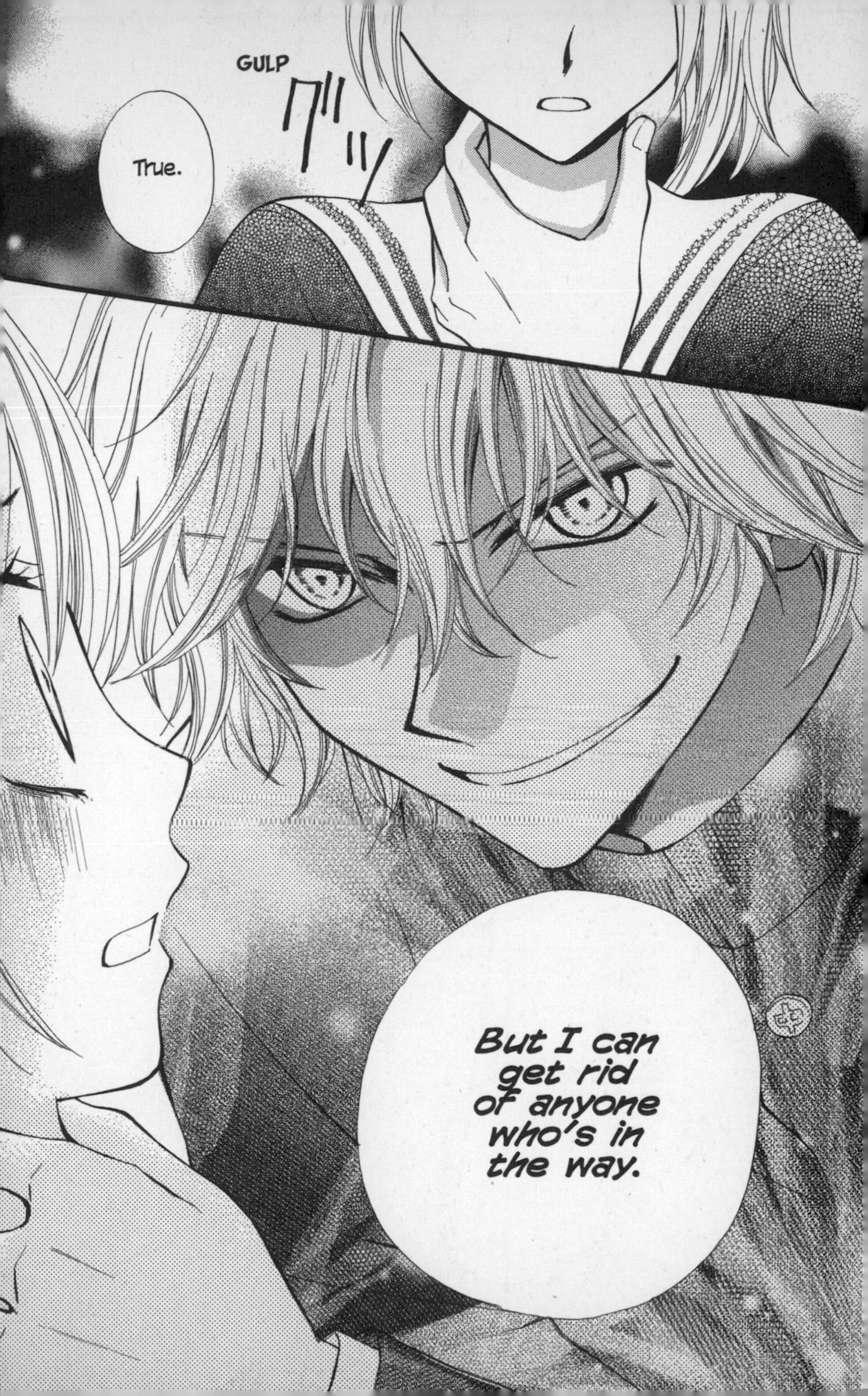
GULP
グッ
True.
But I can get rid of anyone who's in the way.

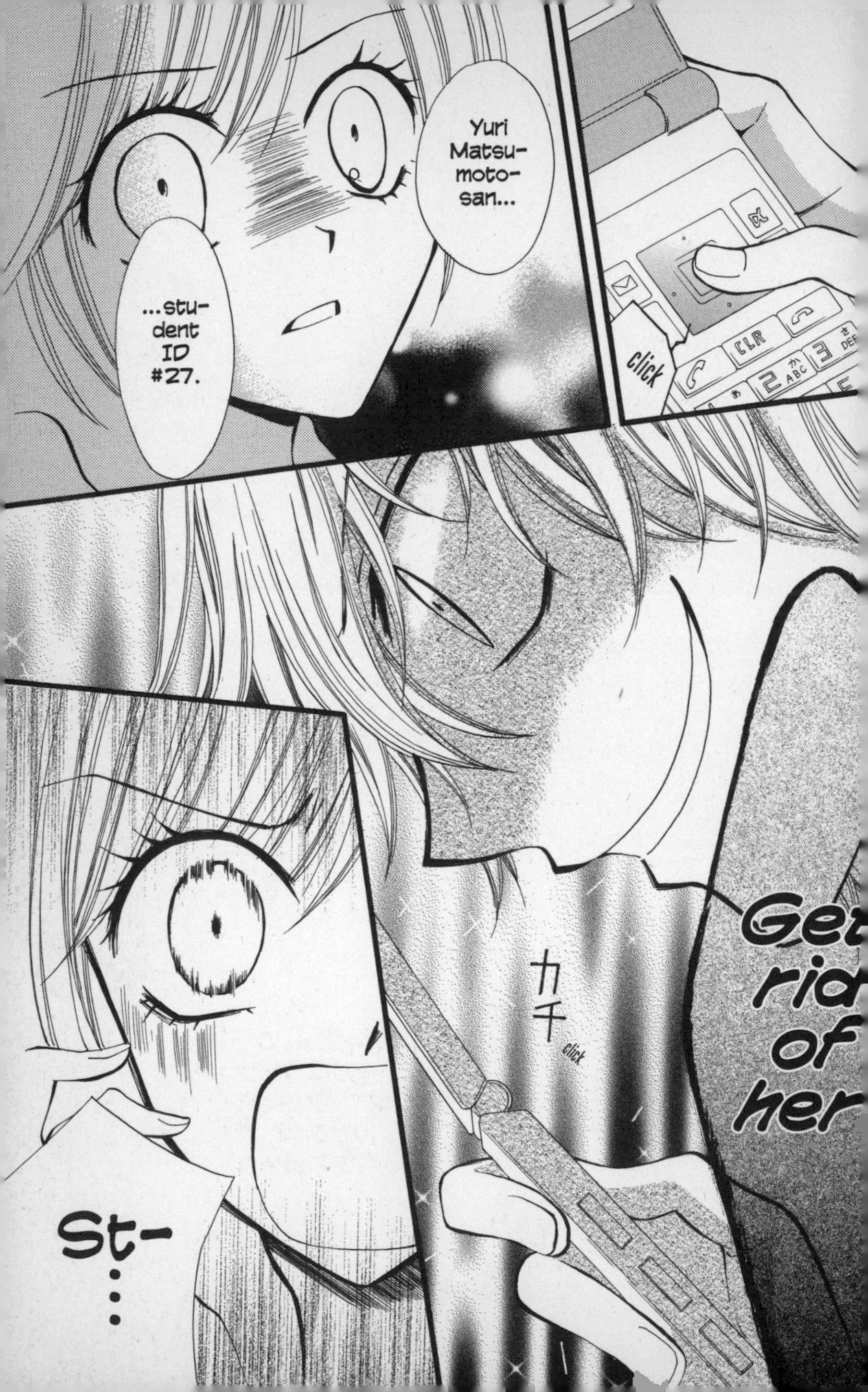
click
Yuri Matsu-moto-san...
...stu-dent ID #27.
Get rid of her
カチ click
St-...

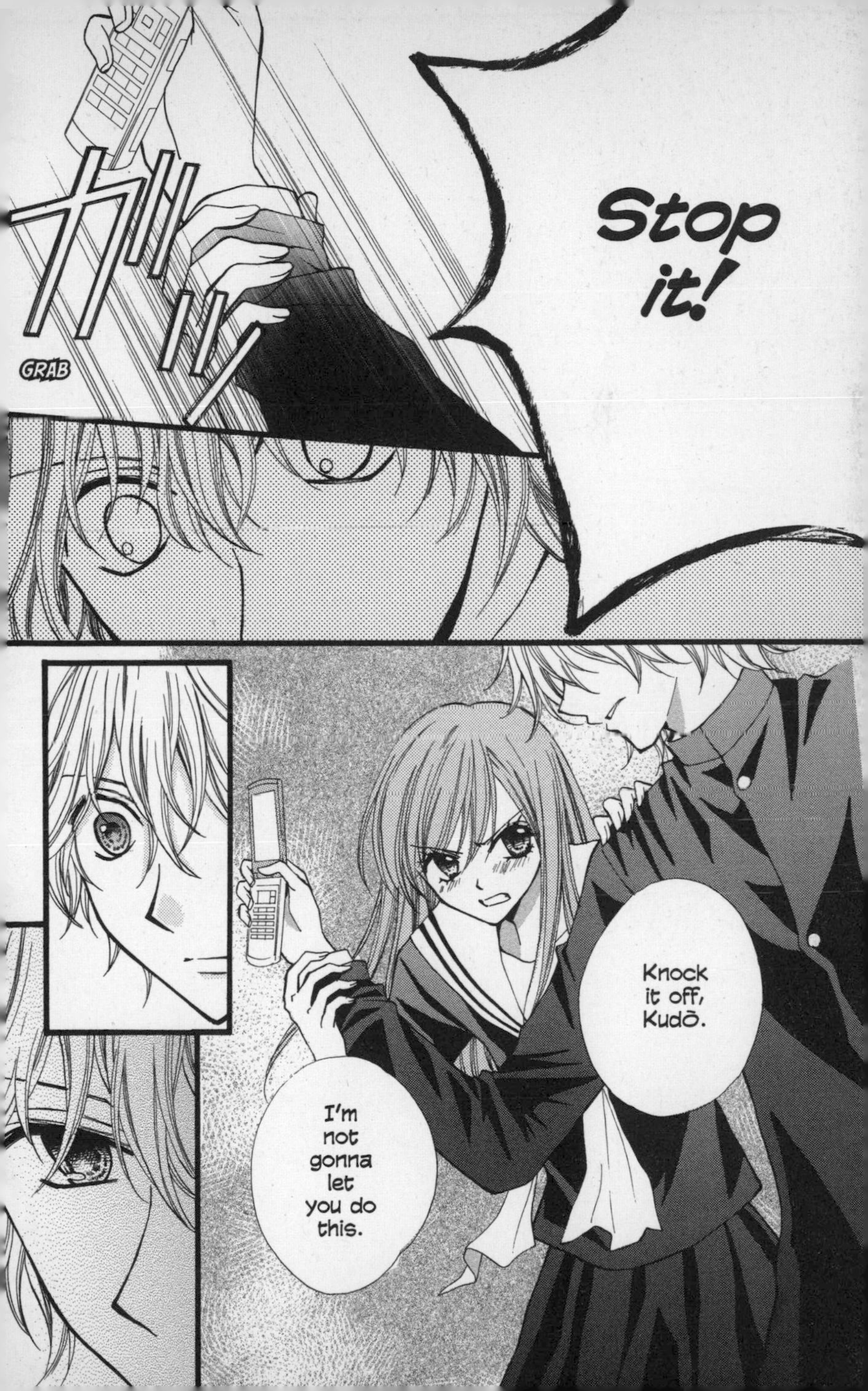
Stop it!
カッ
GRAB
Knock it off, Kudō.
I'm not gonna let you do this.

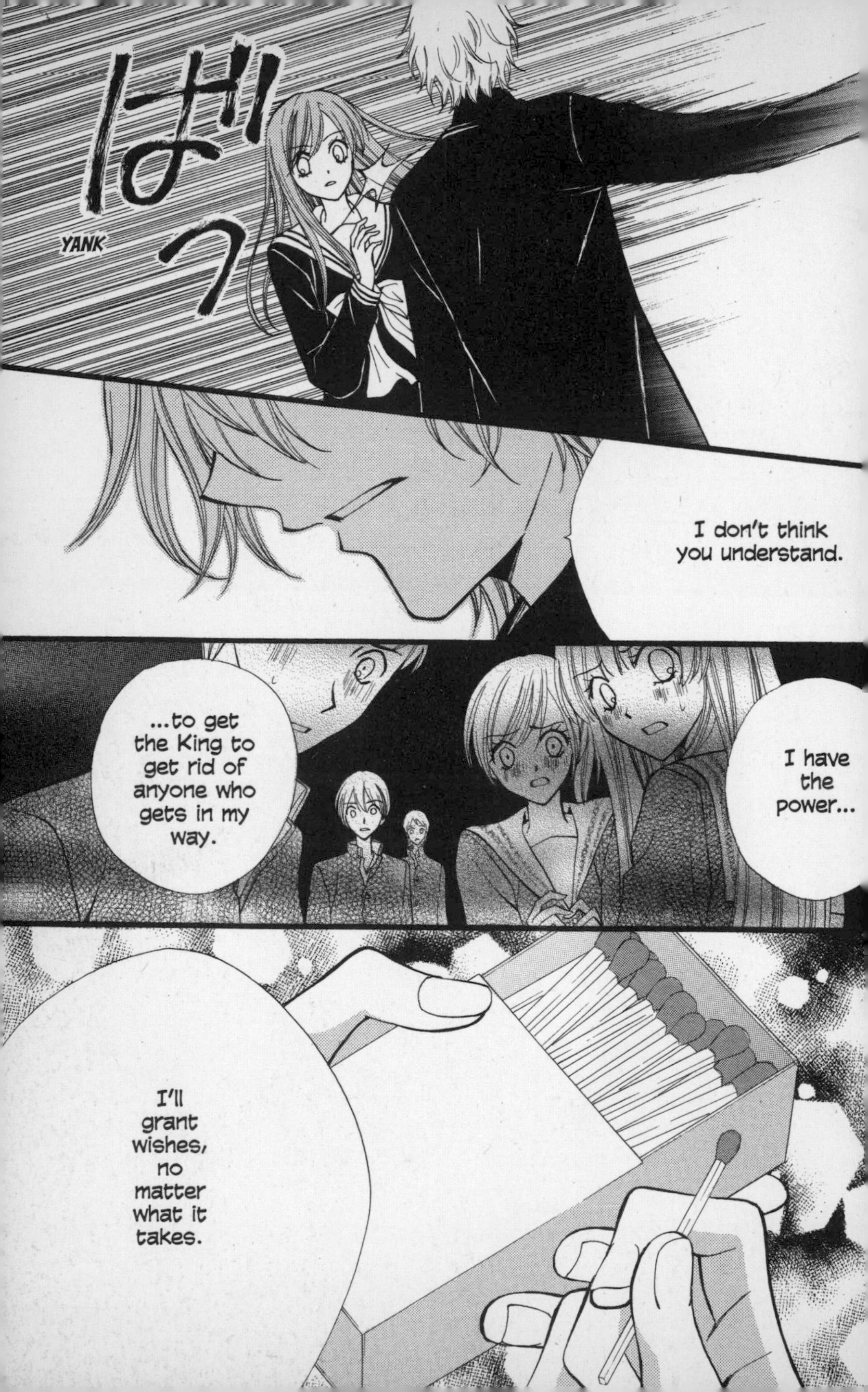
はっ
YANK
I don't think you understand.
I have the power...
...to get the King to get rid of anyone who gets in my way.
I'll grant wishes, no matter what it takes.

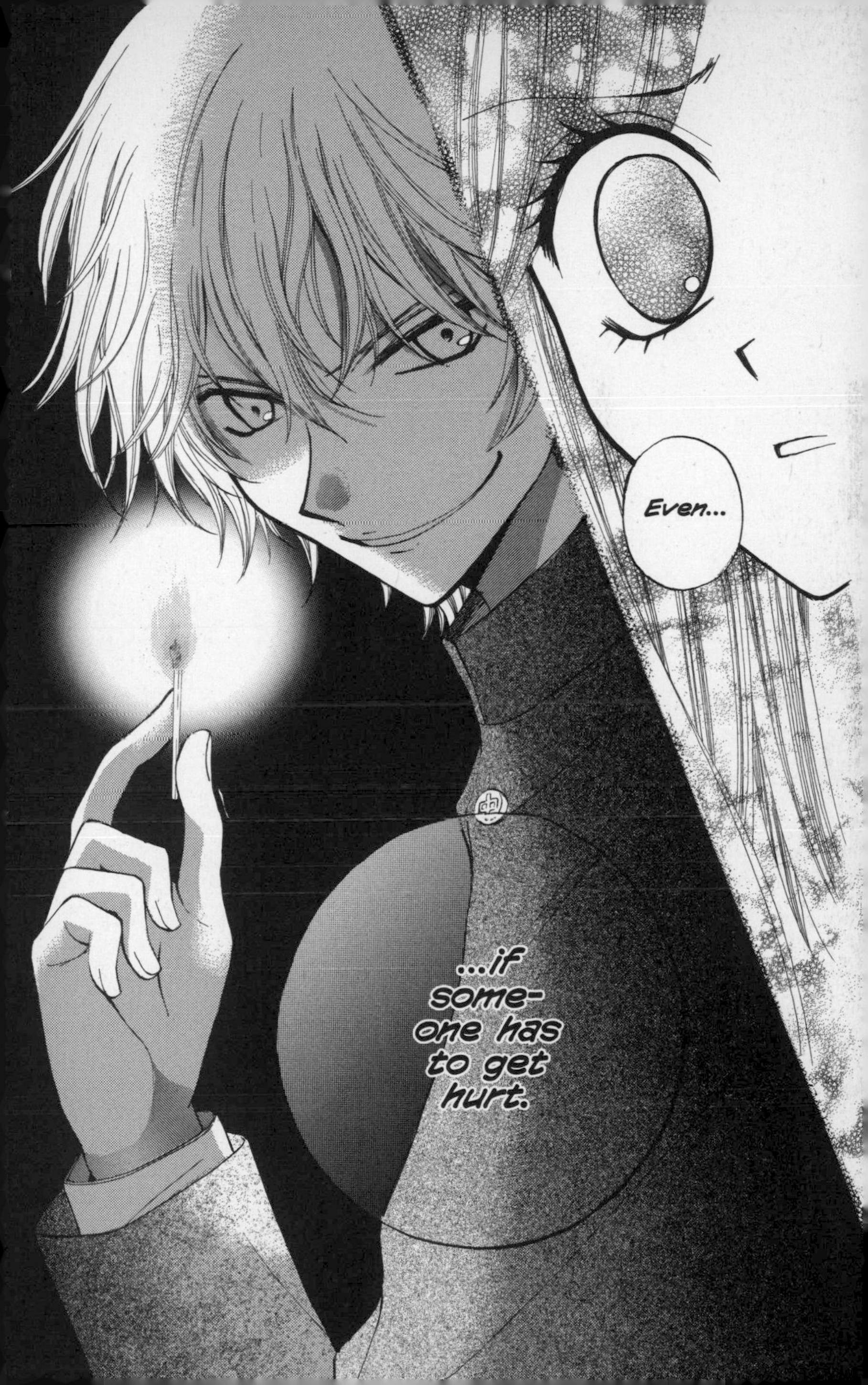
Even...
...if someone has to get hurt.

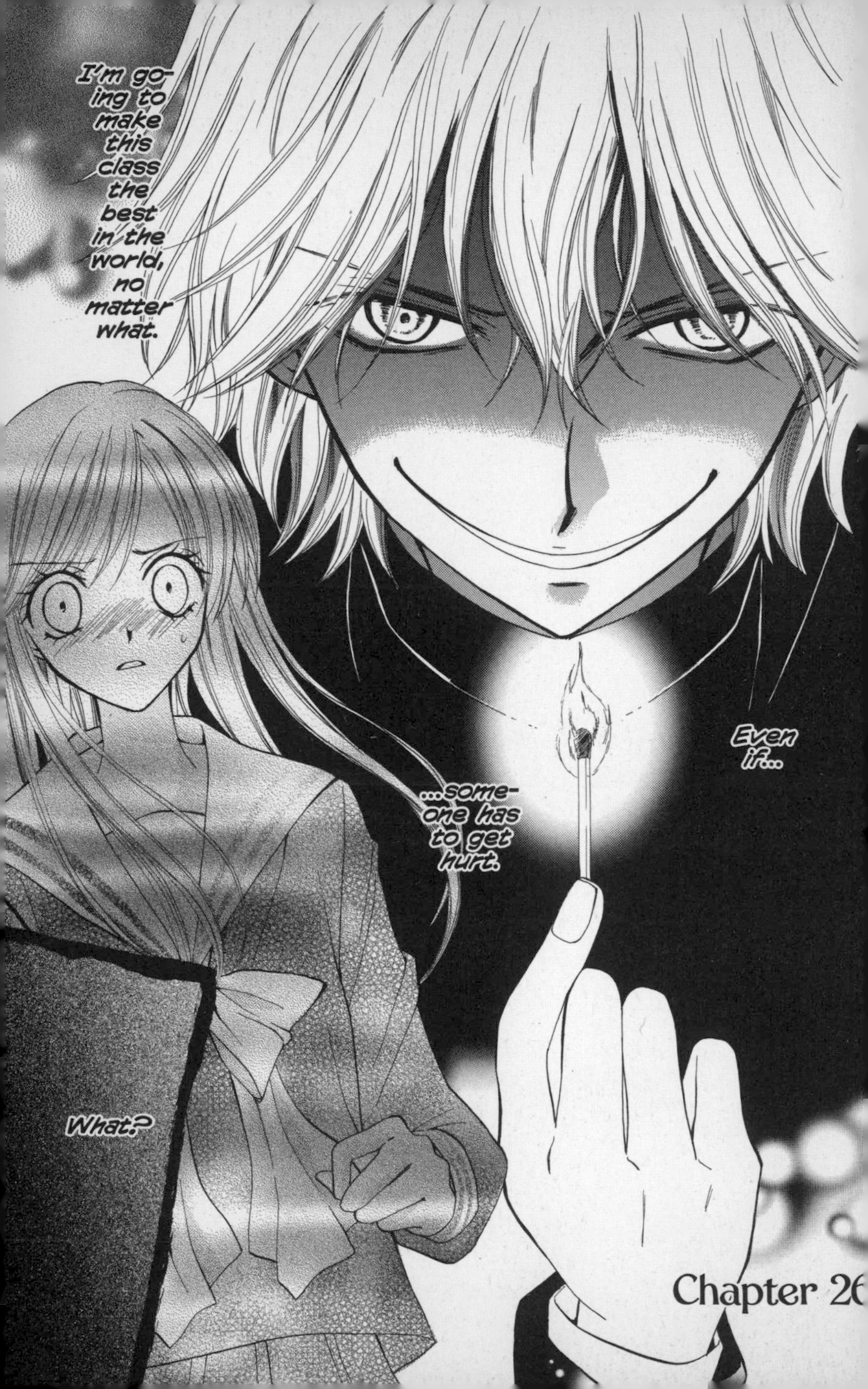
I'm go-ing to make this class the best in the world, no matter what.
Even if...
...some-one has to get hurt.
What?
Chapter 26

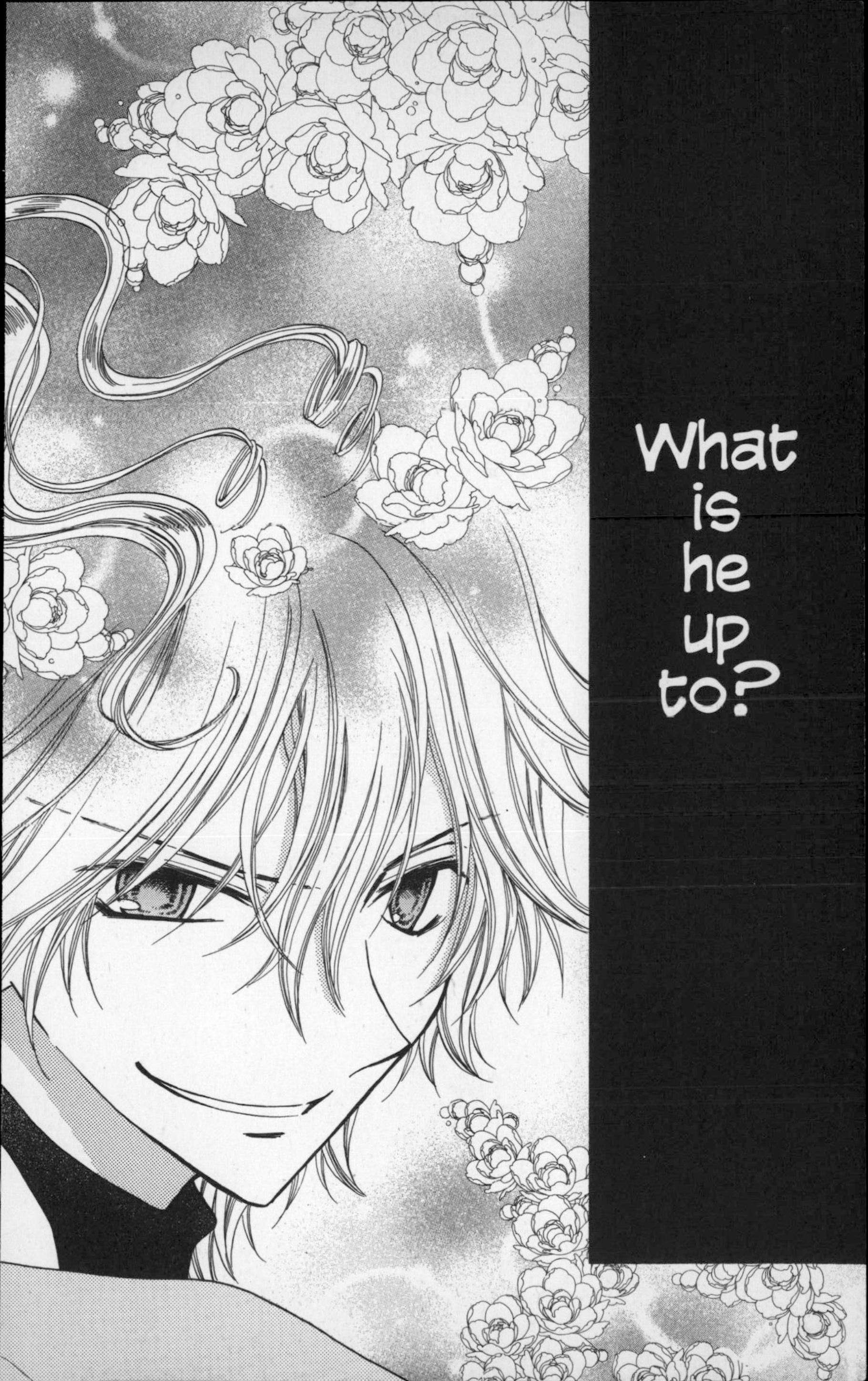
What is he up to?

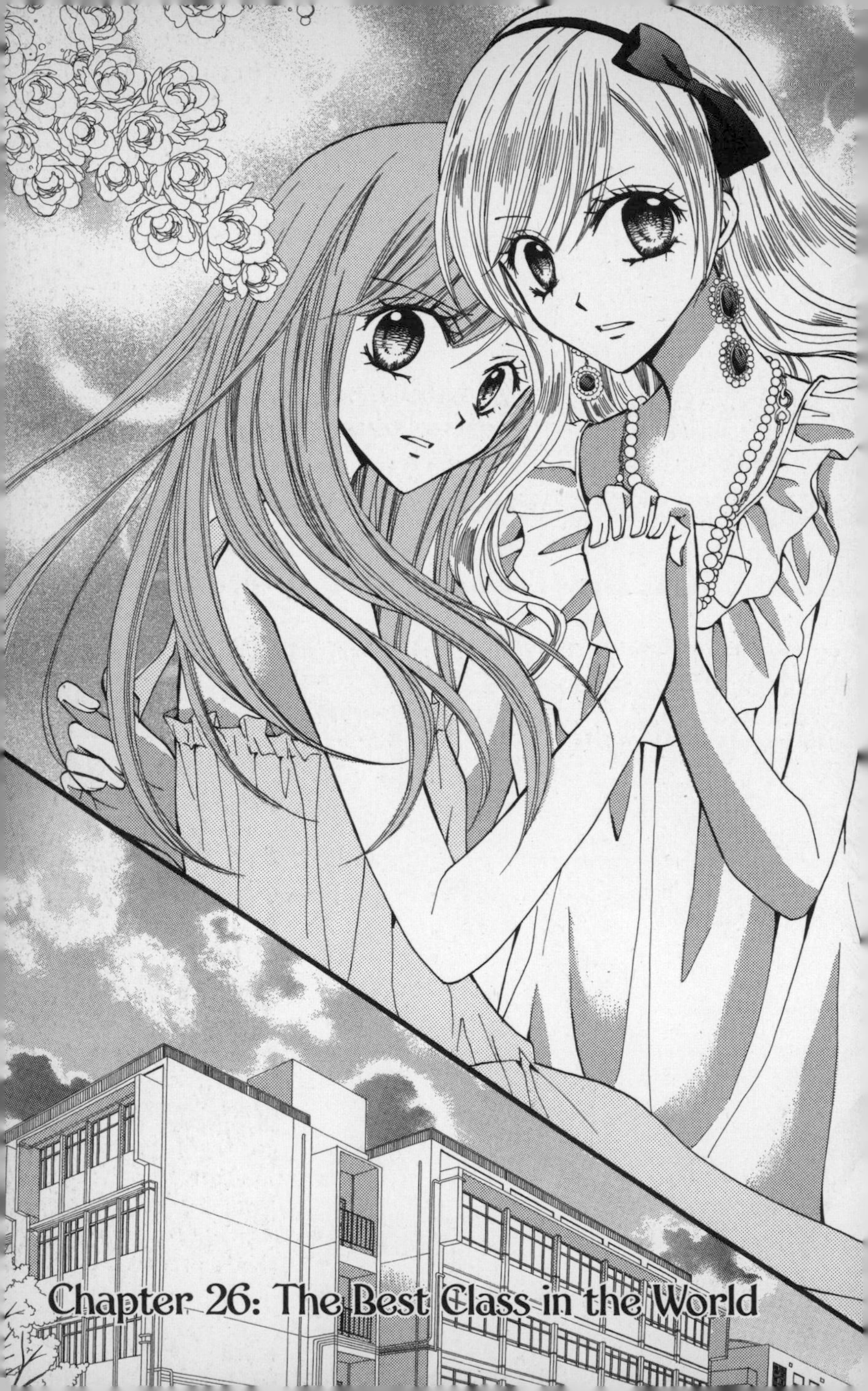
Chapter 26: The Best Class in the World

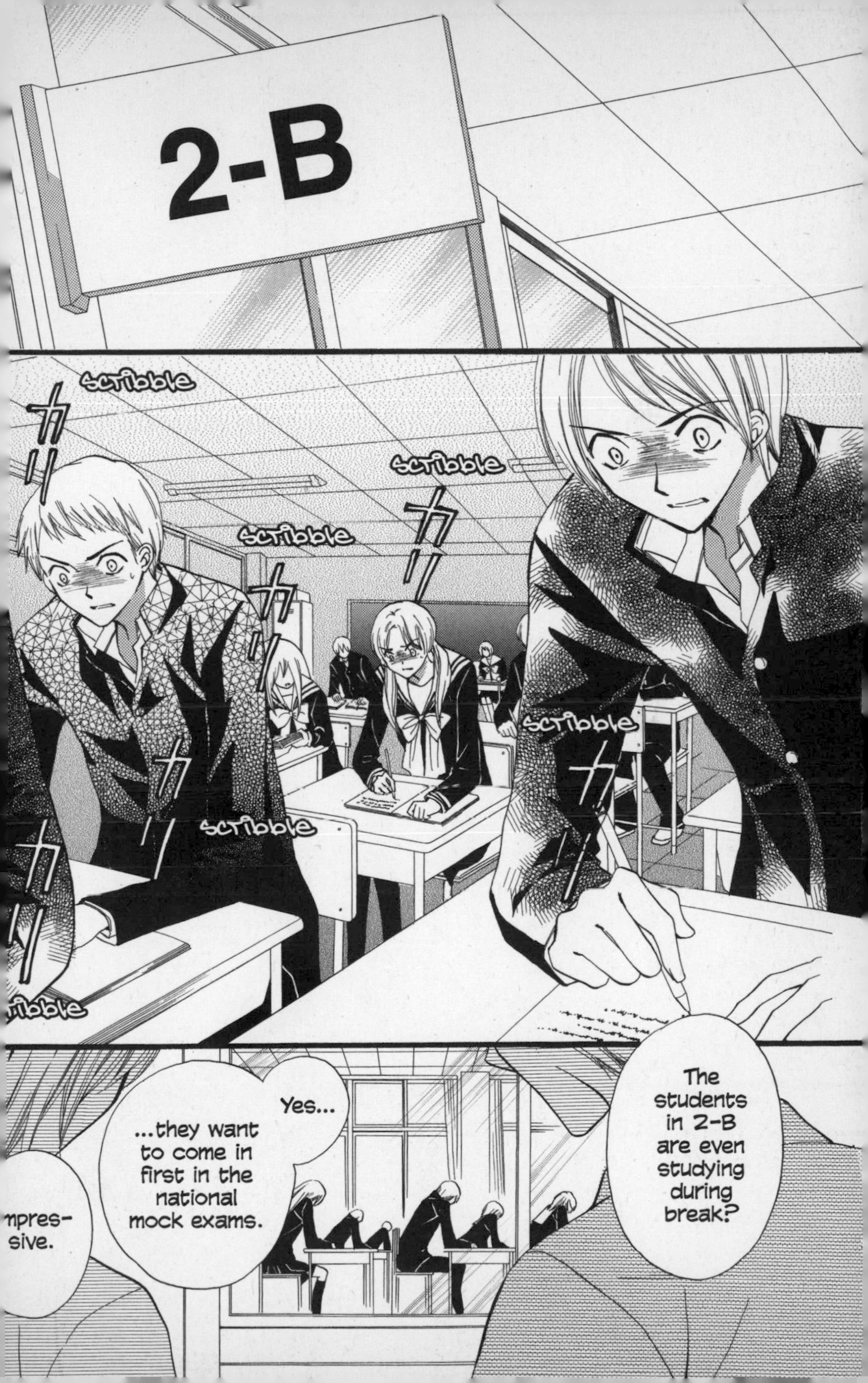
2-B
scribble
scribble
scribble
scribble
scribble
ribble
The students in 2-B are even studying during break?
Yes...
...they want to come in first in the national mock exams.
mpres-sive.

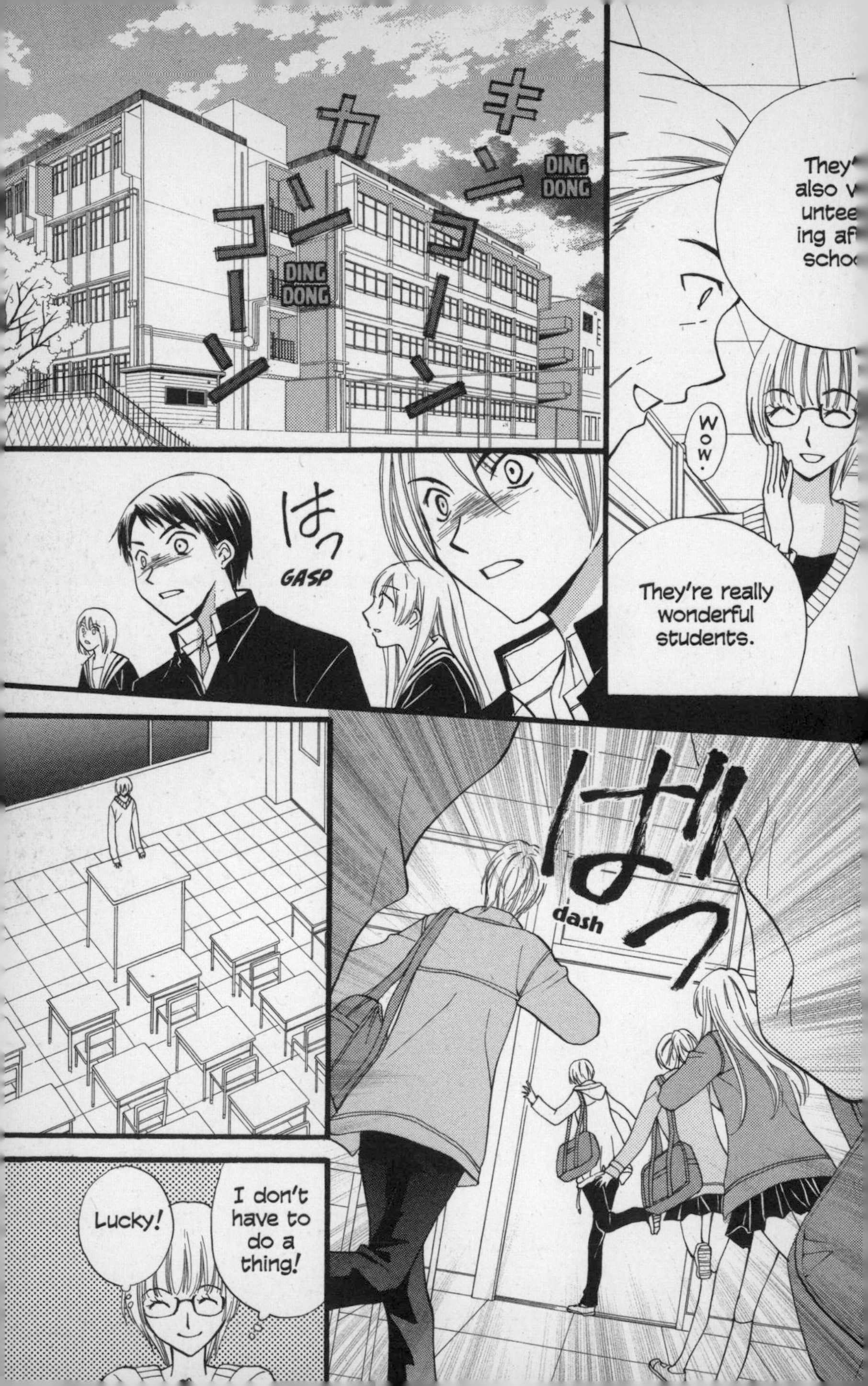
They' also v untee ing af schoo
Wow.
They're really wonderful students.
キーンコーンカーンコーン
DING DONG
DING DONG
はっ
GASP
はっ
dash
I don't have to do a thing!
Lucky!

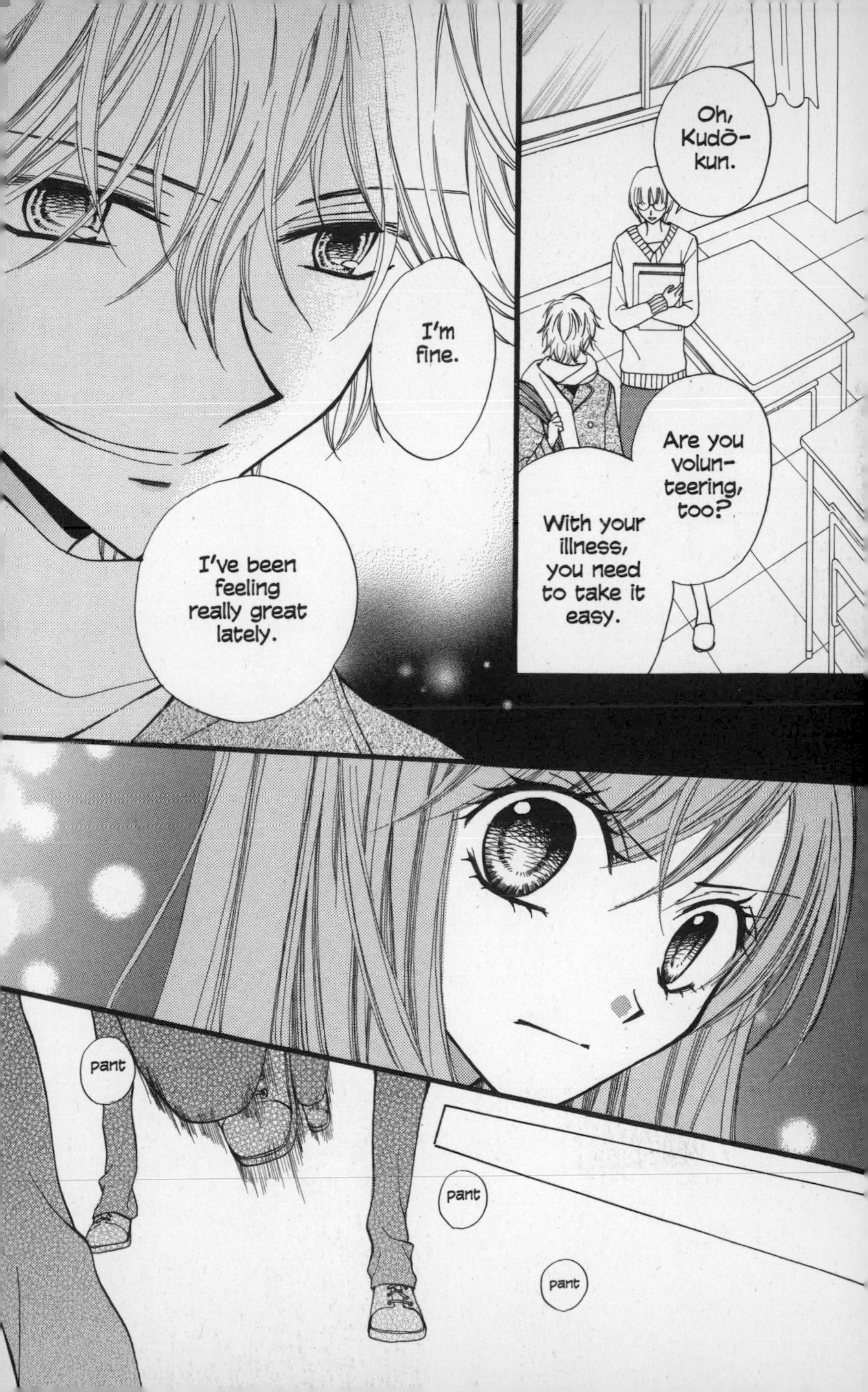
Oh, Kudō-kun.
Are you volunteering, too?
With your illness, you need to take it easy.
I'm fine.
I've been feeling really great lately.
pant
pant
pant

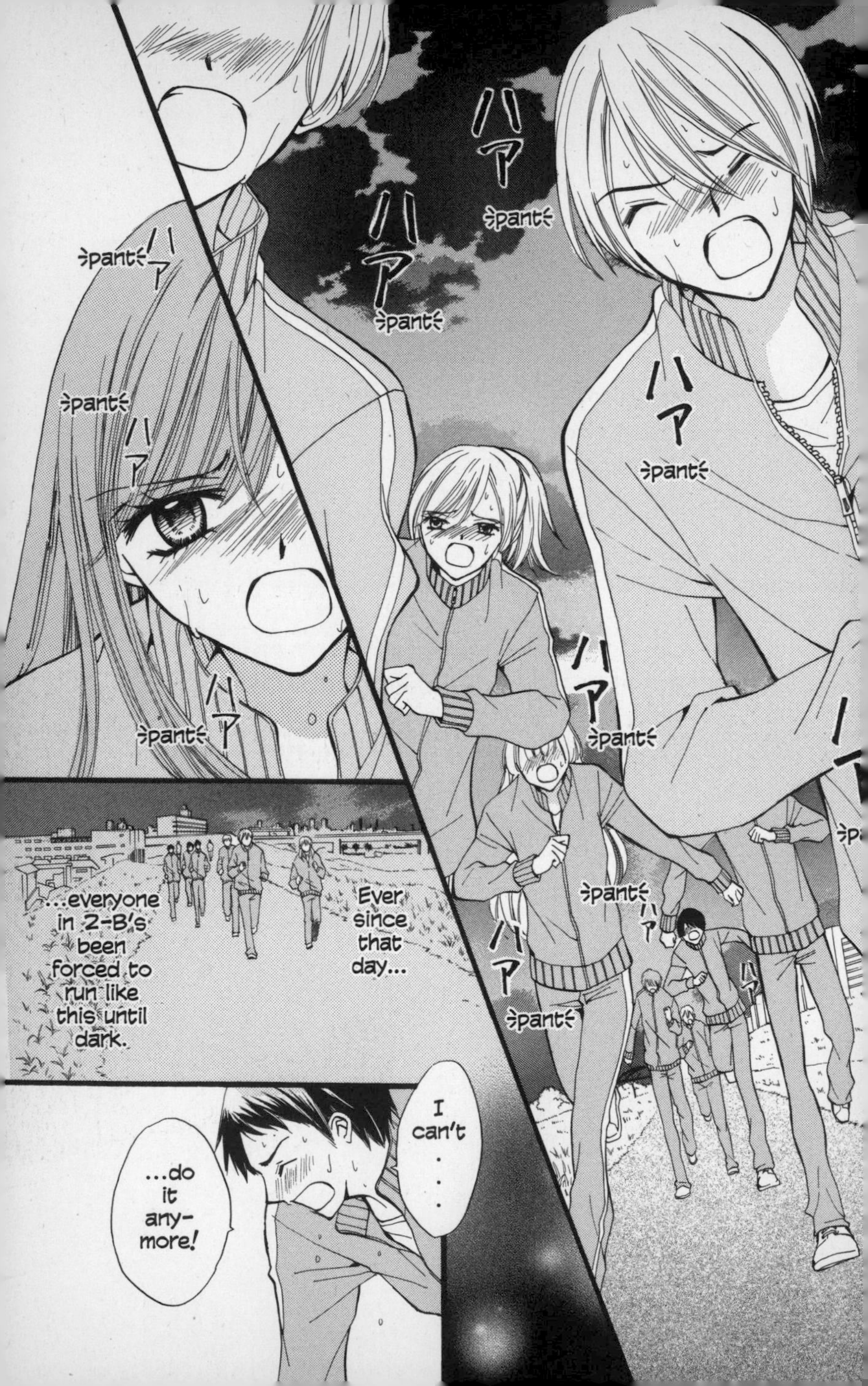

ハア
pant
ハア
pant
ハア
pant
ハア
pant
pant
ハア
ハア
pant
pant
ハア
pant
ハア
ハア
pant
Ever since that day...
...everyone in 2-B's been forced to run like this until dark.
I can't...
...do it anymore!

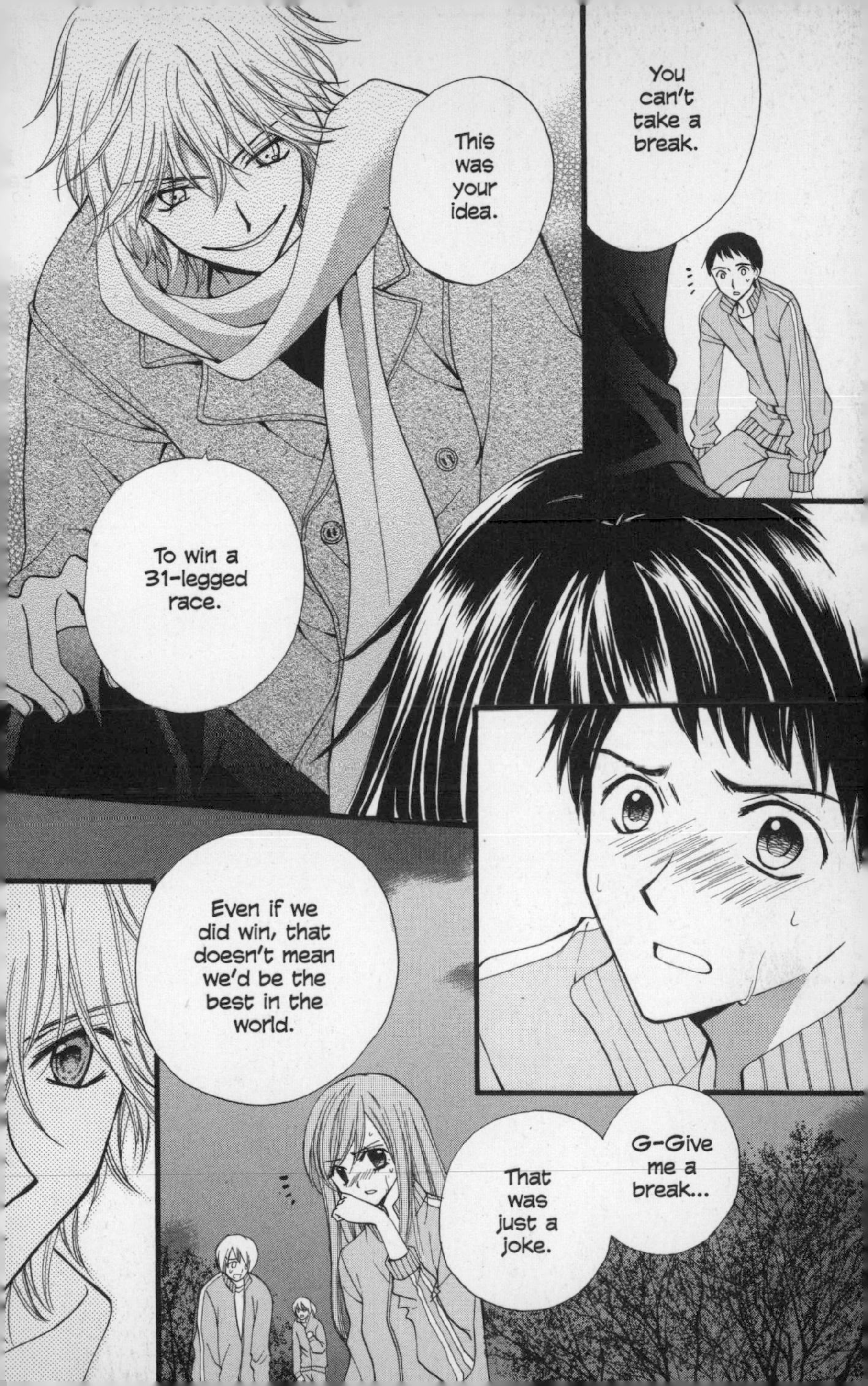
You can't take a break.
This was your idea.
To win a 31-legged race.
Even if we did win, that doesn't mean we'd be the best in the world.
G-Give me a break...
That was just a joke.

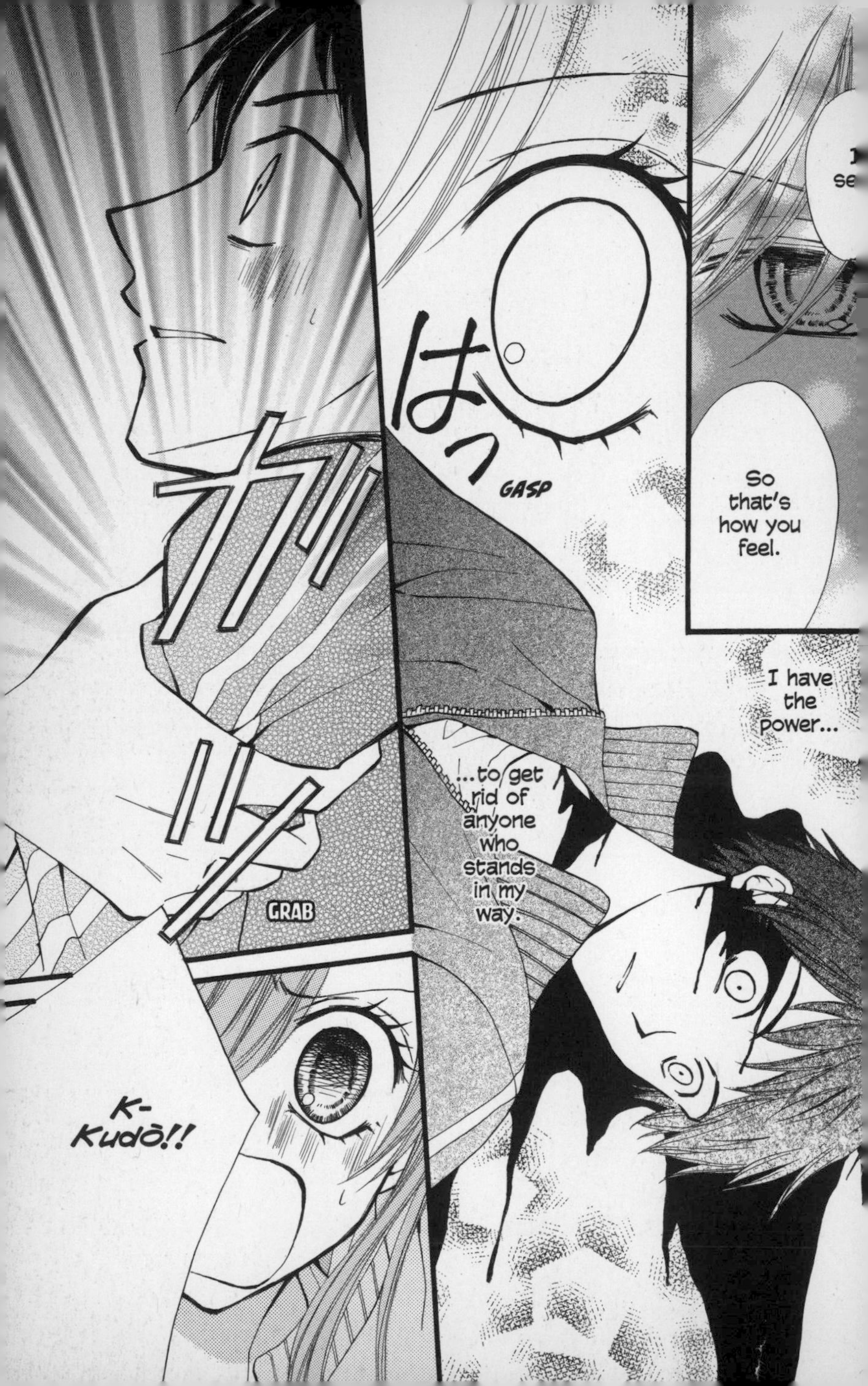
So that's how you feel.
はっ
GASP
ガッ
GRAB
I have the power...
...to get rid of anyone who stands in my way.
K-Kudō!!

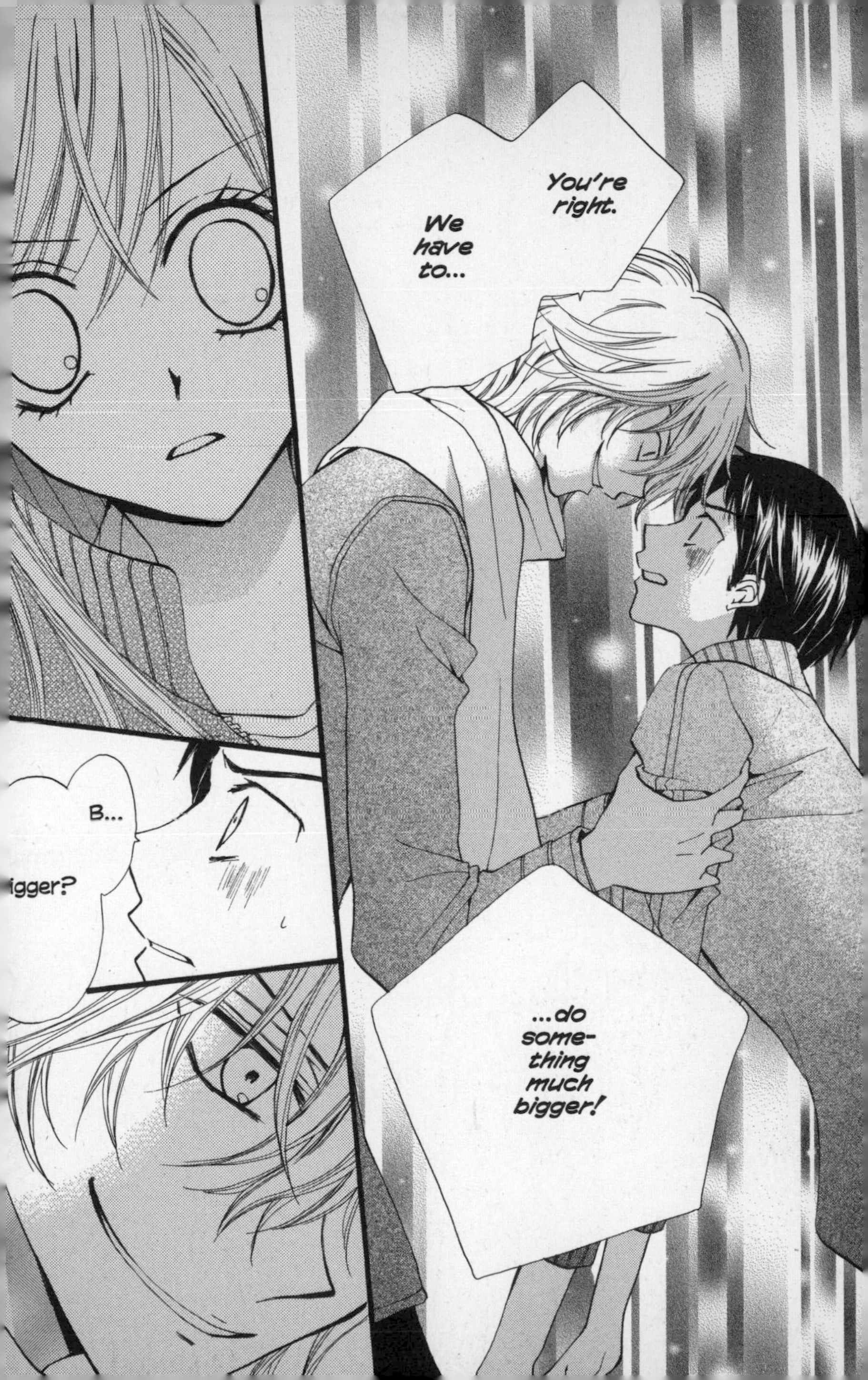
You're right.
We have to...
...do something much bigger!
B...
igger?

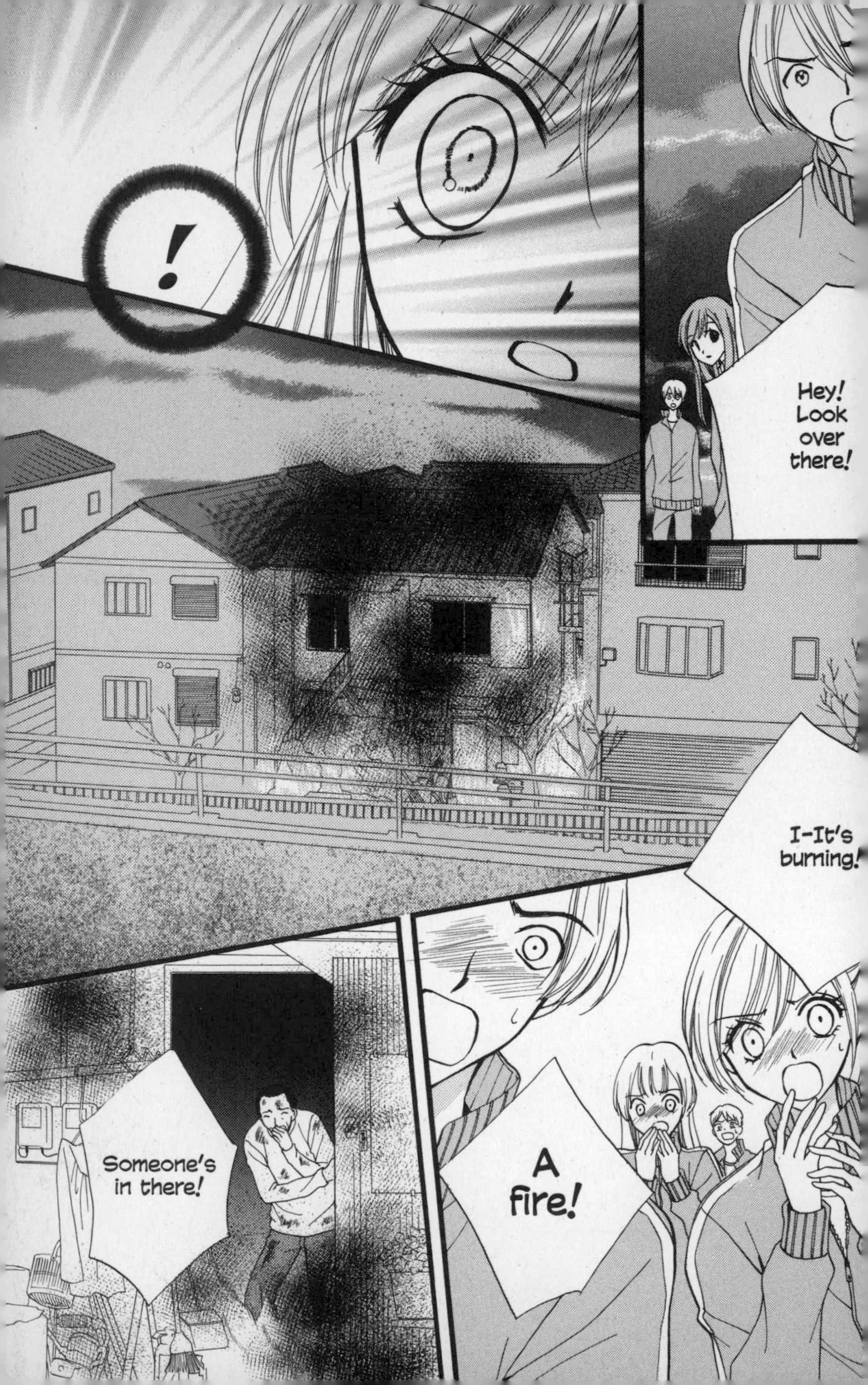
Hey! Look over there!
!
I-It's burning!
A fire!
Someone's in there!

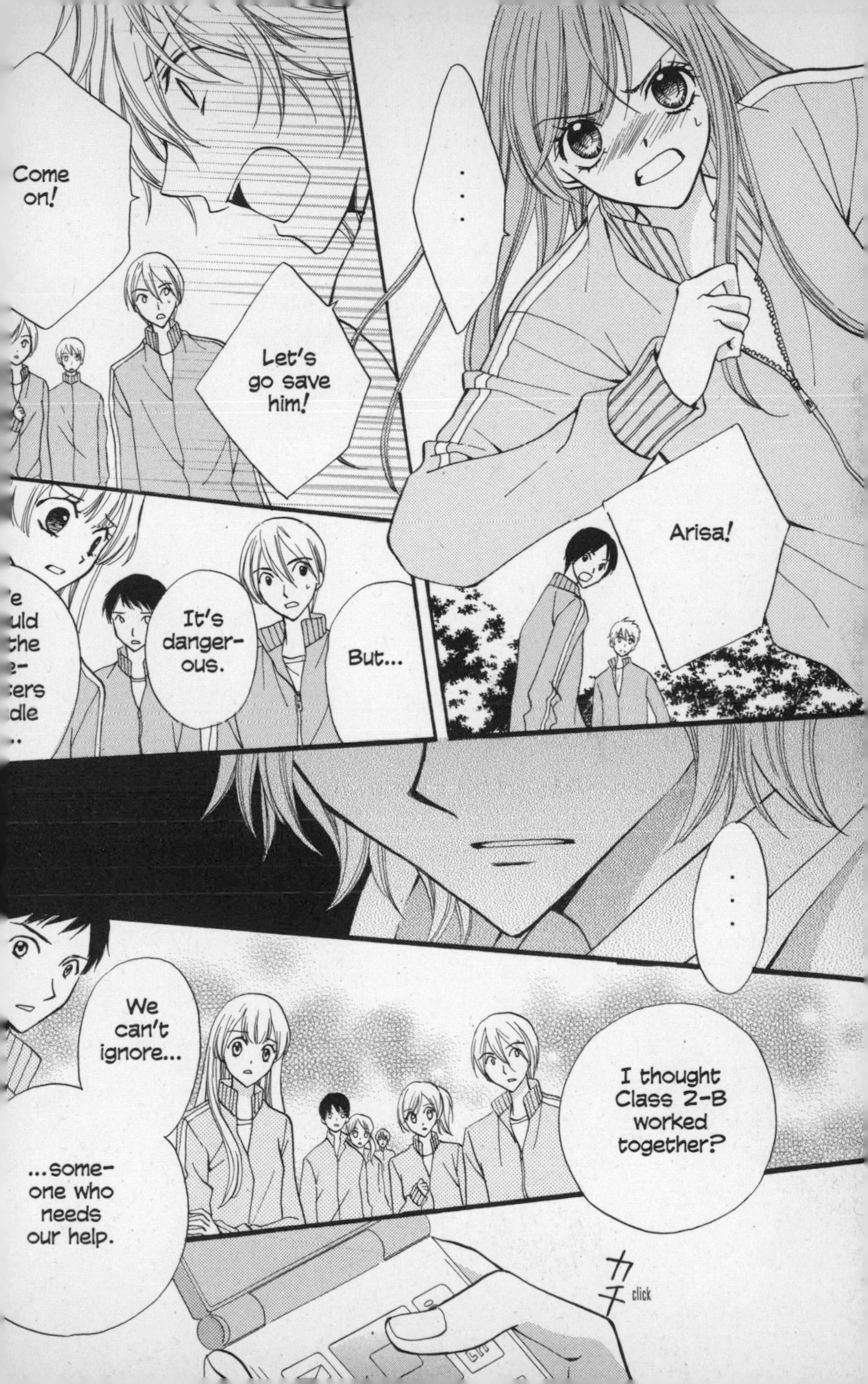

...
Come on!
Let's go save him!
Arisa!
But...
It's dangerous.
...
I thought Class 2-B worked together?
We can't ignore...
...someone who needs our help.
カチ click

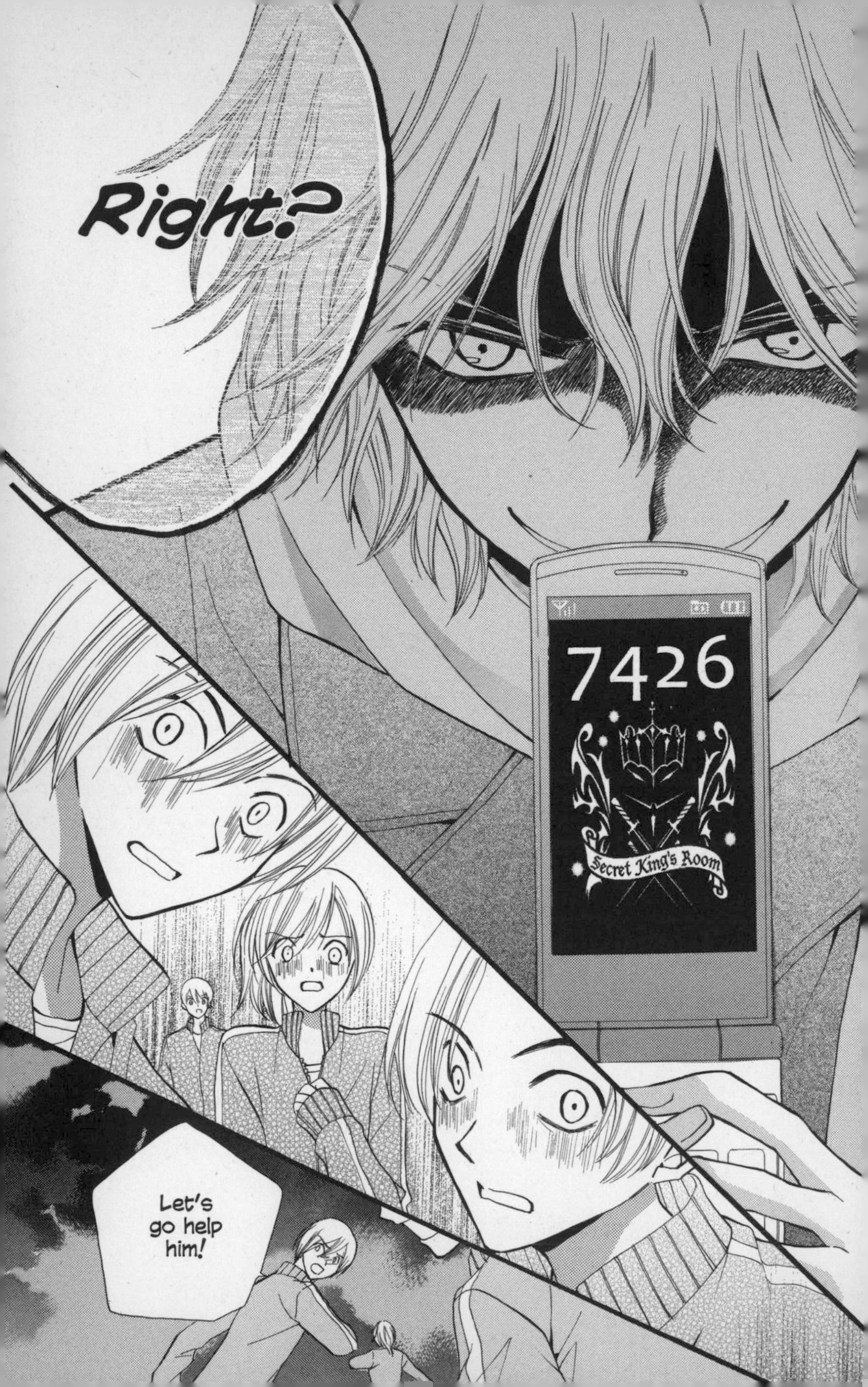
Right?
7426
Secret King's Room
Let's go help him!

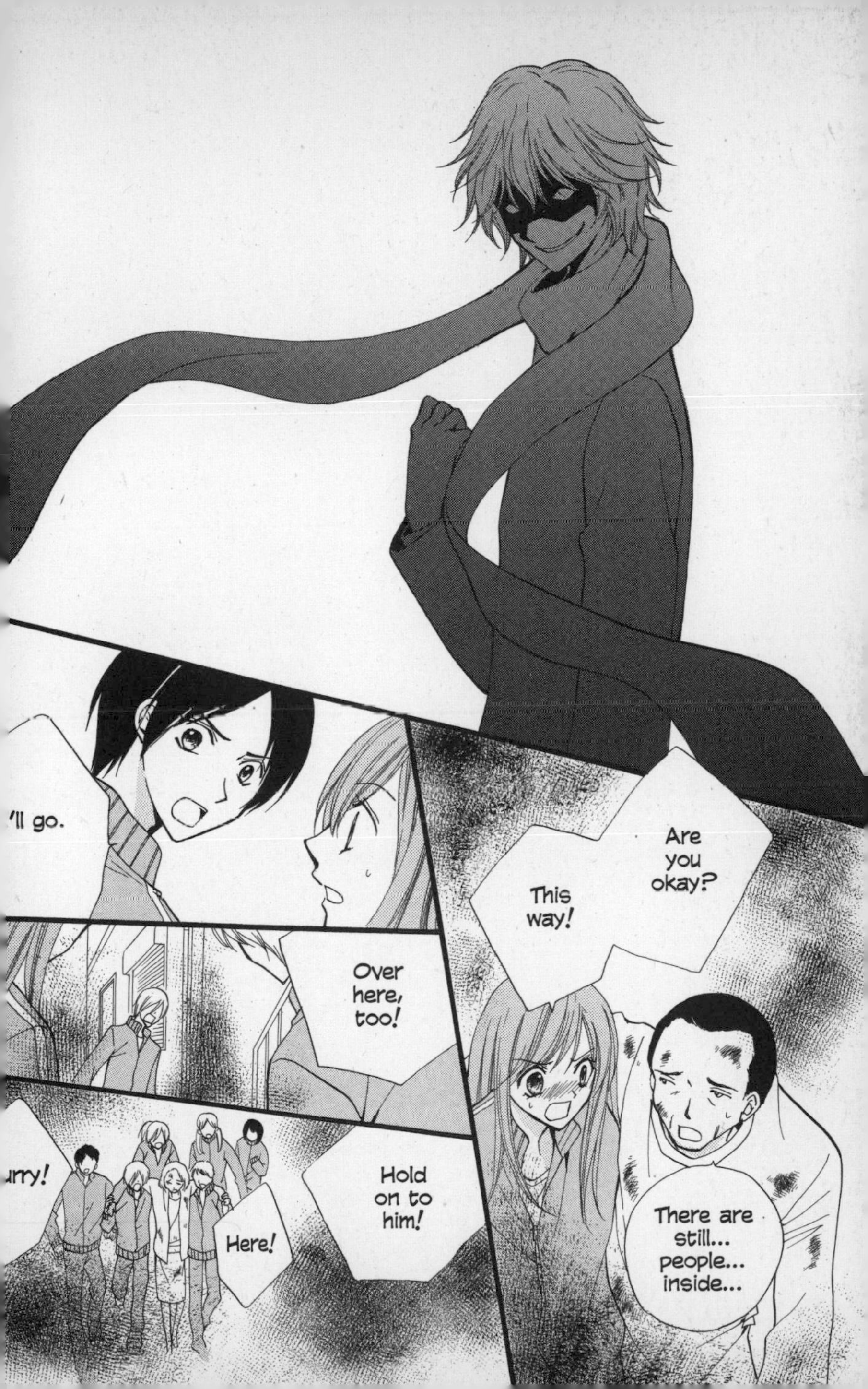
Are you okay?
This way!
There are still... people... inside...
'll go.
Over here, too!
Hold on to him!
Here!
urry!

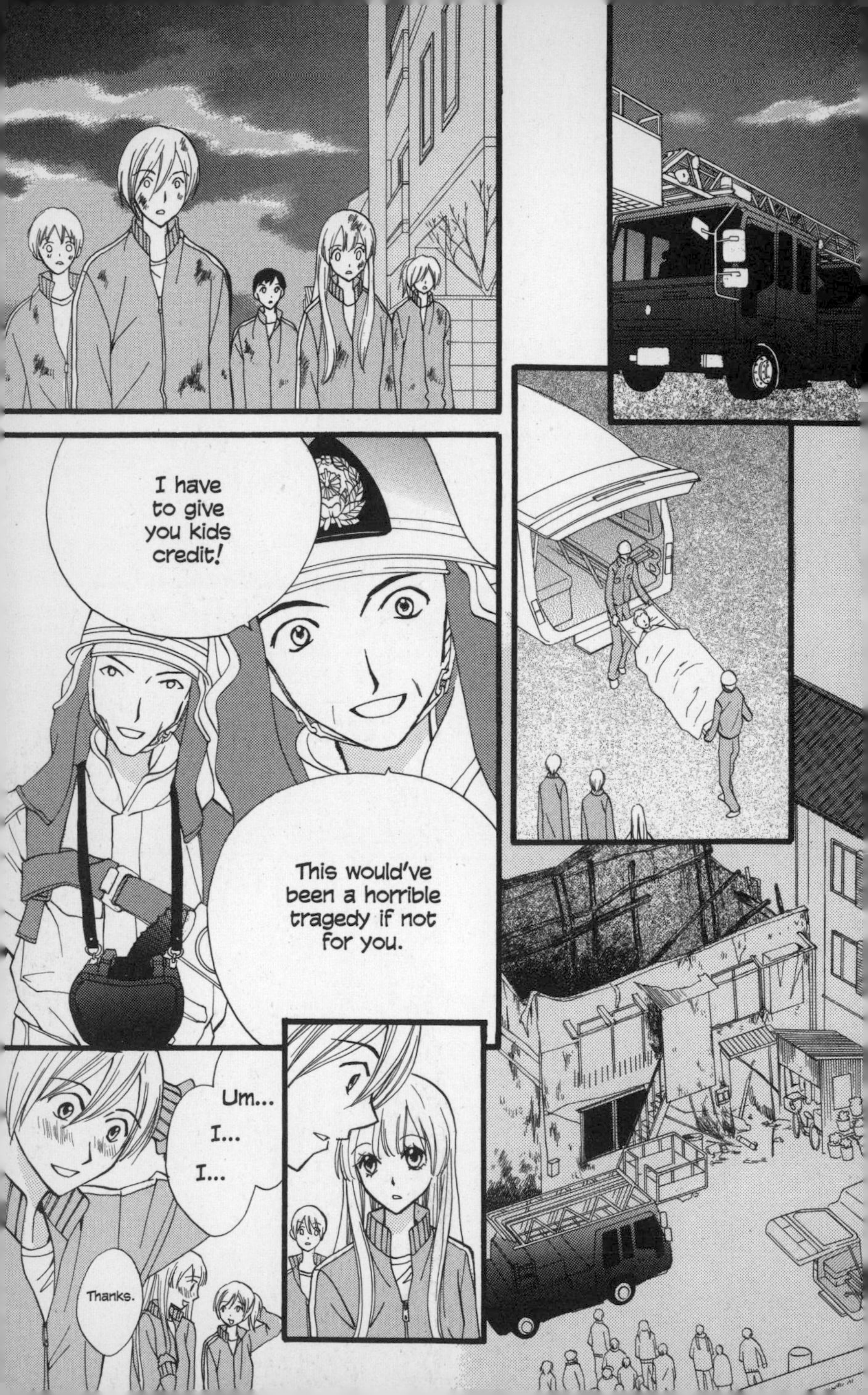
I have to give you kids credit!
This would've been a horrible tragedy if not for you.
Um... I... I...
Thanks.

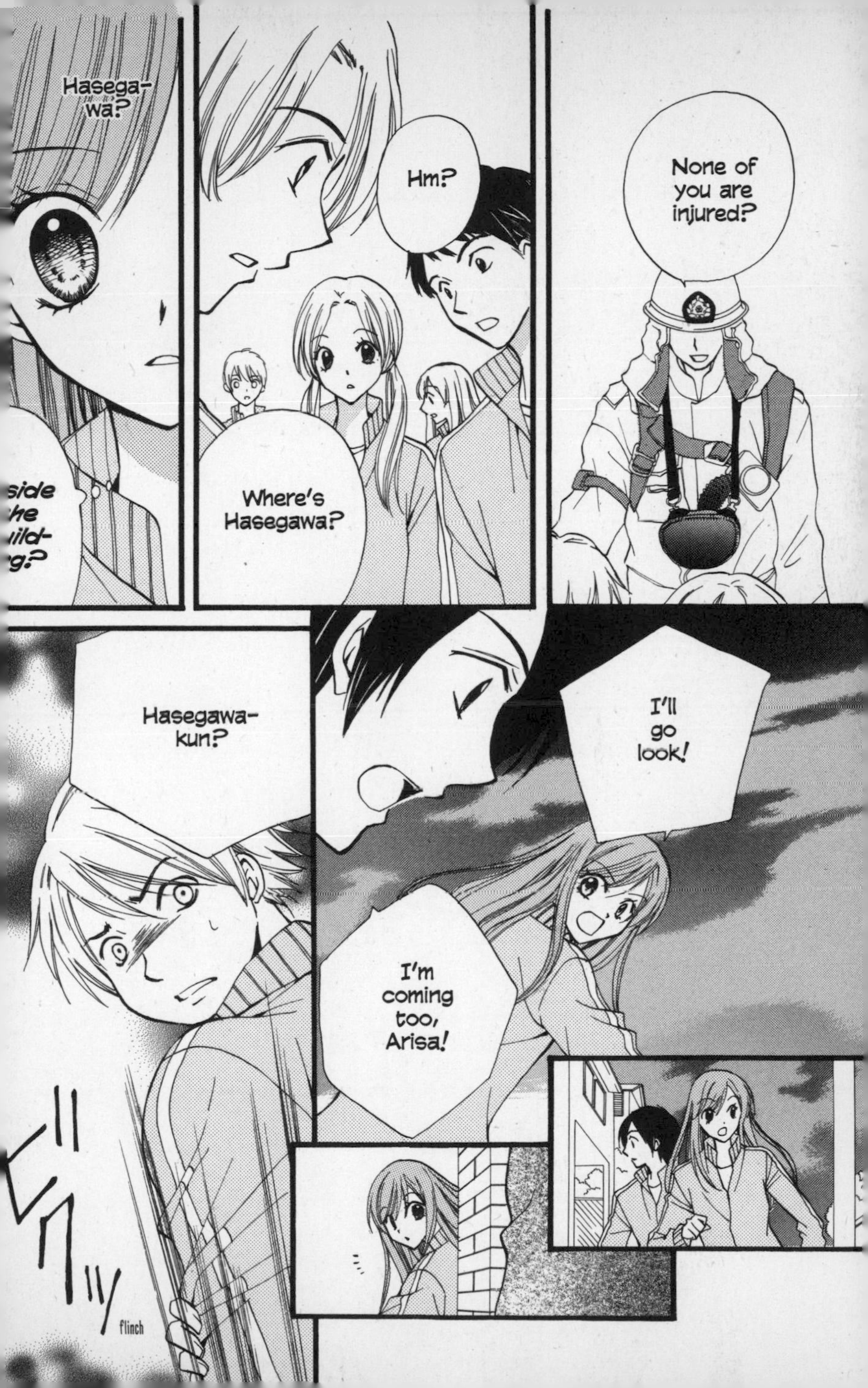
None of you are injured?
Hm?
Where's Hasegawa?
Hasega-wa?
side he uild- g?
I'll go look!
I'm coming too, Arisa!
Hasegawa-kun?
flinch

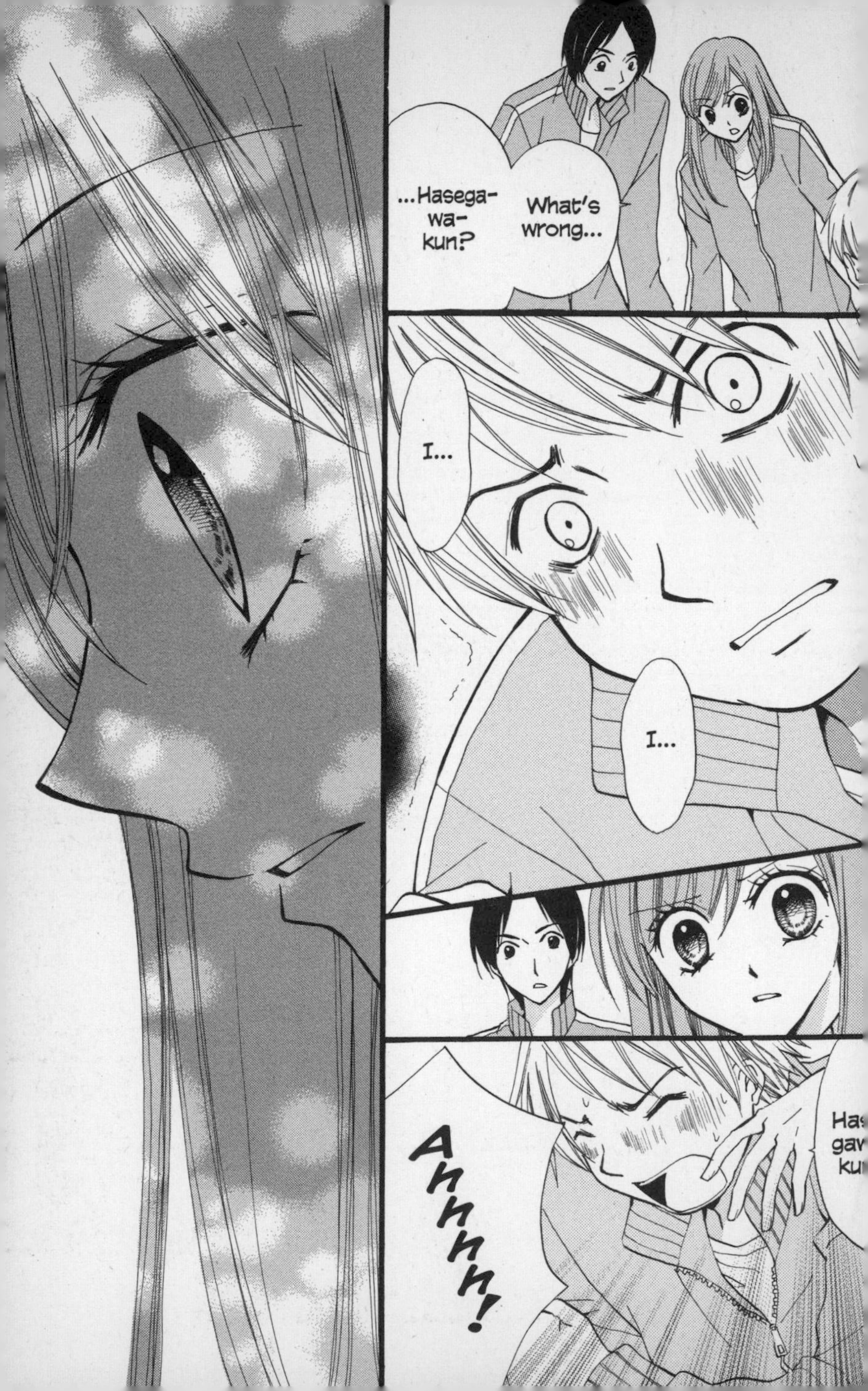
What's wrong...
...Hasega-wa-kun?
I...
I...
Annnn!

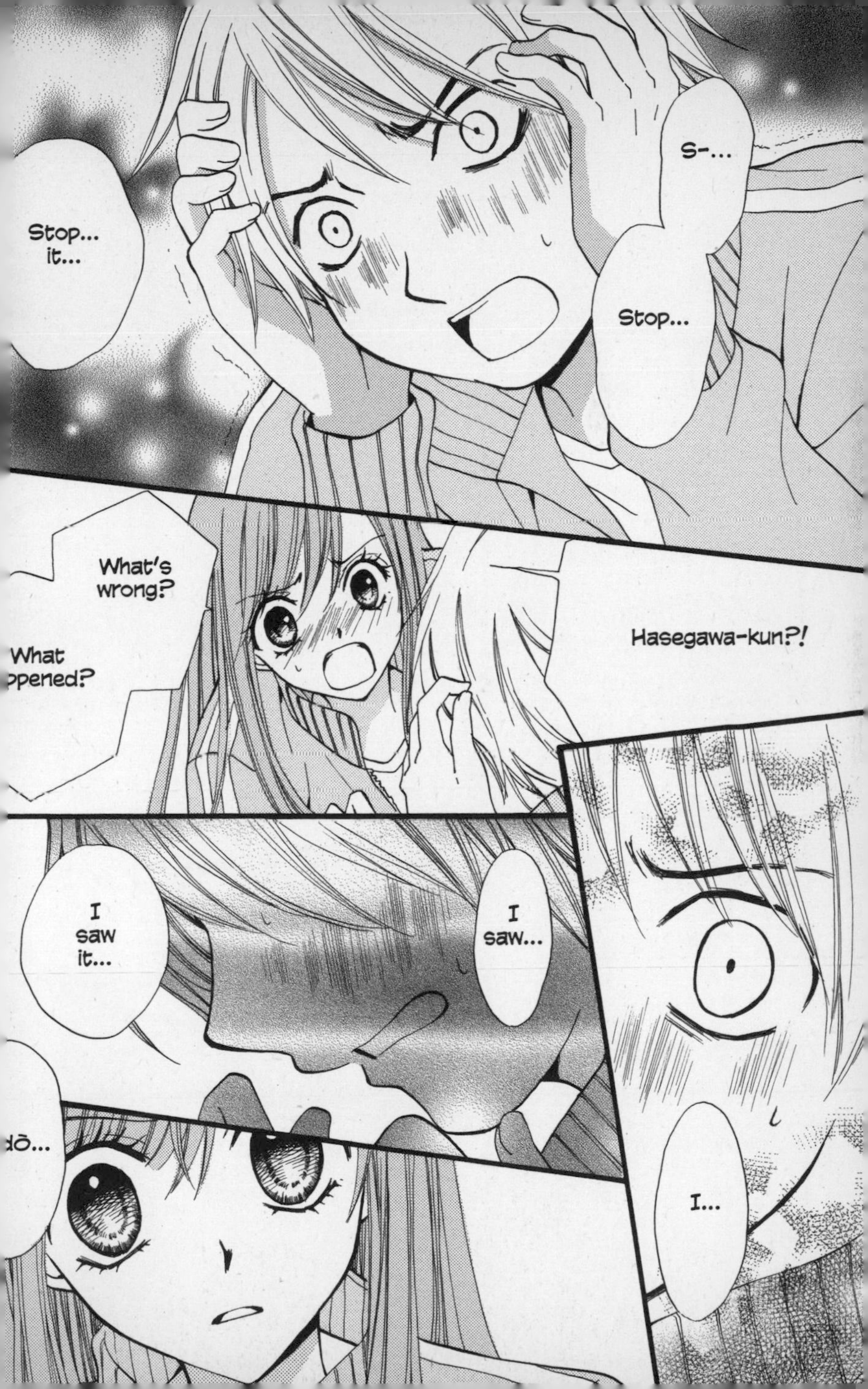
S-...
Stop...
Stop... it...
Hasegawa-kun?!
What's wrong?
What ppened?
I...
I saw...
I saw it...
dō...

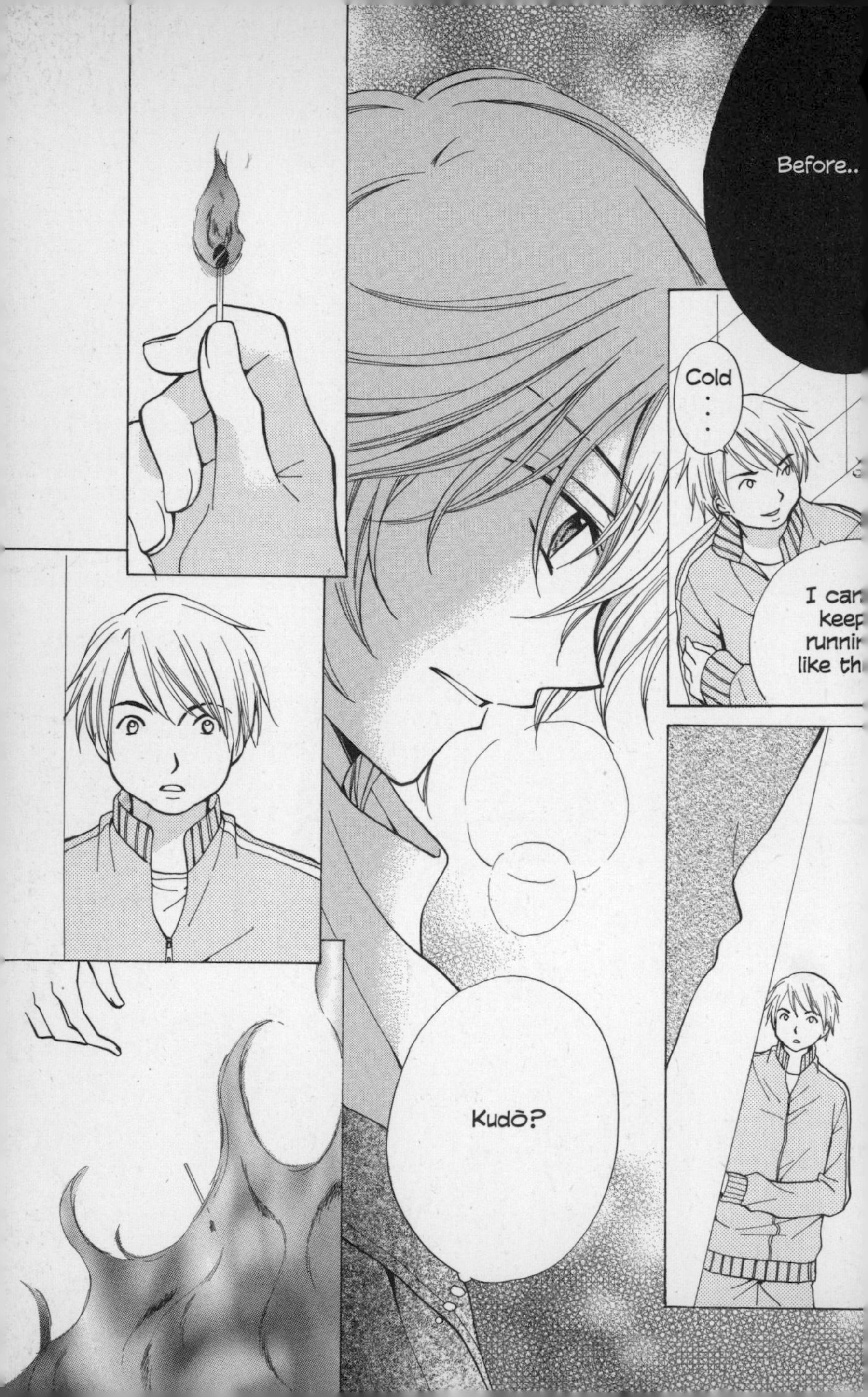
Before..
Cold...
I can
keep
runnir
like th
Kudō?

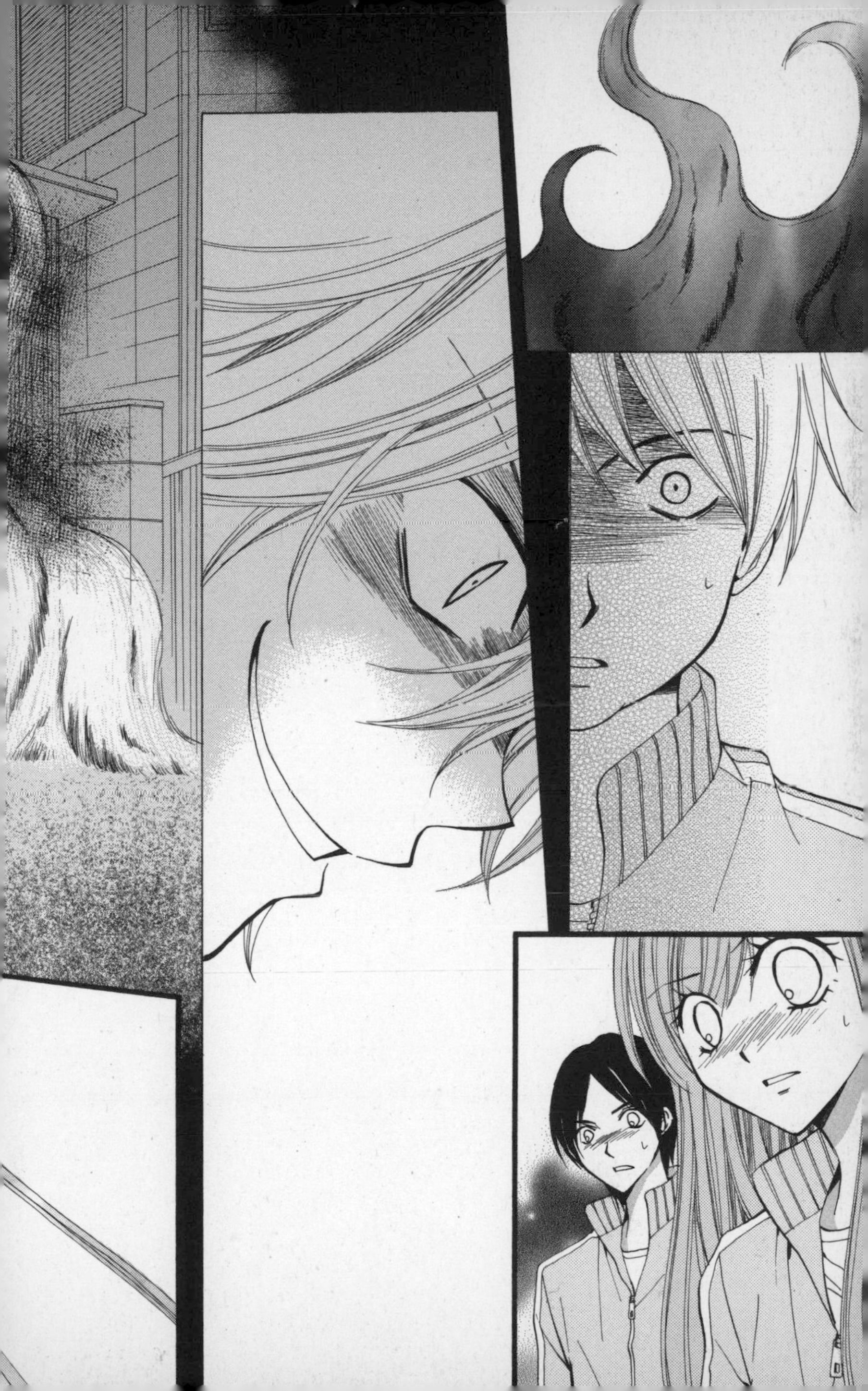

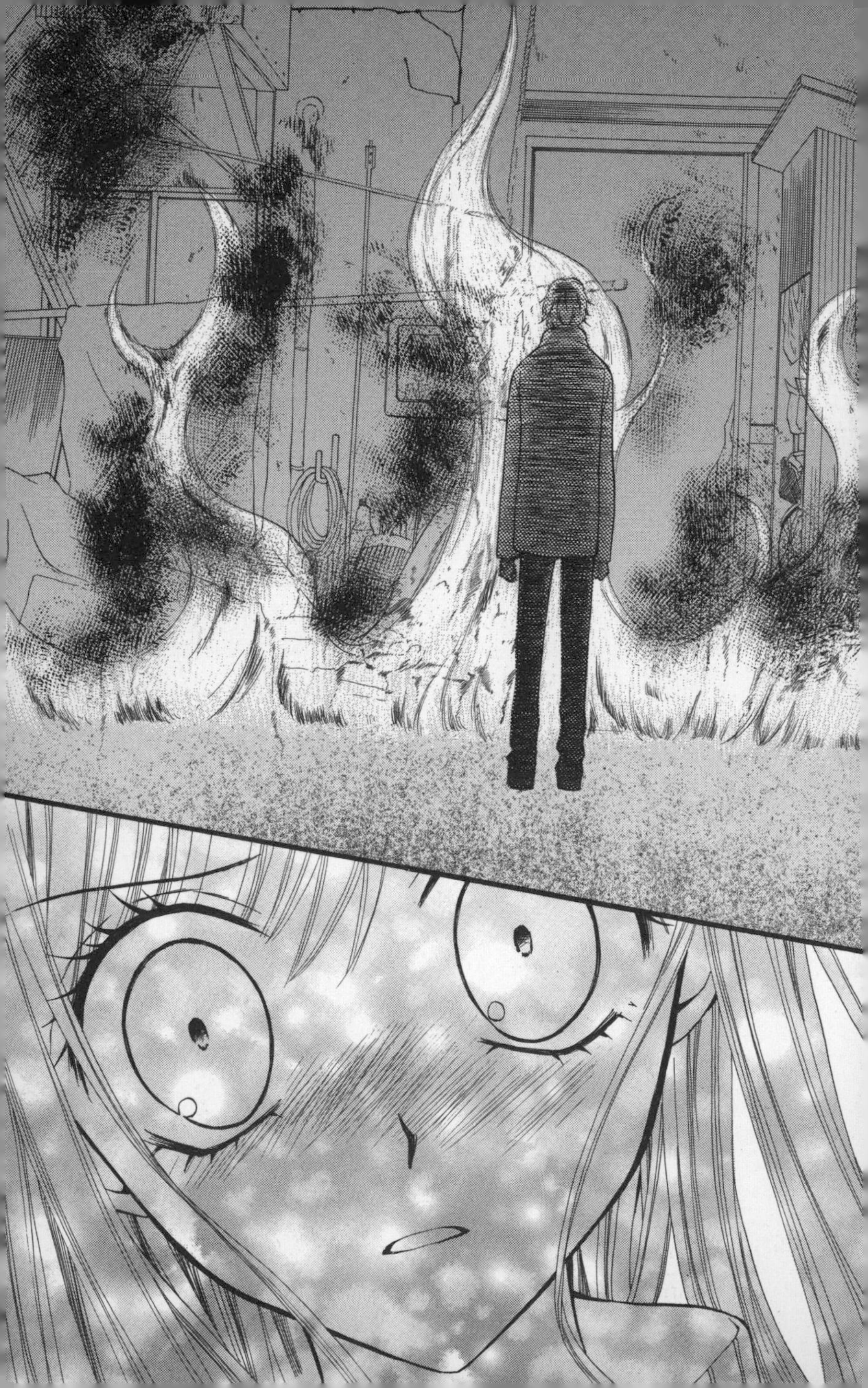

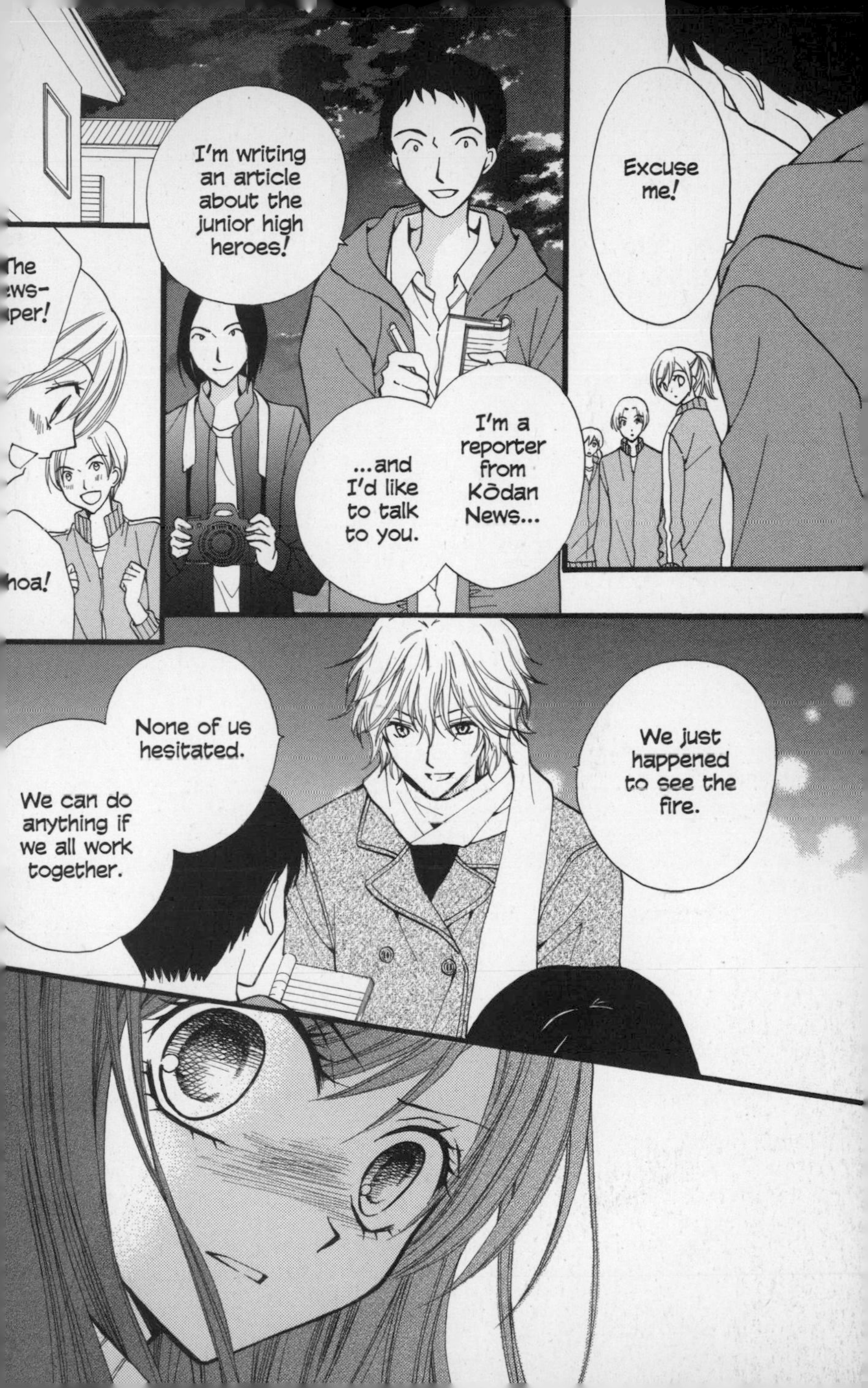
Excuse me!
I'm a reporter from Kōdan News...
...and I'd like to talk to you.
I'm writing an article about the junior high heroes!
The ews- per!
hoa!
We just happened to see the fire.
None of us hesitated.
We can do anything if we all work together.

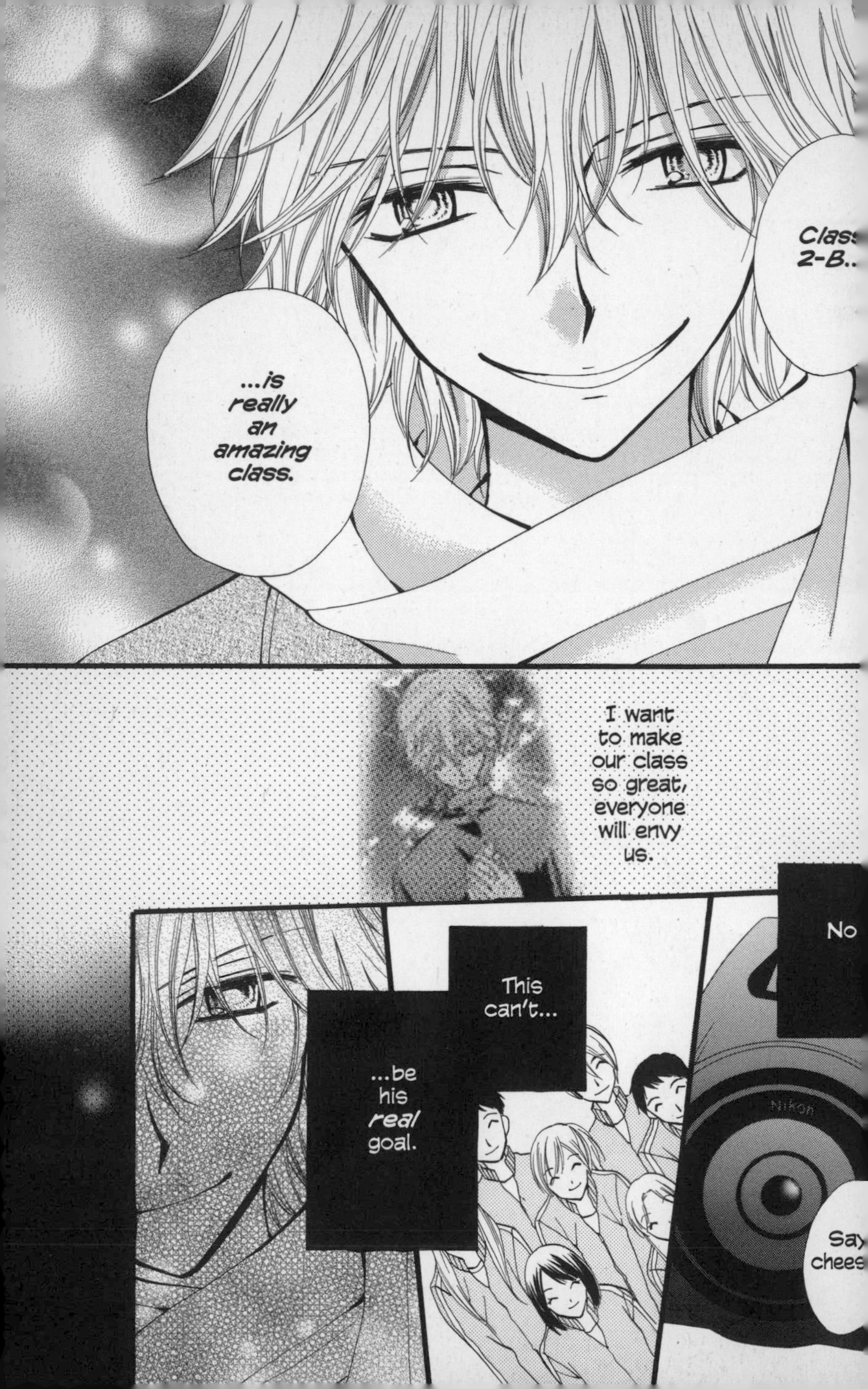
Class 2-B..
...is really an amazing class.
I want to make our class so great, everyone will envy us.
No
Say chees
This can't...
...be his *real* goal.

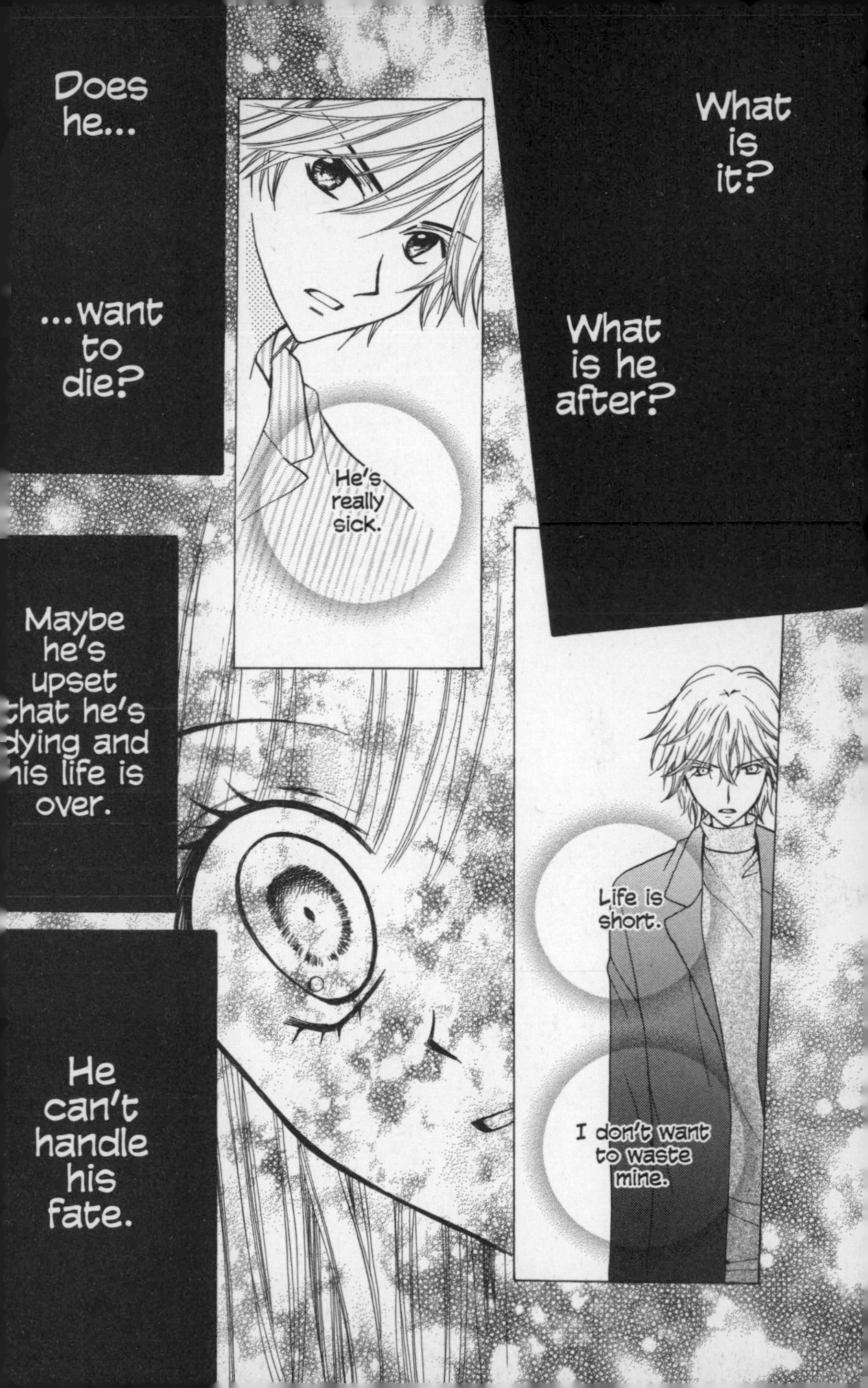
What is it?
What is he after?
He's really sick.
Does he...
...want to die?
Life is short.
I don't want to waste mine.
Maybe he's upset that he's dying and his life is over.
He can't handle his fate.

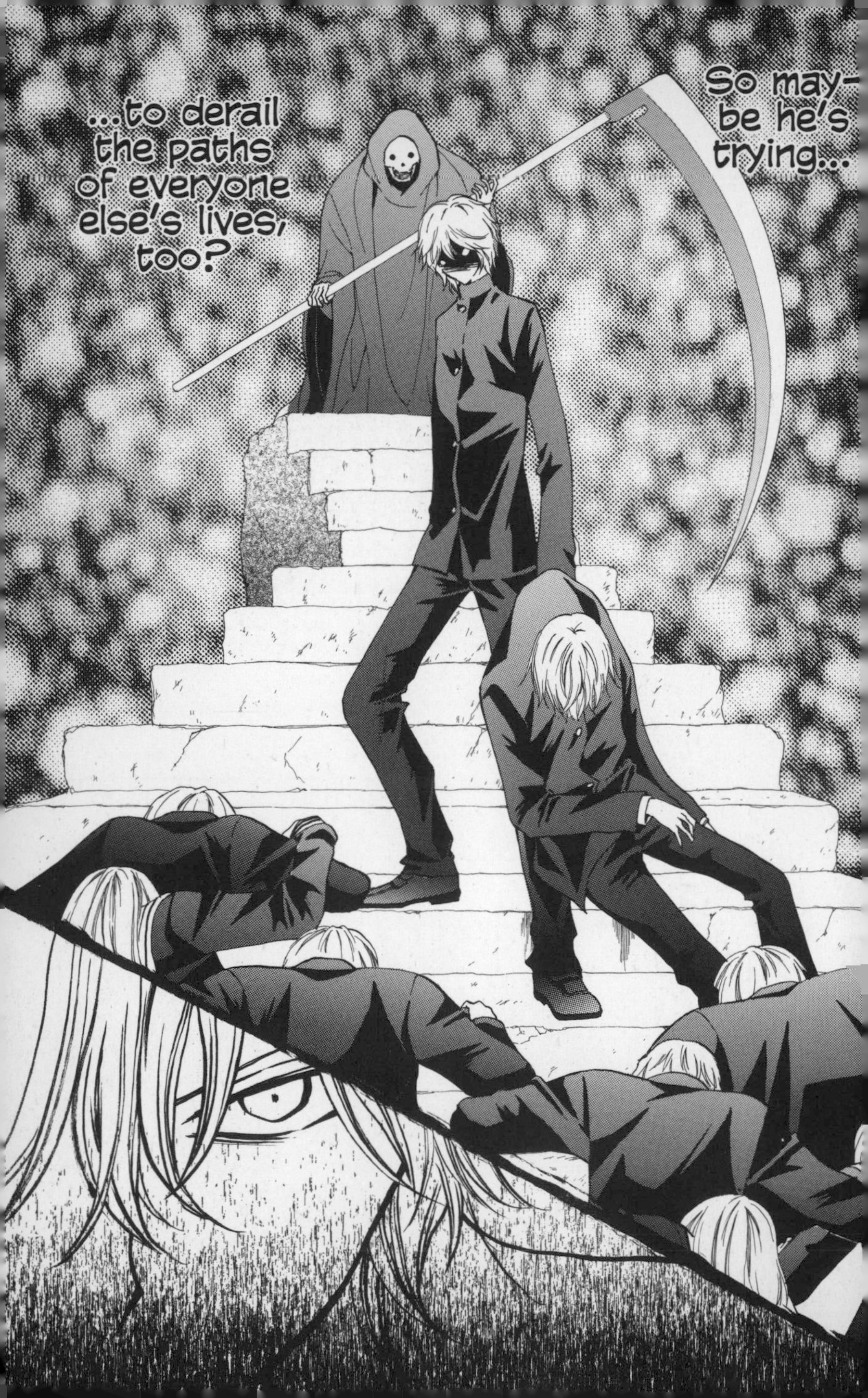
So may-be he's trying...
...to derail the paths of everyone else's lives, too?

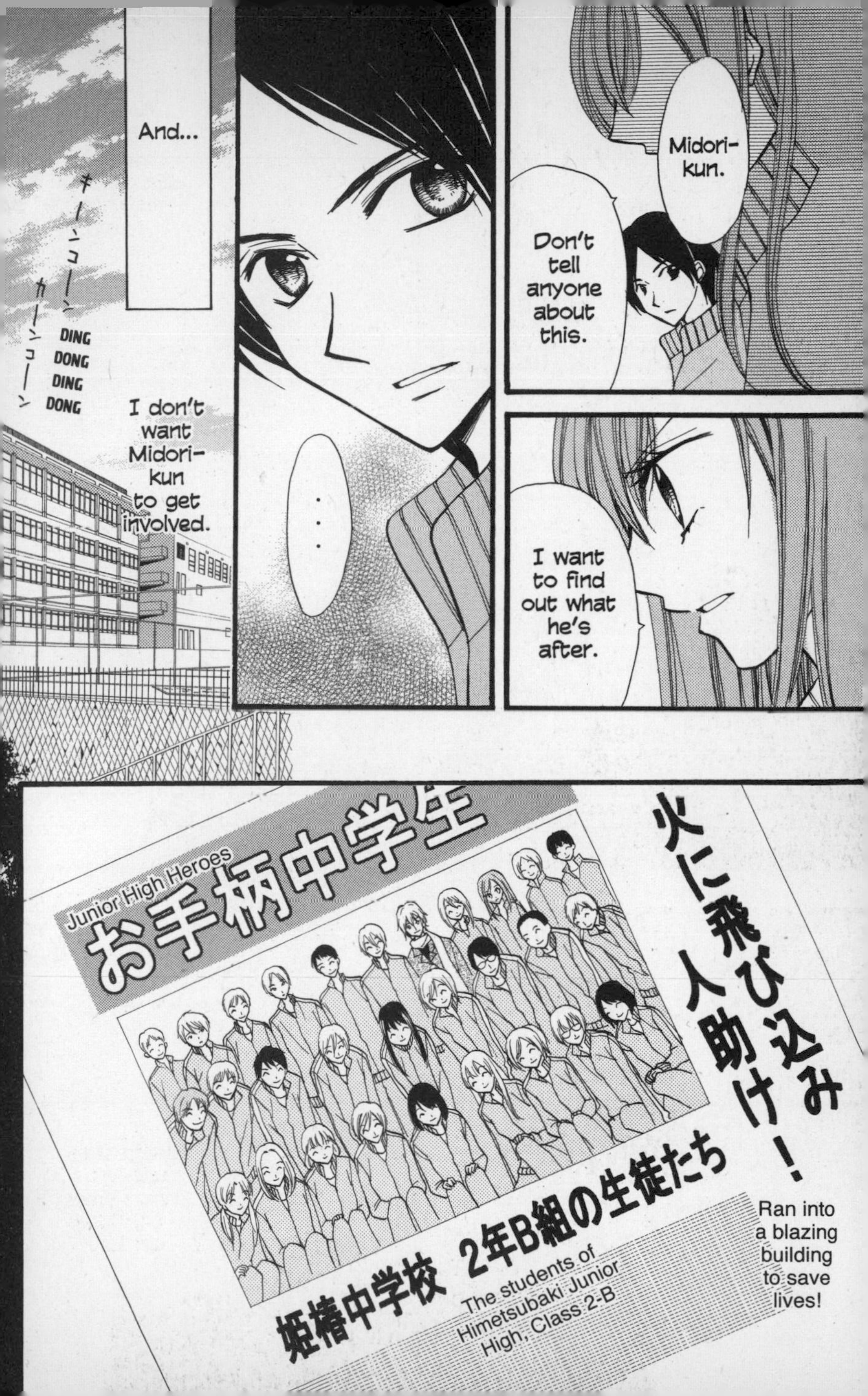
Midori-kun.
Don't tell anyone about this.
I want to find out what he's after.
...
And...
キーンコーン
カーンコーン
DING DONG DING DONG
I don't want Midori-kun to get involved.
火に飛び込み人助け！
Ran into a blazing building to save lives!
お手柄中学生
Junior High Heroes
姫椿中学校　2年B組の生徒たち
The students of Himetsubaki Junior High, Class 2-B

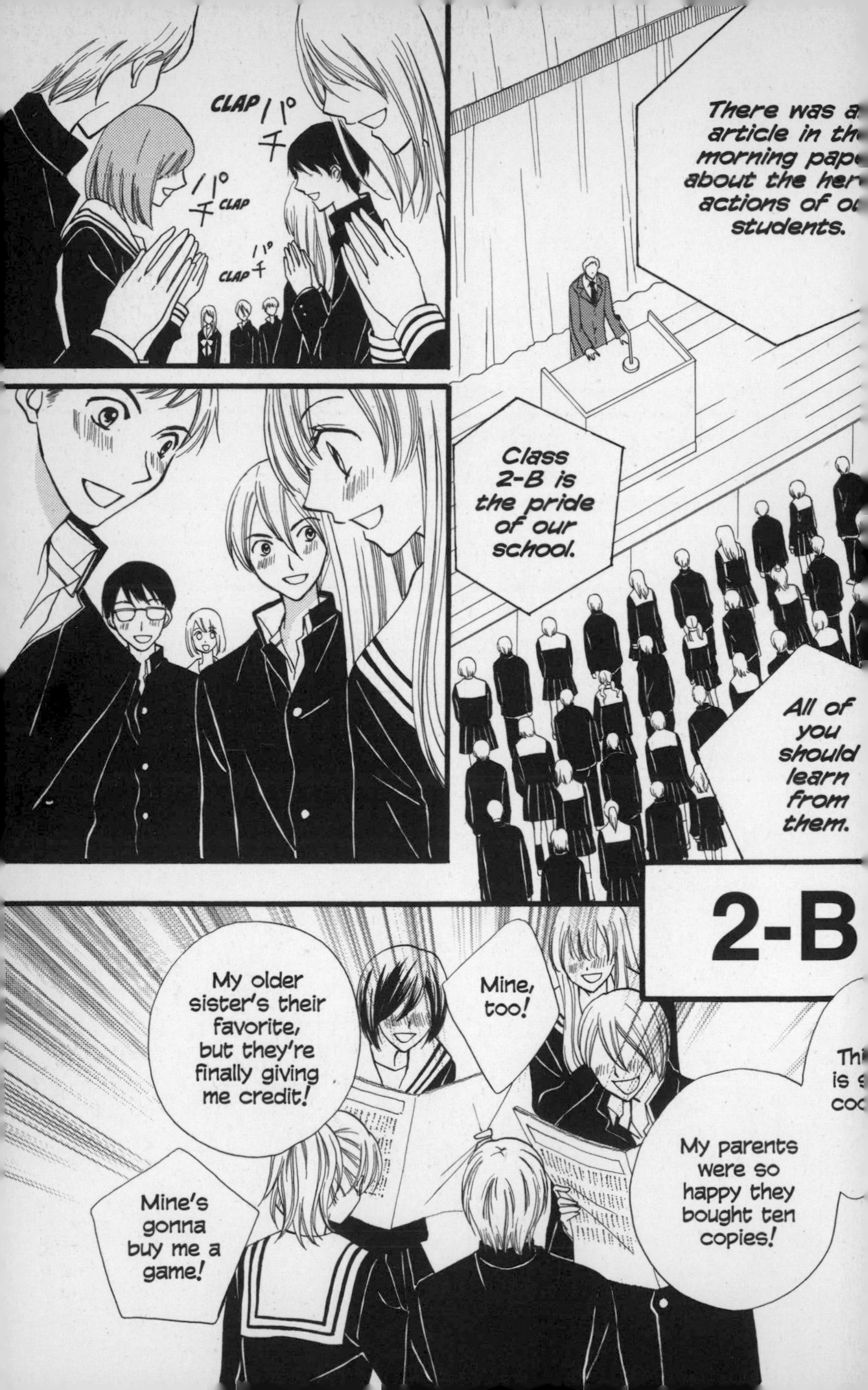

There was a article in th morning pape about the her actions of o students.
Class 2-B is the pride of our school.
All of you should learn from them.
CLAP パチ
パチ CLAP
パチ CLAP
2-B
My parents were so happy they bought ten copies!
Mine, too!
My older sister's their favorite, but they're finally giving me credit!
Mine's gonna buy me a game!

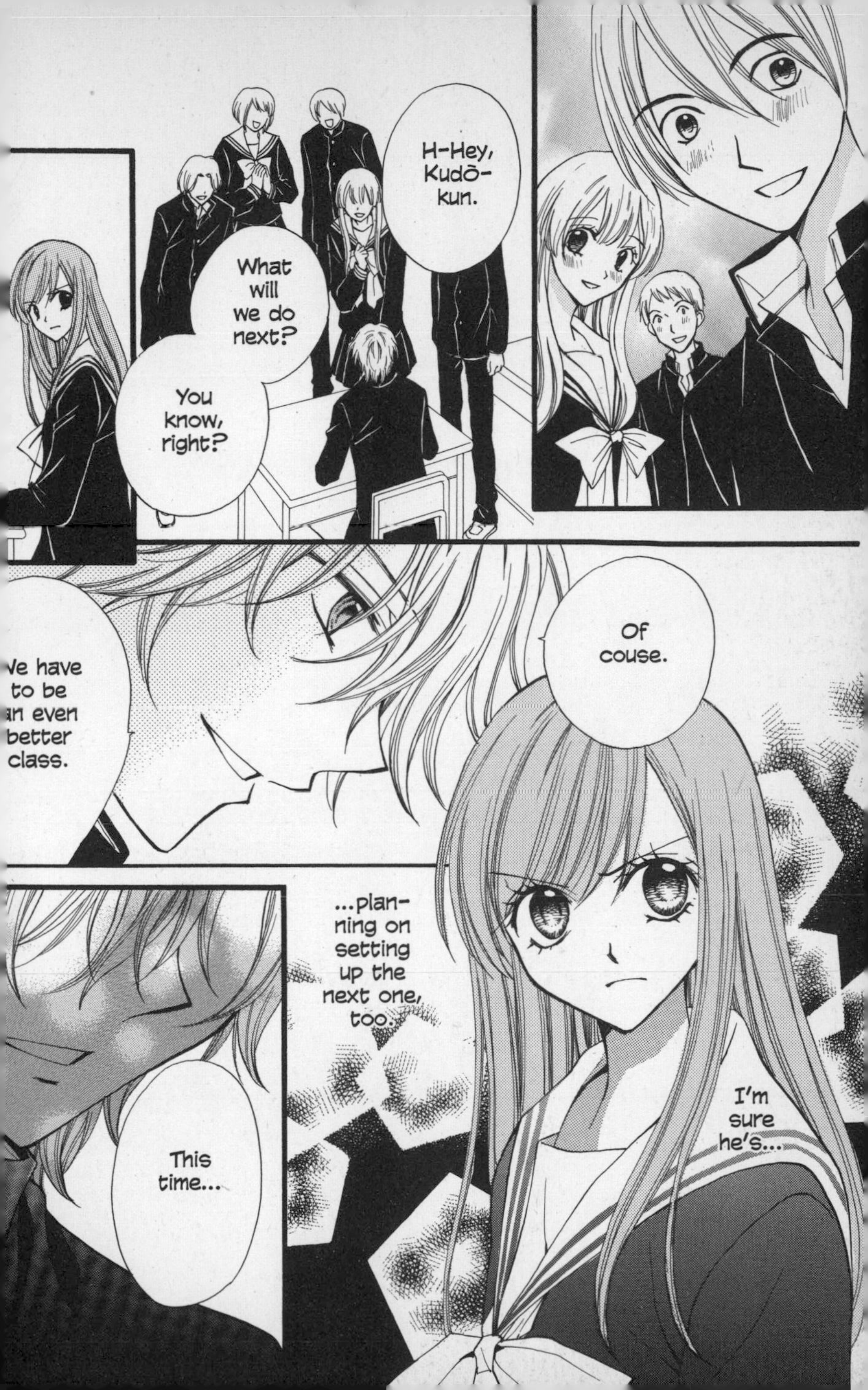
H-Hey, Kudō-kun.
What will we do next?
You know, right?
Of couse.
We have to be an even better class.
I'm sure he's...
...plan-ning on setting up the next one, too.
This time...

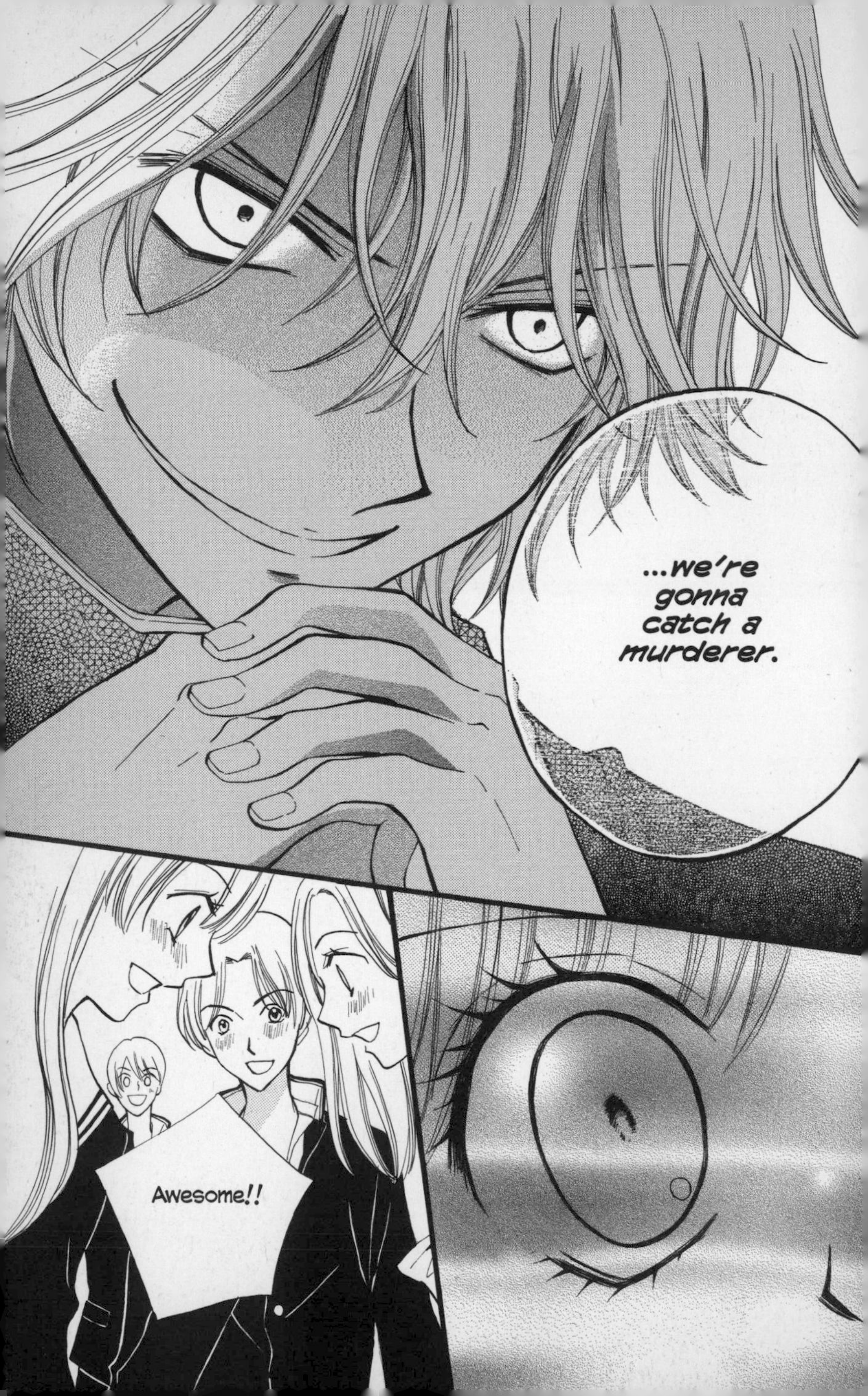
...we're gonna catch a murderer.
Awesome!!

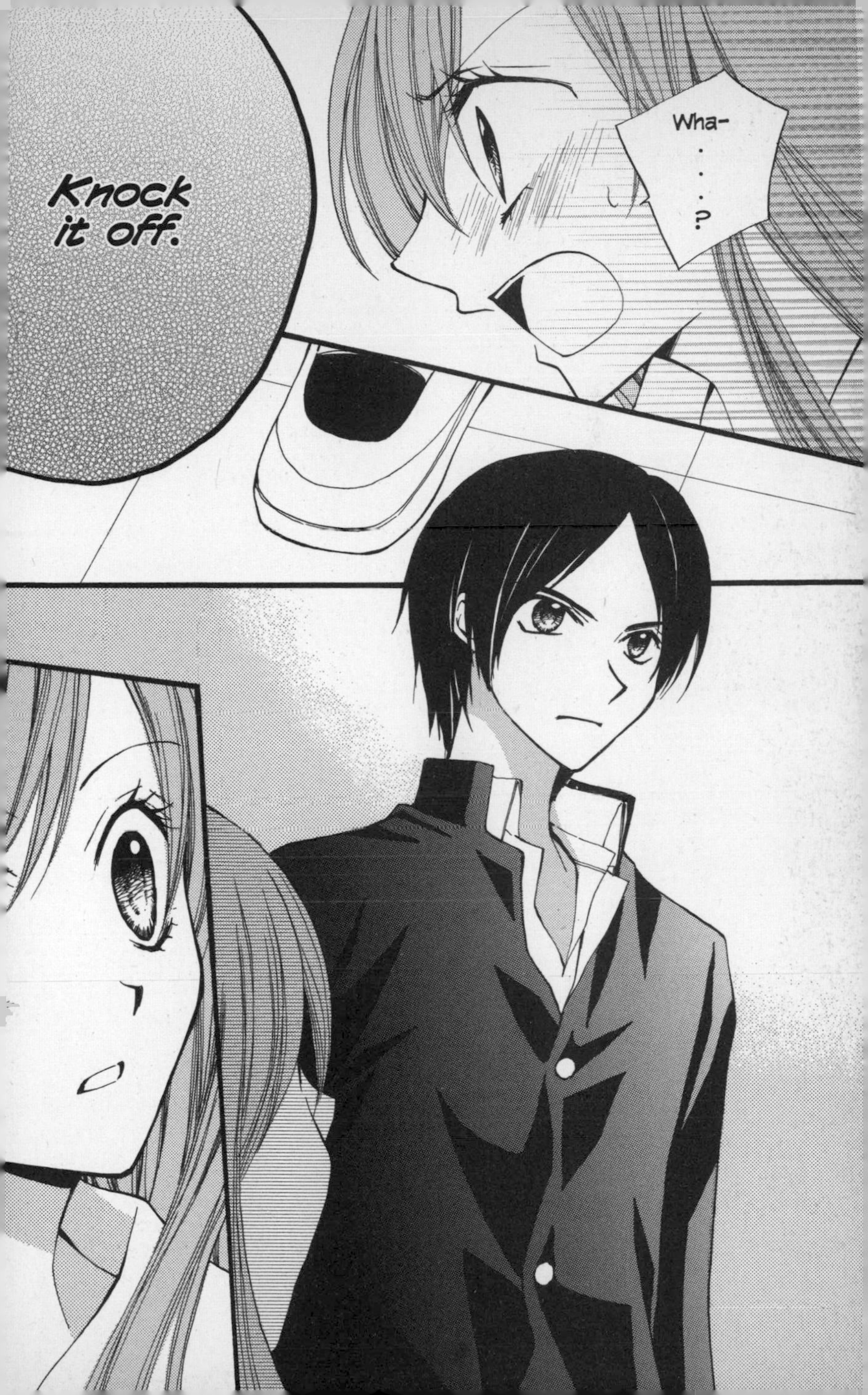
Wha- . . . ?
Knock it off.

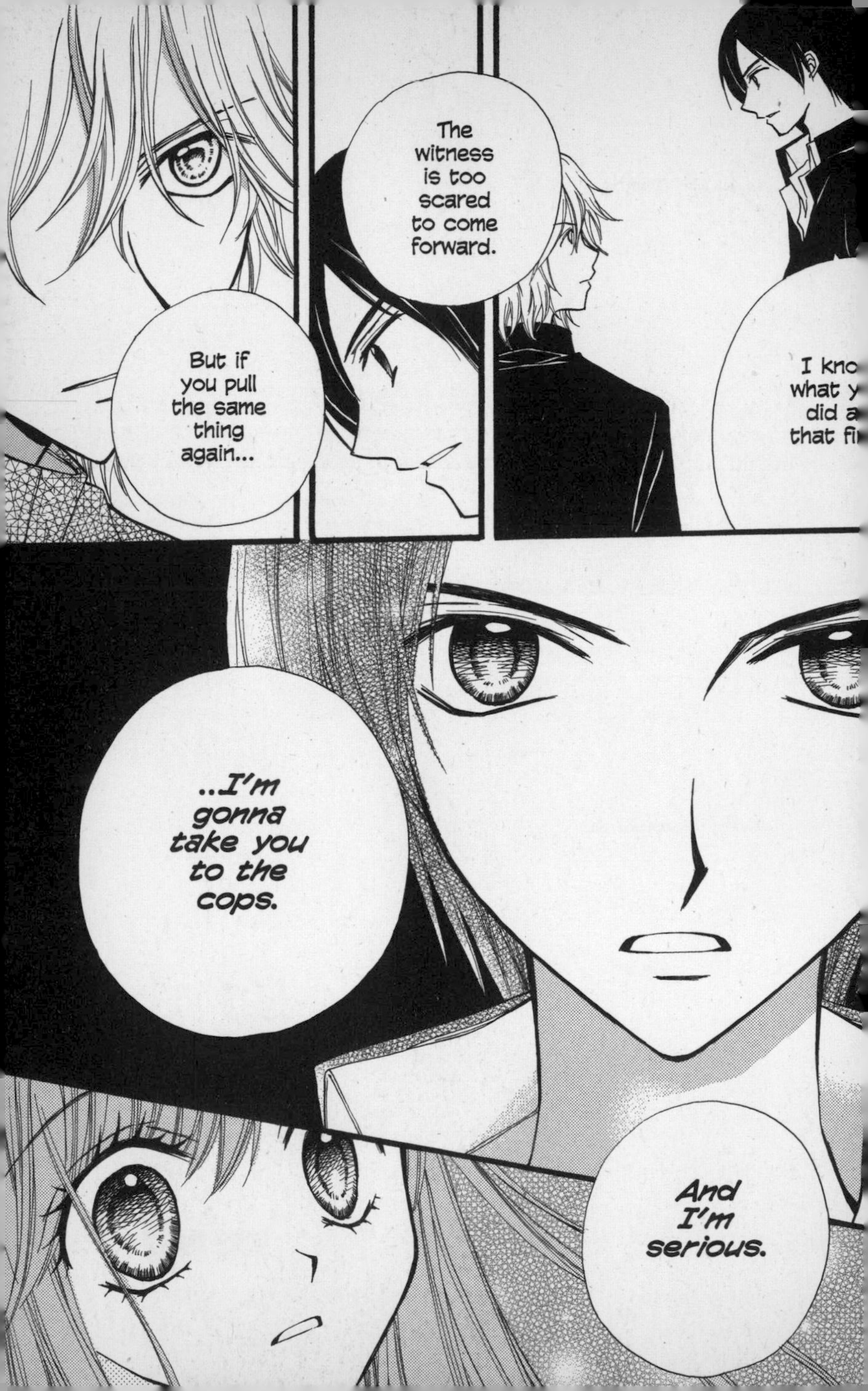
I kno what y did a that fi
The witness is too scared to come forward.
But if you pull the same thing again...
...I'm gonna take you to the cops.
And I'm serious.

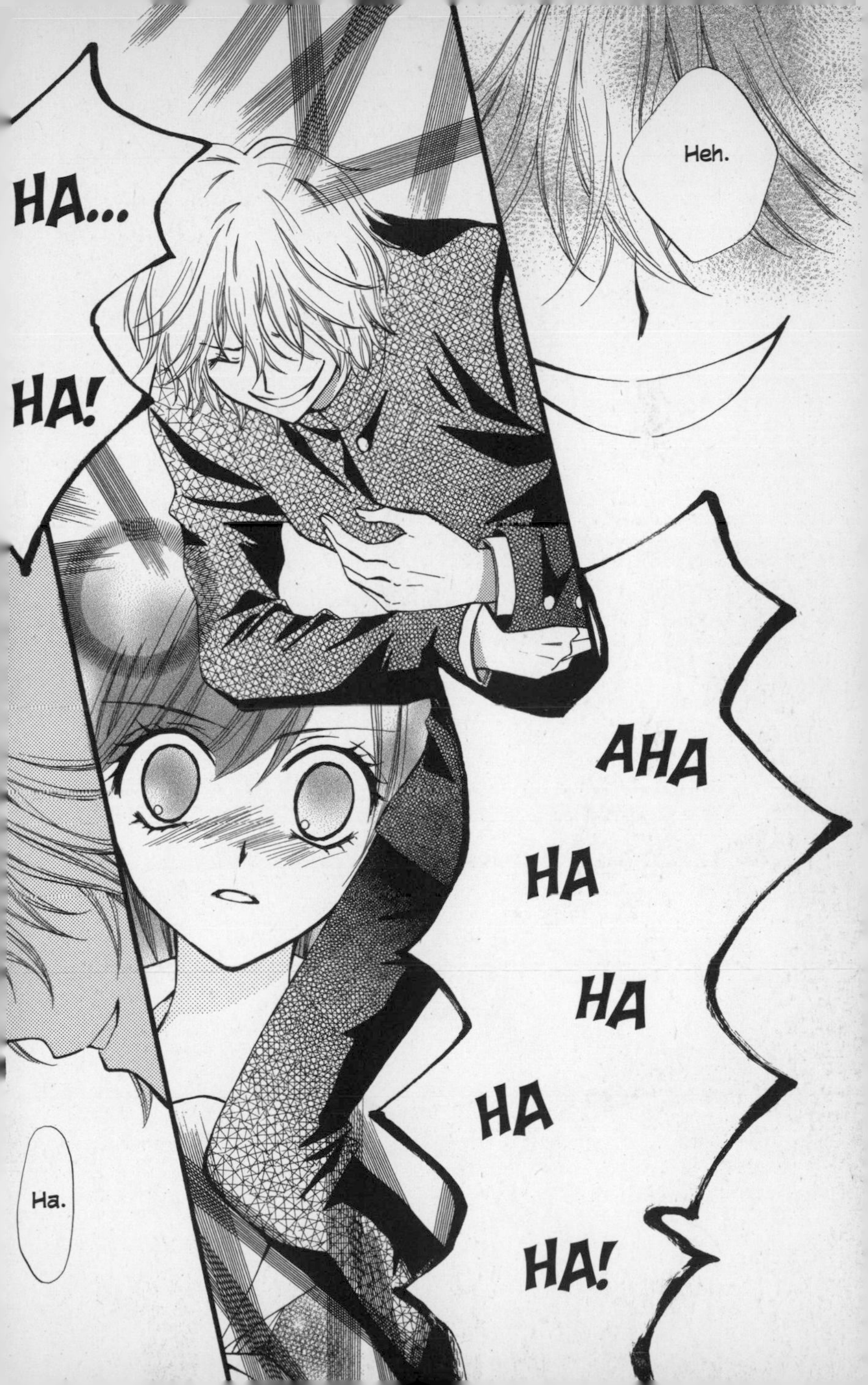
Heh.
HA... HA!
AHA HA HA HA HA!
Ha.

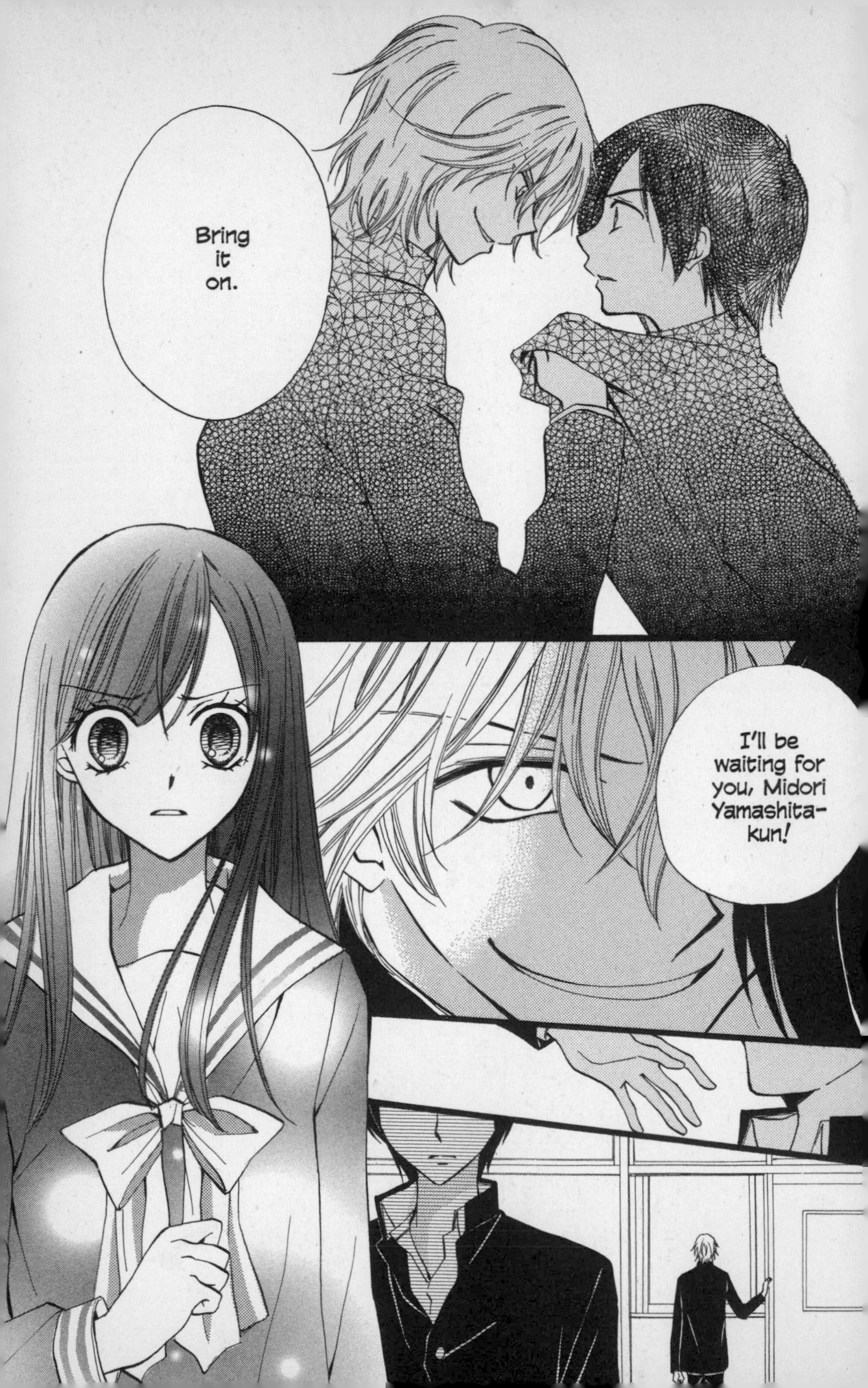
Bring it on.
I'll be waiting for you, Midori Yamashita-kun!

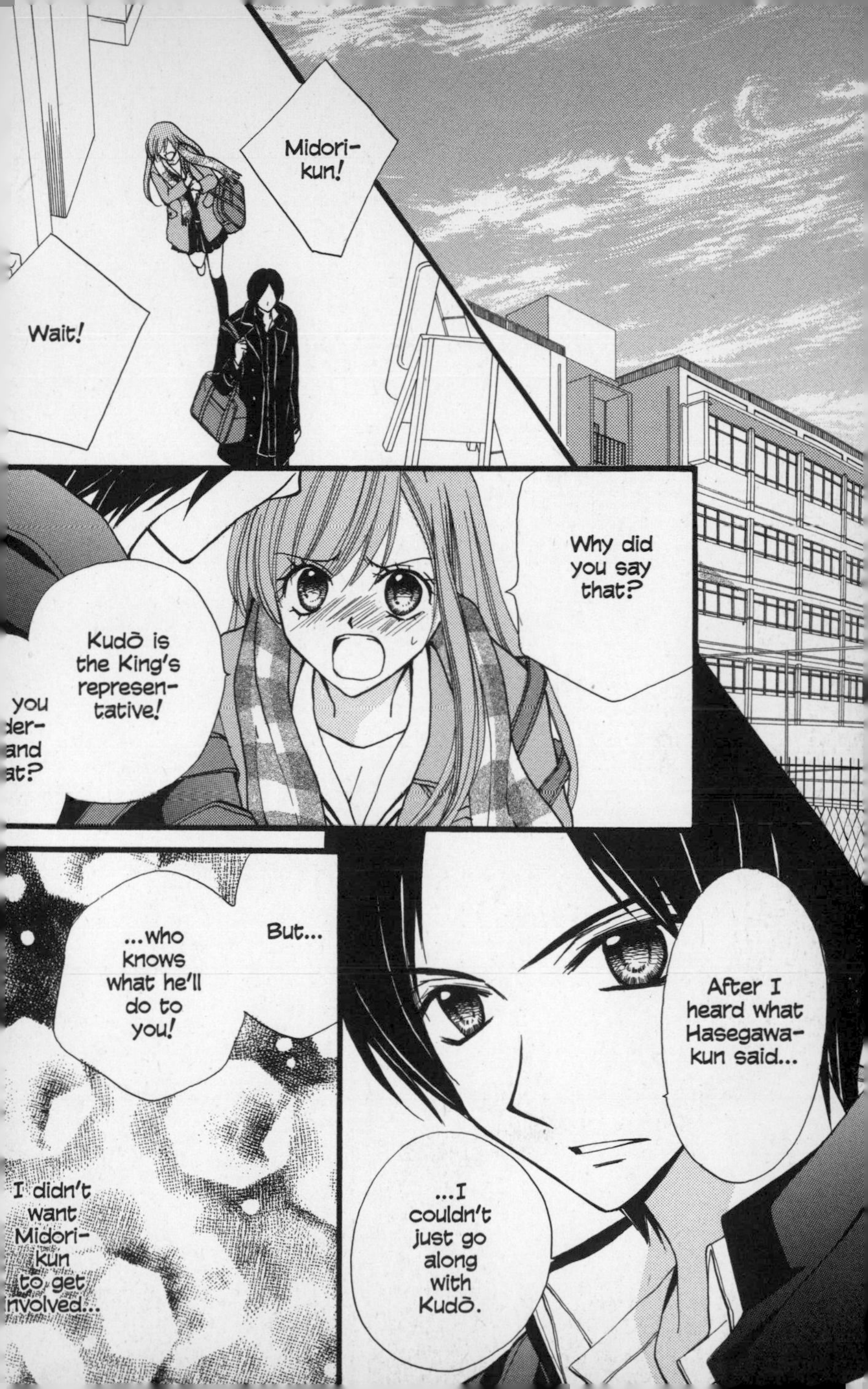
Midori-kun!
Wait!
Why did you say that?
Kudō is the King's representative!
you der- and at?
After I heard what Hasegawa-kun said...
...I couldn't just go along with Kudō.
But...
...who knows what he'll do to you!
I didn't want Midori-kun to get nvolved...

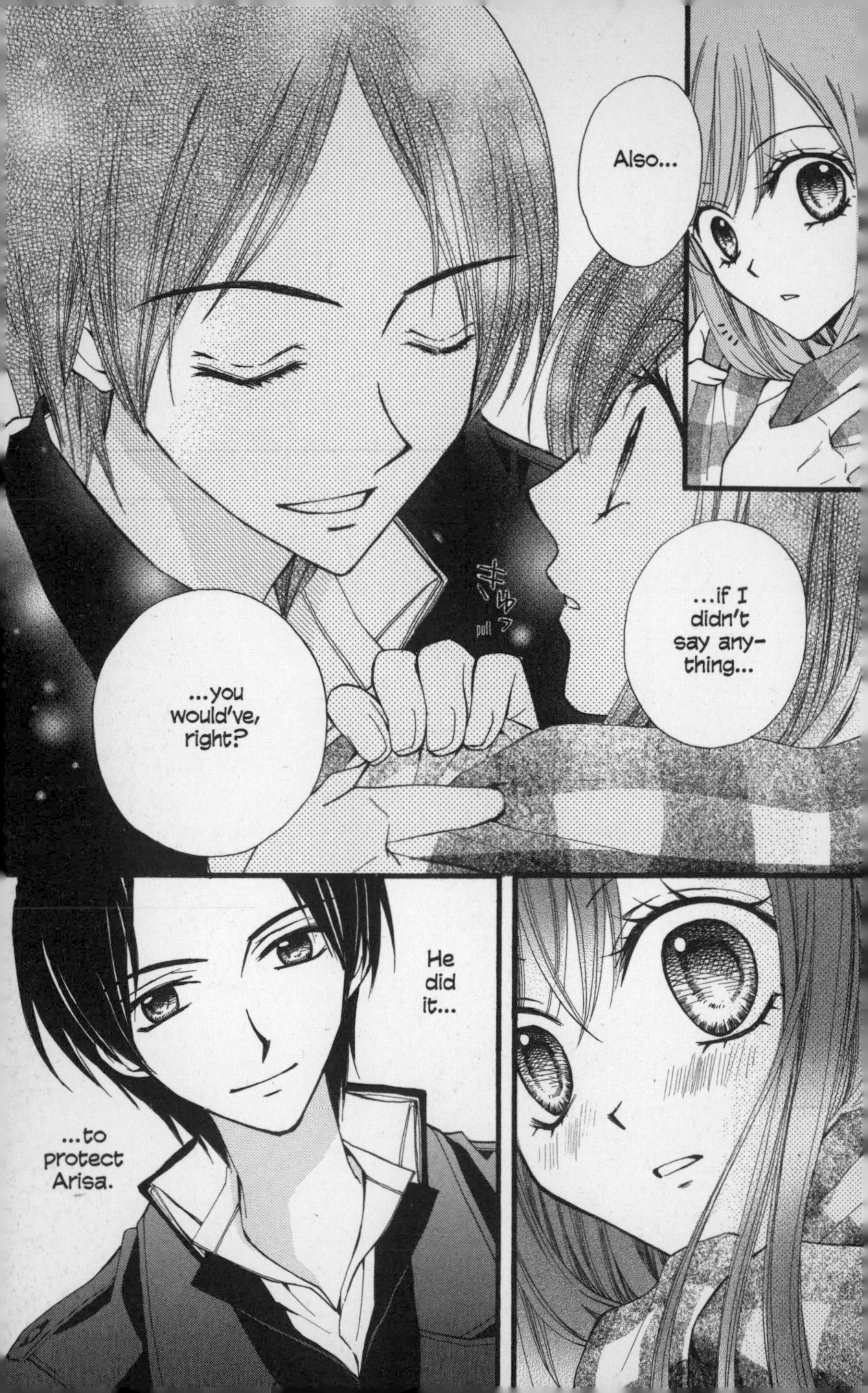
Also...
...if I didn't say any-thing...
pull
...you would've, right?
He did it...
...to protect Arisa.

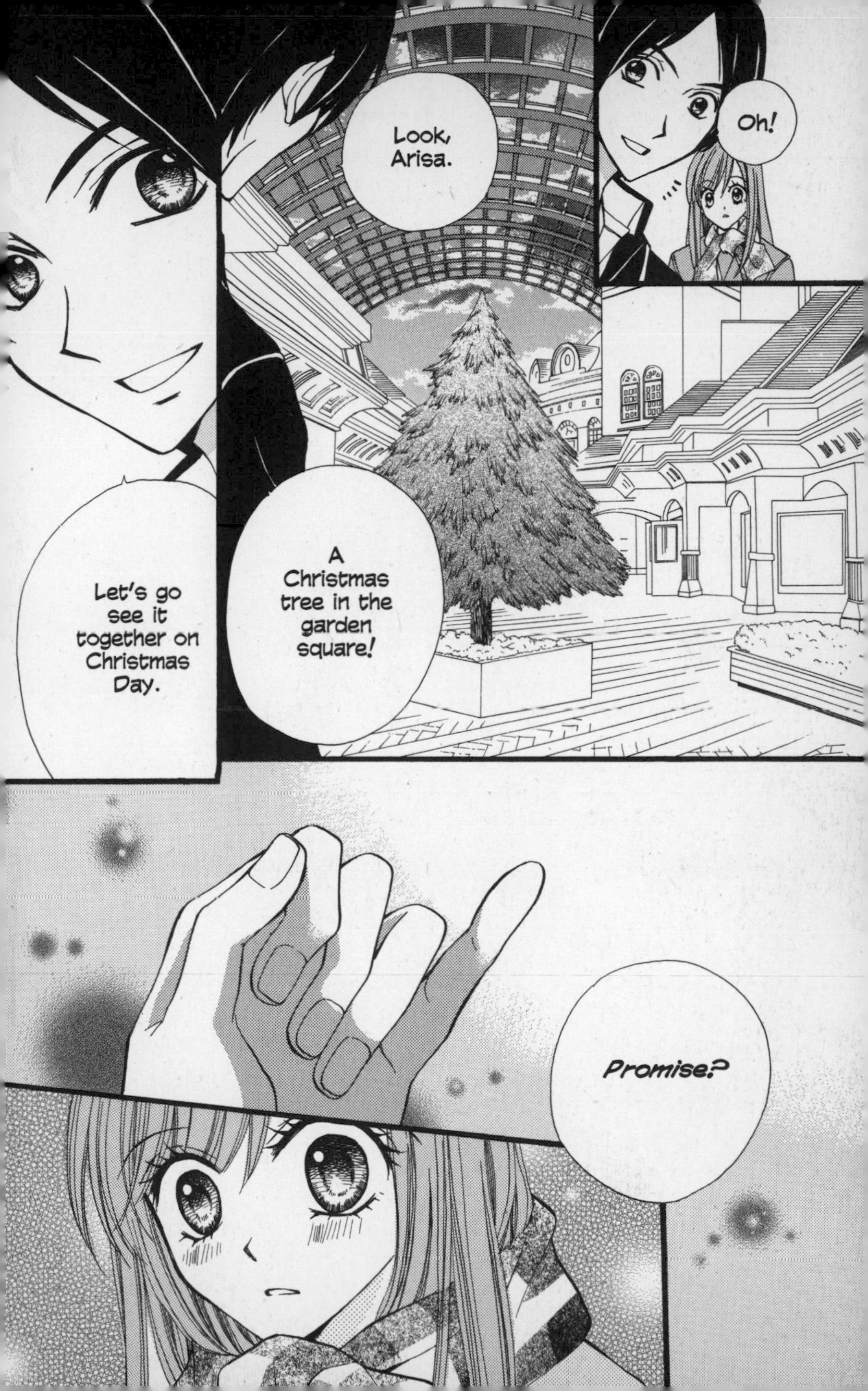
Look, Arisa.
Oh!
A Christmas tree in the garden square!
Let's go see it together on Christmas Day.
Promise?

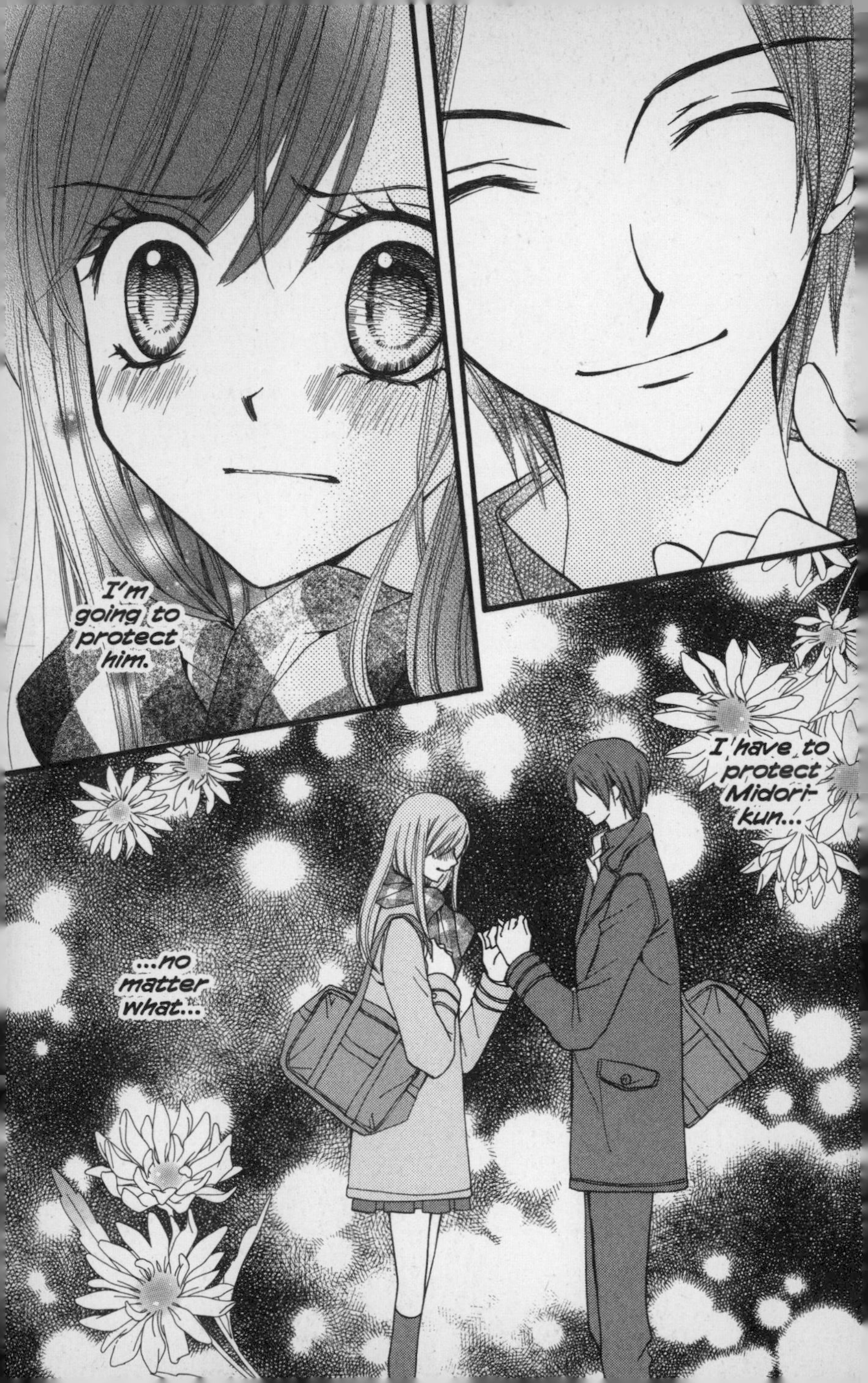
I'm going to protect him.
I have to protect Midori-kun...
...no matter what...

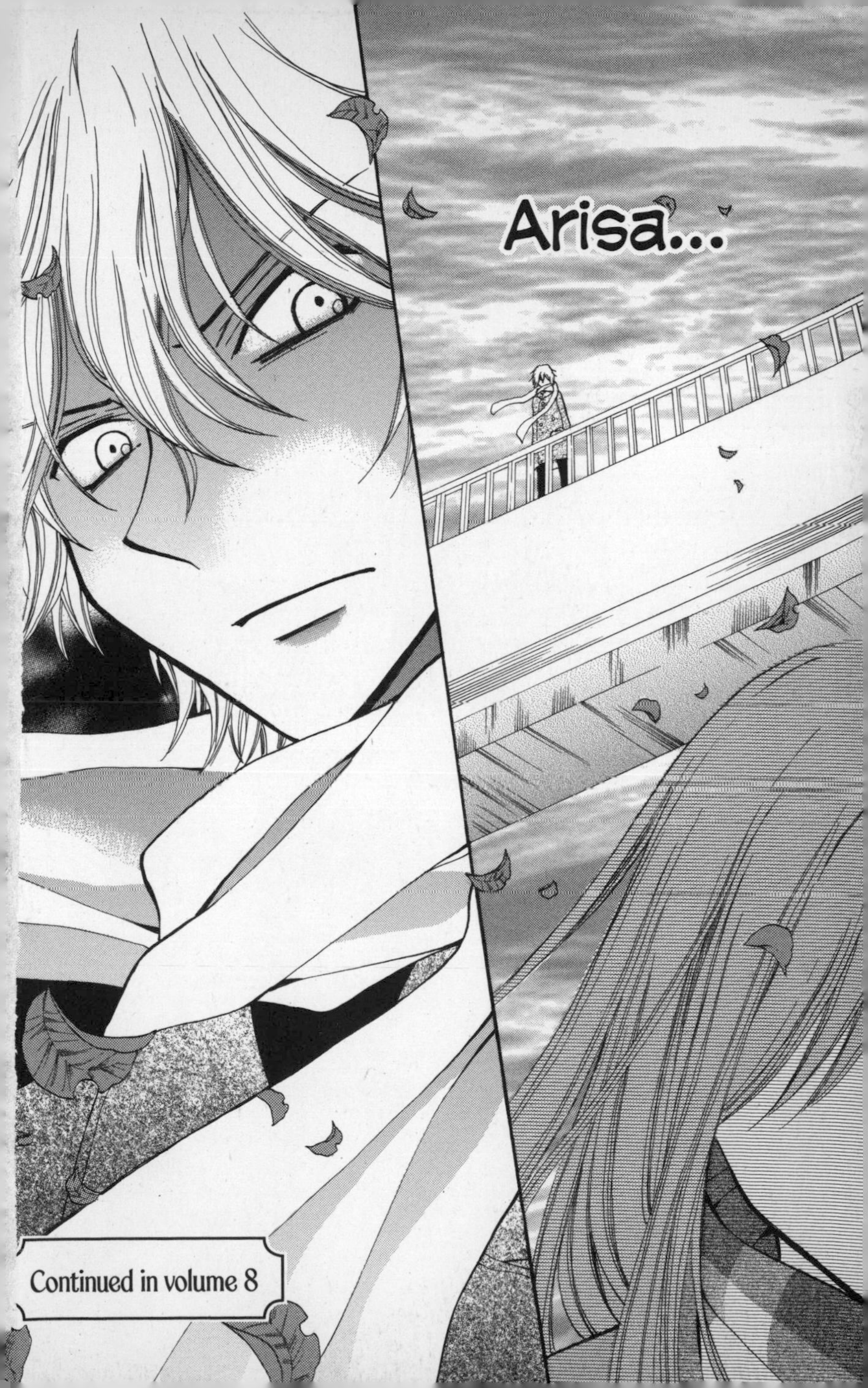
Arisa...
Continued in volume 8

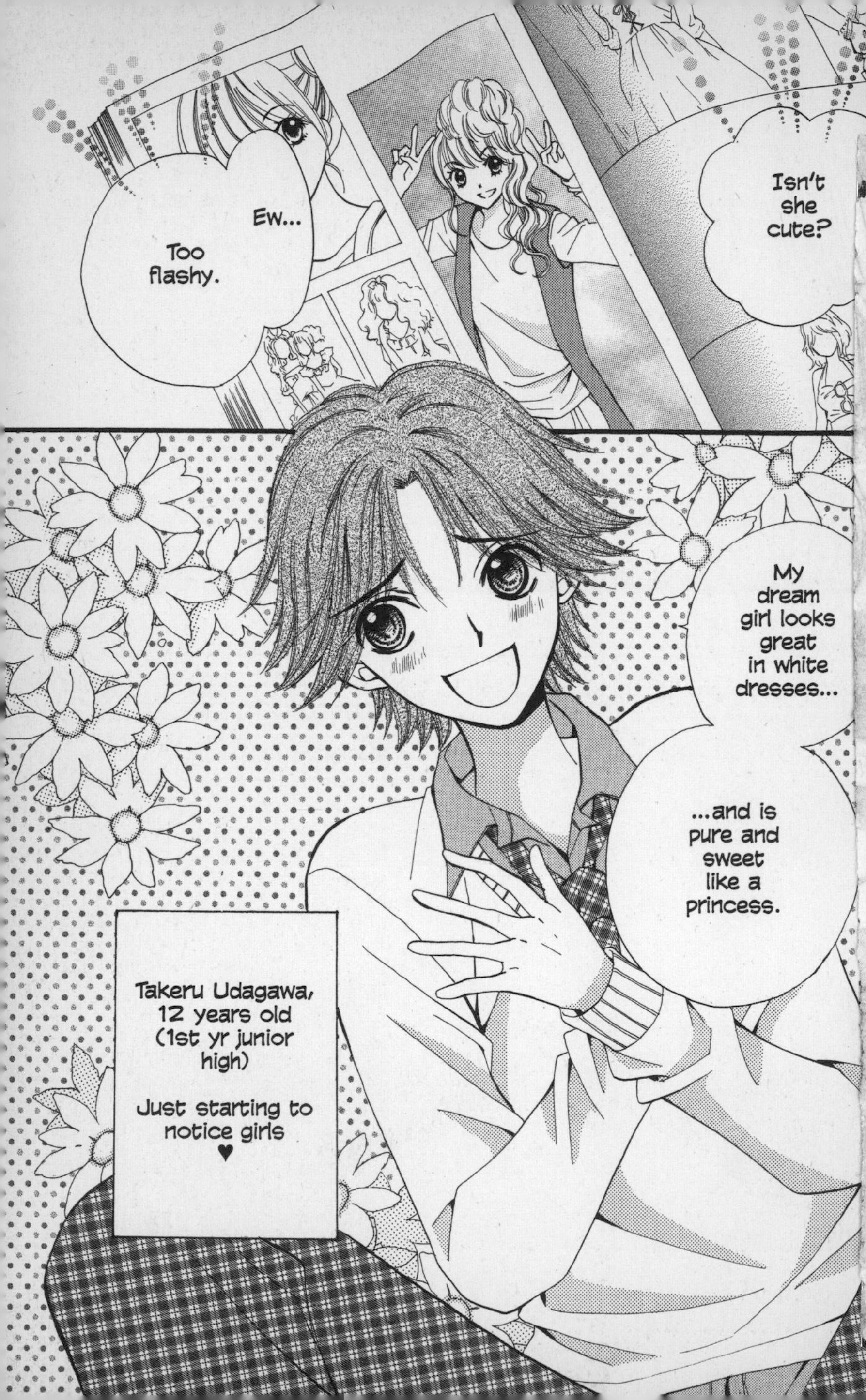
Isn't she cute?
Ew... Too flashy.
My dream girl looks great in white dresses...
...and is pure and sweet like a princess.
Takeru Udagawa, 12 years old (1st yr junior high) Just starting to notice girls ♥

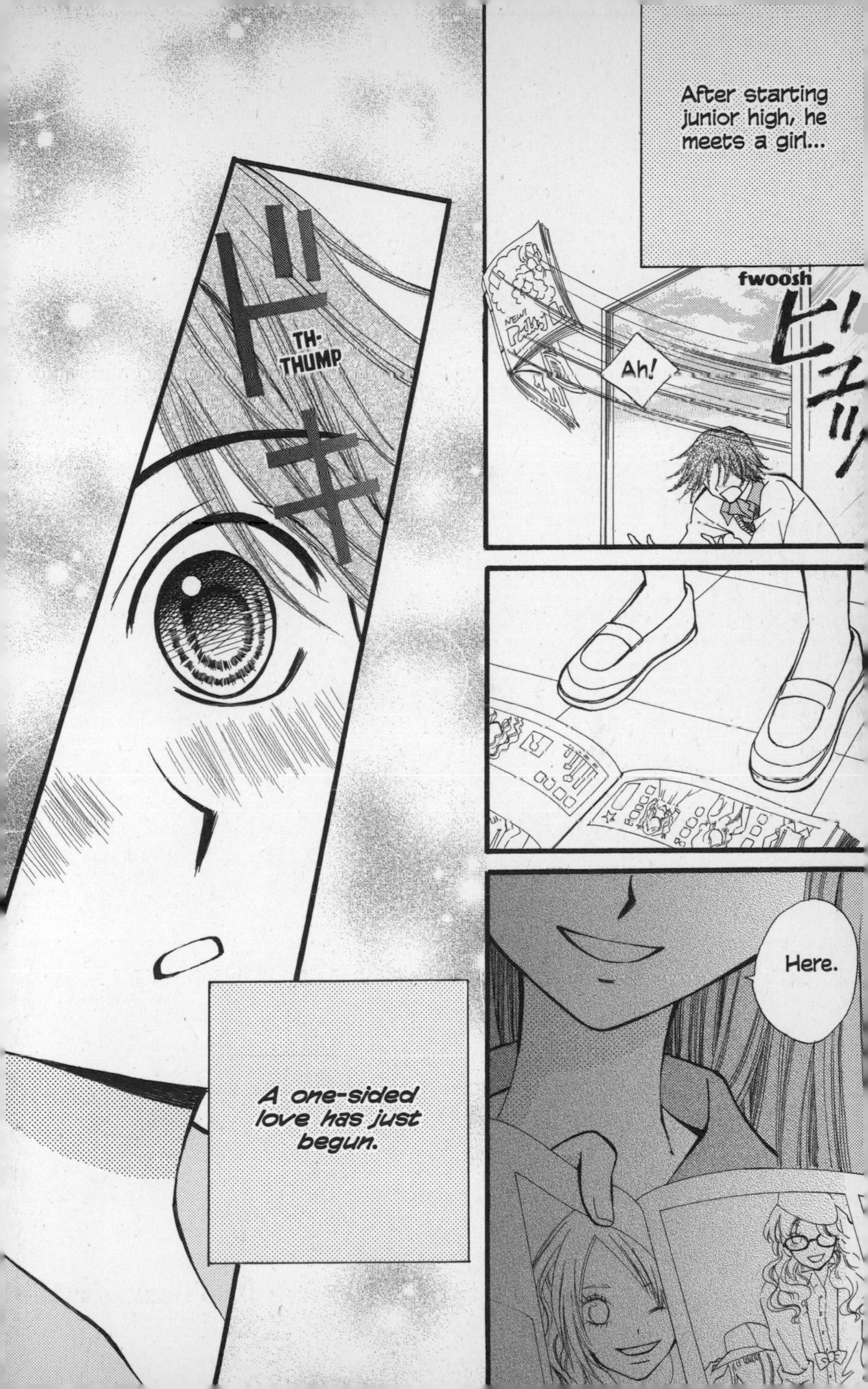

After starting junior high, he meets a girl...
fwoosh
Ah!
Here.
ドキ
TH-THUMP
A one-sided love has just begun.

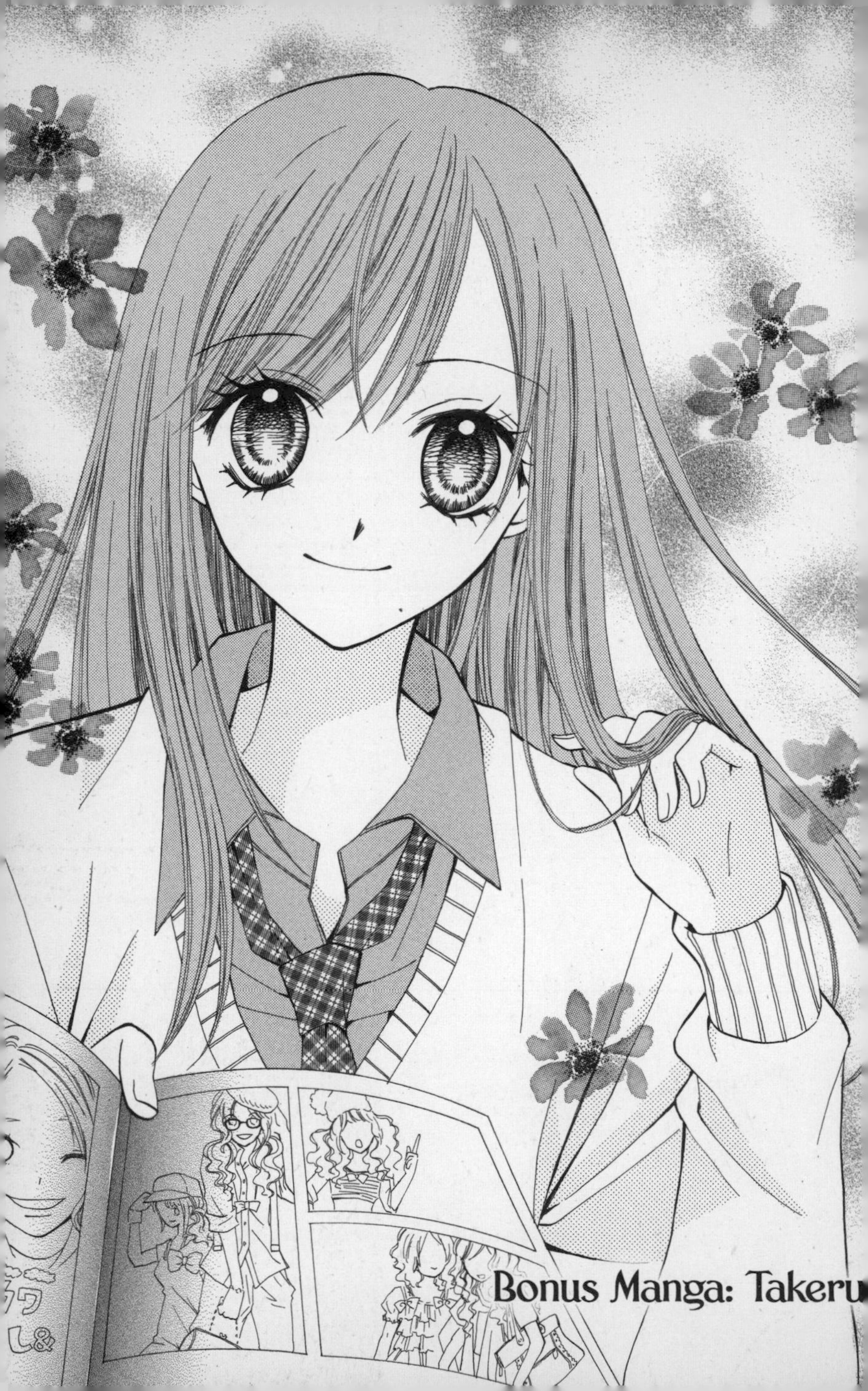
Bonus Manga: Takeru

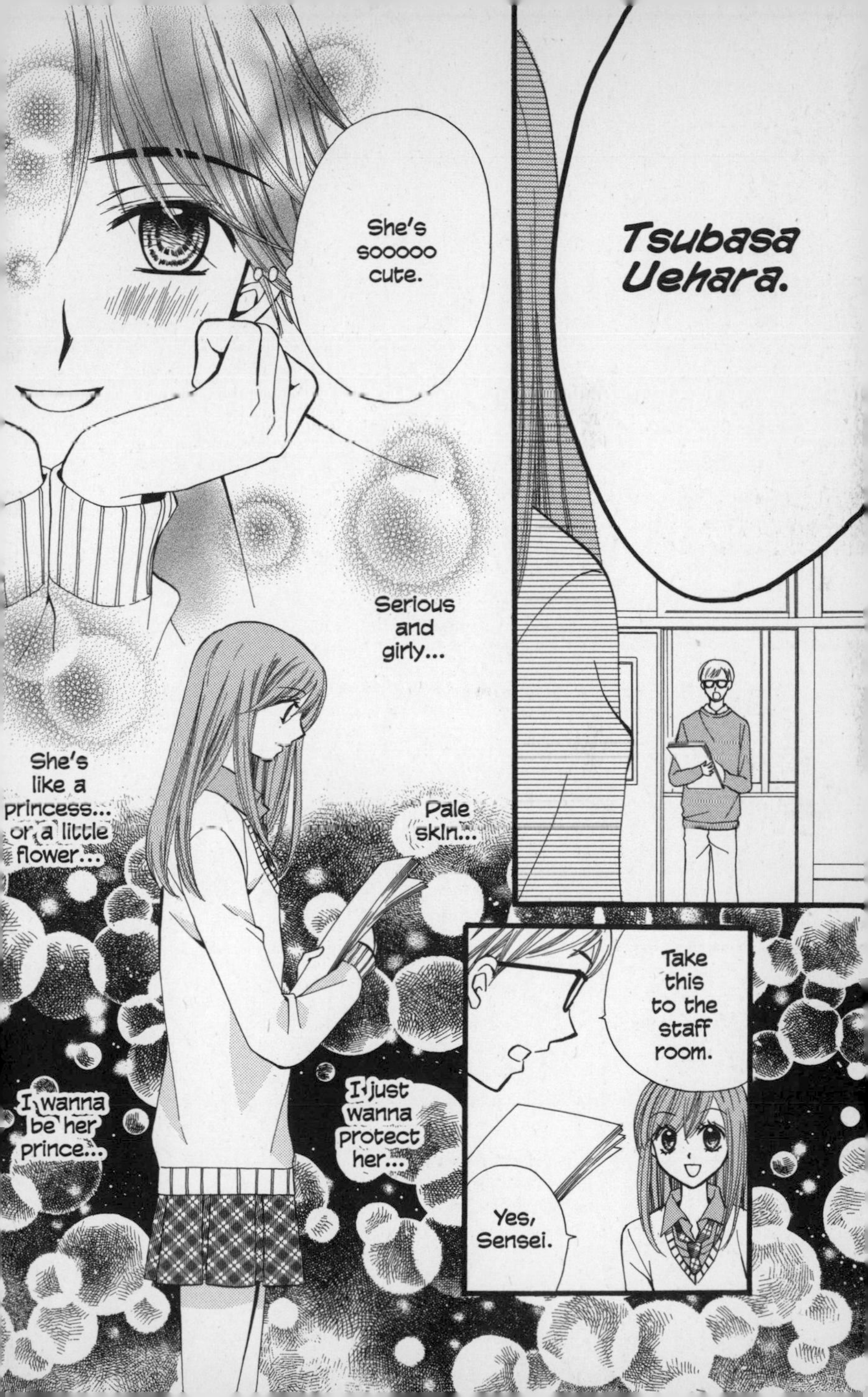
Tsubasa Uehara.
Take this to the staff room.
Yes, Sensei.
She's sooooo cute.
Serious and girly...
Pale skin...
She's like a princess... or a little flower...
I just wanna protect her...
I wanna be her prince...

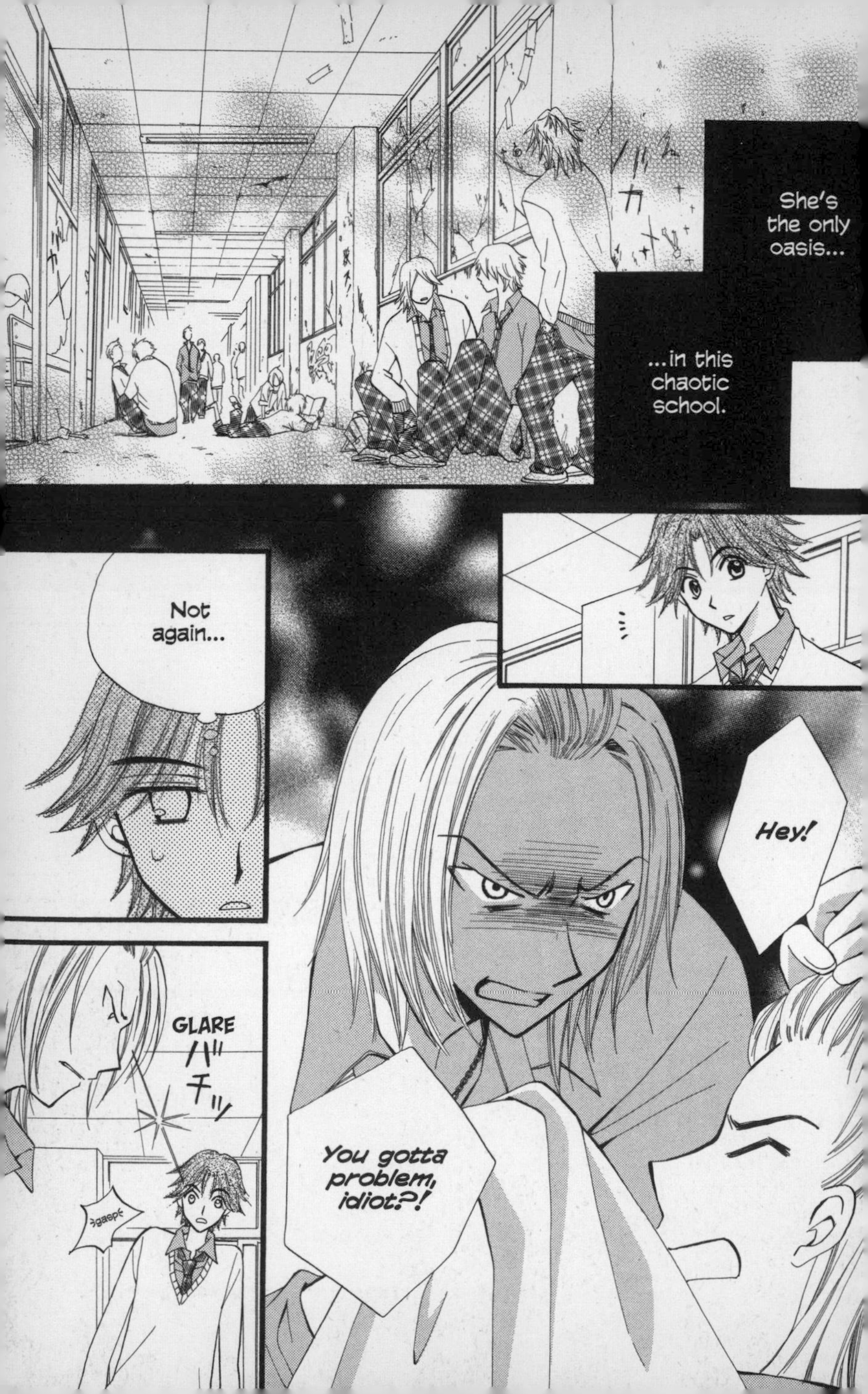
She's the only oasis...
...in this chaotic school.
...
Not again...
Hey!
You gotta problem, idiot?!
GLARE
バチッ
gasp

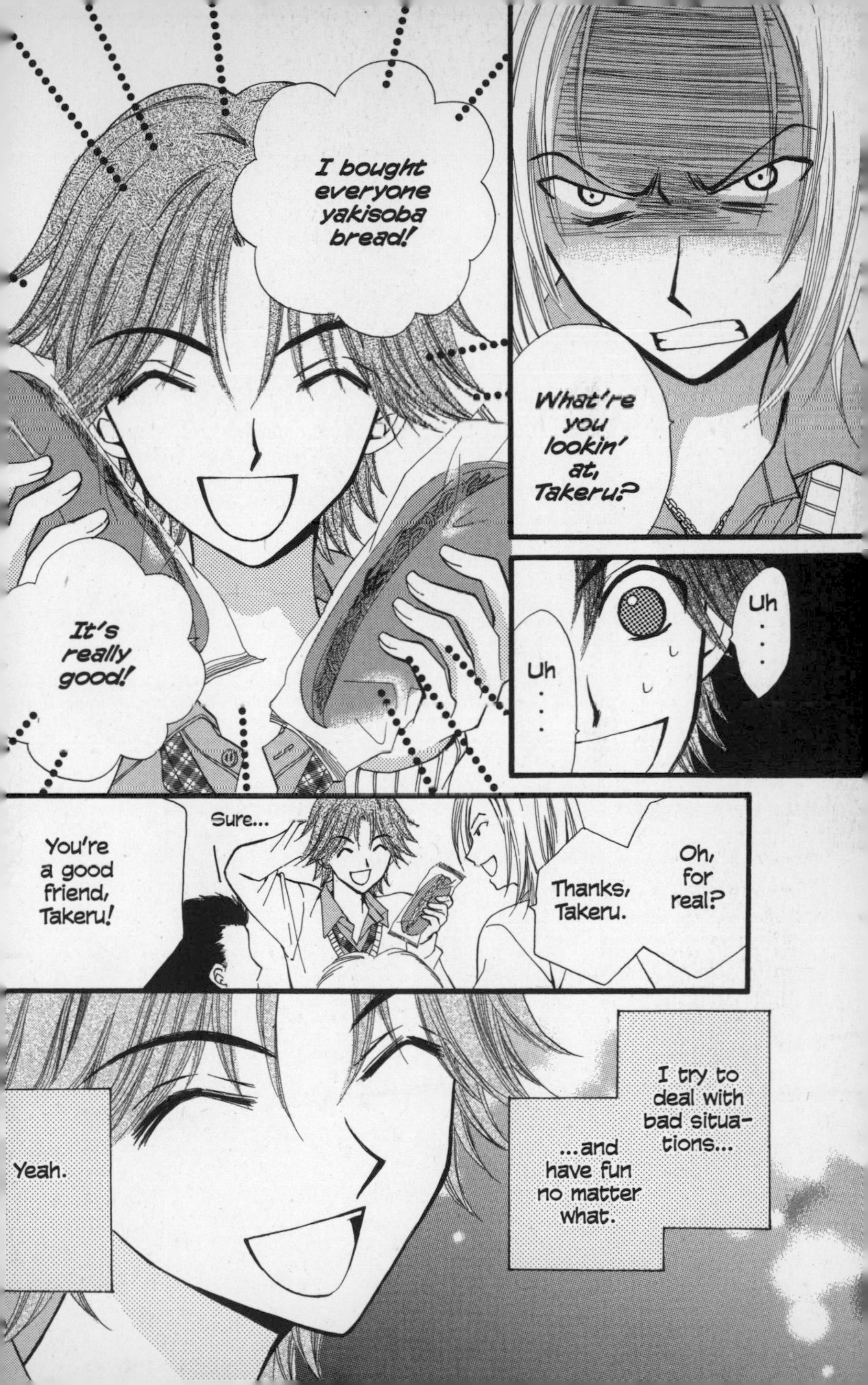
What're you lookin' at, Takeru?
Uh...
Uh...
I bought everyone yakisoba bread!
It's really good!
Oh, for real?
Thanks, Takeru.
Sure...
You're a good friend, Takeru!
I try to deal with bad situations...
...and have fun no matter what.
Yeah.

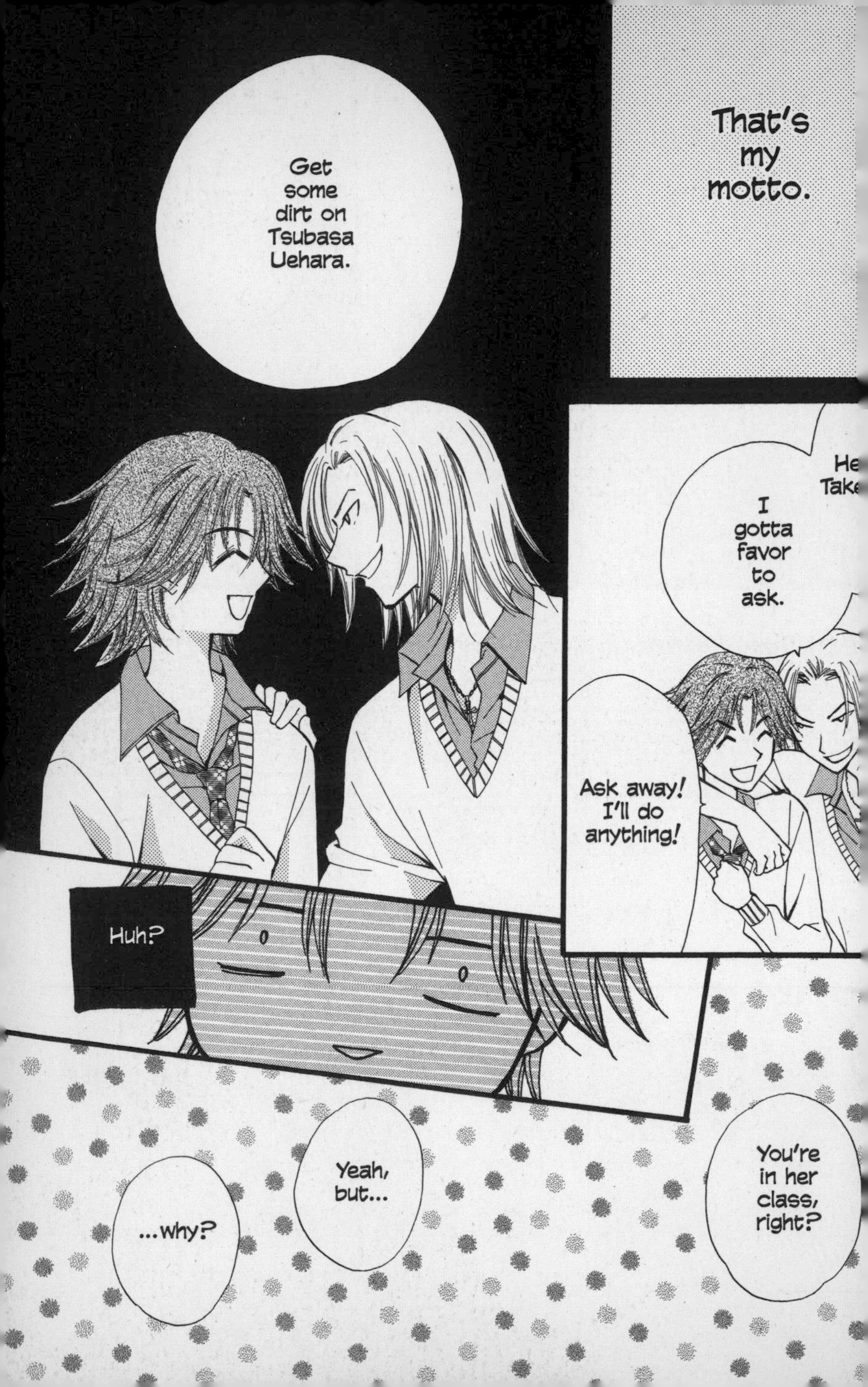
That's my motto.
Get some dirt on Tsubasa Uehara.
I gotta favor to ask.
Ask away! I'll do anything!
Huh?
You're in her class, right?
Yeah, but...
...why?

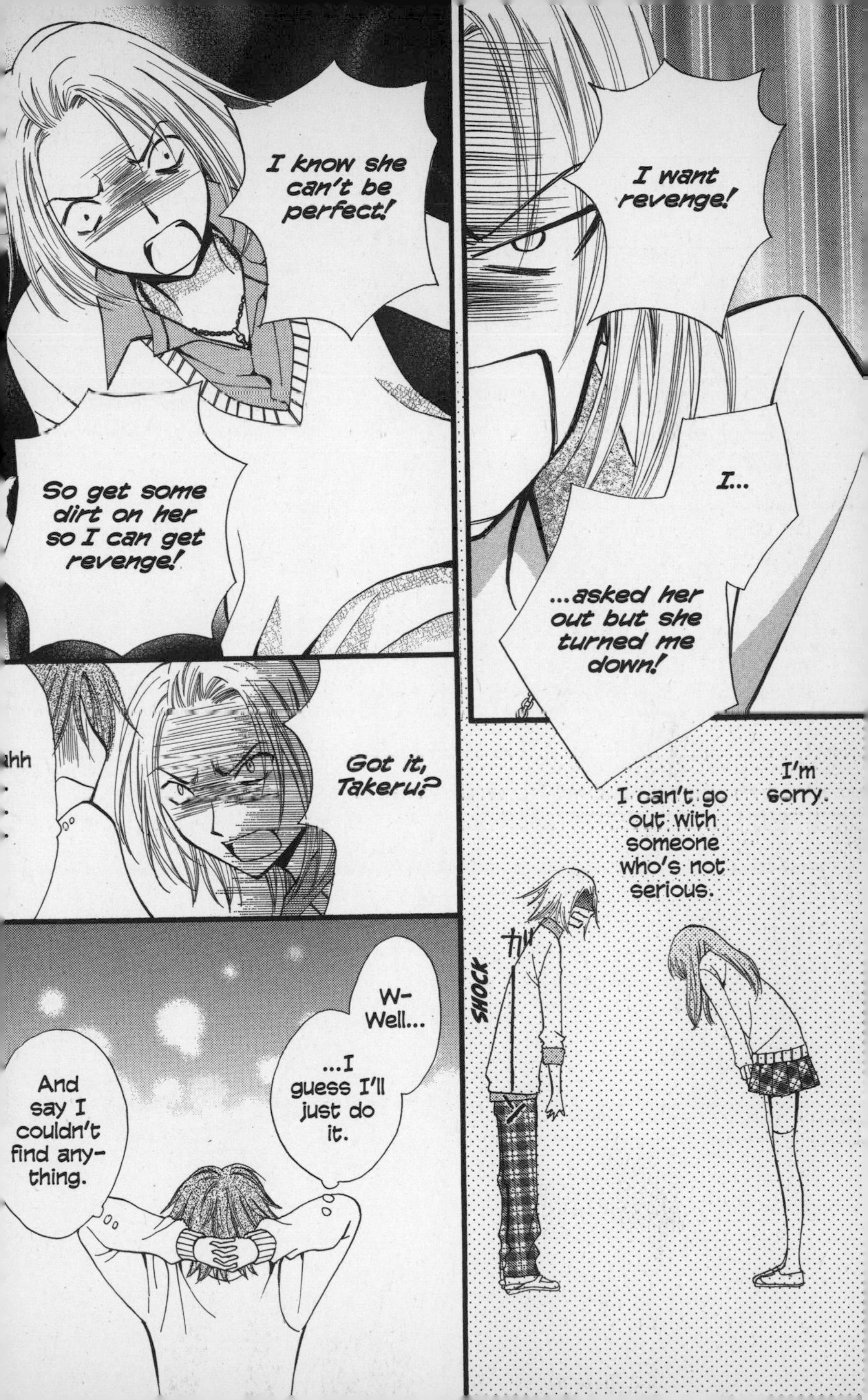

I want revenge!
I...
...asked her out but she turned me down!
I'm sorry.
I can't go out with someone who's not serious.
SHOCK
I know she can't be perfect!
So get some dirt on her so I can get revenge!
Got it, Takeru?
ahh
W-Well...
...I guess I'll just do it.
And say I couldn't find any-thing.

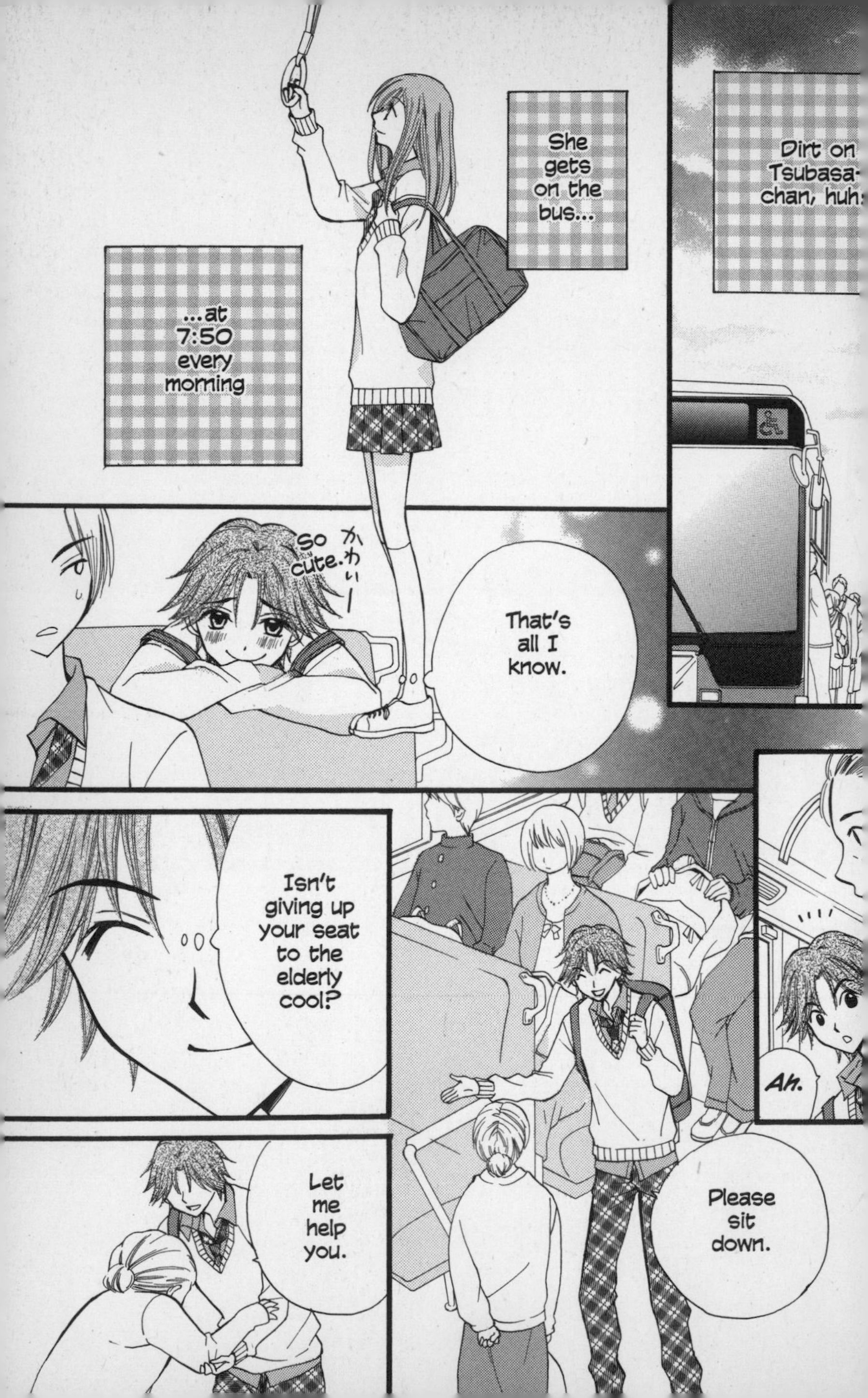
Dirt on Tsubasa-chan, huh
She gets on the bus...
...at 7:50 every morning
That's all I know.
So cute.
かわいー
Ah.
Please sit down.
Isn't giving up your seat to the elderly cool?
Let me help you.

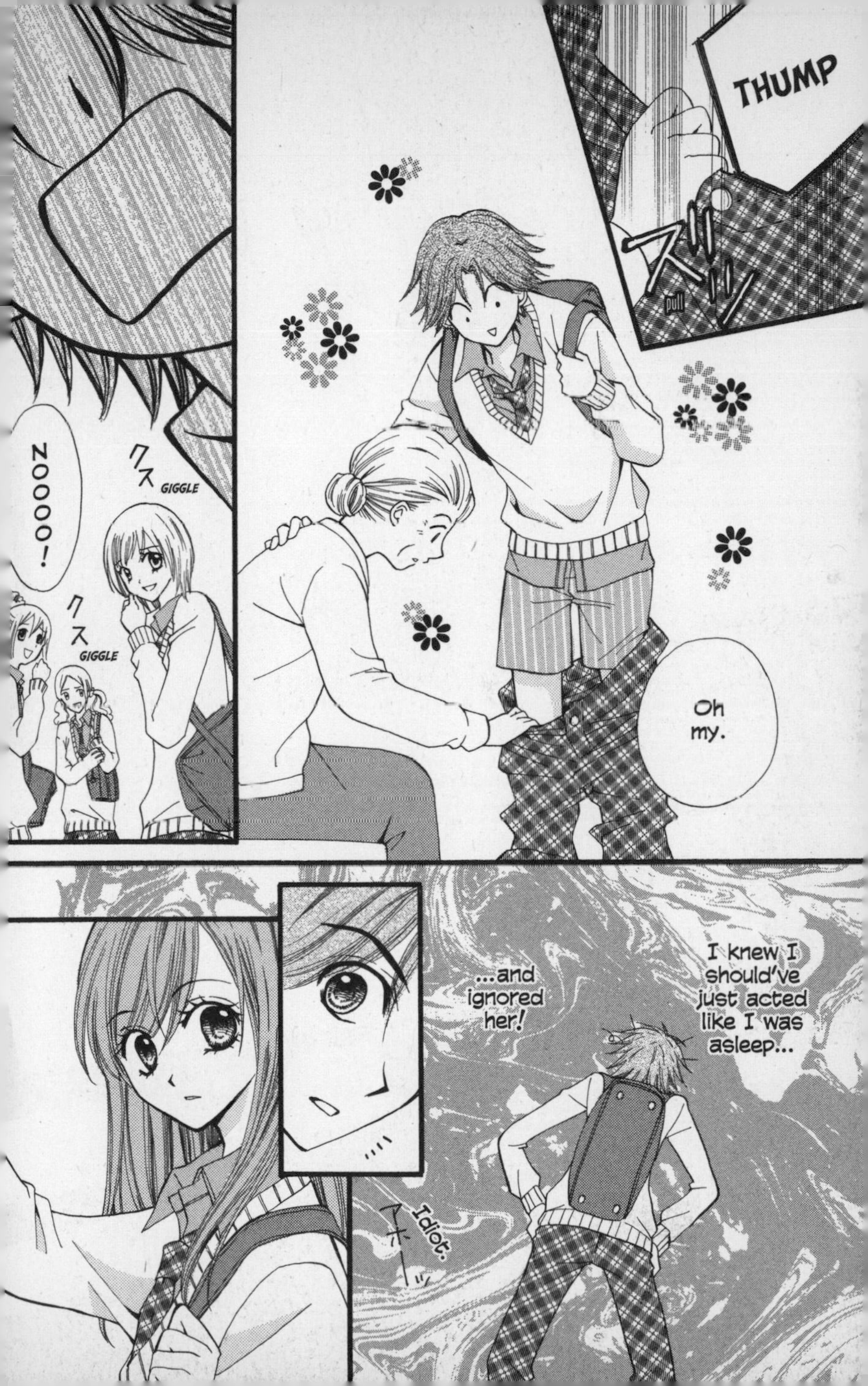
THUMP
pull
Oh my.
NOOOOO!
GIGGLE
GIGGLE
I knew I should've just acted like I was asleep...
...and ignored her!
Idiot.

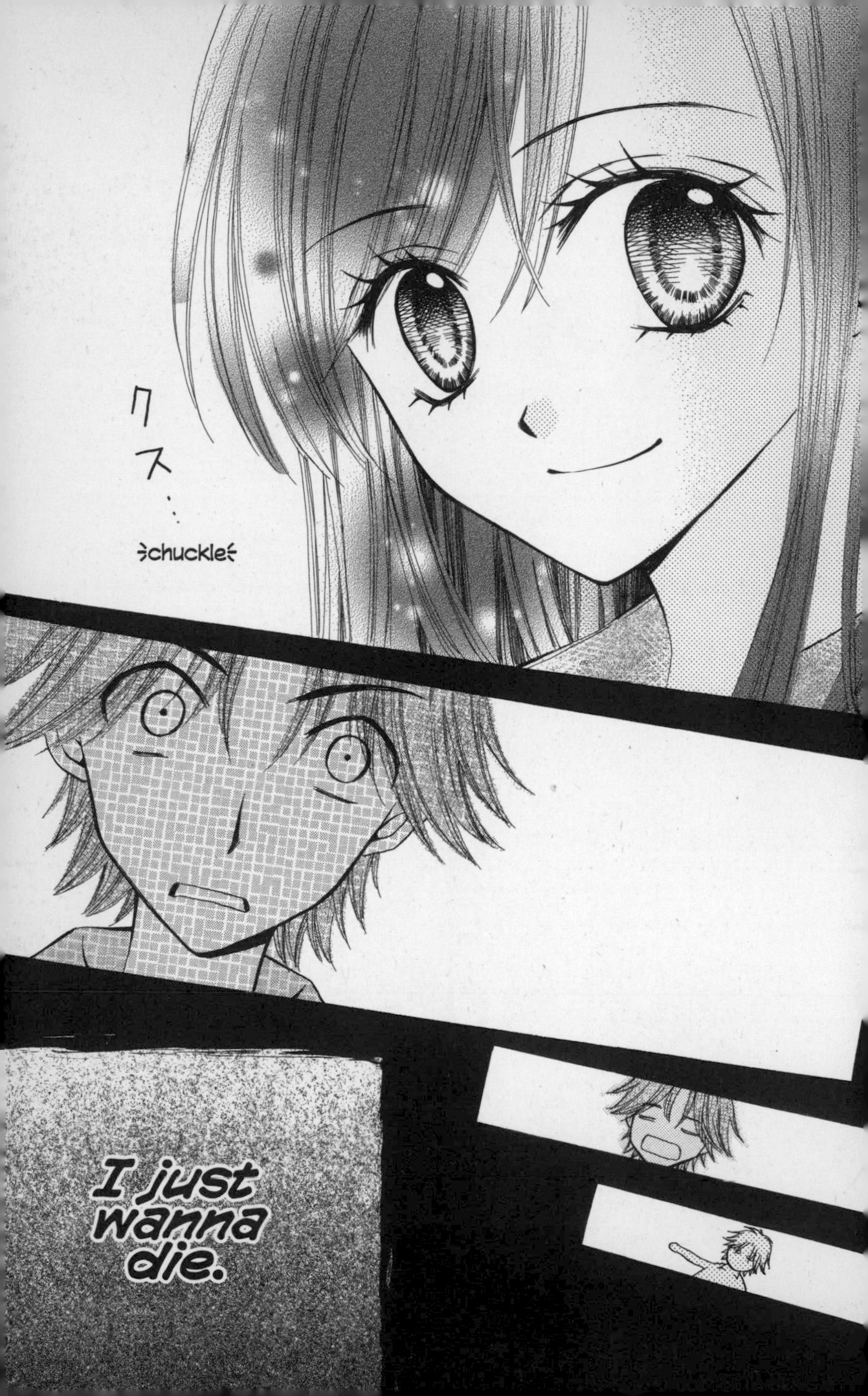

クス…
chuckle
I just wanna die.

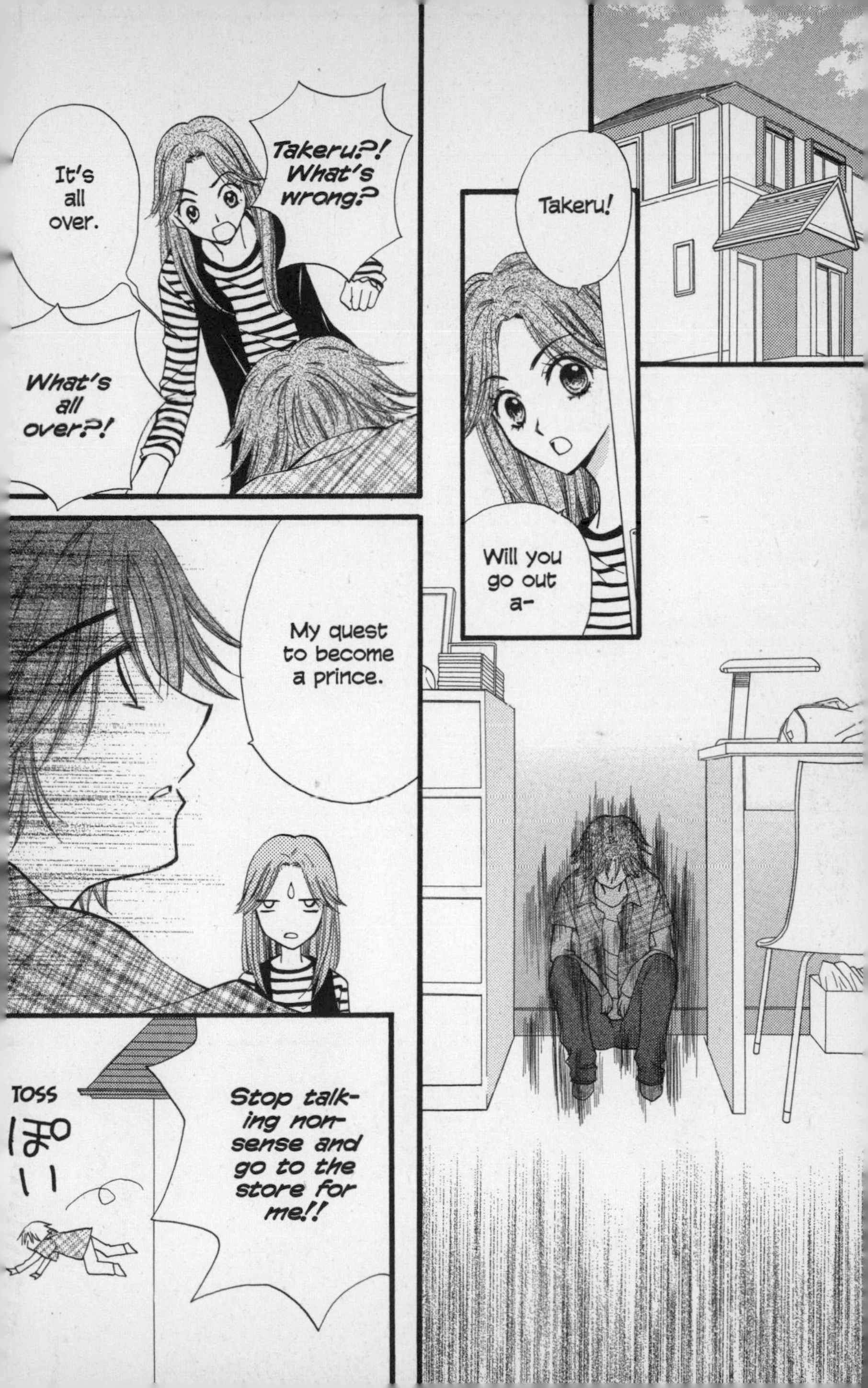
Takeru!
Will you go out a-
Takeru?! What's wrong?
It's all over.
What's all over?!
My quest to become a prince.
Stop talking nonsense and go to the store for me!!
TOSS
ぽい

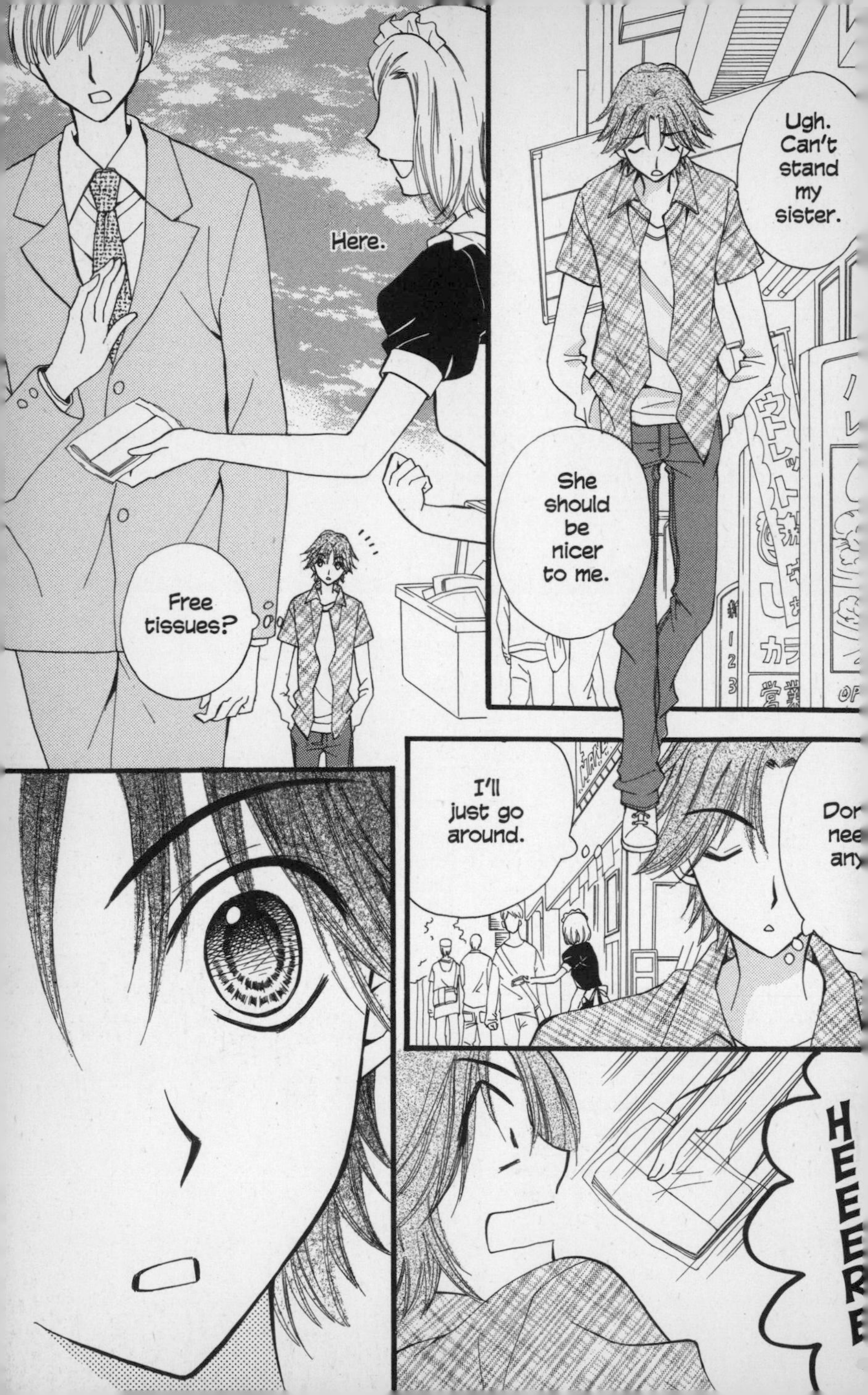
Ugh. Can't stand my sister.
She should be nicer to me.
Here.
Free tissues?
Dor nee any
I'll just go around.
HEEERE

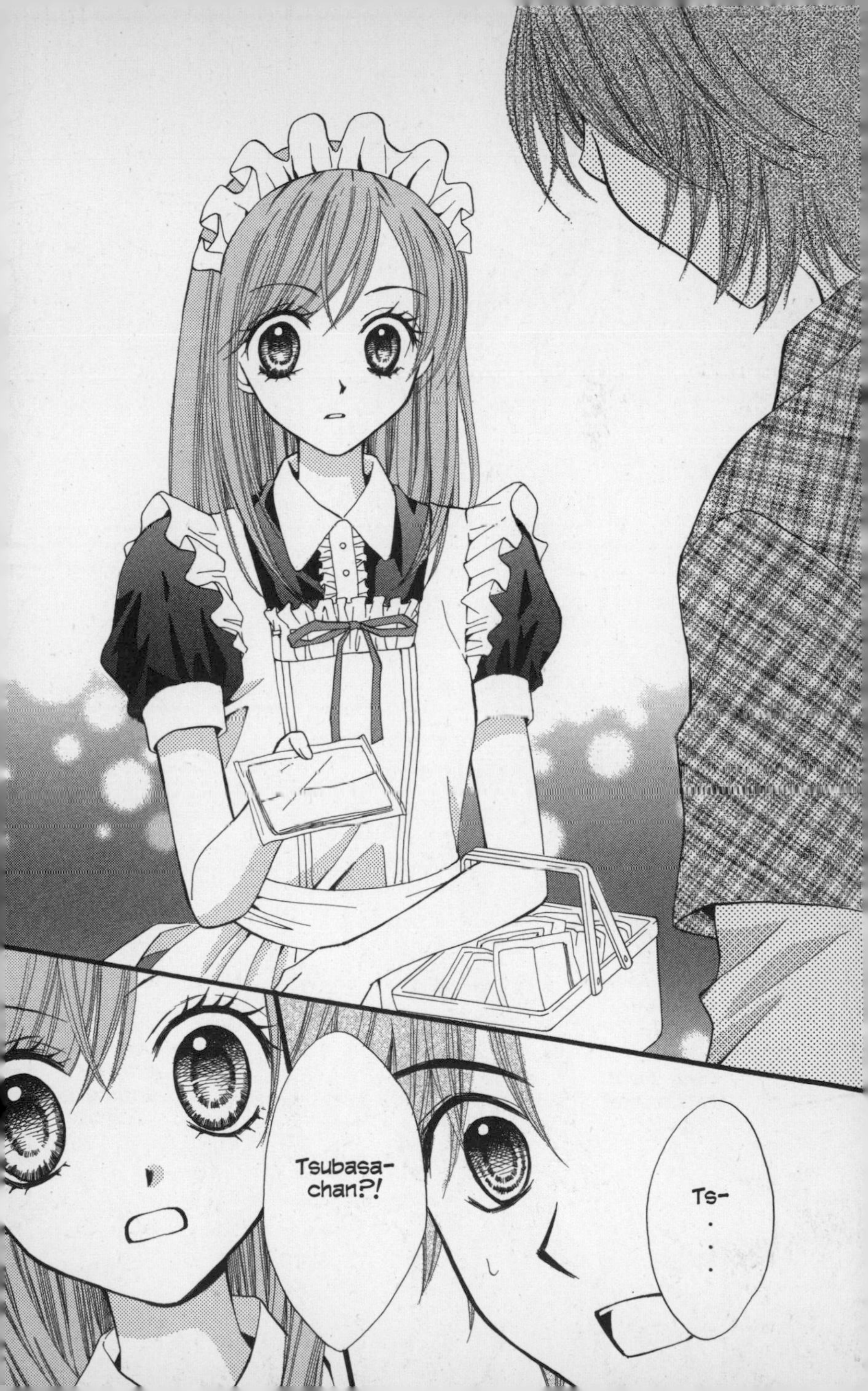
Ts- . . .
Tsubasa-chan?!

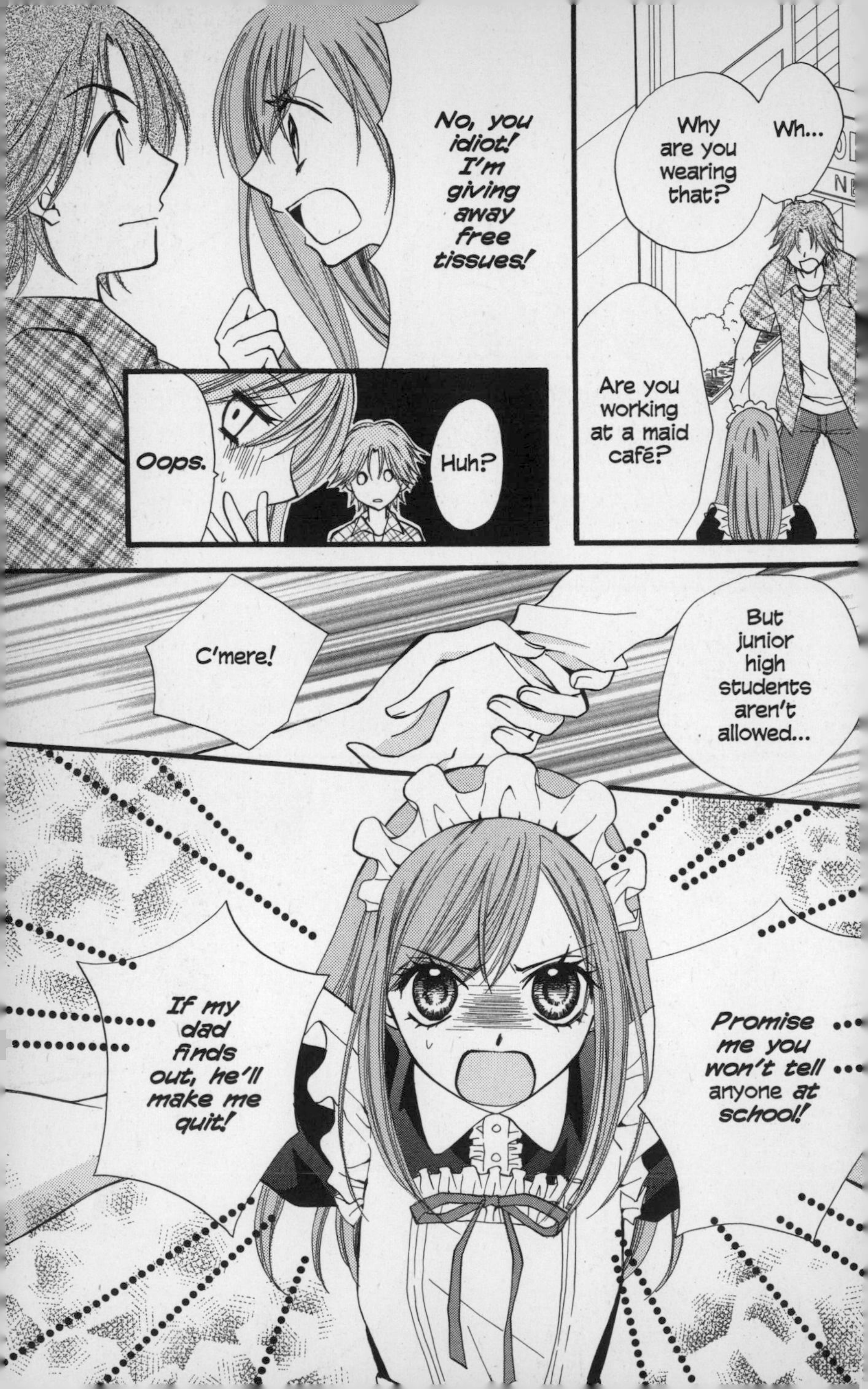
Wh...
Why are you wearing that?
Are you working at a maid café?
No, you idiot! I'm giving away free tissues!
Huh?
Oops.
But junior high students aren't allowed...
C'mere!
Promise me you won't tell anyone at school!
If my dad finds out, he'll make me quit!

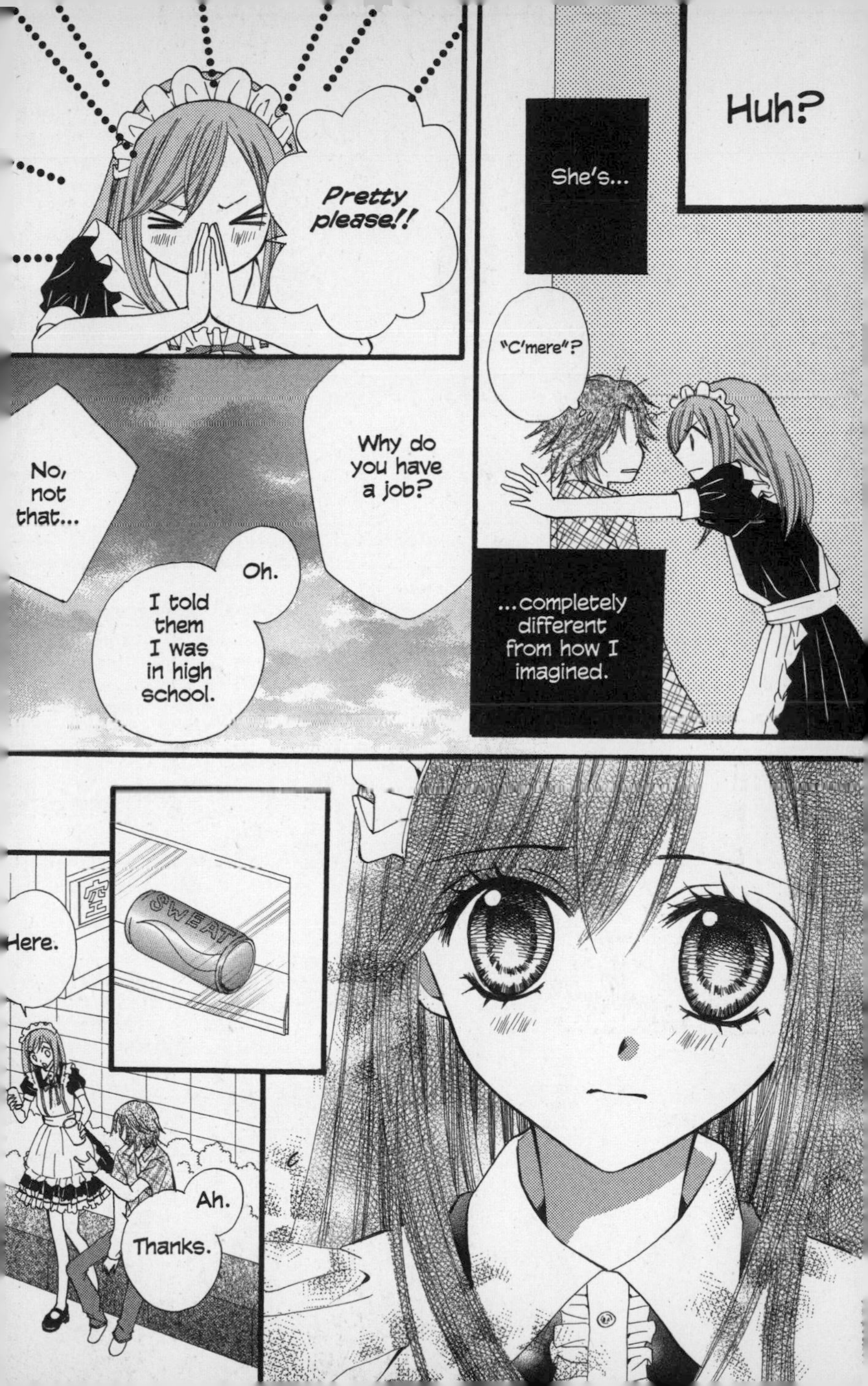

Huh?
She's...
"C'mere"?
...completely different from how I imagined.
Pretty please!!
Why do you have a job?
Oh.
I told them I was in high school.
No, not that...
SWEAT
Here.
Ah.
Thanks.

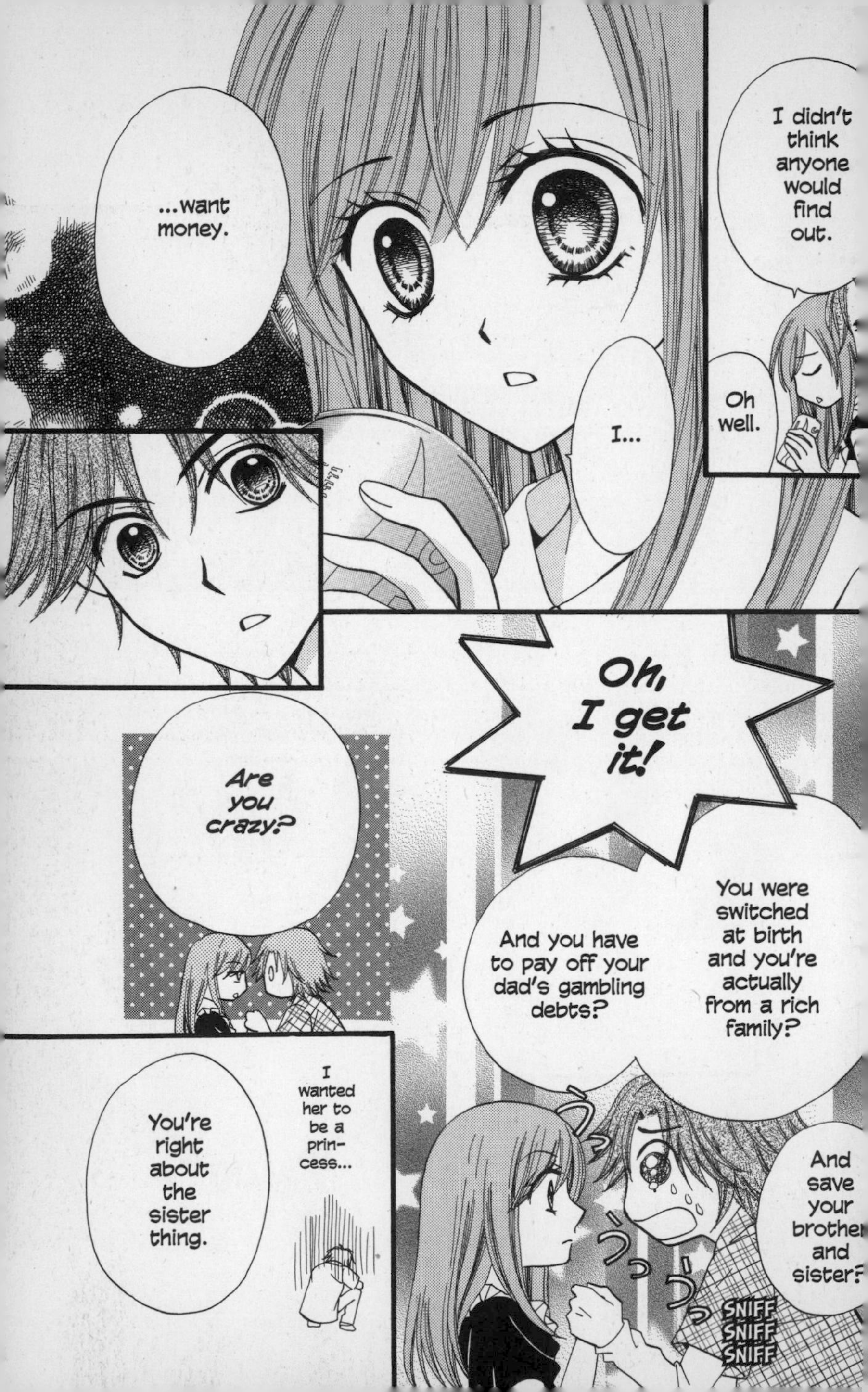

I didn't think anyone would find out.
Oh well.
I...
...want money.
Oh, I get it!
You were switched at birth and you're actually from a rich family?
And you have to pay off your dad's gambling debts?
And save your brothe and sister?
SNIFF SNIFF SNIFF
Are you crazy?
I wanted her to be a prin-cess...
You're right about the sister thing.

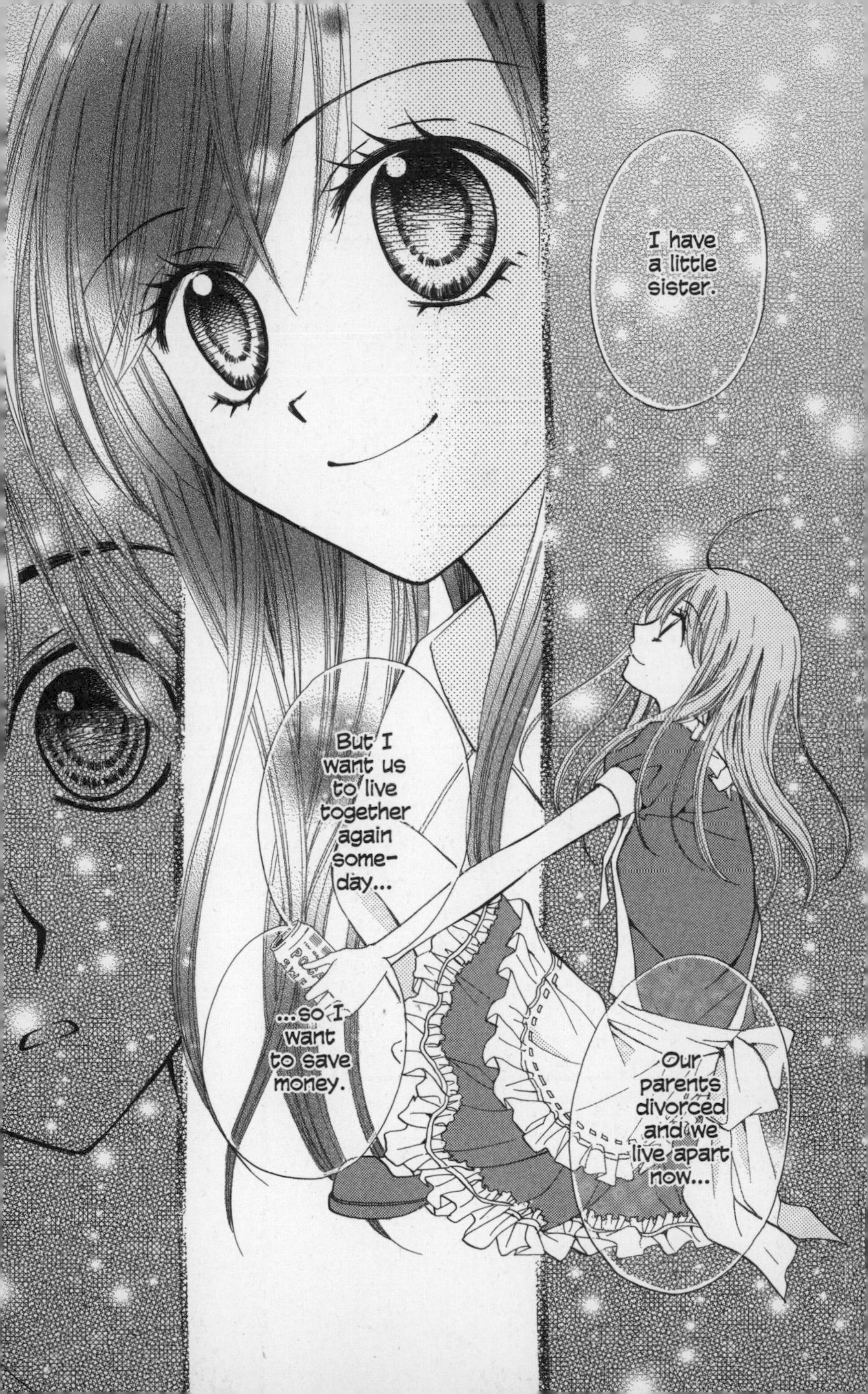
I have a little sister.
Our parents divorced and we live apart now...
But I want us to live together again someday...
...so I want to save money.

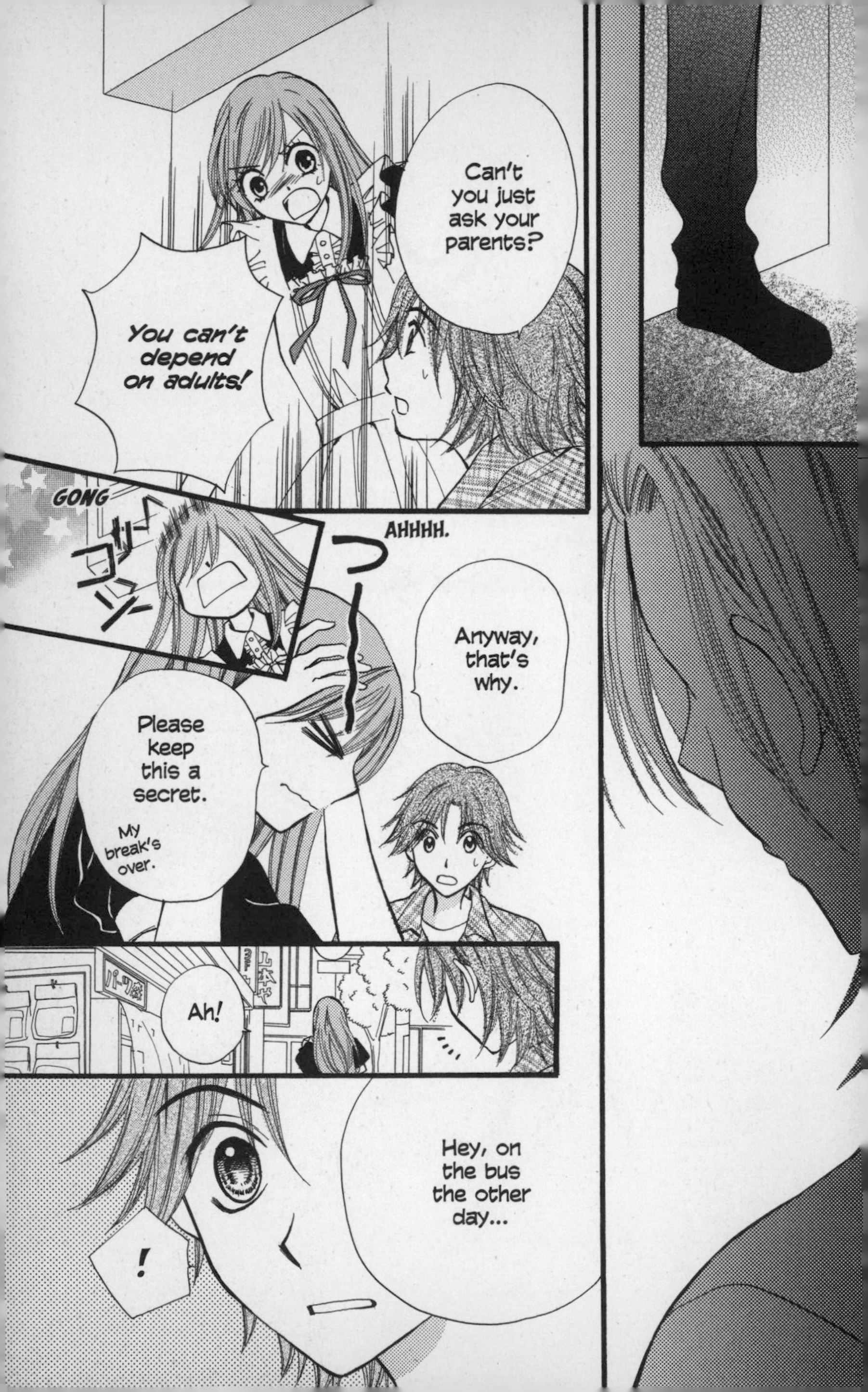
Can't you just ask your parents?
You can't depend on adults!
GONG
AHHHH.
Anyway, that's why.
Please keep this a secret.
My break's over.
Ah!
Hey, on the bus the other day...
!

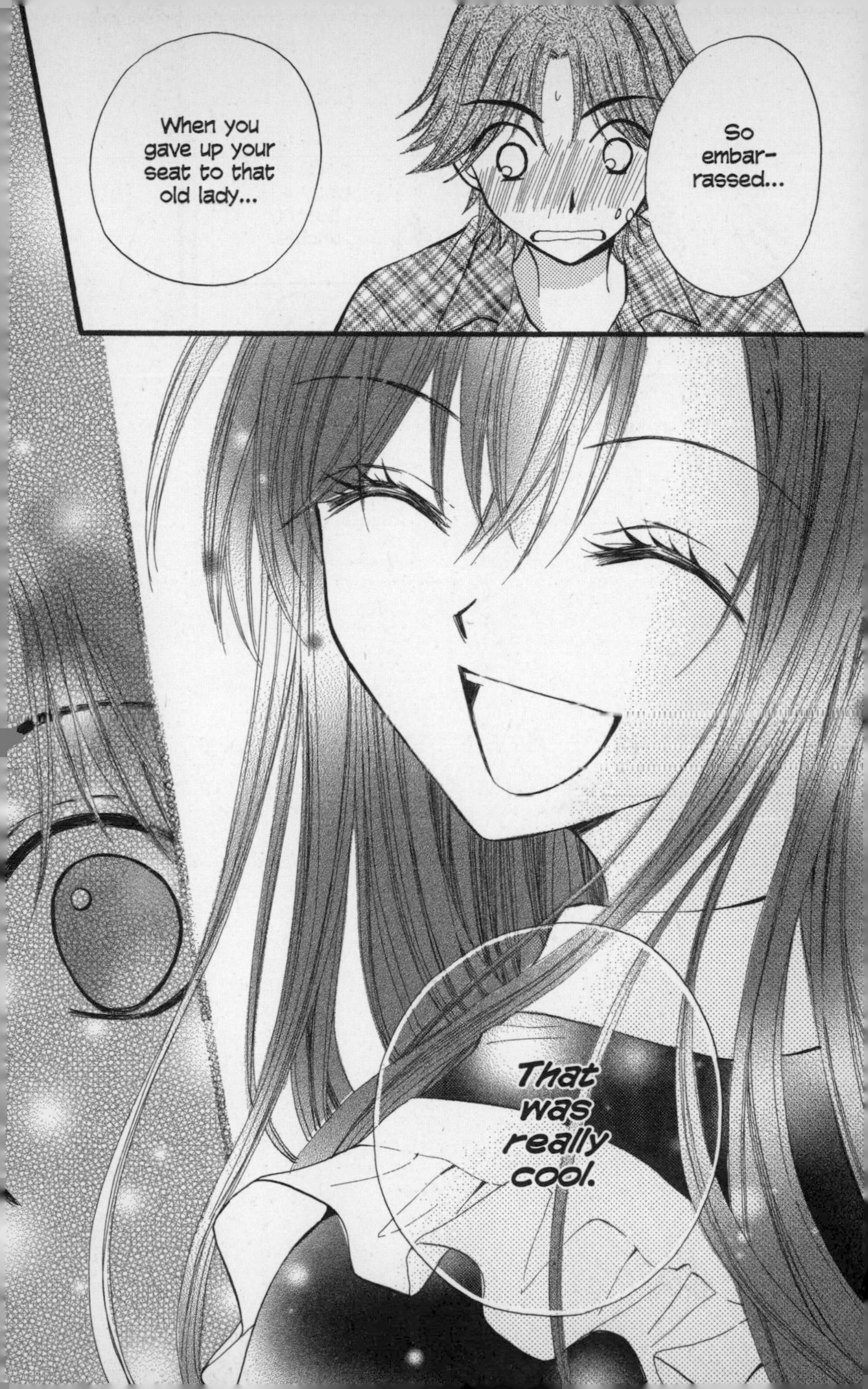
So embarrassed...
When you gave up your seat to that old lady...
That was really cool.

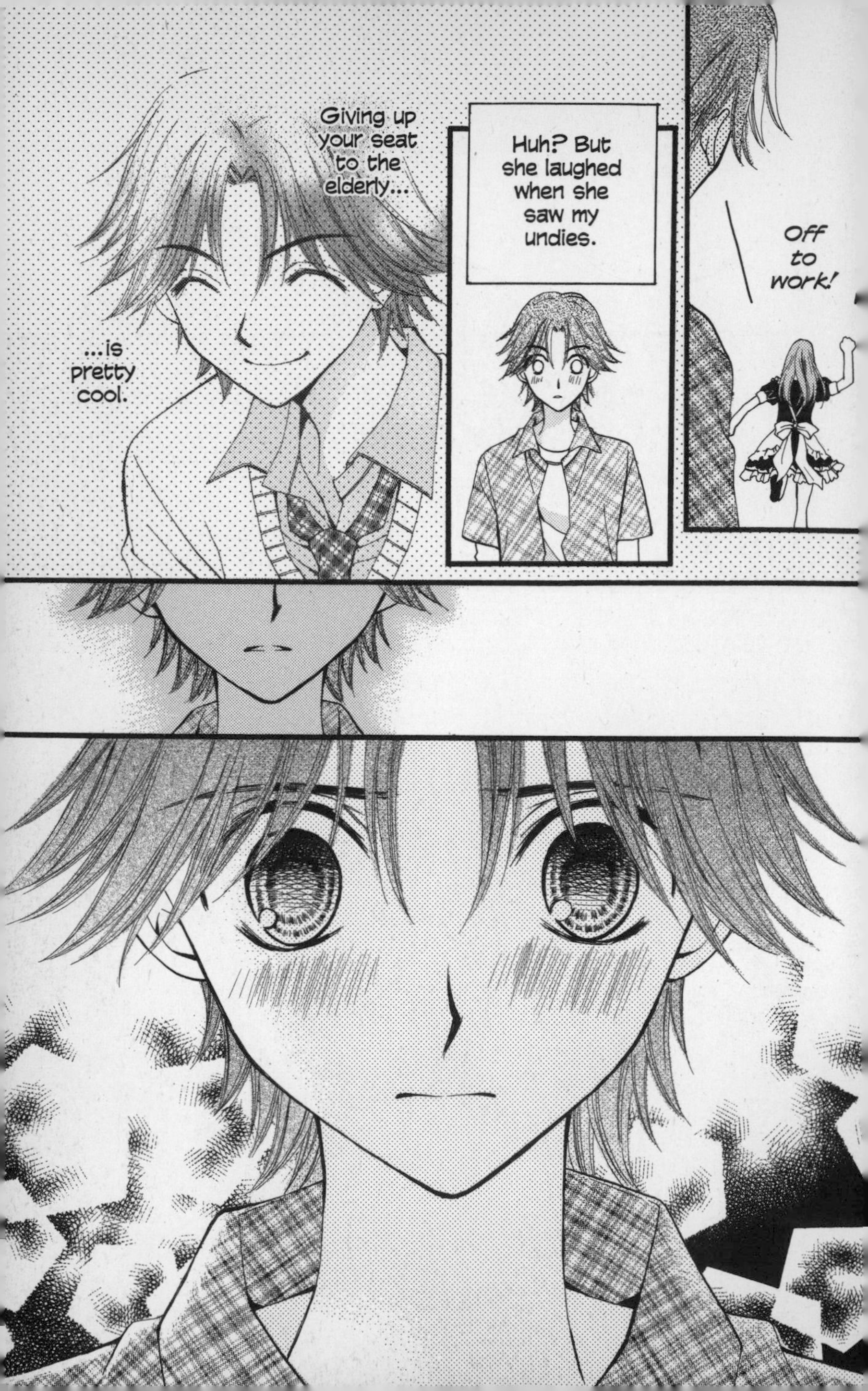
Off to work!
Huh? But she laughed when she saw my undies.
Giving up your seat to the elderly...
...is pretty cool.

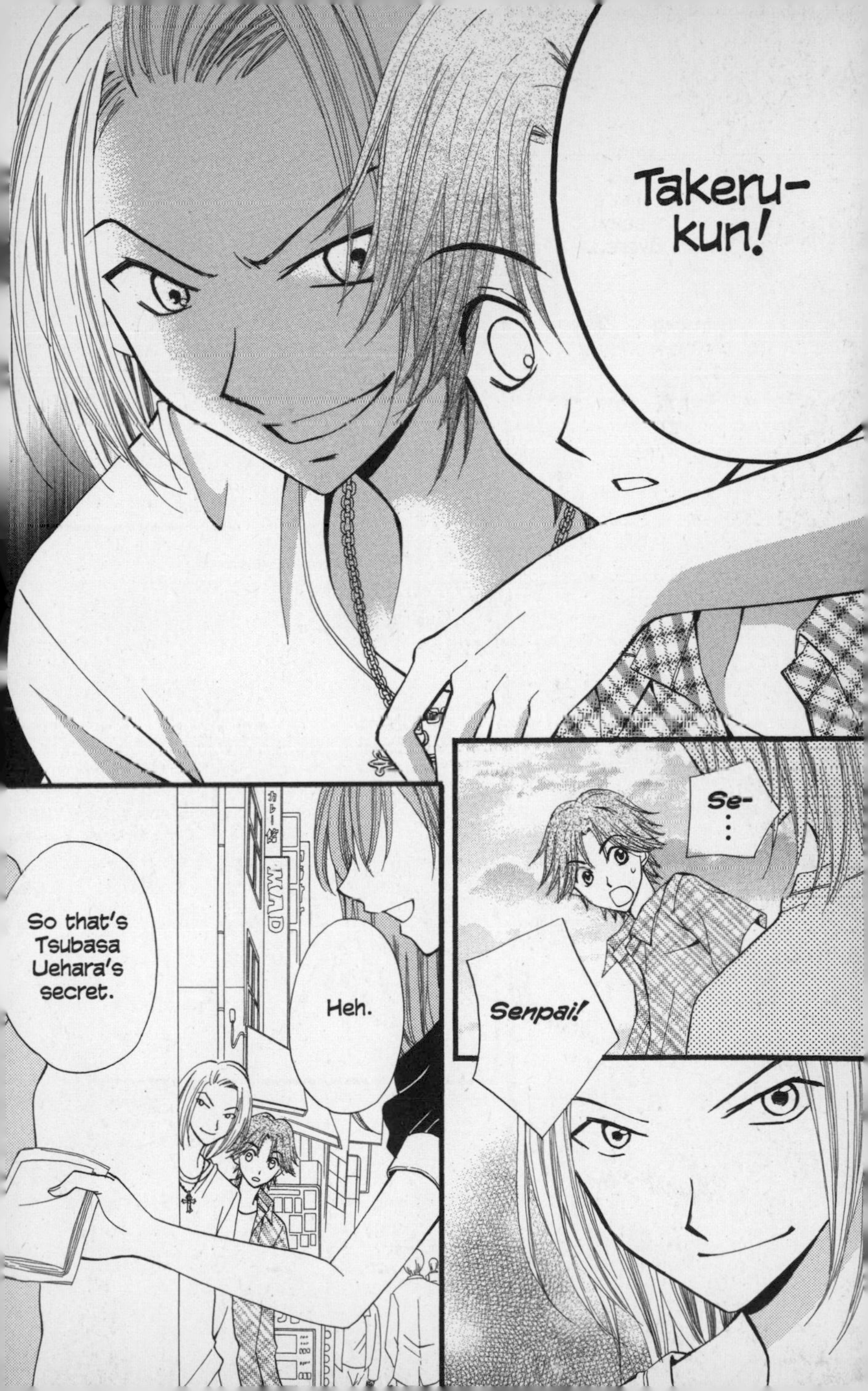
Takeru-kun!
Se-...
Senpai!
Heh.
So that's Tsubasa Uehara's secret.

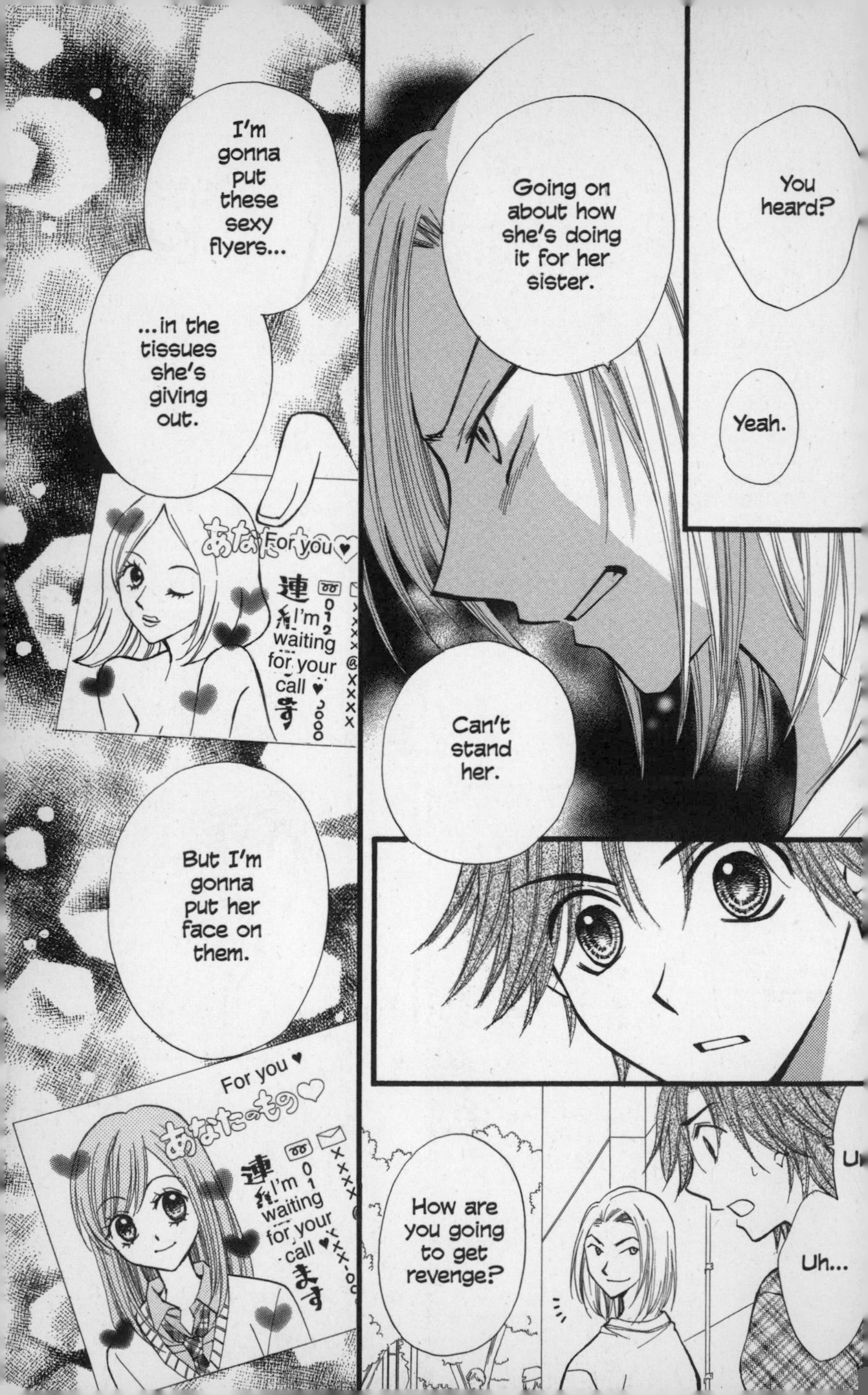

You heard?
Yeah.
Going on about how she's doing it for her sister.
Can't stand her.
Uh...
How are you going to get revenge?
I'm gonna put these sexy flyers...
...in the tissues she's giving out.
For you ♥
I'm waiting for your call ♥
But I'm gonna put her face on them.
For you ♥
I'm waiting for your call ♥

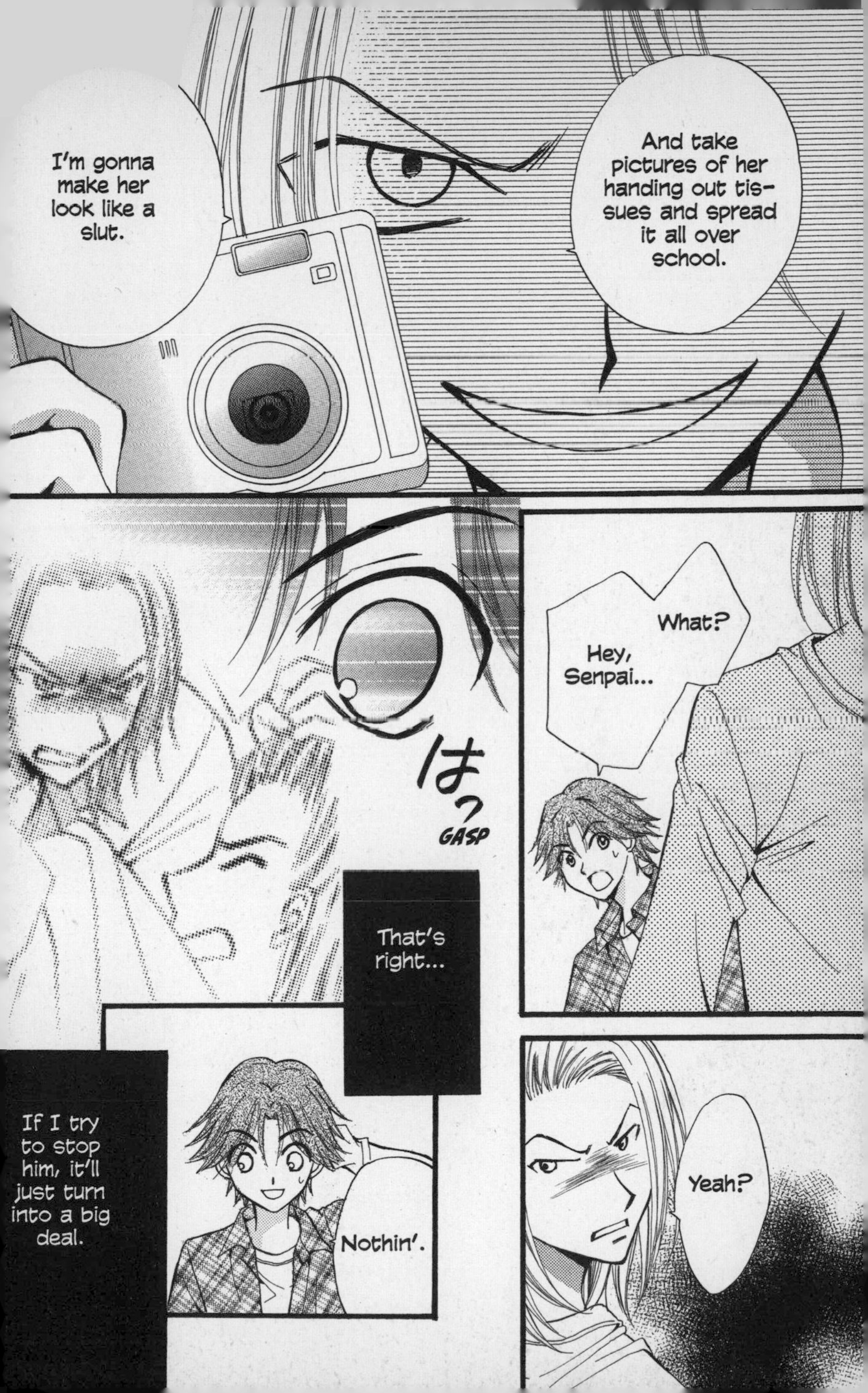
I'm gonna make her look like a slut.
And take pictures of her handing out tissues and spread it all over school.
What?
Hey, Senpai...
はっ
GASP
That's right...
Yeah?
Nothin'.
If I try to stop him, it'll just turn into a big deal.

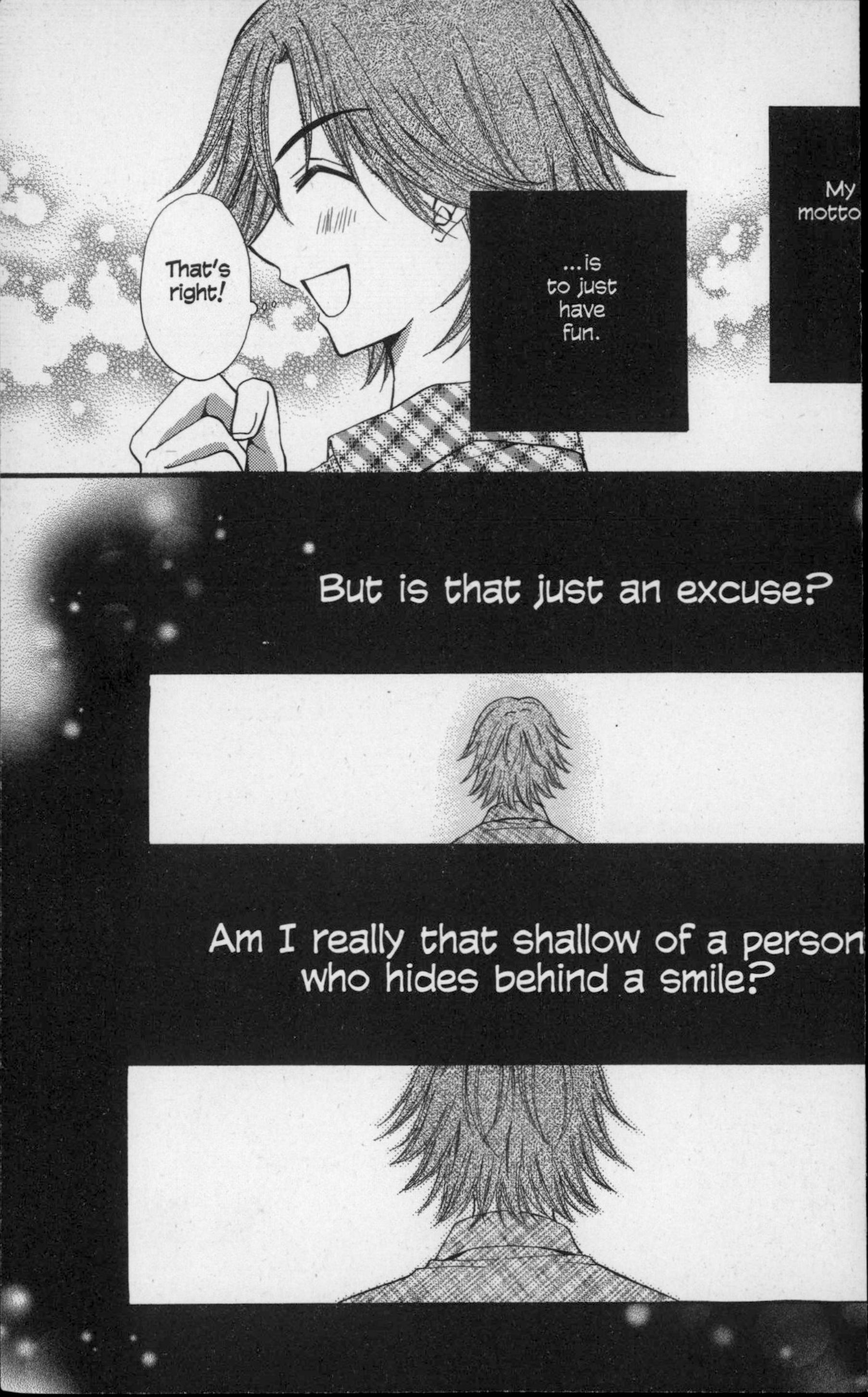
My motto
...is to just have fun.
That's right!
But is that just an excuse?
Am I really that shallow of a person who hides behind a smile?

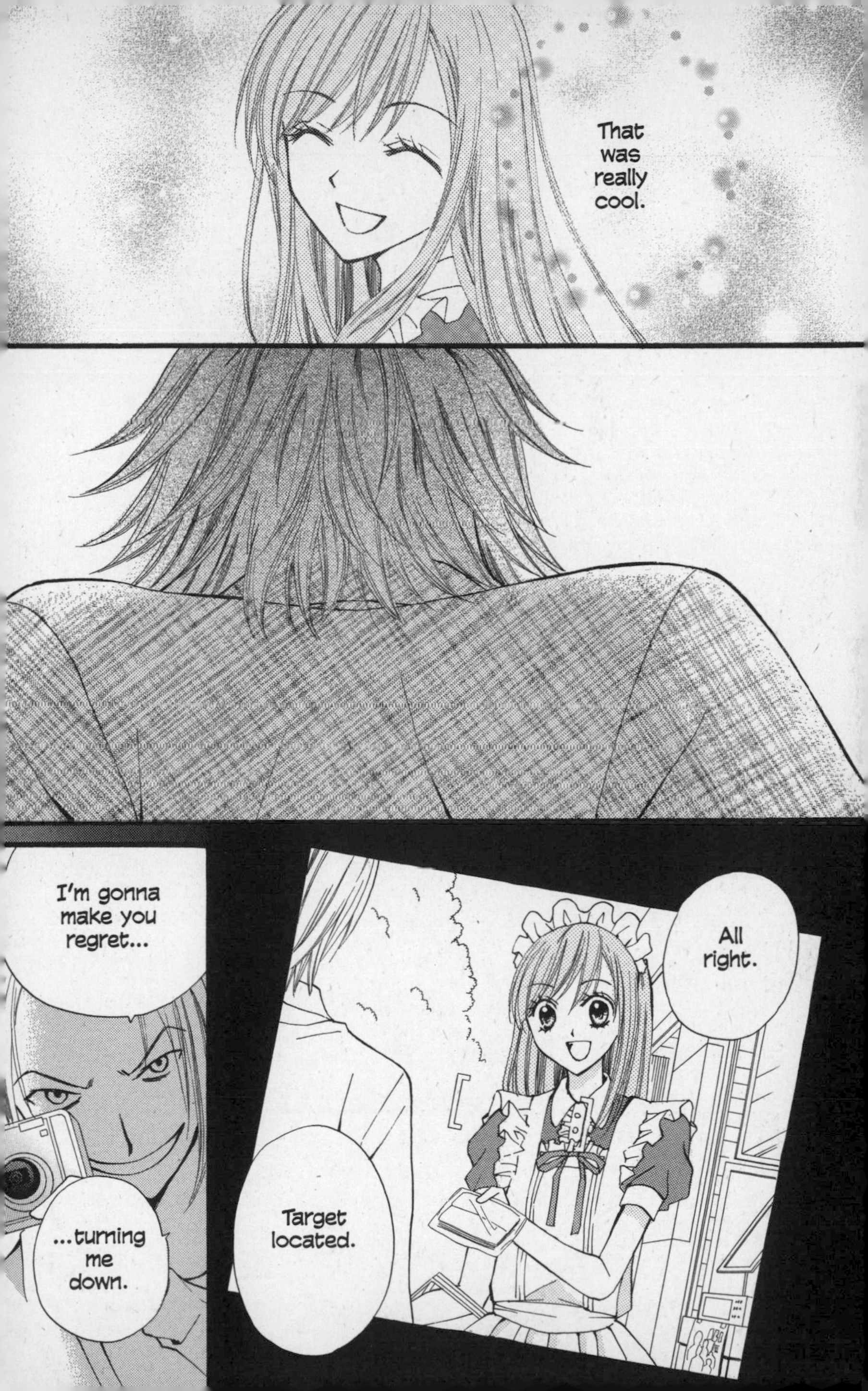
That was really cool.
All right.
Target located.
I'm gonna make you regret...
...turning me down.

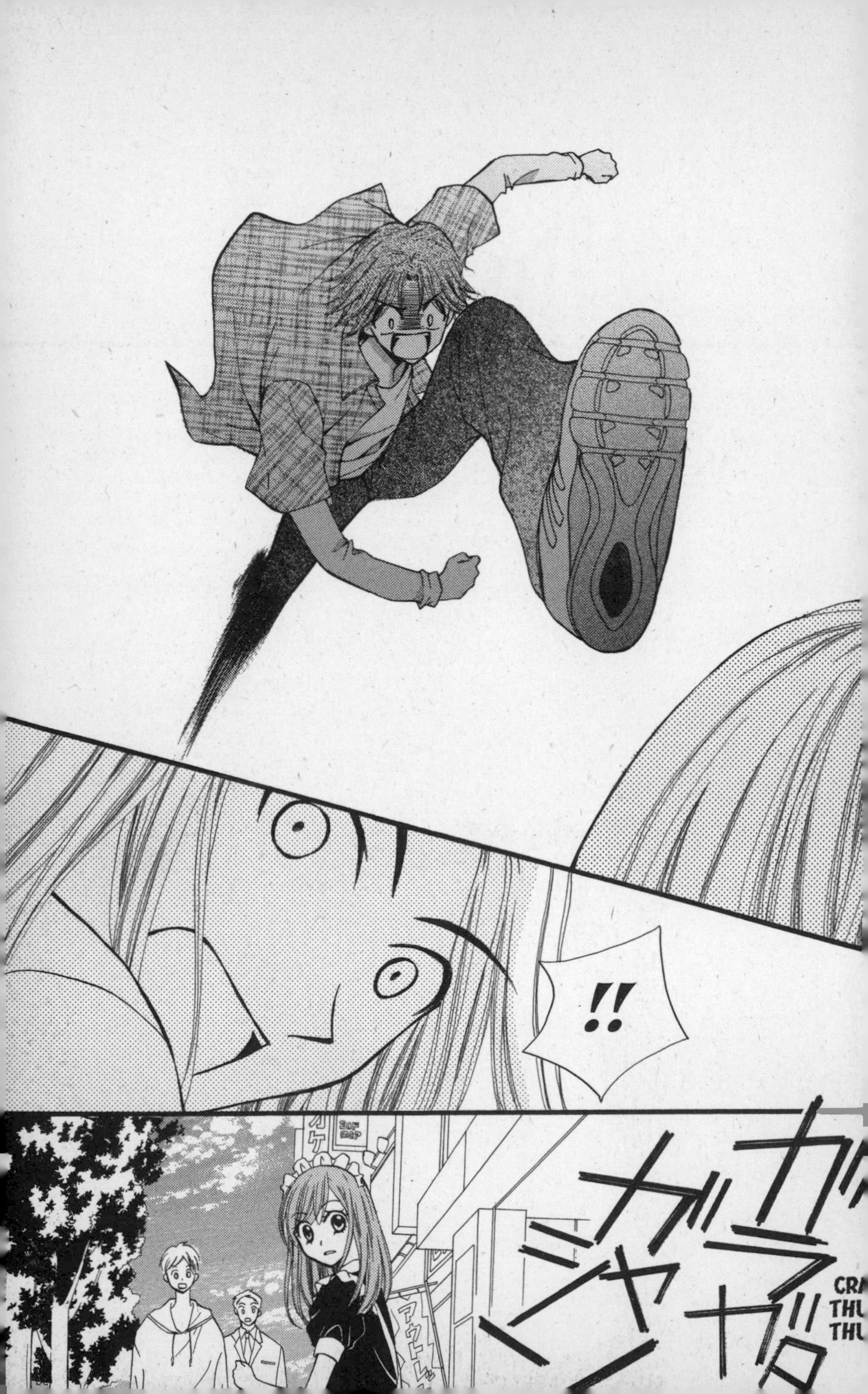
!!
ガシャン
CRA
THU
THU

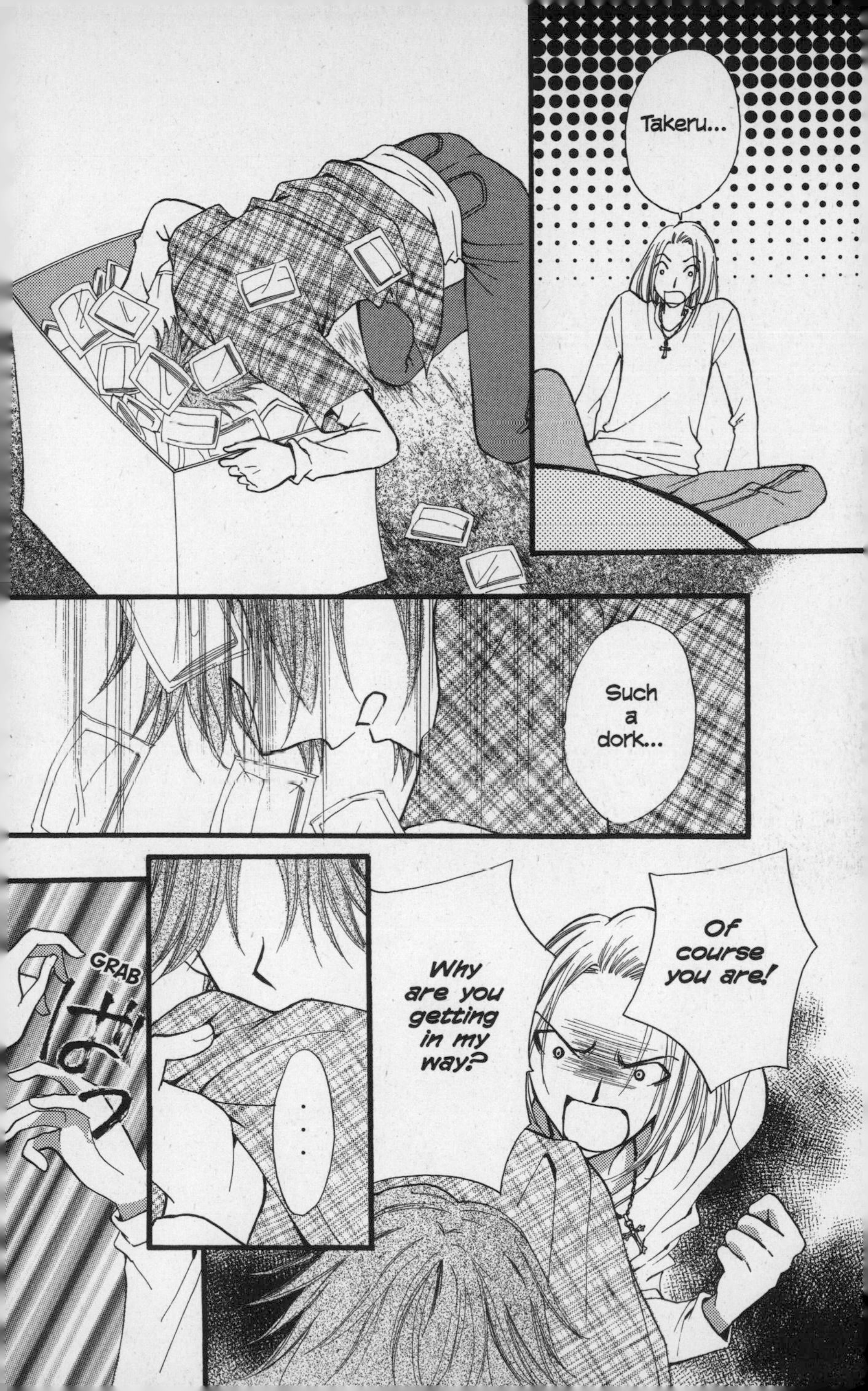
Takeru...
Such a dork...
Of course you are!
Why are you getting in my way?
...
GRAB

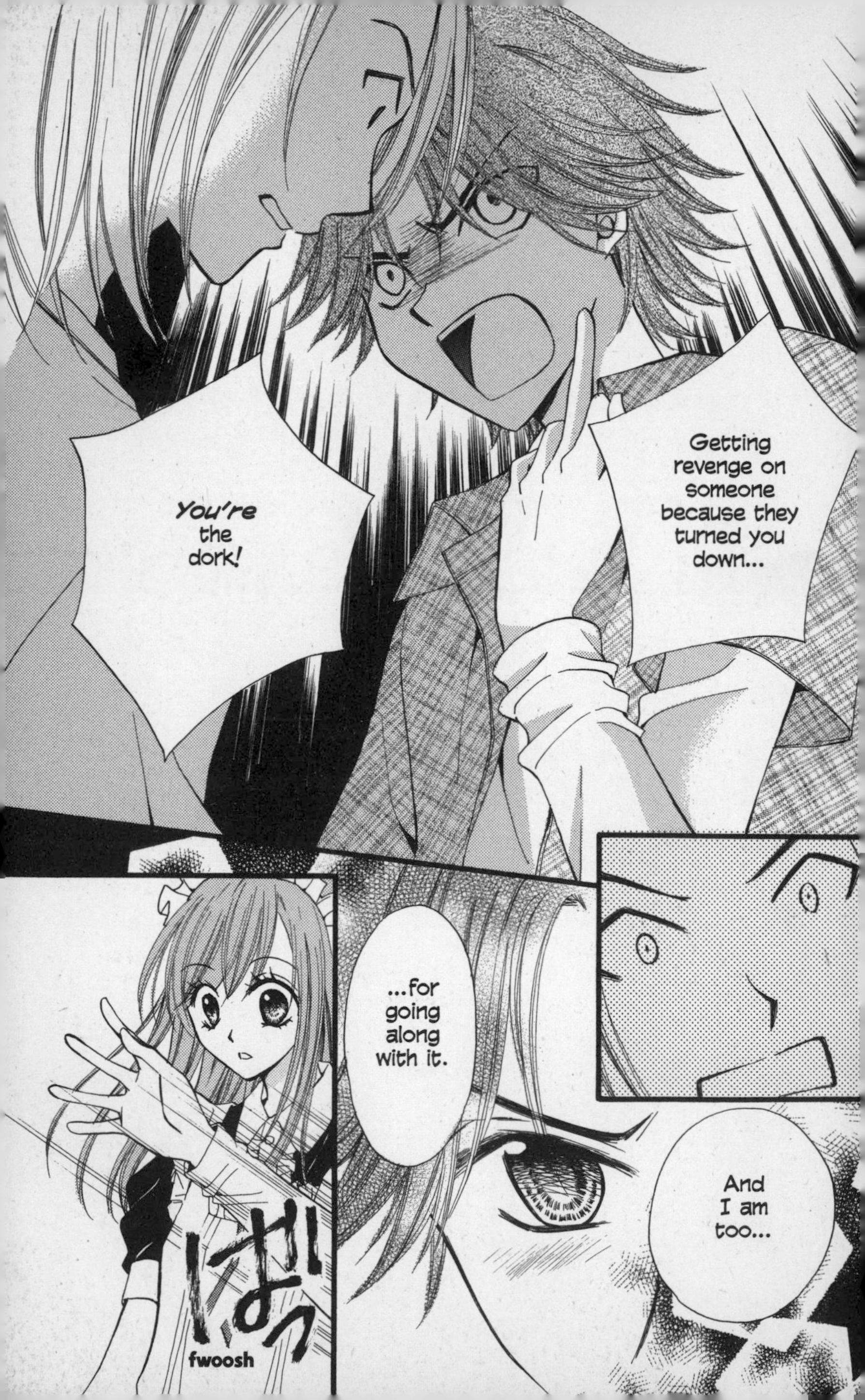
Getting revenge on someone because they turned you down...
You're the dork!
...for going along with it.
And I am too...
はっ
fwoosh

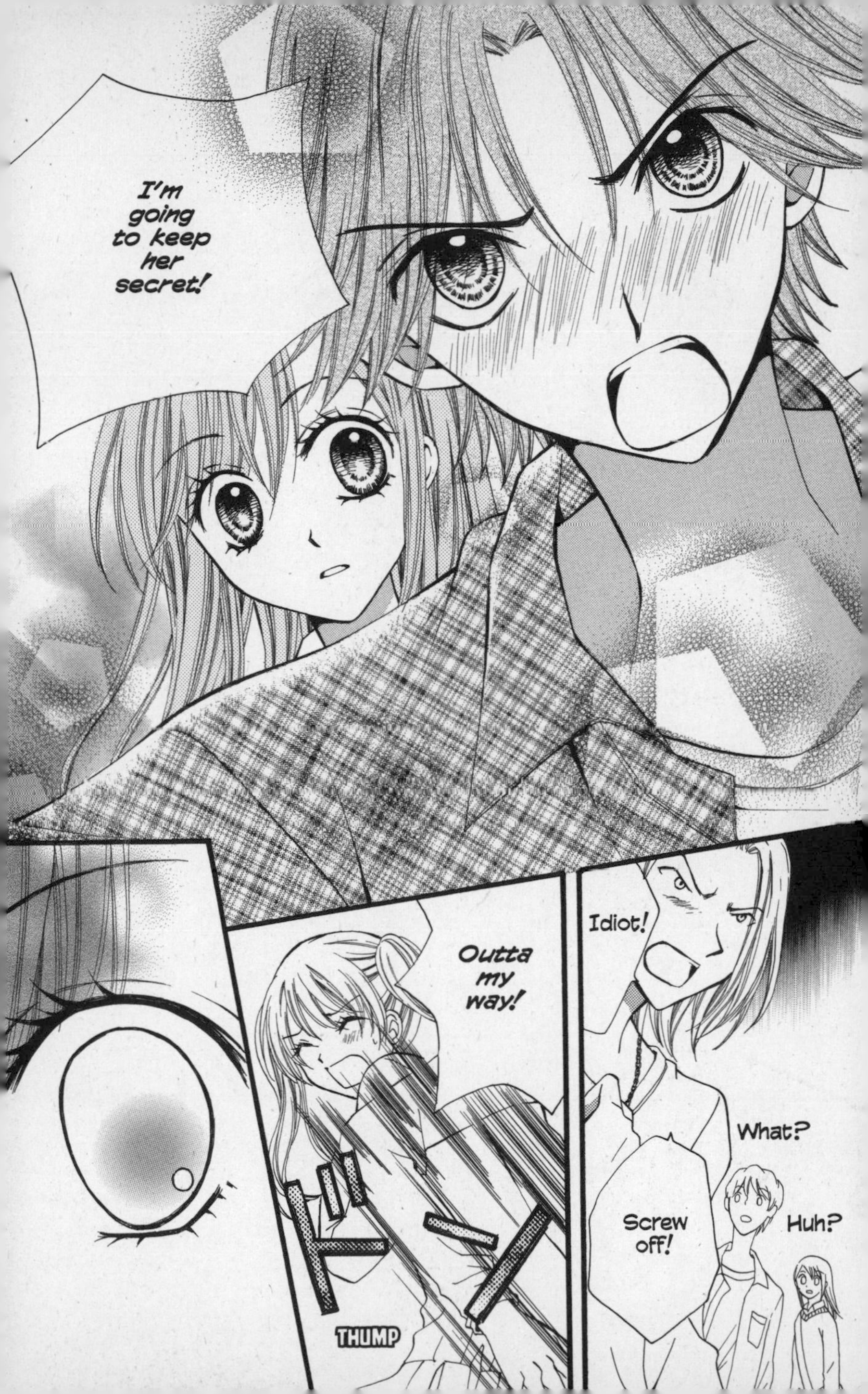
I'm going to keep her secret!
Idiot!
What?
Huh?
Screw off!
Outta my way!
THUMP

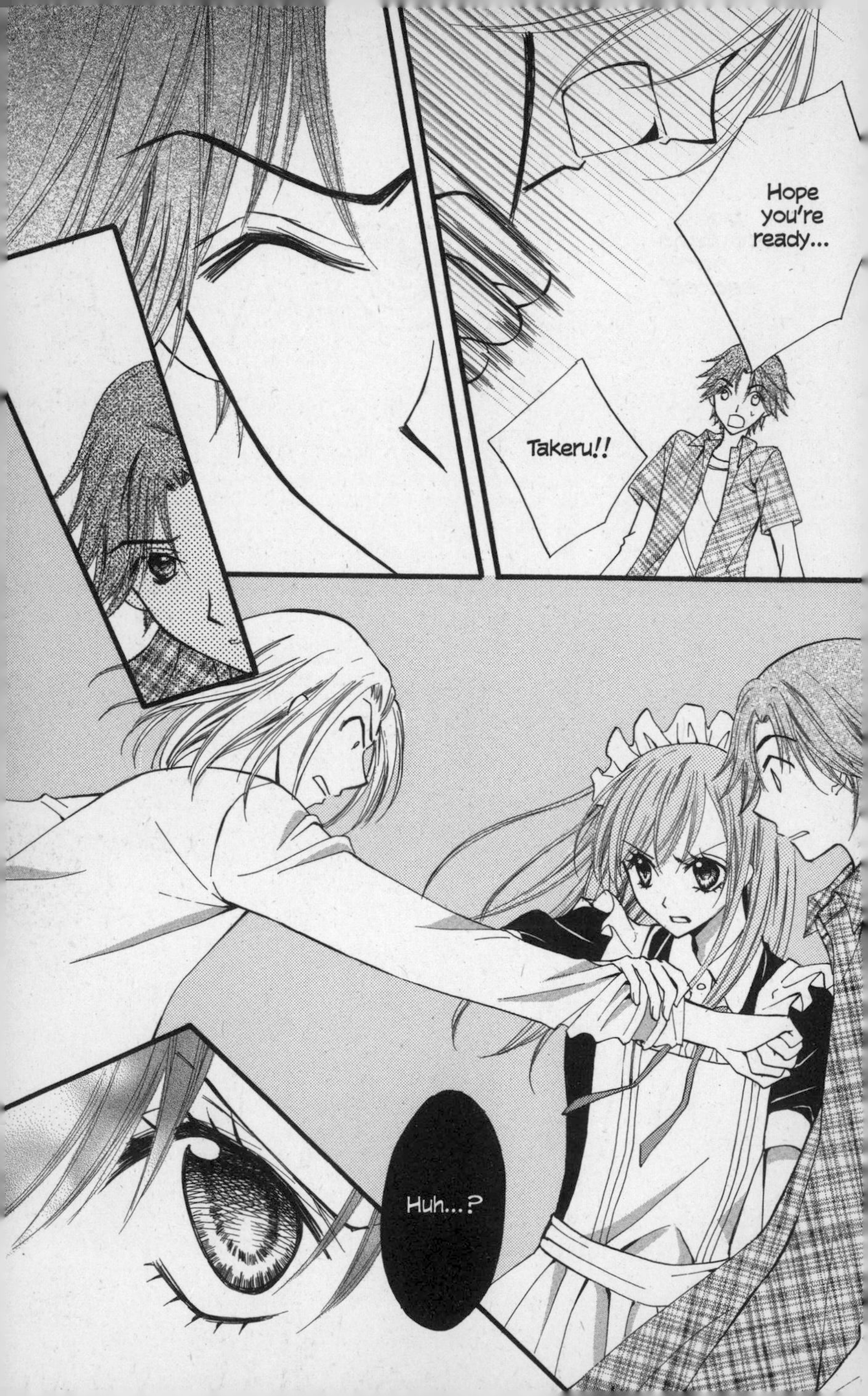
Hope you're ready...
Takeru!!
Huh...?

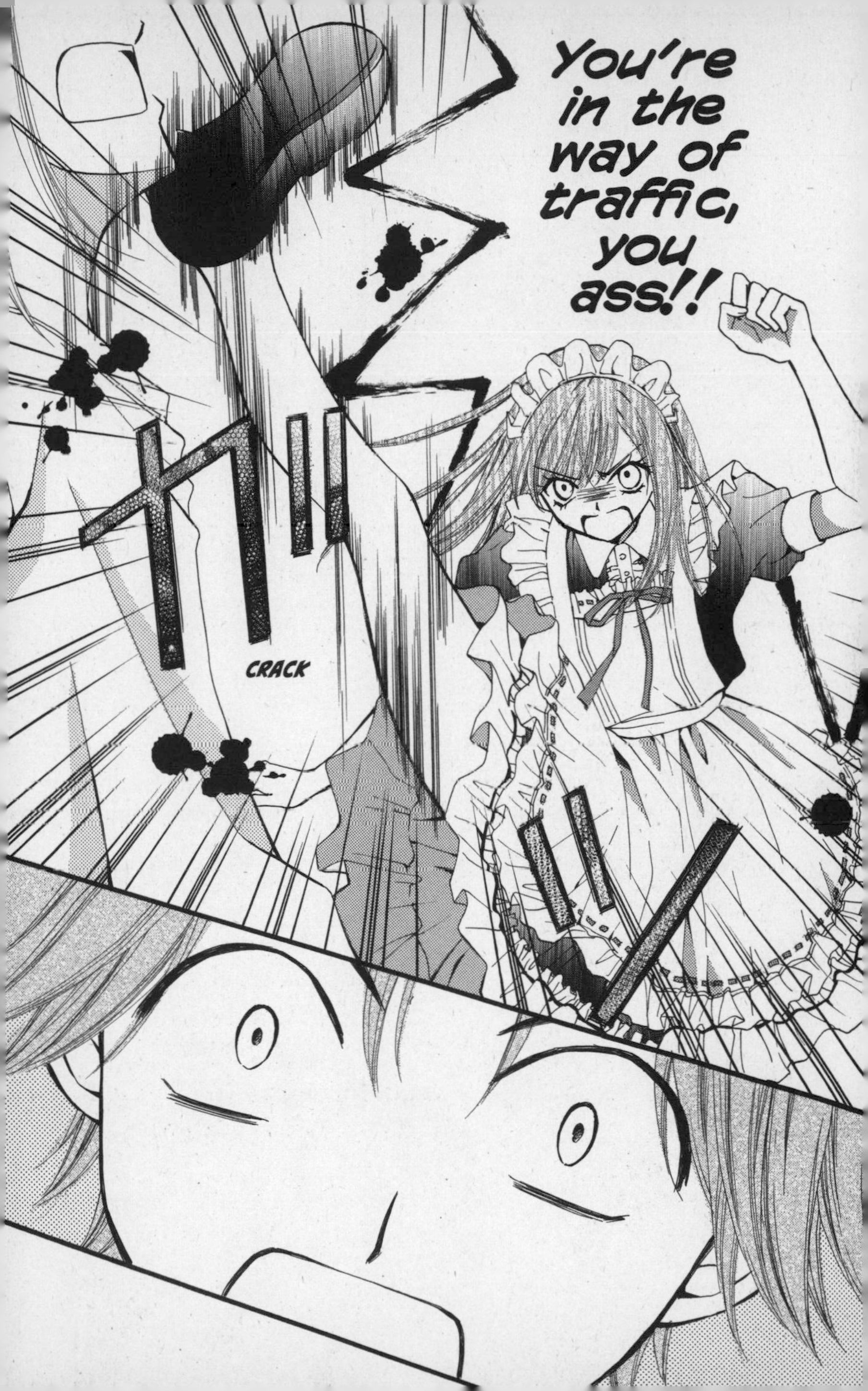
You're in the way of traffic, you ass!!
CRACK

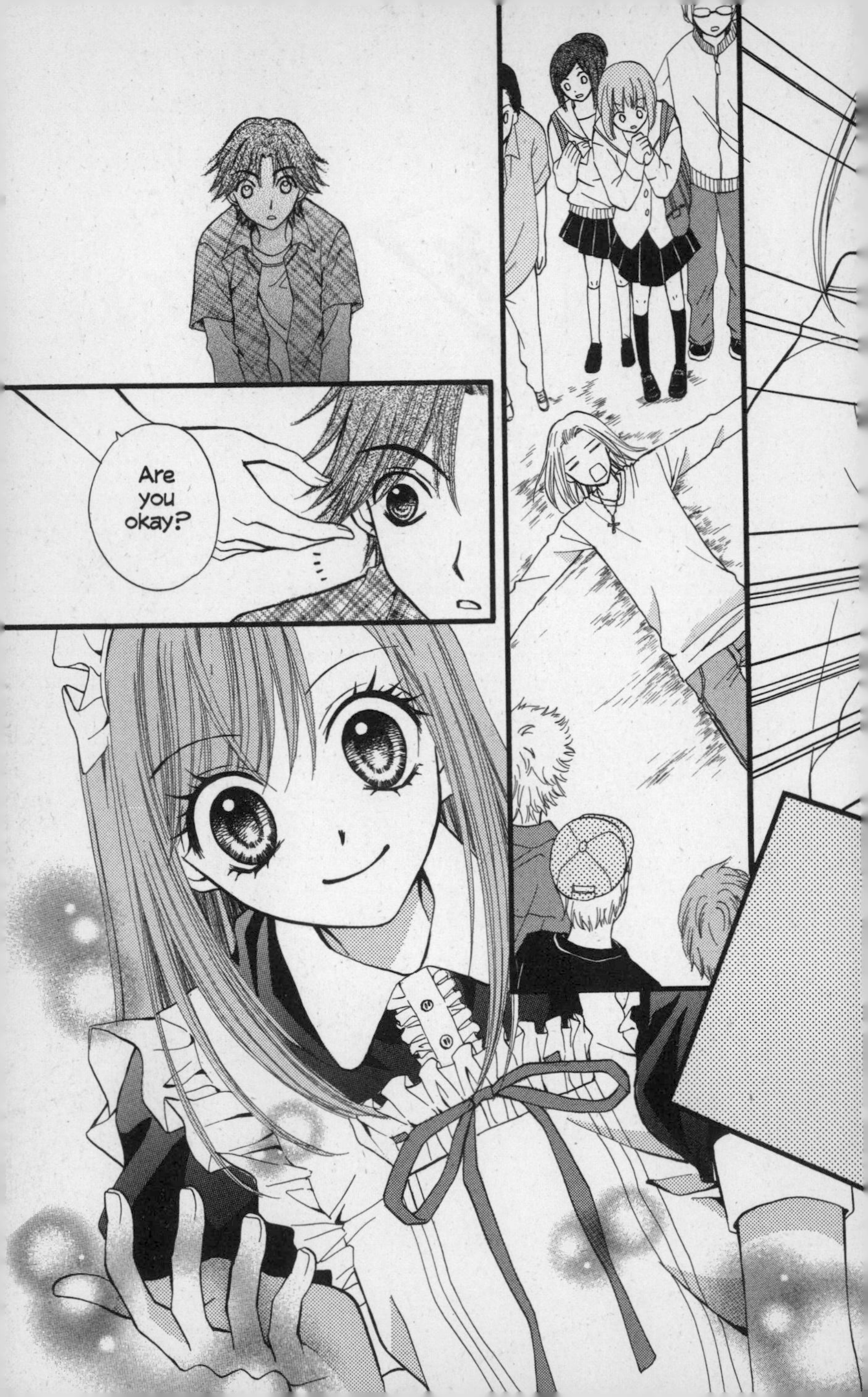
Are you okay?

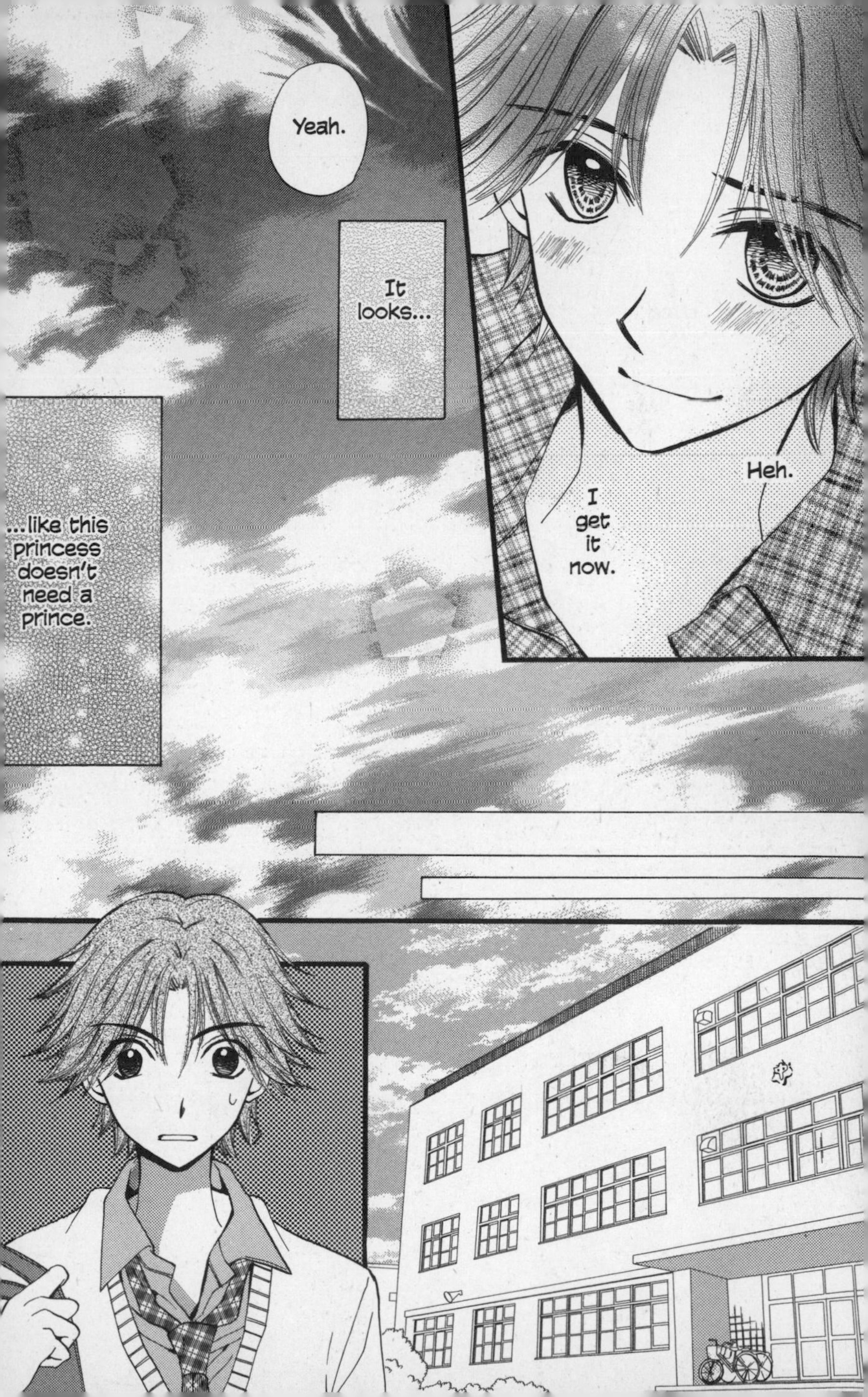
Heh.
I get it now.
Yeah.
It looks...
...like this princess doesn't need a prince.

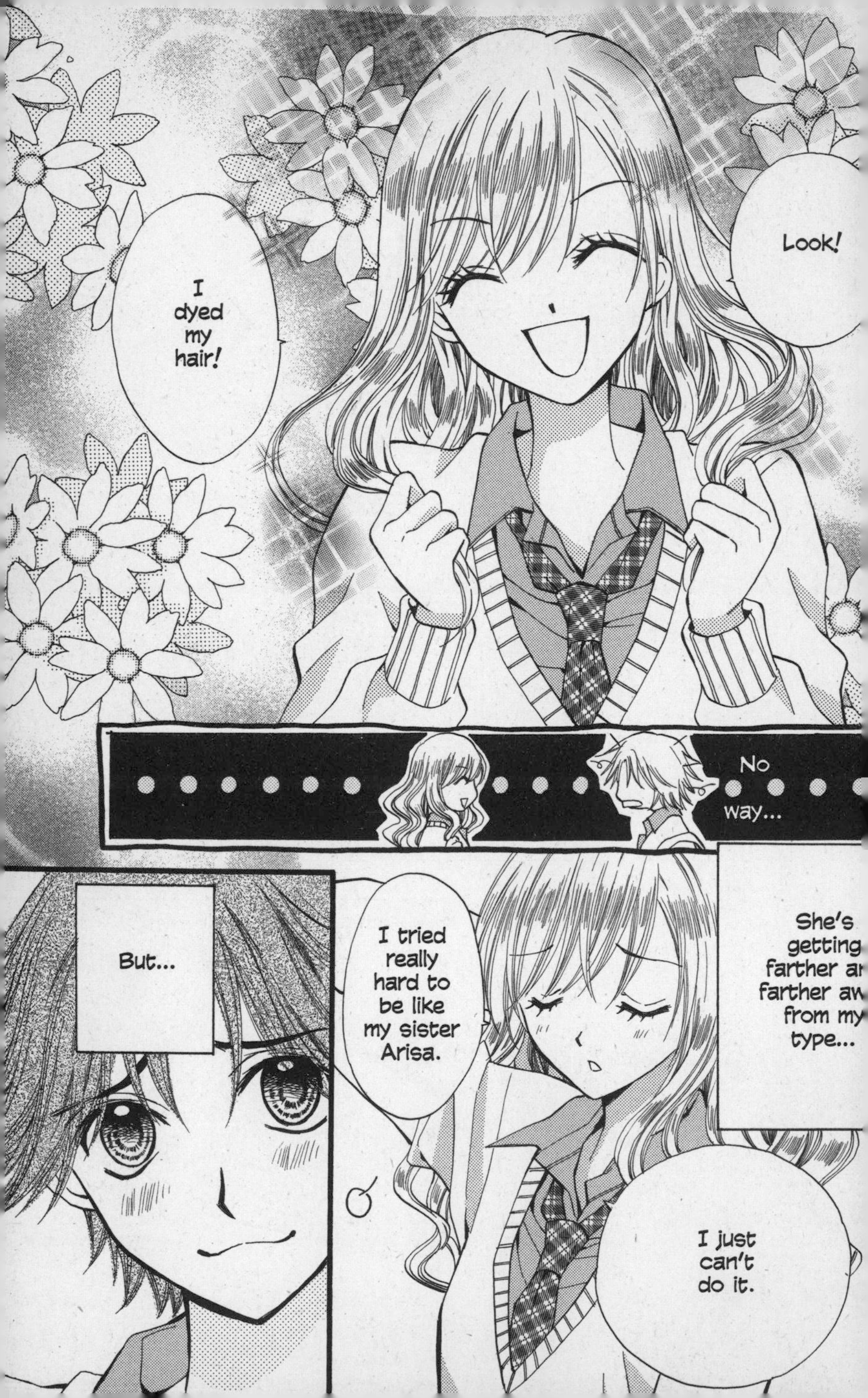
Look!
I dyed my hair!
No way...
She's getting farther a farther aw from my type...
I tried really hard to be like my sister Arisa.
I just can't do it.
But...

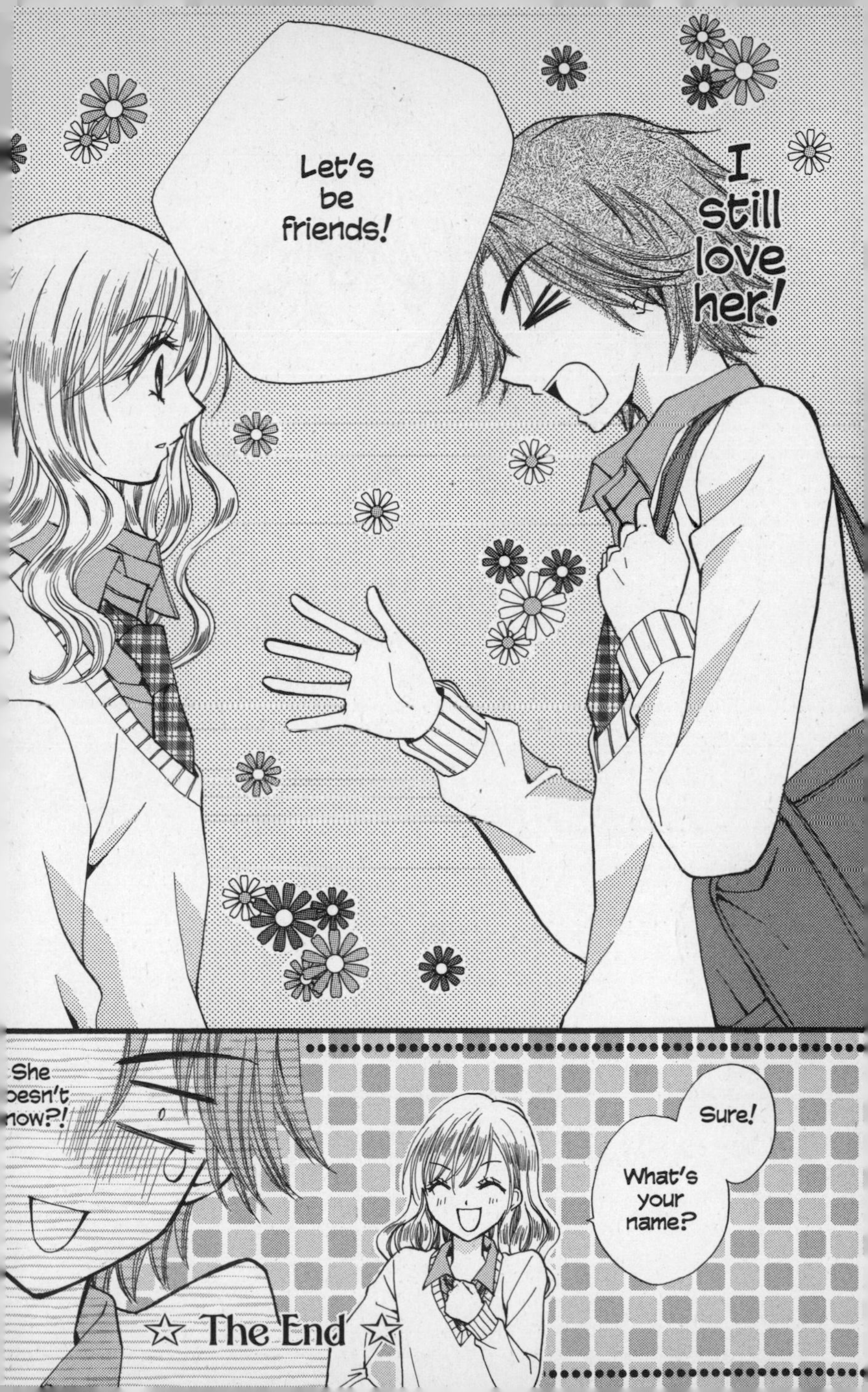
I still love her!
Let's be friends!
Sure!
What's your name?
She oesn't now?!
☆ The End ☆

Please send mail to:
Natsumi Andō
c/o Kodansha Comics
1745 Broadway
New York, NY 10019

Special Thanks:

T. Nakamura
H. Kishimoto
M. Nakata
My assistants and editors at Nakayoshi
Takeda~sama
Red rooster
Takashi Shimoyama
GINNANSHA
And all my readers who support me.

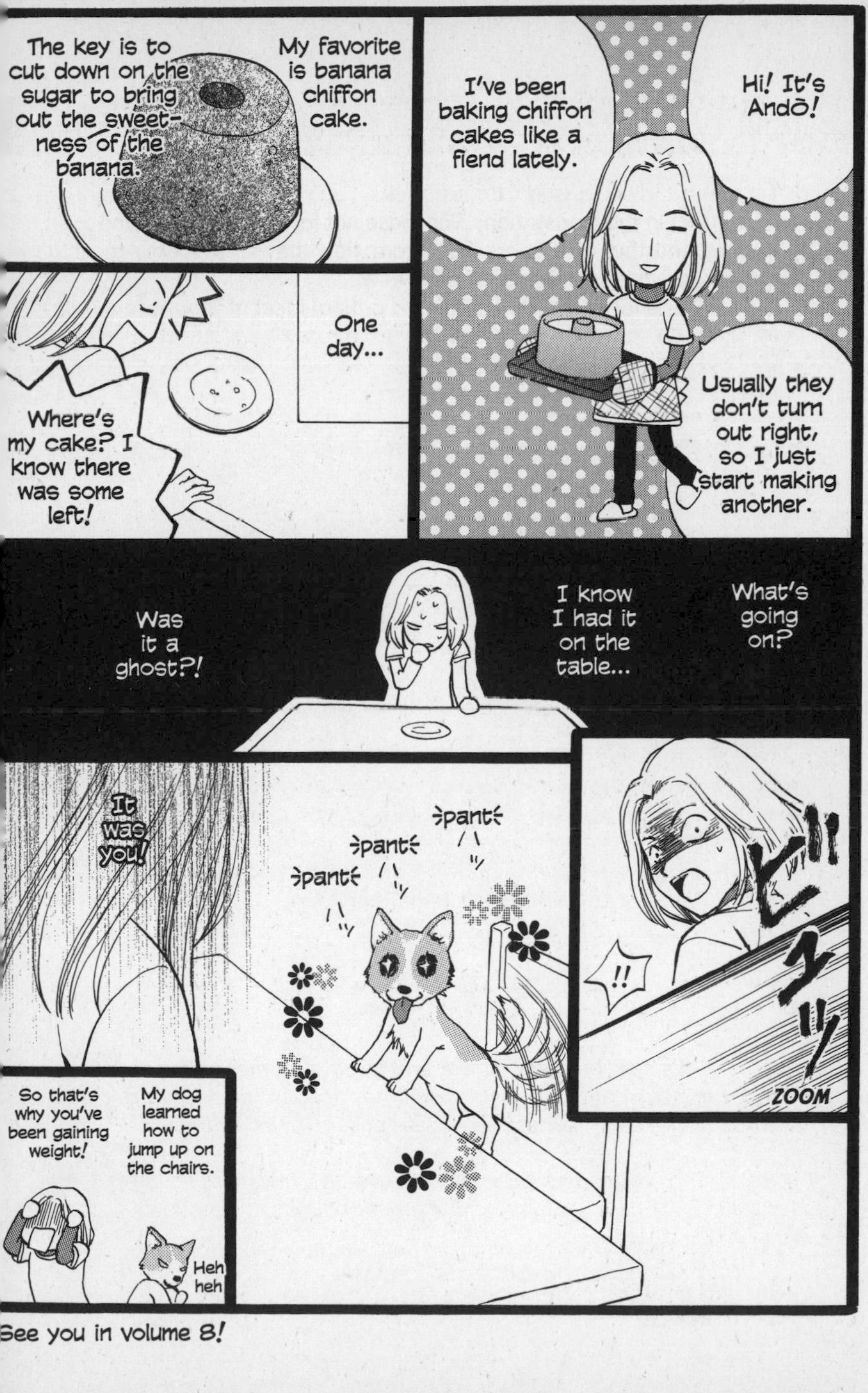
Hi! It's Andō!
I've been baking chiffon cakes like a fiend lately.
Usually they don't turn out right, so I just start making another.
My favorite is banana chiffon cake.
The key is to cut down on the sugar to bring out the sweetness of the banana.
One day...
Where's my cake? I know there was some left!
What's going on?
I know I had it on the table...
Was it a ghost?!
!!
ZOOM
pant
pant
pant
It was you!
My dog learned how to jump up on the chairs.
So that's why you've been gaining weight!
Heh heh

See you in volume 8!

HONORIFICS EXPLAINED

Throughout the Kodansha Comics books, you will find Japanese honorifics left intact in the translations. For those not familiar with how the Japanese use honorifics and, more important, how they differ from American honorifics, we present this brief overview.

Politeness has always been a critical facet of Japanese culture. Ever since the feudal era, when Japan was a highly stratified society, use of honorifics—which can be defined as polite speech that indicates relationship or status—has played an essential role in the Japanese language. When addressing someone in Japanese, an honorific usually takes the form of a suffix attached to one's name (example: "Asuna-san"), is used as a title at the end of one's name, or appears in place of the name itself (example: "Negi-sensei," or simply "Sensei!").

Honorifics can be expressions of respect or endearment. In the context of manga and anime, honorifics give insight into the nature of the relationship between characters. Many English translations leave out these important honorifics and therefore distort the feel of the original Japanese. Because Japanese honorifics contain nuances that English honorifics lack, it is our policy at Kodansha Comics not to translate them. Here, instead, is a guide to some of the honorifics you may encounter in Kodansha Comics books.

-san: This is the most common honorific and is equivalent to Mr., Miss, Ms., or Mrs. It is the all-purpose honorific and can be used in any situation where politeness is required.

-sama: This is one level higher than "-san" and is used to confer great respect.

-dono: This comes from the word "tono," which means "lord." It is an even higher level than "-sama" and confers utmost respect.

-kun: This suffix is used at the end of boys' names to express familiarity or endearment. It is also sometimes used by men among friends, or when addressing someone younger or of a lower station.

-chan: This is used to express endearment, mostly toward girls. It is also used for little boys, pets, and even among lovers. It gives a sense of childish cuteness.

Bozu: This is an informal way to refer to a boy, similar to the English terms "kid" and "squirt."

Sempai/Senpai: This title suggests that the addressee is one's senior in a group or organization. It is most often used in a school setting, where underclassmen refer to their upperclassmen as "sempai." It can also be used in the workplace, such as when a newer employee addresses an employee who has seniority in the company.

Kohai: This is the opposite of "sempai" and is used toward underclassmen in school or newcomers in the workplace. It connotes that the addressee is of a lower station.

Sensei: Literally meaning "one who has come before," this title is used for teachers, doctors, or masters of any profession or art.

-[blank]: This is usually forgotten in these lists, but it is perhaps the most significant difference between Japanese and English. The lack of honorific means that the speaker has permission to address the person in a very intimate way. Usually, only family, spouses, or very close friends have this kind of permission. Known as yobisute, it can be gratifying when someone who has earned the intimacy starts to call one by one's name without an honorific. But when that intimacy hasn't been earned, it can be very insulting.

Translation Notes

Japanese is a tricky language for most Westerners, and translation is often more art than science. For your edification and reading pleasure, here are notes on some of the places where we could have gone in a different direction with our translation of the work, or where a Japanese cultural reference is used.

The King

In Japanese, there is no pronoun used to refer to the King. It is not clear in the Japanese whether the King is male or female. This is more difficult in English, so the King is referred to as "he" in this translation. Keep in mind this does not necessarily mean the identity of the King is a male (or isn't).

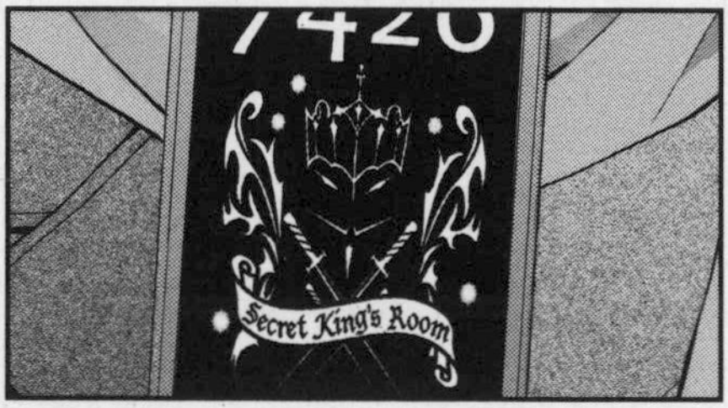
Secret King's Room

Third-person, page 25.6

Tsubasa saying "Arisa" here isn't giving away her identity. It's fairly common in Japanese for young girls to refer to themselves in third person, so Midori wouldn't have been suspicious.

31-legged race, page 76.2

Like a 3-legged race, except 30 people (the entire class) tie their legs together and run the race at the same time.

yakisoba bread, page 126

Fried noodles with sauce stuffed into a bun topped with mayonnaise and pickled ginger.

Preview of *Arisa* Volume 8

We're pleased to present you a preview from volume 8. Please check our website, www.kodanshacomics.com, to see when this volume will be available!

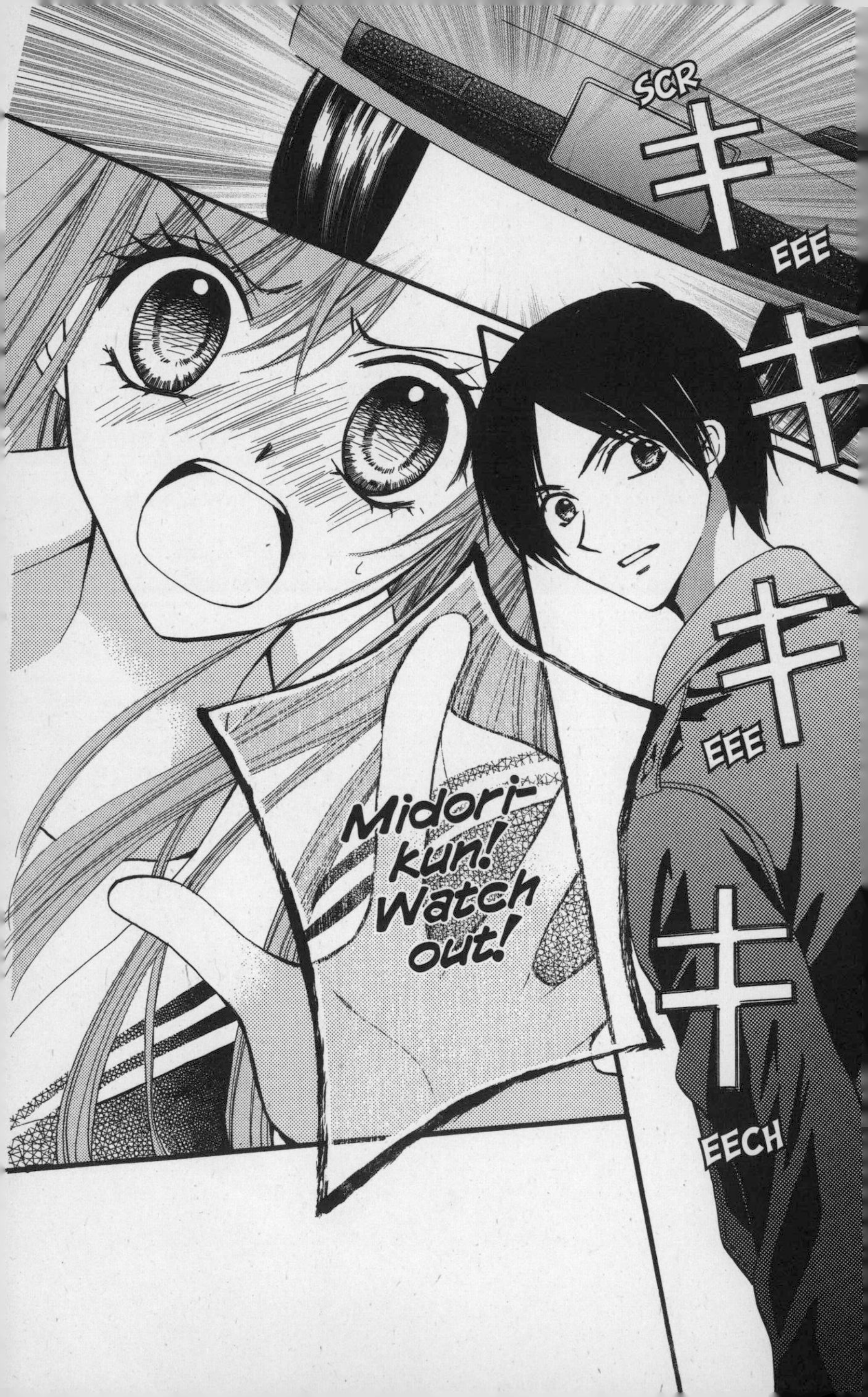
SCR
EEE
EEE
EECH
Midori-kun! Watch out!

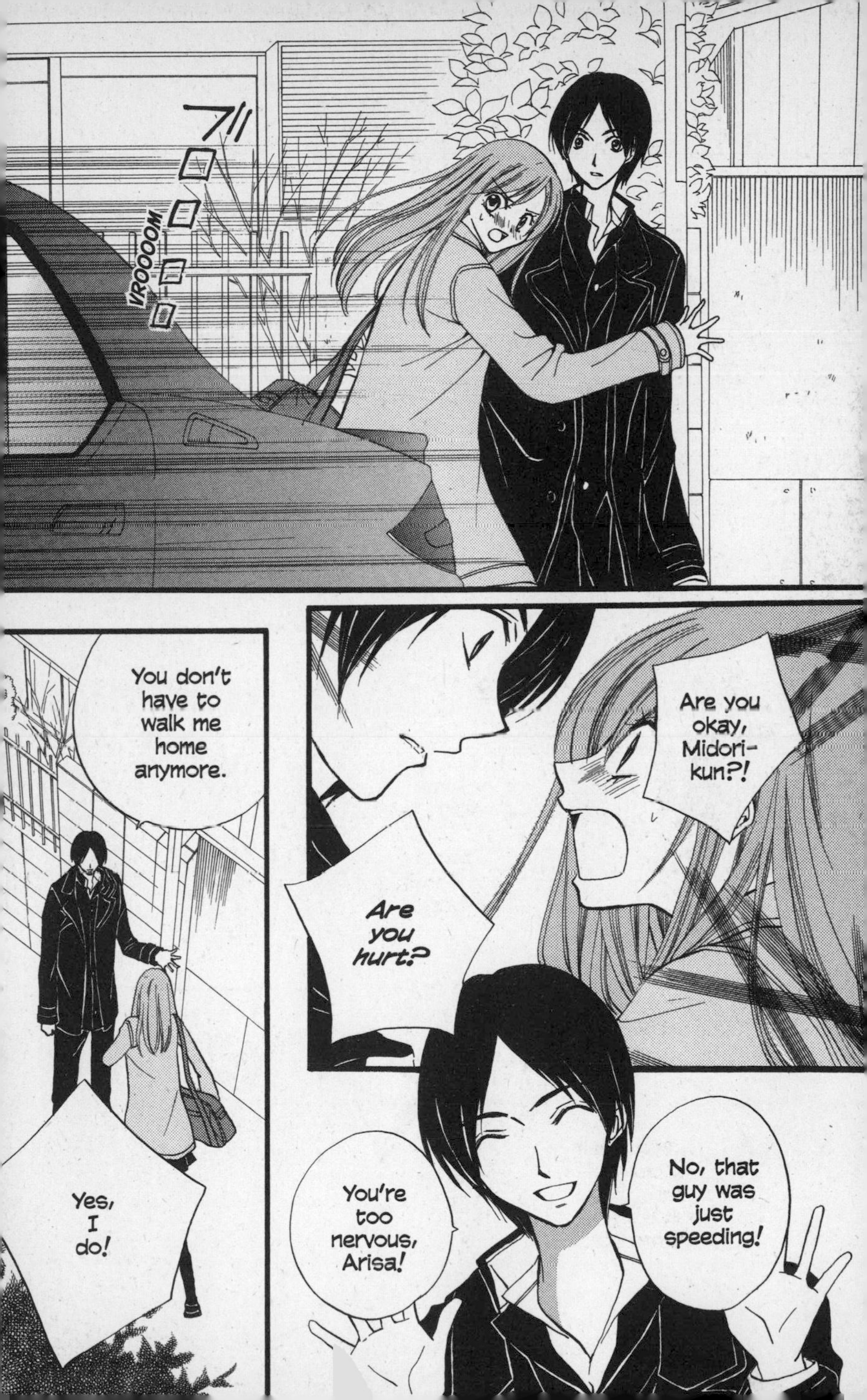
VROOOOM
Are you okay, Midori-kun?!
Are you hurt?
No, that guy was just speeding!
You're too nervous, Arisa!
You don't have to walk me home anymore.
Yes, I do!

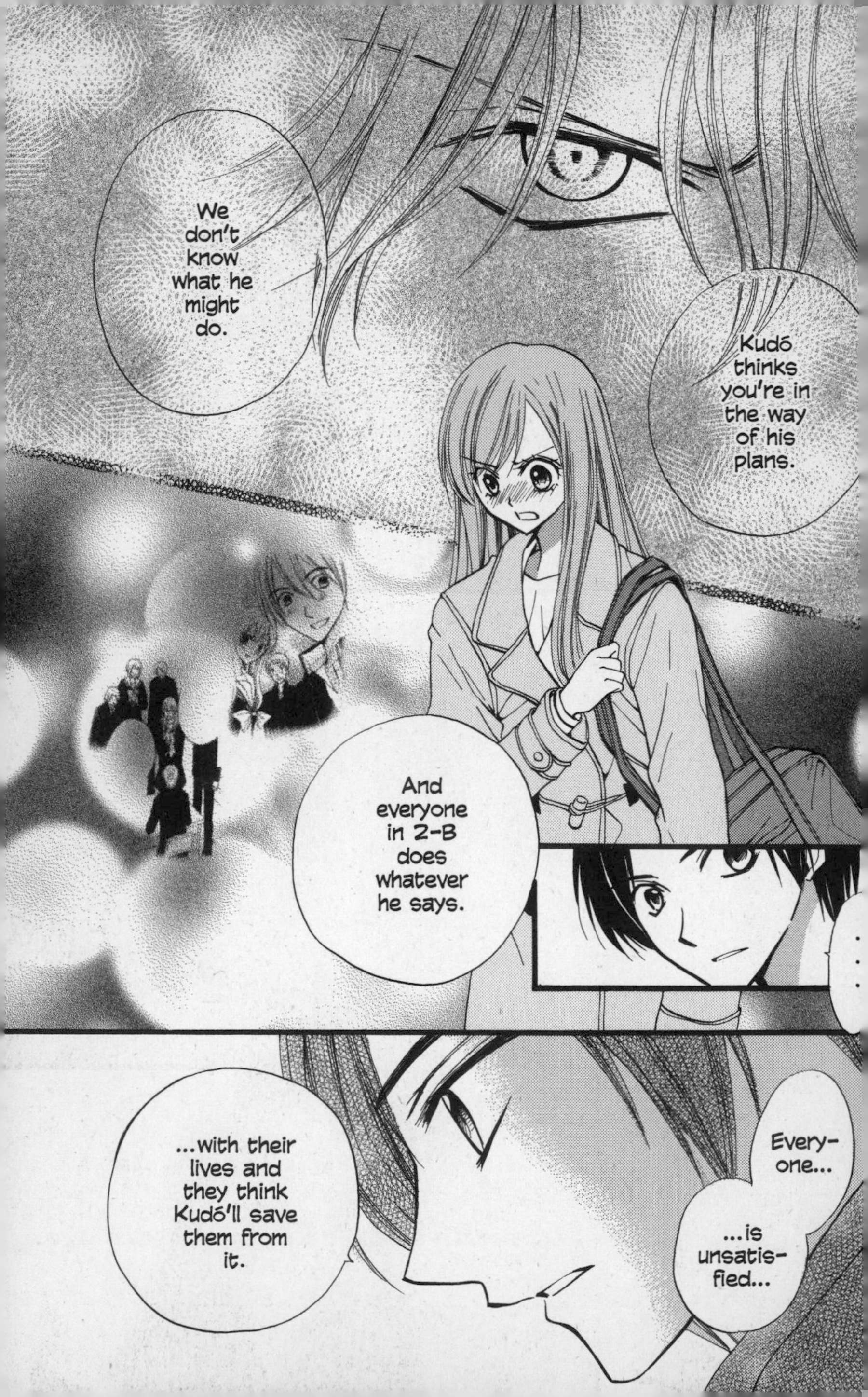
Kudō thinks you're in the way of his plans.
We don't know what he might do.
And everyone in 2-B does whatever he says.
...
Every-one...
...is unsatis-fied...
...with their lives and they think Kudō'll save them from it.

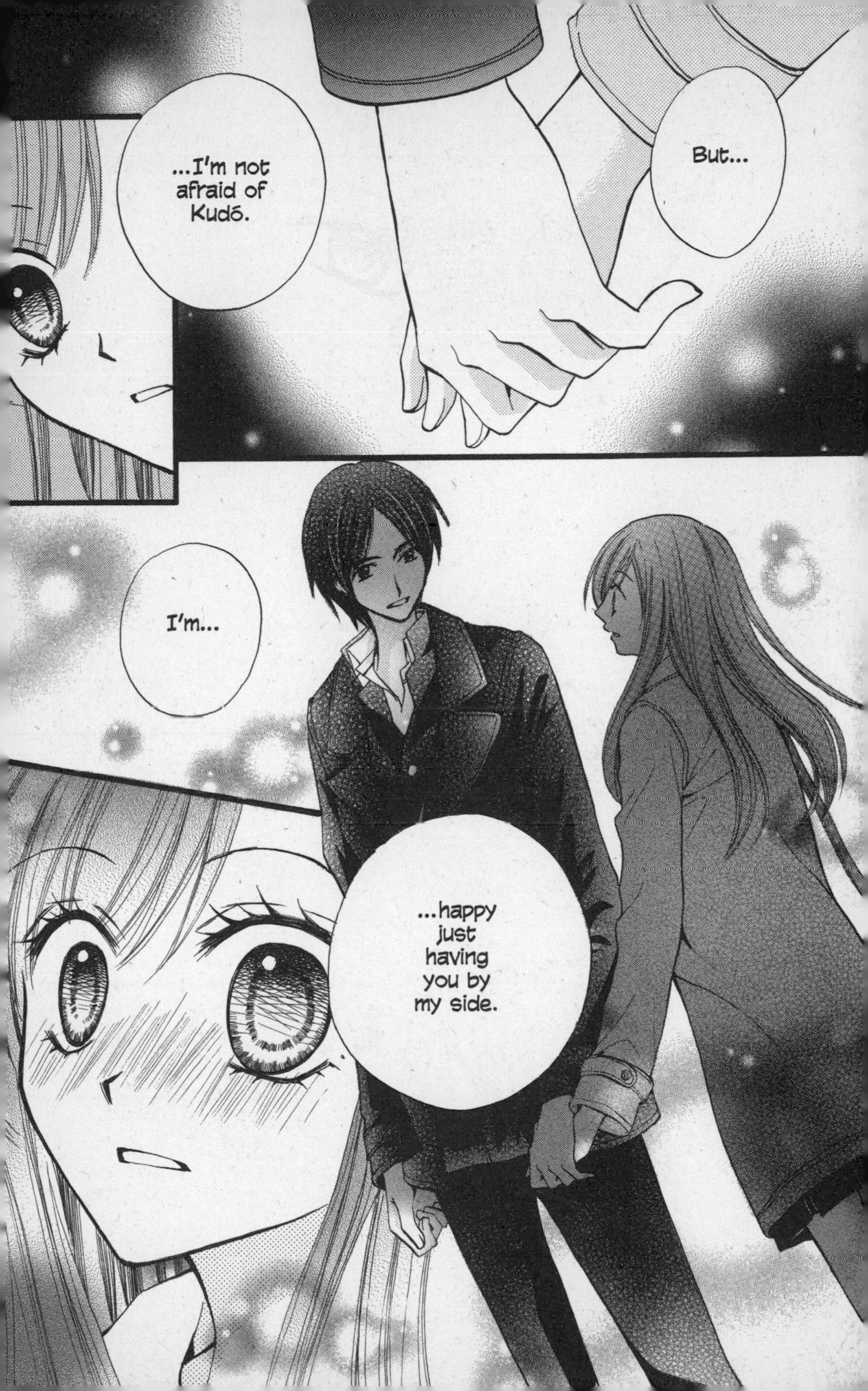
But...
...I'm not afraid of Kudō.
I'm...
...happy just having you by my side.

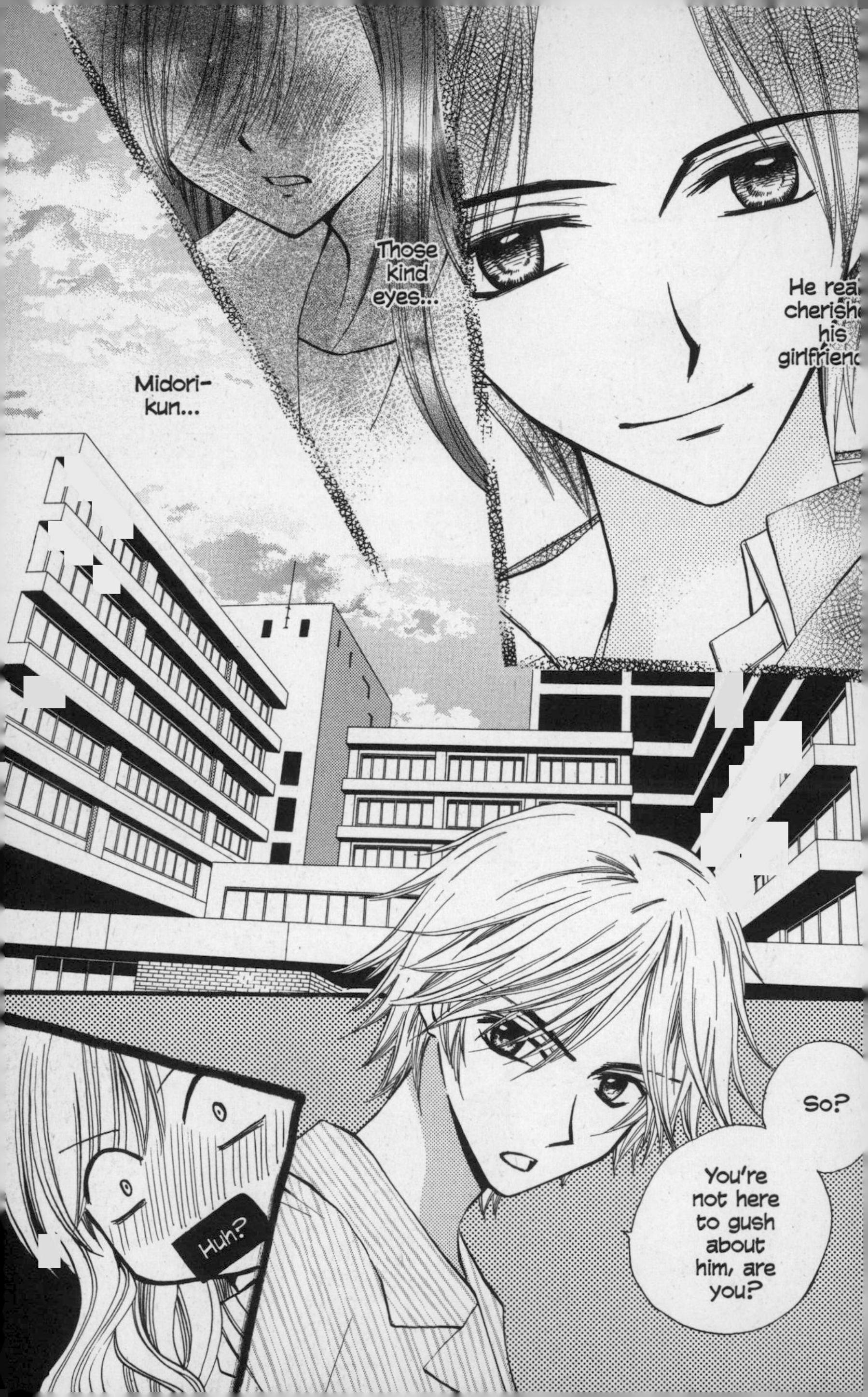
He rea cherishe his girlfrien
Those kind eyes...
Midori-kun...
So?
You're not here to gush about him, are you?
Huh?

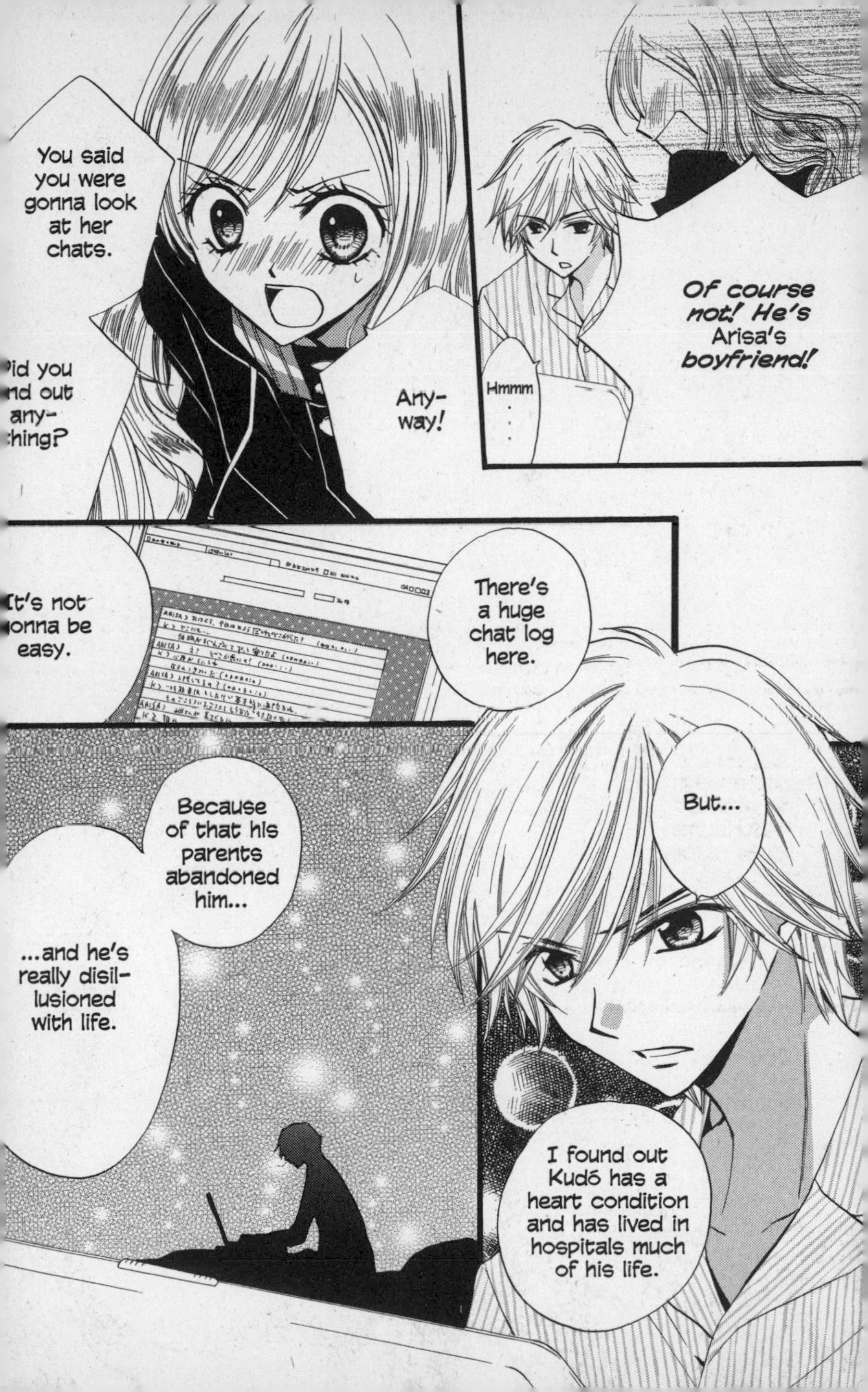
Of course not! He's Arisa's boyfriend!
Hmmm...
You said you were gonna look at her chats.
Any-way!
id you nd out any- hing?
There's a huge chat log here.
t's not onna be easy.
But...
I found out Kudō has a heart condition and has lived in hospitals much of his life.
Because of that his parents abandoned him...
...and he's really disil-lusioned with life.

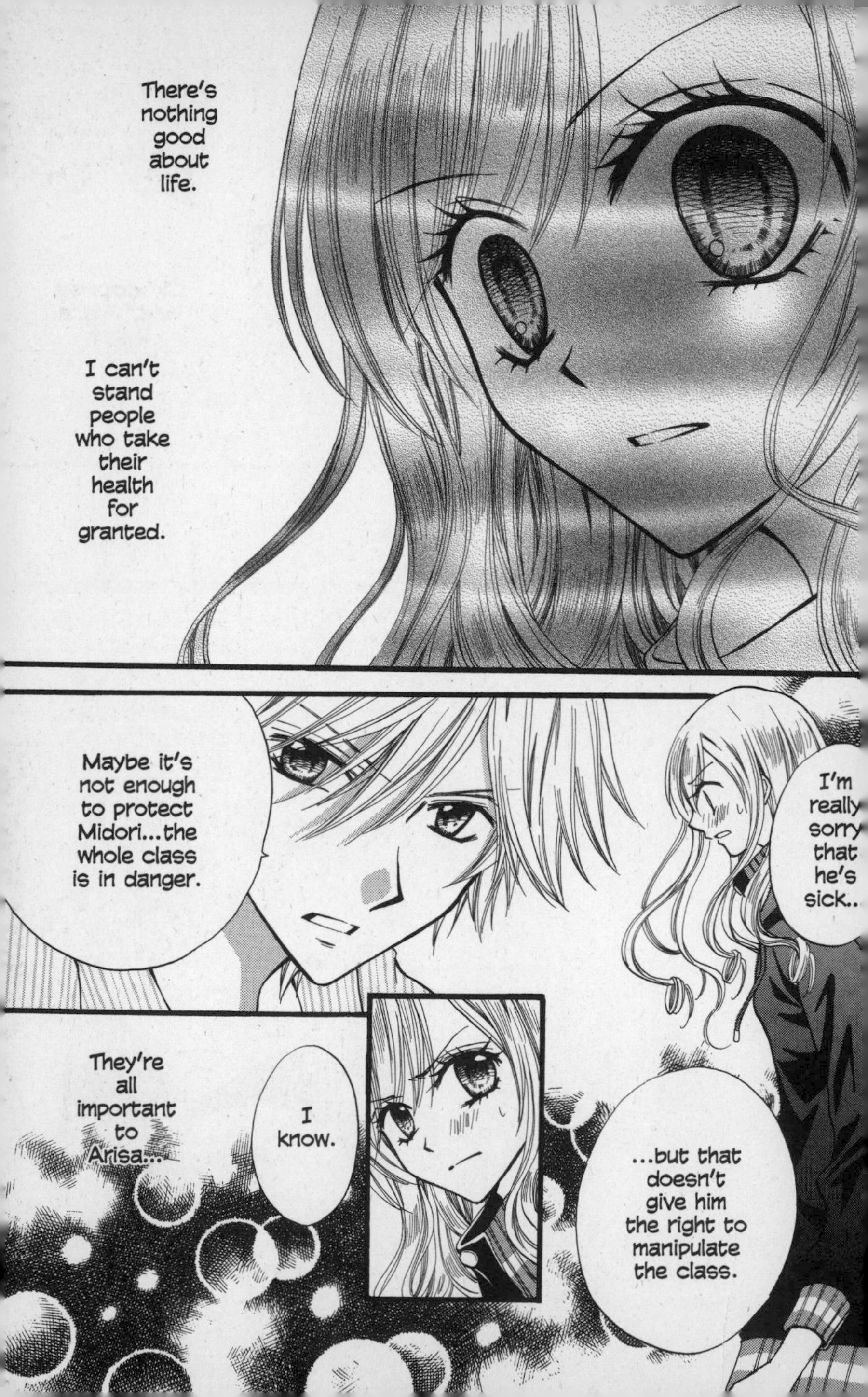
There's nothing good about life.
I can't stand people who take their health for granted.
I'm really sorry that he's sick...
Maybe it's not enough to protect Midori...the whole class is in danger.
...but that doesn't give him the right to manipulate the class.
I know.
They're all important to Arisa...

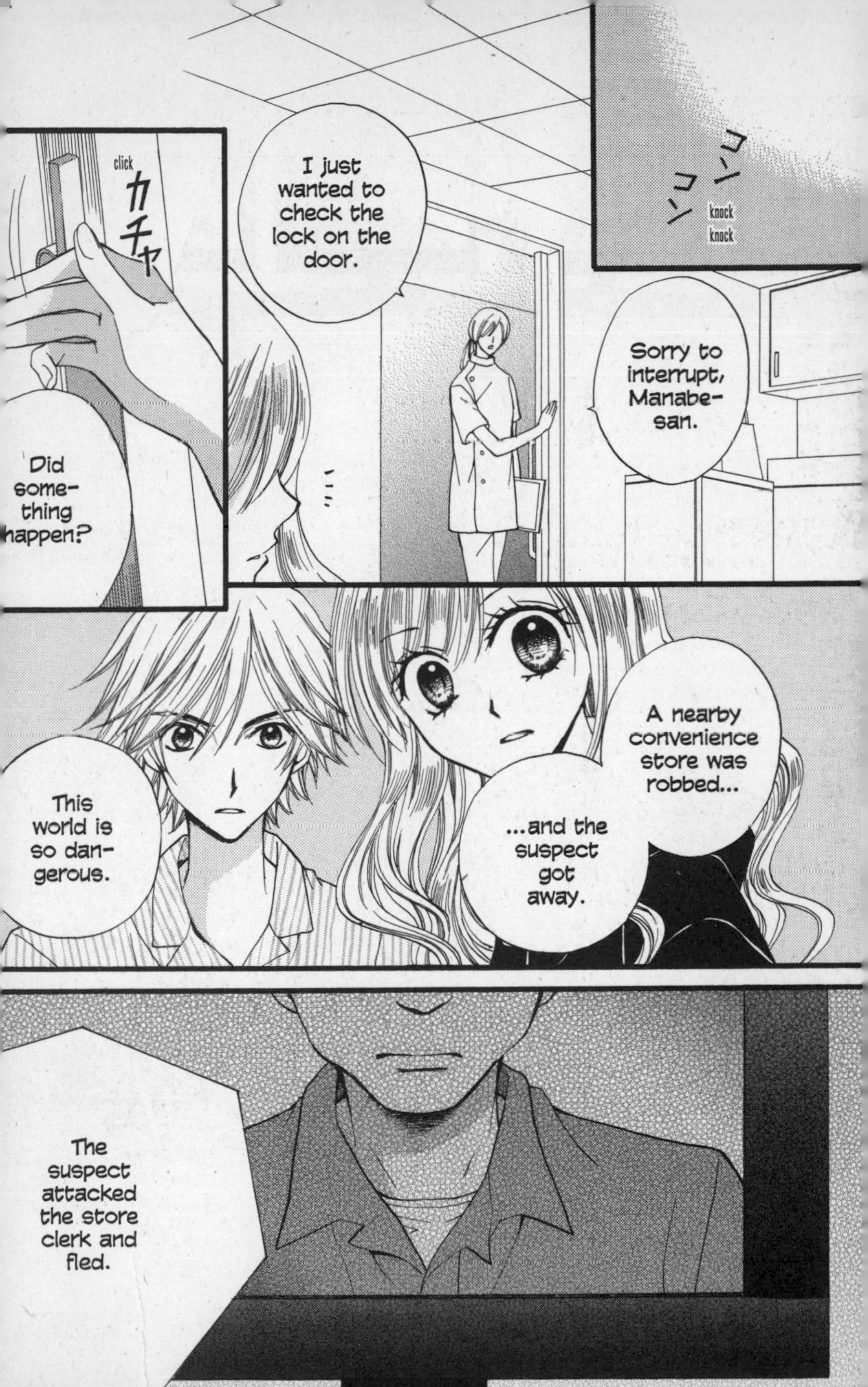
コンコン
knock
knock
Sorry to interrupt, Manabe-san.
I just wanted to check the lock on the door.
...
click
カチャ
Did something happen?
A nearby convenience store was robbed...
...and the suspect got away.
This world is so dangerous.
The suspect attacked the store clerk and fled.

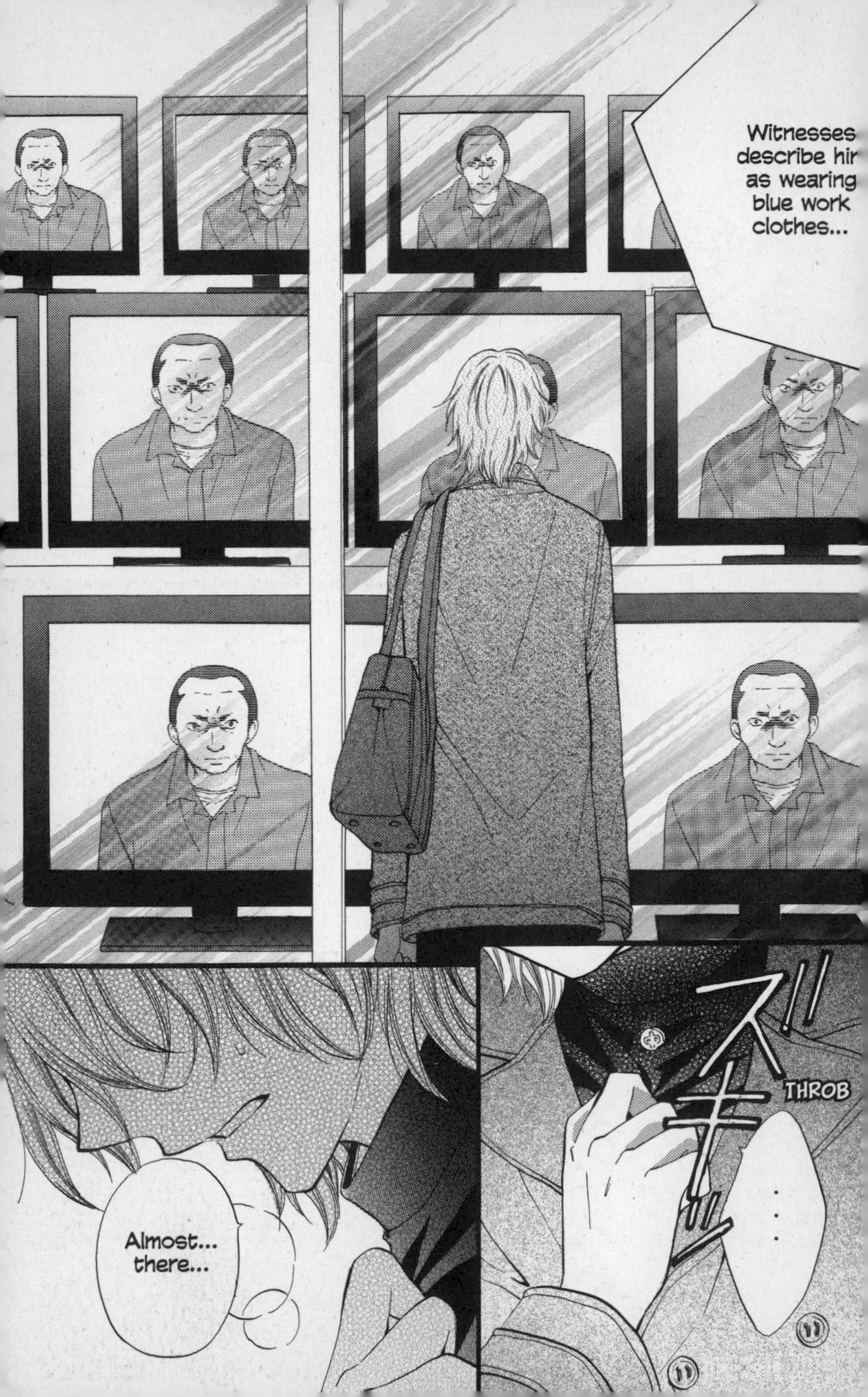

Witnesses describe hi
as wearing blue work clothes...
ズキ!!
THROB
. . .
Almost... there...

The Pretty Guardians are back!

Kodansha Comics is proud to present *Sailor Moon* with all new translations.

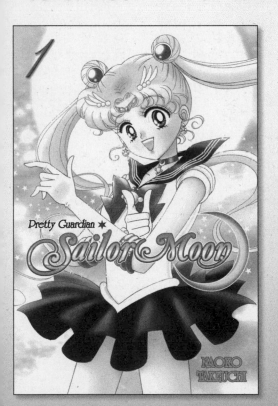

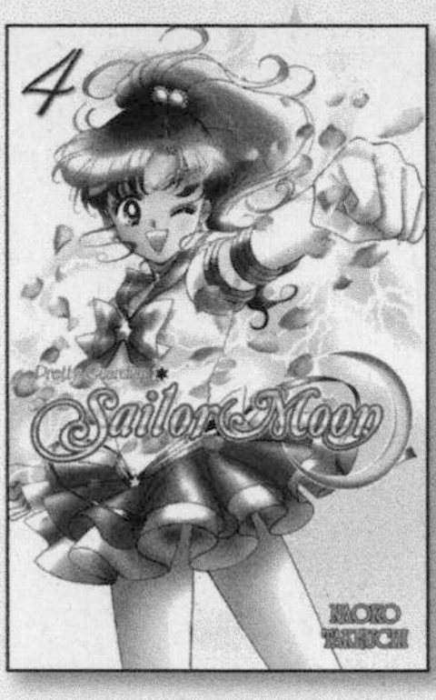
4
Pretty Guardian
Sailor Moon
NAOKO TAKEUCHI

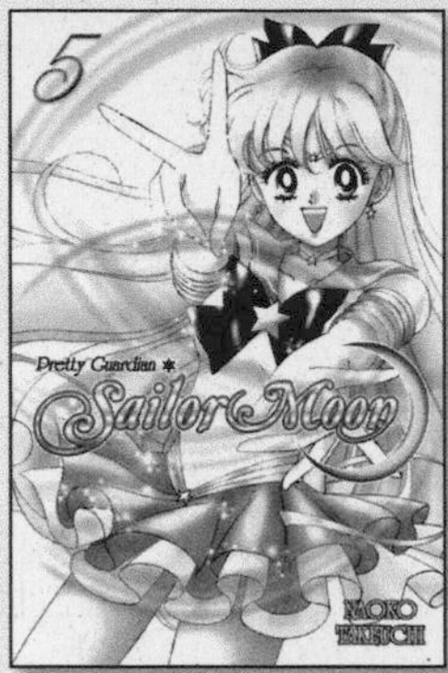
5
Pretty Guardian
Sailor Moon
NAOKO TAKEUCHI

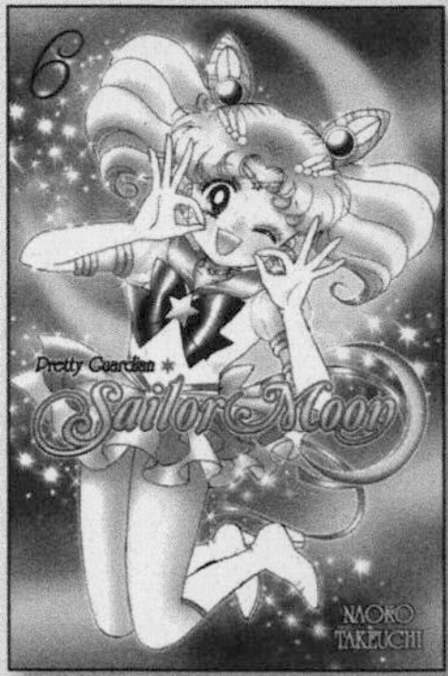
6
Pretty Guardian
Sailor Moon
NAOKO TAKEUCHI

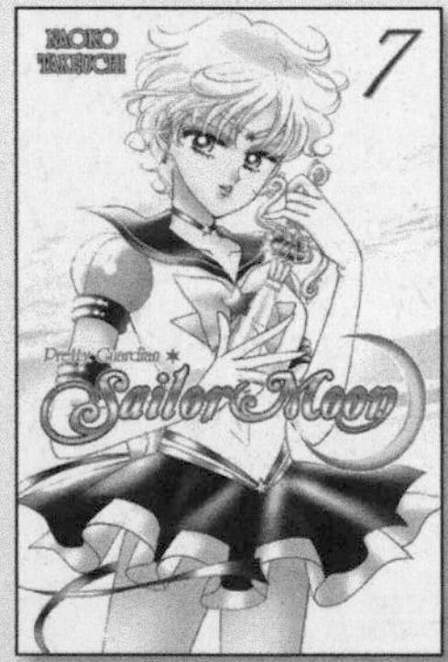
NAOKO TAKEUCHI
7
Pretty Guardian
Sailor Moon

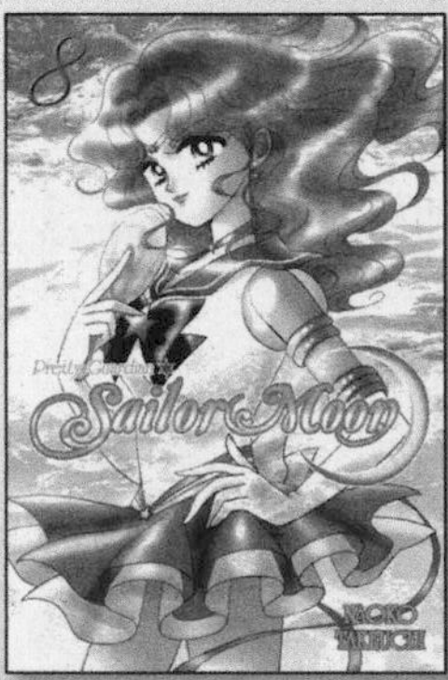
8
Sailor Moon
NAOKO TAKEUCHI

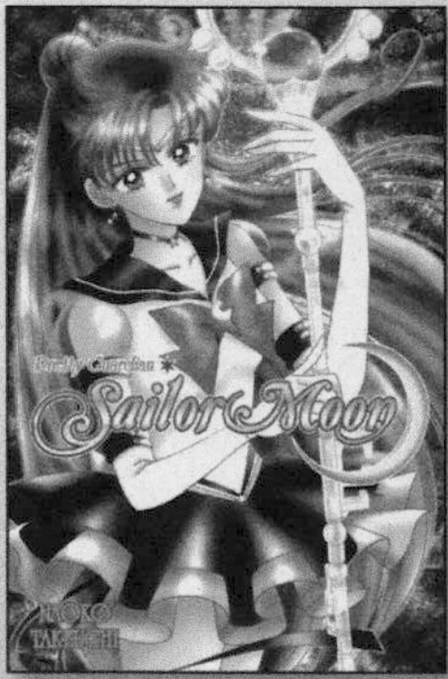
Pretty Guardian
Sailor Moon

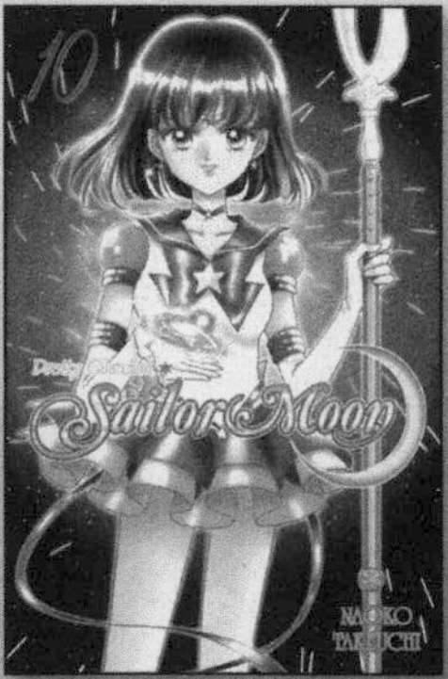
10
Sailor Moon
NAOKO TAKEUCHI

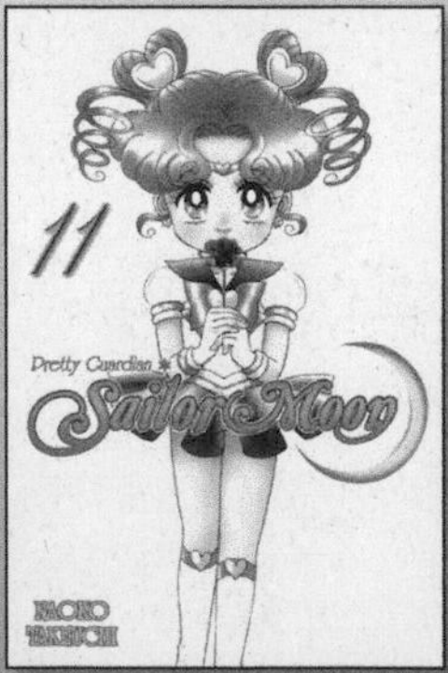
11
Pretty Guardian
Sailor Moon
NAOKO TAKEUCHI

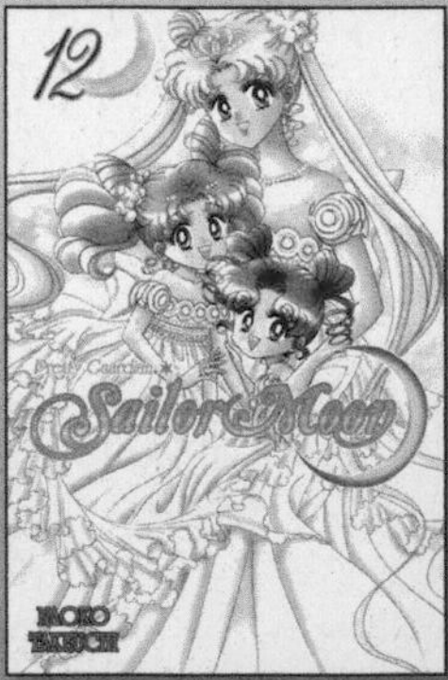
12
Pretty Guardian
Sailor Moon
NAOKO TAKEUCHI

KC
KODANSHA COMICS

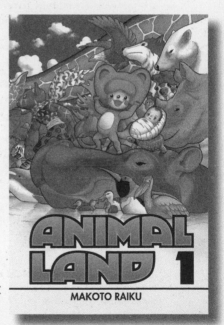

Arisa volume 7 is a work of fiction. Names, characters, places, and incidents are the products of the author's imagination or are used fictitiously. Any resemblance to actual events, locales, or persons, living or dead, is entirely coincidental.

A Kodansha Comics Trade Paperback Original

Published in the United States by Kodansha Comics, an imprint of Kodansha USA Publishing, LLC, New York.

Publication rights for this English edition arranged through Kodansha Ltd., Tokyo.

First published in Japan in 2011 by Kodansha Ltd., Tokyo.

ISBN 978-1-61262-114-2

Printed in the United States of America.

www.kodanshacomics.com

9 8 7 6 5 4 3 2 1

Translator/Adapter: Andria Cheng
Lettering: Scott O. Brown

P9-BJK-864

TOMARE!

[STOP!]

You're going the wrong way!

Manga is a completely different type of reading experience.

To start at the *beginning*, go to the *end*!

That's right! Authentic manga is read the traditional Japanese way—from right to left. Exactly the *opposite* of how American books are read. It's easy to follow: Just go to the other end of the book, and read each page—and each panel—from the right side to the left side, starting at the top right. Now you're experiencing manga as it was meant to be!